D1451026

WHY CUBA MATTERS

WHY CUBA MATTERS

MATTERS

New Threats
in
America's Backyard

NÉSTOR T. CARBONELL

ARCHWAY
PUBLISHING

Archway Publishing books may be ordered through booksellers or by contacting:

Archway Publishing
1663 Liberty Drive
Bloomington, IN 47403
www.archwaypublishing.com
1 (888) 242-5904

ISBN: 978-1-4808-8585-1 (sc)
ISBN: 978-1-4808-8586-8 (hc)
ISBN: 978-1-4808-8884-5 (hc color)
ISBN: 978-1-4808-8587-5 (e)

Library of Congress Control Number: 2020900332

Printed in the United States of America.

Archway Publishing rev. date: 03/03/2020

*To Rosa, Rosa María, Néstor Gastón, José Manuel and
the rest of our family, with my love and pride.*

A SENSE OF THE PAST

"A sense of the past is far more basic to the maintenance of freedom than hope for the future. The former is concrete and real; the latter is necessarily amorphous and more easily guided by those who can manipulate human actions and beliefs. Hence the relentless effort by totalitarian governments to destroy memory. And hence the ingenious techniques for abolishing the social allegiances within which individual memory is given strength and power of resistance."

Robert A. Nisbet

CONTENTS

SECTION III
The Promising Future

PREFACE

My Cuban Journey

The recent passing of Fidel Castro brought back painful memories of the day I left Cuba. It was a breezy summer day in June 1960 when I climbed the steep metal steps to a Pan American Airways flight that would take me from Communist-controlled Cuba, the island of my birth, to what became my safe haven, Miami, Florida.

I was not lured by the American dream. I was driven by a nightmare: the oppressive regime of Fidel Castro.

When I arrived in Miami I was twenty-four, penniless, and deeply distraught about leaving my family and about the bleak situation gripping my country. Still, I was hopeful of soon returning to a Cuba once again free.

Sadly, that never happened. My involvement in the failed Bay of Pigs operation and in subsequent efforts to liberate the island had foreclosed any opportunity to return to Cuba under the Castro regime without risking prison—or worse. But regardless of the risks, I would not go back if I had to bow to the despots who had enslaved my homeland and imprisoned and executed members of my family.

In the nearly sixty years since leaving, I have built with my family a wonderful life, blessed in so many ways, and have become a proud citizen of the United States. Yet I have never forgotten my beloved Cuba, which to this day remains a captive nation yearning for freedom.

There are many reasons why Cuba remains so close to my heart: fond memories of a blissful youth; a rich and vibrant culture; the rhythm of its music; the warmth and passion of its people; vivid images of the island's natural splendor, the same ones that dazzled Christopher Columbus; and, of course, the dream of what Cuba, unshackled from communism, could be in the future—a free and prosperous nation with potential to emerge as a regional powerhouse. All of that helped to preserve my "Cubanía" or Cubanness. But nothing forged my bond to the island more powerfully than the values instilled in me by my parents and grandparents, in particular the supreme importance of integrity and an abiding devotion to family and *patria* or homeland.

My commitment to those values, in large measure, led me to write *Why Cuba Matters*. My goal has been to shed new light on Cuba's complex saga, drawing on extensive research and personal recollections to clarify pivotal episodes in the island's history, dispel myths of the past, and correct fallacies of the present. At the same time, I have looked to the future, projecting the eventual end of the Castro tyranny and the start of a new era with its manifold challenges and opportunities.

Where they added substance and perspective, I have woven some of my direct experiences into the text. Beyond simply growing up in Havana, I witnessed at close range, in some cases as an active participant, a number of critical developments in the island's history and have known many of the players involved.

This stems in part from being born into a wonderful, politically active family with not only a deep attachment to the patria but also a very strong sense of history, often conveyed through inspiring stories shared at family gatherings. Listening to those stories, usually over dinner in Havana, I learned of the epic of my great-grandfather Néstor Leonelo Carbonell, a veteran of Cuba's first war of independence against Spain (the 1868–78 "Ten Years' War"), who later emigrated with his family to Tampa, Florida, and remained committed to the liberation of the island. It was he who invited Cuba's foremost hero, José Martí, to address the large exile community in Tampa for the first time. The two speeches Martí delivered there electrified the Cubans and laid the groundwork for the final independence war of 1895–98, which triggered US military intervention against the colonial power of Spain.

At those family gatherings, which often sparked spirited discussions on a wide variety of issues, I became aware of the challenges and achievements of my two grandfathers, José Manuel Carbonell and José Manuel Cortina. Carbonell, when he was sixteen, fought in the final war of independence and subsequently pursued a diplomatic and literary career. In the late 1930s and early '40s, he was Cuba's ambassador to Mexico and became the dean of the Diplomatic Corps in that country. A renowned poet, he used to regale me with his patriotic and romantic sonnets. Carbonell crowned his literary endeavors serving as president of the Cuban Academy of Arts and Letters and authoring the monumental eighteen-volume work *Evolución de la Cultura Cubana*.

Cortina, known for his powerful oratory, was a leader of Cuba's Liberal Party. He was elected to the senate, served twice as secretary of state, and headed Cuba's delegation to the League of Nations. Perhaps his greatest achievement was the decisive role he played at the Constitutional Convention of 1940, which adopted one of the most advanced democratic charters of its time. Reading the transcripts of his debates against the very astute and articulate Communist delegates helped me later to unveil the stratagems of Fidel and Raúl Castro and their Marxist cohorts.

Both grandfathers devoted more time to public service than to their legal profession and business interests. And so did my father, Néstor Carbonell-Andricaín, who at a very young age was elected to the House of Representatives, rose through the ranks, and became Speaker of the House. He subsequently was elected senator and served as majority whip. An ebullient and popular legislator with a disarming sense of humor, he was very effective at harmonizing opposing views to achieve consensus.

All of these men provided historical perspective to the young members of our family, myself included, who tended to be superficial and overly negative in our appraisals of Cuba's rocky path. While candidly acknowledging setbacks and frustrations, the elders pointed out the remarkable progress made in just fifty years as a republic.

Despite political turmoil and endemic corruption (Havana had been harshly and unfairly labeled "the mob-controlled nightclub and brothel capital of the world"), the island before Castro topped most Latin American countries in standards of living. The Cuban peso was on par with the dollar, and the organized labor force benefited from progressive social legislation.

An entrepreneurial middle class was driving the growth of the economy—still too dependent on sugar—and was narrowing the glaring inequities between the urban and rural areas. All in all, flaws and vices notwithstanding, Cuba was rapidly moving from the underdeveloped to the near-developed takeoff stage.

The uplifting assessment of Cuba's trajectory conveyed by my parents and grandparents drastically changed following Fulgencio Batista's egregious military coup in 1952, which disrupted the constitutional process and opened a bloody cycle of civil strife. Our elders viewed the ensuing polarization with great concern. They feared that without a peaceful, democratic solution, the country would face a dreadful dilemma: Batista or Castro—the despot in power or the rambunctious firebrand with totalitarian tendencies.

My grandfathers were too old and too frail to enter the fray, so the responsibility fell to my father. In mid-1958, after obtaining my law degrees from the University of Villanueva in Havana and Harvard, I joined him and other former Cuban senators and political leaders in the formation of a "third force" (the Free People's Party). Our mission: to beat Batista's candidates in the November general election and avert a Castro takeover. Unfortunately the initiative failed, torpedoed by Fidel and his allies with violence and death threats, and nullified by Batista with fraud.

I witnessed the fall of the republic following the flight of Batista on January 1, 1959, and the unconditional surrender of the demoralized army. I also saw how Castro filled the power vacuum that ensued. Through firsthand experience and reliable sources, I came to understand the tragic dynamic. Castro ensnared the Cuban people with a lethal combination of charisma, false promises, and terror, while Washington unwittingly facilitated his takeover by pushing Batista out without supporting a democratic alternative.

Following Castro's ascent with absolute power, my father, convalescing from a heart attack, was ostracized by the regime for having fostered a third force. So, with my father barred from politics and exposed to arrest, the family's civic duty to take a stand on democratic principles fell to me and several of my cousins.

The commitment Castro publicly reiterated in January 1959 to restoring democracy eased somewhat my lingering concern, but not for long. By March, I realized it was a sham. I called for the rule of law in an article in Cuba's leading newspaper, *Diario de la Marina*. Fidel responded (fortunately without naming me): yes, the rule of law, but based on the "new" law that the revolution will pass, not the "old" law, which has no validity.

I took a riskier step in a speech to the National Cattle Ranchers' Association in May 1959 on the Agrarian Reform Law passed by the revolutionary government. Denouncing it as a prelude to the obliteration of free enterprise and private property in Cuba (which turned out to be the case), I warned the ranchers: "If you do not rise, you will be crushed by the uncontainable avalanche of state interventionism."

In August, the first major conspiracy against the regime was aborted. Among those arrested were prominent cattlemen, former officers of Cuba's pre-Castro standing army, several rebel army chiefs, and young prodemocracy activists, including my twenty-eight-year-old cousin Eddy Arango. Although I did not participate in the conspiracy, I was detained, interrogated at army headquarters, and released under surveillance. Given my article and the speech to the cattlemen, I was lucky to have escaped imprisonment.

After that, I was more cautious. When I wrote a sixty-page paper highlighting the similarities between the steps prescribed by Karl Marx and Vladimir Lenin for a Communist takeover and the revolutionary measures taken by Castro, I made sure copies were secretly delivered to the main opposition leaders and the US Embassy without my name.

By early 1960, Fidel had accelerated the radicalization of the regime, snuffing out the free press, confiscating properties, arresting or executing dissidents, and excoriating Yankee imperialism. Meanwhile US relations with Castro's Cuba had taken a sharp turn for the worse. So the State Department, which had failed to engage the Cuban ruler despite repeated attempts, accepted an offer by the Argentine ambassador Julio Amoedo to try to persuade Castro to halt his anti-US tirades and explore a rapprochement with Washington. By luck we were privy to the secret negotiations—the ambassador had rented our house and become close with my parents.

The collapse of this last-ditch effort to reach an understanding, scuttled by Castro, who was just buying time to seal his pact with Moscow, set in motion the Program of Covert Action Against the Castro Regime, authorized by President Eisenhower. This prompted my abrupt departure to the United States in June 1960 to serve as executive assistant to the leader of the CIA– and White House–backed anti-Castro coalition based in Miami, the former prime minister of Cuba Manuel Antonio "Tony" Varona.

Armed only with freshly minted law degrees, I did my best to carry out my assignments in areas that were new to me: intelligence activities, propaganda, agitation, geopolitics, and diplomacy. Then in early 1961, I felt that the time had come for me to enroll in the anti-Castro Cuban brigade being trained in the jungles of Guatemala. I joined a unit called Operation 40, which was supposed to help establish law and order in the cities and towns that were to be set free by the brigade, and embarked on the secret journey to Guatemala.

Just before the brigade was flown to Puerto Cabezas, Nicaragua, to board the flotilla that would take us to Cuba, Operation 40 was split into two groups. Mine, part of a second wave of reinforcements aboard the *Lake Charles*, was instructed to wait near the coast of Cuba for the green light to head to the Bay of Pigs, only to be called back when the beachhead fell. The other group landed with the brigade—with tragic consequences. Its chief (Colonel Vicente León) was killed, and several of my Operation 40 brothers-in-arms died or were wounded.

When I returned to Miami after my near–Bay of Pigs experience, the trauma of the disaster was compounded by family tragedy. Manuel "Ñongo" Puig, an underground leader who was married to my cousin Ofelia Arango, had been executed by the Castro regime. Also executed was Antonio "Tony" Ramirez-Núñez, my maternal grandmother's nephew, who conspired against the regime from the air base of San Julian, where he was stationed. Three other cousins who had been involved in the resistance remained in prison. Along with Eddy Arango, arrested in 1959, were Ramón "Rino" Puig, married to my cousin Ileana Arango and serving fifteen years, and Humberto Cortina, seriously wounded during the Bay of Pigs invasion.

I grieved with my parents and grandparents in Miami, but not for long. The Cuban Revolutionary Council in exile—the enlarged anti-Castro coalition semiofficially recognized by the White House and headed by the distinguished attorney and former prime minister with Castro, José Miró-Cardona—appointed me as its special representative to the Organization of American States (OAS). So I traded my camouflage uniform for a diplomat's suit and headed for Washington.

My mission was to design and implement a strategy to obtain enough votes to condemn and sanction the Castro regime for its repeated violations of human rights, subversive activities, and alignment with the Sino-Soviet bloc. At the time, eight Latin American countries had severed diplomatic relations with Cuba, and nine had recalled their ambassadors.

While the State Department seemed satisfied with a generic and toothless declaration that Marxism-Leninism was incompatible with the inter-American system, we had something more ambitious in mind.

Having ourselves aligned the hard-line anti-Castro governments and secured the critical vote of Uruguay, host of the January 1962 OAS conference, a resolution was passed not just condemning the Castro regime but also expelling it from the organization. Communist Cuba was in effect declared a pariah and deprived of OAS protection. This could have provided legal cover for collective military action under the Inter-American Treaty of Reciprocal Assistance (Rio Treaty) against the Castro regime; however, the United States never stepped up to lead the charge.

By mid-1962, the underground movement reported to us a veiled and alarming shift in the Soviet military buildup in Cuba. Soviet ships were being unloaded at night by foreign civilian-clothed personnel in quasi-military formation who moved out in truck convoys carrying large cylindrical armaments covered with canvas. We also were informed that there was suspicious activity going on in cordoned-off areas of the island, including remote valleys surrounded by caves.

When the Cuban Revolutionary Council on August 20 publicly denounced with harder data the onset of the "Soviet invasion of Cuba" with troops and large concealed arms, the State Department ridiculed our report. President Kennedy himself stated on August 30 that "we do not have information that troops have come into Cuba" and that "the main [Soviet] thrust, of course, is assistance because of the mismanagement of the Cuban economy." To our dismay, he implicitly justified the buildup by adding, "I think the situation was critical enough that they needed to be bolstered up."

We were deeply alarmed by the passive attitude of the White House, which was persistently in denial. So, at the suggestion of my grandfather Cortina, we discreetly initiated a bipartisan initiative to pass a congressional joint resolution that committed the United States to repel Soviet military intervention in Cuba and support the aspirations of freedom-loving Cubans for self-determination. The joint resolution, broadly supported by Congress, was signed into law by the president on October 3, 1962.

Under strong pressure from CIA director John McCone, New York senator Kenneth Keating, and other legislators we and others had briefed, the president agreed to resume low-level U-2 reconnaissance flights over suspected areas in Cuba, which had been suspended for almost one month to avoid a clash with Moscow.

Those first aerial photographs after the hiatus proved highly consequential. They triggered the Cuban Missile Crisis. The photos clearly showed that the Soviets had built a strategic missile base in Pinar del Río, the far-western province of Cuba. A CIA intelligence report correctly pointed out that the base was located near the towns of San Cristobal and San Diego de los Baños, in a hacienda that belonged to "Dr. Cortina" (my maternal grandfather). The location, we knew full well, was ideal for the base given the spacious valley surrounded by rugged limestone hills (*mogotes*) with caves.

After thirteen days of agonizing deliberations, marked by growing concern and shifting views, President Kennedy finally charted a decisive course of action. With the backing of our allies, he mobilized US forces and forged an awesome ring of steel around Cuba: a total blockade euphemistically called "quarantine."

The twenty-seventh of October, the most portentous day of the crisis, remains etched in my memory. After US major Rudolf Anderson, on a return U-2 flight over Cuba, had been downed by a Soviet-manned SA-2 antiaircraft battery, and after work at the missile bases had been stepped up, White House emissaries advised the exile leader Miró-Cardona that the US invasion could be imminent and that he should prepare to land with the troops.

That evening, Miró-Cardona asked me to draft an uplifting proclamation in Spanish that he would broadcast upon landing. The proclamation, wholeheartedly approved by the exile leader, was of course never used. The Missile Crisis ended without an invasion or a head-on nuclear confrontation. That was great news. But the belated US response to the Soviet challenge, after the missiles had already been emplaced on Cuban soil and were virtually operational, had very serious consequences.

Having to negotiate under those conditions, Kennedy traded the dismantling of the Soviet bases on the island for the removal of US missiles in Turkey and a pledge not to invade Cuba. Regrettably, Kennedy failed to get a reciprocal commitment from Nikita Khrushchev that the island would not be used as a sanctuary for Communist subversion in other countries. As a result, the Soviets ended up with a strategic bulwark ninety miles off the US coast, one that for three decades wreaked havoc from the Horn of Africa to the Caribbean Basin to Cape Horn in South America.

In 1964, realizing with a broken heart that it would take a long time for Cuba to regain its freedom, I headed for New York to rebuild my life. There, I met my Cuban-born wife-to-be, Rosa Arellano, granddaughter of Dr. Raúl de Cárdenas, a highly respected jurist who had honorably served as Cuba's duly elected vice president from 1944 to 1948. To this day Rosa remains my source of inspiration and steadfast companion.

After a short stint as an attorney for Schering Corporation, I embarked on an exhilarating forty-year journey with PepsiCo, shifting gears from the Cold War to the Cola Wars. That journey opened exciting professional opportunities for me, both in the United States and abroad, in various fields: law, operations, and general management. I also became vice president of the corporation, responsible for international public and government affairs.

This last post, as PepsiCo's ambassador-at-large, enabled me to meet and gain valuable insights from many world leaders, among them the triumphant triad of the free world—Ronald Reagan, Margaret Thatcher, and Pope John Paul II—who conceived and executed the crucial strategy that helped to end the Cold War, a strategy not only to contain, but also to undermine, roll back, and dismantle, the Soviet empire.

Although I was fully occupied professionally, my commitment to the cause of freedom in Cuba never abated. I closely followed developments on the island and wrote several books in Spanish about the Communist takeover. One in English, *And the Russians Stayed: The Sovietization of Cuba*, was published by William Morrow in 1989. Given my responsibilities at PepsiCo, I had no time to promote this latter book, but I was honored with the accolades of former president Richard Nixon and other foreign affairs luminaries, including Zbigniew Brzezinski, Jeane Kirkpatrick, and Brent Scowcroft.

Since retiring from PepsiCo in 2008, I have delved deeper into the deceptions and delusions that have made it possible for the Castro brothers to subjugate the Cuban people and defy twelve US presidents. I also have reflected on the factors that could advance—or hold back—the inevitable dawn of freedom in Cuba.

Five years prior to President Obama's announcement of his new Cuba policy, I wrote an article titled "Bailing Out the Castro Regime? Not Unless Communist Cuba Makes Concrete Democratic Changes," which *Forbes* posted on April 21, 2009. In this article, I referred to the many failed attempts by US presidents to normalize relations with the Castro regime and warned of a new ploy hatched in Havana to obtain the lifting of the US embargo on Cuba without introducing any meaningful economic and political reforms. I also called for stronger and better-coordinated efforts to stimulate and support the emerging civil society and the dissident movement on the island, as Washington successfully did with Solidarity in Poland.

More than a few leading minds of the foreign policy community took note of this view. For example, Richard Haass, president of the Council on Foreign Relations, who favors increased engagement with Havana, commented, "Your analysis of what has worked (and more often not worked) in the past is invaluable as the United States seeks the policy that can most effectively generate positive changes in Cuba."

Dr. Henry Kissinger wrote to me: "We are in substantial agreement that the United States should be wary of concessions without some positive indication that the Castro regime is committed to moving toward greater openness, including free elections. When and if that happens, we should then be slowly and conditionally supportive, which I believe to be your position as well."

Unfortunately this caveat was not heeded by the Obama administration, which seemed to have accepted most of the Castro regime's demands to normalize relations with the United States without obtaining any significant quid pro quo.

Since the key to the eventual resurgence of a free Cuba lies in the up-and-coming generations, I have been in touch with young dissidents, independent journalists, human rights activists, economists, and bloggers on the island who are taking a courageous stand in support of a peaceful democratic transition. I also have engaged Cuban American college students who wish to keep the flame of their family traditions alive and play a role in the future reconstruction of Cuba. While their views differ on how best to accelerate fundamental change on the island, their goals are pretty much the same: a free and democratic Cuba without hatred or fear, offering its citizens the opportunity to chart their own future and grow in a fair, dynamic, and inclusive environment. They all wish to understand the past, not to go back to it, but to learn from it.

Today the subject of Cuba still comes up in my family gatherings, just as it did when I was a teenager in Havana. True to their heritage, the young Carbonells—our daughter, Rosa María, and our two sons, Néstor Gastón and José Manuel—enjoy discussing whatever book or article I may be writing about my country of birth, and they are not shy to express their thoughts. Recently their questions have mostly centered on Cuba's entanglement in Venezuela and its collusion with Russia and China in the United States' backyard; the dissident movement in Cuba; and Raúl Castro's succession plans. Will they hasten or retard the anxiously awaited democratic opening of the captive island?

I have tried to respond to this and other queries as best I could. There is one question, however, they never ask—one I know is on their minds: Will my wife and I still be around to take all of them to a free Cuba? I don't have the answer. All I know is that, despite looming clouds on the horizon, hope still flickers in my heart.

INTRODUCTION

Sixty years after Fidel Castro seized power, there remains much confusion about the Cuban Communist tyranny and its remarkable longevity. Far more concerning, however, is the fact that few are aware of the looming threats the island poses today in collusion with hostile powers.

Perhaps we shouldn't be surprised, because Cuba in many ways is an enigma. What happened there defied all odds. A seemingly local political strife on a sun-drenched Caribbean island grew into a vexing geopolitical conflict involving the world's most powerful nations—not for a year or two, but for decades.

Moreover, it is difficult to fathom how a radical bearded Stalinist disguised as a liberator could subjugate for generations a people who cherished individualism, entrepreneurship, and freedom. It is also hard to imagine how he managed to subvert other countries, defy US presidents, and impose a dynastic succession.

This highly improbable chapter of history could not have occurred without two intertwined elements: Fidel Castro's mastery of deceit and his unbridled exercise of absolute power.

Modern totalitarian tyrants from Vladimir Lenin to Joseph Stalin, Benito Mussolini, Adolf Hitler, and Mao Tse-tung have used deception to confound enemies, win friends or "useful idiots," and deflect blame for their heinous crimes. But none did it with as much impudence and gusto, or for as long, as Fidel Castro. This is a man who promised a democratic revolution, consolidated his hold on power, and then unabashedly announced he was, and always would be, a Marxist-Leninist. That brazen duplicity—a constant in his life—sprang naturally from his schizoid narcissistic personality.

Raúl, Fidel Castro's younger brother, compliant partner, and pre-ordained successor, shares that penchant for deception—less histrionic and imposing than Fidel's, but no less ingrained.

It would, of course, be wrong to attribute the Castros' longevity in power—from their awe-inspiring apogee in 1959 to today's lackluster regime—solely to deception. Their dynasty surged, struggled, and survived through a confluence of internal and external circumstances, including notorious miscalculations by Cuban opponents and by leaders and pundits in the United States and elsewhere.

Sadly, the miscalculations persist. Even highly regarded foreign policy experts, who should know better, don't see Communist Cuba today as a brewing national security issue. Apparently they have forgotten the island's outsized geopolitical importance, driven largely by its "choke point" location. Sitting astride the so-called American Mediterranean, Cuba dominates the main entrances to the Gulf of Mexico. It commands the Caribbean Sea and the Atlantic approaches to the Panama Canal. And it lies ninety miles from the United States.

Its strategic value is borne out by history. Spain fought long and hard to keep the island it called "bulwark of the Indies and key to the New World." The conquistadors used it as launchpad for their historic forays, and renowned pirates and buccaneers assaulted its coastal cities to catch their prey. Spain lost Havana to England in 1782 and traded Florida for it one year later—such was the importance that Spain attached to the island.

Several US presidents coveted Cuba. Thomas Jefferson viewed the island "as the most interesting addition which could ever be made to our system of States." President James Monroe, unable to acquire it, preferred Cuba to remain in the hands of a weakened Spain (pending later purchase by the United States or independence) rather than those of a stronger England, France, or Russia. Hence the 1823 Monroe Doctrine, which declared that the Americas would not be considered open to further colonization by any European powers.

Alfred Thayer Mahan, considered the most influential American strategist of the nineteenth century, stressed the national security importance of the Caribbean (of which Cuba was the gateway). If the Caribbean were controlled by hostile powers, he warned, the Panama Canal, the Atlantic seaboard, and the great Mississippi Valley—the heartland of North America—would be at risk. Mahan's sway may explain why decades after the Spanish-American War and two brief US military occupations of Cuba, Washington has kept the naval base at Guantánamo Bay.

During the critical Battle of the Atlantic in World War II, Nazi submarines around Cuba ravaged the Caribbean Basin and undermined Allied war efforts until the United States blunted the attacks with a major counteroffensive.

In the midst of the Cold War, the Soviet Union, at great cost and even greater risk, sought to turn the island into a nuclear stronghold in 1962. Moscow failed in that endeavor but was able to convert the island into a formidable base for military assaults and subversion throughout the Americas, Africa, and other regions.

But that was several decades ago, some may say, at the peak of the Cold War. So does Cuba really matter now? Given its sinister intervention in Venezuela to support dictator Nicolás Maduro, and its collusion with Russia, China, and rogue states to undermine US leadership and national security—as revealed in the February 15, 2018, report to Congress by then commanding general of the US Southern Command, Admiral Kurt Tidd—there should be no doubt that Cuba matters today, more than many people may think.

———

Why Cuba Matters is history entwined with a living saga. It delves into new angles of the momentous events triggered by the Castro-Communist regime in concert with hostile powers. It also evokes the suffering of the Cuban people and their courageous struggle to end the tyranny and usher in a democratic and prosperous new era.

The in-depth history draws on declassified government documents, relevant reports, and reliable testimonies. And the saga relies on vivid experiences of witnesses and key players (including the author and his family) who have been involved on many fronts of the struggle.

In the interest of fairness and transparency, it is important to note that the record of some of those who have opposed the Castro regime, both on the island and abroad, is not spotless. At times their actions have been reprehensible. Yet, when passing judgment, it would be un-conscionable to equate the noble pursuit of freedom, even with its lamentable excesses, with the vile stranglehold of tyranny.

Why Cuba Matters is divided into three parts. It starts with "The Critical Present," probing key issues and new threats posed by the Castro regime in our backyard. It then flashes back to "The Daunting Past," shedding fresh light on pivotal episodes of the revolution. It ends with "The Promising Future"—projecting possible post-Castro scenarios and the outlook for a free Cuba.

The Critical Present

Cuba is facing a bleak situation—its economy is in or near recession; the shortages of food, medicine, and power are increasing; the state welfare system is in shambles; and the curtailed Venezuelan lifeline is at risk. And yet the Castro regime continues to block the opening of the economy and to suppress human rights.

Although Raúl Castro stepped down as president in 2018 and anointed as his successor a fifty-nine-year-old apparatchik (Miguel Díaz-Canel), Raúl will still control the regime until 2021 as first secretary of the Communist Party and de facto head of the armed forces. The new Communist constitution introduced numerous "reforms," but as *The Economist* correctly pointed out, "the twin pillars of Fidel Castro's [decadeslong] rule—the Communist monopoly on power and the state's domination of the economy—remain in place."

Hopes for a sustainable US-Cuba thaw, following the restoration of diplomatic relations in 2015 and the unilateral concessions made by the Obama administration to the Raúl Castro regime, were dashed by mysterious attacks that caused brain injuries to twenty-six US diplomats and security officers based in Cuba. These targeted attacks over more than one year, still under investigation, triggered countermeasures by the Trump administration, which further increased tensions.

Even after Cuba was removed from the US list of state sponsors of terrorism, Castro continued to support terrorist organizations and harbor fugitives from the United States and other countries.

Drawing on fresh information, this section describes the metastasizing of the Cuban Communist cancer in Venezuela and the Castro regime's role as strategy, intelligence, and repression mainstay of the Maduro dictatorship—now widely ostracized by democratic governments and facing strong internal opposition. It recounts Cuba's development of offensive bioweapons, its sale of dual-use biotechnology to Iran, and even a plot with North Korea to smuggle heavy weapons under tons of sugar.

Largely overlooked or downplayed by Washington until recently is China's growing economic, geopolitical, and military clout in Latin America. This is evidenced in Cuba, where China has become the island's largest trading partner on soft credits. Beijing reportedly uses the electronic eavesdropping base of Bejucal near Havana. Experts suspect that the new steerable parabolic antenna close to the base could potentially be used to intercept signals, track missiles, and disrupt satellite communications.

Even more worrisome is Russia's strategic reengagement with Cuba, particularly after President Vladimir Putin wrote off 90 percent ($32 billion) of Cuba's old debt to the Soviet Union. Although Moscow has not yet followed through on its reported intent to reopen the old Lourdes electronic surveillance station close to Havana or establish a new military outpost on the island to service its nuclear submarines and strategic bombers, it is actively developing cyberwarfare capability there.

Russia's high-tech spy ship *Viktor Leonov*, armed with missiles, has frequently docked in Havana. And in 2015, the Russian spy ship *Yantar*, equipped with self-propelled deep-sea submersible crafts, cruised the area where a major underwater cable lands near the US naval base at Guantánamo.

As reported by the *New York Times*, this became a source of major concern in the Pentagon since underwater cables, currently targeted by Russia for espionage and, potentially, sabotage, carry the lifeblood of global electronic communications, including national security data.

The Cold War may be over, but new threats from Castro's Cuba, in collusion with major adversaries of the United States, are looming in our backyard. And we ignore them at our peril.

The Daunting Past

This section starts with the March 1952 Fulgencio Batista military coup that derailed the republic and led to the Castro-Communist takeover in January 1959. Drawing on declassified documents and firsthand testimonies, it sheds new light on a number of puzzling questions not fully addressed by Cuba experts.

Given Castro's university record of gangster-type violence and crime, his egotistical personality, and his radical tendencies, how did he gain national and international standing during the struggle against the Batista dictatorship? Why did Batista spare his life and set him free, and why did most of Cuba's democratic leaders and some prominent businessmen eventually support or join forces with Castro during the insurgency?

And, finally, why did midlevel US State Department officials, who then called the shots on Cuba policy, press Batista to leave without supporting a democratic alternative, thereby creating a power vacuum filled by Castro?

This section also unveils three startling documents missed by most historians: Fidel Castro's psychological profile, written by one of Cuba's leading psychiatrists; the confidential findings of a Vatican emissary (Castro's Jesuit school mentor), who stayed three days with Castro in his mountain hideout; and President Eisenhower's angry instructions when he was belatedly apprised of the growing Communist influence over Castro's movement just days before Castro seized power.

Acclaimed as a savior by most of the frenzied population after Batista fled the country on January 1, 1959, Fidel Castro manipulated the masses with incessant harangues and false promises of democracy and social justice; penalized dissent with arbitrary arrests and firing squad executions; and covertly started laying the foundations of his totalitarian regime through a secret shadow government of loyal Marxists.

Even as Castro excoriated Yankee imperialism, harassed American companies, and suppressed human rights, the US ambassador to Cuba pursued through all of 1959 a policy of "patience and forbearance." As State Department declassified documents reveal, he even tipped off Castro about the first major conspiracy against the regime.

Much has been written about the botched Bay of Pigs invasion launched by the United States in April 1961 after Castro had sealed his fate with Moscow. *Why Cuba Matters* zeroes in on some of the still-perplexing questions, among them: Why didn't President Eisenhower, who strongly supported military action against the Castro regime, finish the job before he left the White House?

Perhaps even more puzzling, why did President Kennedy neither commit the necessary resources to ensure the success of the operation nor cancel it outright to avoid disaster?

The CIA and the Joint Chiefs of Staff raised red flags when Kennedy changed the recommended landing site and called off the vital air cover. Nonetheless, they agreed to go ahead with the invasion. Why?

Still unclear to many is how Castro was able to arrest the five heads of the underground prior to the invasion, preempt an internal uprising, and corral and eventually crush anti-Communist guerrillas in the mountains.

Finally, why were the Cuban exile chiefs marginalized and reportedly misled by US authorities and even held incommunicado during the invasion?

Several months after Cuban exile leaders were instrumental in having the Castro regime expelled from the Organization of American States in January 1962, with scant State Department support, the world was shocked by the Cuban Missile Crisis. Most historians focused on the ominous thirteen days in October 1962 when the two superpowers went eyeball-to-eyeball on the brink of a nuclear conflict. But few have fully explored why the United States failed to detect and deter the nearly four-month Soviet invasion of Cuba involving over one hundred shipments of offensive missiles and other lethal weapons and more than forty thousand Soviet soldiers and military personnel.

Following an unparalleled show of US power and Western solidarity, Kennedy negotiated with Khrushchev the withdrawal of the Soviet offensive missiles without unleashing a nuclear war, for which the president was praised. But given his belated response to the threat posed by the missiles—mostly emplaced and virtually operational—Kennedy had to pay a steep price for the settlement. He got the missiles out, but with his "no invasion of Cuba" pledge, he allowed the Soviets in. And in they stayed for thirty years, bolstering the Castro regime and turning the strategic island of Cuba into a launchpad for Communist aggression and subversion throughout this hemisphere and beyond.

Why Cuba Matters delves into the circumstances surrounding the tragic assassination of President Kennedy and provides declassified information and reliable testimonies pointing to a possible Castro connection, suspected by Lyndon Johnson and others.

After Kennedy's death, there were various attempts to reach an accommodation with Castro. All failed. In fact, the Cuban ruler's

Soviet-backed forays forced numerous US presidents to deploy military troops, intelligence operatives, and special forces in the Dominican Republic, Bolivia, Chile, Angola, Ethiopia, Grenada, Nicaragua, and Panama, among other countries. And yet the Castro-Soviet safe haven in the Caribbean was left untouched.

To complete "The Daunting Past," *Why Cuba Matters* details the regime's horrifying record of crimes against humanity and the living hell inside Castro's prisons. It also recounts the harrowing and often deadly flight of Cuban refugees, including the daring rafters and fourteen thousand unaccompanied children who were spirited out of the island to avoid Communist indoctrination. Finally it highlights the courageous struggle of peaceful dissidents to keep the flame of resistance alive.

The Promising Future

This final section ponders the prospects of a peaceful democratic transition in post-Castro Cuba, after the octogenarian diehards are no longer in power. It describes possible scenarios and points out what could accelerate, or retard, the process. It also highlights the likely role of the dissident movement and the young reformists within the government and the military, along with the involvement of militant organizations in the Cuban diaspora. This section also points out what the United States and other countries should do to avert the meddling of hostile powers and support the advent of a free Cuba.

The transition from totalitarian rule to democratic governance in Cuba will likely be staggered and bumpy and will require a broad-based unity government to ensure stability and justice without vendettas. The dismantling of the repressive apparatus, preceded by the release of all political prisoners and the approval of an interim constitutional framework that guarantees human rights, will be critically important.

Also urgent will be an emergency relief program, followed by the liberalization of the economy and an orderly privatization of the state monopolies—essential to attract foreign investment and know-how. The interim government will also have to establish a multiparty political system as a prelude to free elections.

Apart from recounting the major challenges that must be tackled to lift Cuba from misery and decay, this section outlines the long-term opportunities that could arise if future generations rein in their divisive passions, leverage their entrepreneurial zeal, and abide by the tenets of freedom under the rule of law.

SECTION I

The Critical Present

CHAPTER 1

Castro's Collusion with Russia, China, and Venezuela

Following the US-Cuba thaw, officially proclaimed in December 2014 by both President Obama and Raúl Castro, thousands of Americans traveled to the hitherto forbidden island. Many were curious to see, before it changes and becomes too commercialized, one of the last remaining totalitarian states frozen in time, a captive yet fascinating country that cloaks its sadness to foreigners with a warm heart and a broad smile.

A string of celebrities frolicked in Havana and attended a Rolling Stones concert and a Chanel runway fashion show along the stunning El Prado boulevard—a Caribbean version of the Champs-Élysées. Other visitors sailed to Cuba on board cruise lines and enjoyed so-called cultural stopovers at several cities choreographed by the government. Most of these visitors were oblivious to the repression on the island, which peaked in 2016 and has now again intensified, and to the Castro regime's entanglement in Venezuela to bolster the dictator Nicolás Maduro.

It seemed to outsiders that the thaw had marked a new beginning in US bilateral relations with Communist Cuba. This tenuous hope—which turned out to be an illusion—was upended by the mysterious brain damage inflicted, over more than a year, on twenty-six US diplomats and security officers based in Havana. The evidence so far suggests that the attacks were targeted. But since the investigations have dragged on with no conclusions, the *Washington Post* wrote that the United States must demand "accountability for whoever did this, and the first step is to find out who, and why." [1]

However, what dispelled the notion of a flexible and harmless post–Cold War Castro regime and pointed to the looming danger of hostile powers in this hemisphere was the startling February 15, 2018, report to the Senate Armed Services Committee delivered by Admiral Kurt W. Tidd, then head of the US Southern Command, responsible for all Department of Defense security cooperation in the forty-five nations and territories of Central and South America and the Caribbean.

Tidd, a four-star admiral who was the longest serving Naval Academy graduate on active duty, warned of the inroads that China, Russia, Iran, and North Korea have made in the region. He also underscored Cuba's "negative" influence on Venezuela and, ultimately, the direct threat the island could pose to US national security in collusion with those hostile states. It was, to say the least, a wake-up call.

There is, said Admiral Tidd, "a perception among our friends [in the region]—and the palpable anticipation among our competitors [he probably meant adversaries]—that we no longer stand by our commitments, that we are relinquishing our strategic position [in Latin America], and that we don't take the challenge in this region seriously."

He cited the menacing advances that China, Russia, and rogue states are making in the region, "courting some of our most strategically important Latin American and Caribbean partners, and supporting authoritarian, anti-American regimes."

The admiral emphasized the threat posed by the Castro regime. He stated that "from a national security standpoint, Cuba has demonstrated clear intent to target US interests through collection, surveillance, and counterintelligence activities in countries throughout the region."

Not deluded by Castro's sly succession moves on the island, the admiral contended that the Cuban military would continue "cooperation with Russia, China, and even North Korea, on a range of security, political, and economic issues." He also underscored "Cuba's negative influence in Venezuela—notably through its intelligence service and armed forces, which play key advisory roles shaping Venezuelan domestic policy. "This is evident," the admiral added, "in the Maduro regime's increasingly authoritarian tactics and human rights abuses. ... The relationship [between the two countries] is symbiotic, as Cuba receives oil and financial support in exchange for keeping the Maduro regime afloat."

Roughly one year after Admiral Tidd's wake-up call, reinforced by his successor, Admiral Craig S. Faller, the United States and other countries took a bold stand for democracy in Venezuela and considered imposing new sanctions against the Castro regime.

CubaZuela or VeneCuba?

The "Cubanization" of Venezuela, dubbed "socialism for the twenty-first century," started under President Hugo Chávez (1999–2013). This populist-cum-authoritarian ruler who publicly extolled the Castro revolution referred to Cuba as an "ocean of happiness" and called Fidel his ideological father. So close was the Castro-Chávez alliance that hard-liners on both sides gave a name to the desired merger of their two countries: "CubaZuela" if you were Cuban and "VeneCuba" if you were Venezuelan.

Now that Venezuela is struggling to regain its freedom, many wonder how that rich and independent country could have fallen under the sway, if not the virtual control, of the Castro-Communist regime. Early warnings from Cuban exiles who witnessed the takeover of their homeland were not lacking. I, for one, wrote in late 1999 an article in Spanish titled "Quo Vadis, Venezuela," signaling that Chávez's early demagogic-autocratic trend pointed to Marxism "à la venezolana." Some of my close friends in Caracas politely dismissed my concern, saying, "This can't happen here." I heard that same answer in Havana many times at the outset of the Castro regime. Unfortunately, what seemed impossible did happen—both in Cuba and, with marked difference, in Venezuela.

It's hard to believe that for close to twenty years Venezuelan oil on credit, along with huge service fees, investments, and financing, bankrolled the Castro regime. Chávez's massive aid escalated over time, reaching a high of nearly $10 billion annually for several years after 2007.[2]

In exchange, Caracas received more than forty thousand Cuban agents, from doctors and teachers to intelligence officers and military personnel. They all performed a wide variety of functions, but with one ultimate goal: to help Chávez consolidate his regime. (Chávez's embattled successor, Nicolás Maduro, reinforced this arrangement with Raúl Castro, but now with less oil and funds to send to Havana because of Venezuela's dire economic, financial, and political crisis.)

According to former intelligence officers of the Castro regime, the mission entrusted to thousands of Cuban medics sent to Venezuela was not just to upgrade and expand the country's health-care system in rural areas. The program, called Barrio Adentro, as originally outlined by Fidel Castro himself, also had two political objectives: strengthen the Venezuelan-Cuban alliance and underscore the virtues of socialism to the lower socioeconomic strata of the population.

The medics also were supposed to perform a quasi-intelligence function, passing on to their bosses information on each of the families they assisted—occupation, relationships, political allegiance, willingness to join the militias. The politicization of the Cubans' medical program became evident during Maduro's fraudulent reelection in May 2018. As corroborated and flagged by the New York Times on March 17, 2019, Cuban doctors were pressed by their superiors to "trade lifesaving treatment for Maduro votes."

Cuban teachers sent by the Castro regime to Venezuela also have been subject to this type of political pressure. Their educational function has generally called for subtle brainwashing and information gathering.

The Castro regime's sway in Venezuela has been particularly strong in such areas as national defense, paramilitary operations, counterintelligence, repression, and immigration. Antonio Rivero, a high-profile Venezuelan general, resigned in 2010 as head of the country's civil protection agency in protest of the insidious intrusion and control exerted by Castro officers in the military. Rivero denounced that Cuban "advisers" were meddling in all of the military fortifications and had direct access to the state's main security equipment, resources, maps, and plans.[3]

To supplement and, if necessary, counterbalance the country's armed forces, Castro combatants stationed in Venezuela were empowered to assist in the event of a popular uprising or a coup. They also trained and armed paramilitary operatives and militias, including Forces of Special Actions or "colectivos"—motorcycle thugs who have been seen in videos assaulting and killing peaceful protestors and unarmed students, and terrorizing the population.[4]

While Russia sold arms to Venezuela ($11 billion worth of weapons between 2001 and 2011), Cuba provided combat forces, training, and intelligence to bolster and safeguard the Chávez–Maduro regime.

What accounted for the extraordinary lopsided power wielded in Venezuela by the rulers of a country (Cuba) much smaller and poorer than the Bolivarian republic? Moisés Naím, Venezuela's former minister of trade and industry and currently a Distinguished Fellow at the Carnegie Endowment for International Peace, provided pertinent insights. He wrote in a column that the late Venezuelan president Hugo Chávez "felt a deep affection, admiration, and trust for the Cuban leader [Fidel Castro], who became a personal adviser, political mentor, and geopolitical guide." According to Naím, Fidel persuaded Chávez that Chávez could not rely on his own military and security forces, not even on his bodyguards, for personal defense. To address the issue, Castro offered Cuban special forces, activists, and propagandists, which Chávez readily accepted and paid for handsomely.

Chávez's successor, Nicolás Maduro, "deepened Caracas's

dependency on Havana even further," added Naím. Faced with a severe economic and financial crisis, along with growing opposition after
losing control of Venezuela's National Assembly, Maduro leaned heavily
"on many of the tools and tactics perfected by the police state that has
run Cuba for too long."[5]

At least one Latin American defense minister was aghast at the
unrestrained clout of the Castro regime's "advisers" in Venezuela. The
minister told Naím: "During a meeting with high-ranking Venezuelan
officers, we reached several agreements on cooperation and other matters. Then three advisers with a distinctive Cuban accent joined the
meeting and proceeded to change all we had agreed. The Venezuelan
generals were ... embarrassed but didn't say a word. ... Clearly, the
Cubans run the show."[6]

One service the Castro regime has provided to Venezuela poses a se-
rious regional threat: drug trafficking. According to the detailed report
issued in March 2014 by the Institute of Cuban and Cuban American
Studies of the University of Miami, Cuban General Leonardo Ramón
Andollo served for over fifteen years as the principal liaison between
Colombia's narco-guerrillas (FARC) and Venezuela's drug cartels.

As disclosed by Cuban defectors, General Andollo spent extended
periods of time in Caracas and met with Colombian guerrilla leaders in
safe areas controlled by the Venezuelan Cartel de los Soles. This cartel
reportedly was masterminded by Diosdado Cabello, former president
of Venezuela's National Assembly.[7]

In this context, it is relevant to point out that General John Kelly,
when he was chief of the Southern Command of the United States,
declared that large amounts of the Colombian cocaine and other drugs
that go to the United States and Europe are shipped from Venezuela via
islands in the Caribbean.[8]

The most senior Venezuelan official yet to face accusations of drug
trafficking is its recent vice president, Tareck El Aissami, forty-three
years of age. The son of Middle Eastern immigrants, he rose rapidly
through the ranks of Venezuela's power structure as a confidant of

Chávez and was appointed vice president of the country by Maduro in January 2017.

According to the US Treasury's Office of Foreign Assets Control, El Aissami "facilitated shipments of narcotics from Venezuela, to include control over planes that leave from a Venezuelan air base," and "oversaw or partially owned narcotics shipments of over 1,000 kilograms." The US Treasury Department imposed sanctions on him and froze assets in the United States, which reportedly amounted to tens of millions of dollars.[9]

The interior and justice minister of Venezuela Néstor Reverol faces federal indictment in Brooklyn, charged with assisting drug traffickers, and two nephews of Venezuela's first lady Cilia Flores were found guilty in a federal district court in Manhattan of conspiring to transport more than seventeen hundred pounds of cocaine to the United States. They each face ten years in prison.[10]

Since more indictments are expected of Venezuelan officials involved in drug trafficking and money laundering, the country has been viewed as a narco-dictatorship with a huge network of "partners" in many countries, including Colombia and Mexico, and liaisons with Iran, Hezbollah, Cuba and others.[11]

The Castro regime's priorities in Venezuela have been to avert the collapse or overthrow of the Maduro government, maintain the supply of oil on credit, and complete the Cubanization of the country. Following Castro's guidelines, Maduro started to lay the foundations of a Marxist totalitarian regime through a rubber-stamp constituent assembly headed by Diosdado Cabello, this while pounding the opposition, provoking the flight or emigration of over four million Venezuelans, and co-opting his two thousand generals with drug money if they remain loyal—and threatening them with prison or death if they double-cross him or rebel.

Maduro felt that he could rely on Cuban forces and spies in Venezuela to neutralize or quell any resistance. The current secretary-general of the Organization of American States, Luis Almagro, said in a US Senate hearing in July 2017 that "there are currently about fifteen thousand Cubans [including intelligence agents, presidential bodyguards, and military personnel] in Venezuela. … It's like an occupation army from Cuba."[12] (The most current estimate is twenty thousand.) Moreover, the former Venezuelan ambassador to the United Nations Diego Arria earlier declared, "Venezuela is an occupied country. The Venezuelan regime is a puppet controlled by the Cubans. It is no longer tutelage; it is control."[13]

Still today, many are baffled by this asymmetrical phenomenon. Angus Berwick dispels the mystery in his Special Report "How Cuba Taught Venezuela to Quash Military Dissent." [14] It all started to gain traction when Chávez, in May 2008, empowered the Castro regime to create and spearhead a directorate general of military counterintelligence, mainly to spy on Venezuela's own armed forces, instill fear, and crush dissension. Pursuant to two secret agreements, Castro trained Venezuelan intelligence agents in Havana and flooded Caracas with Cuban spies armed with the latest surveillance technology.

María Werlau, in her current well-documented book *Cuba's Intervention in Venezuela*, broadens the assessment of Castro's sway beyond the military. She explains how the Cubans, drawing on extensive digitized data banks and identity cards with biometric identification, have established in Venezuela "an electronic police-state or Big Brother system." In this nefarious science, Chinese-trained agents have served as effective teachers for both Cuba and Venezuela.

But the Castro regime provides more than spying and repression. Cuban troops, which had been kept under wraps, were displayed in October 2018 when the Maduro regime announced that the Venezuelan Army and Cuba's Special Forces, known as "Avispas Negras" (Black Wasps), held a combined strategic military exercise near the Colombian border. According to the Venezuelan general Remigio Ceballos-Ichaso, the operation was also supported by Russia and China.[15]

The overall situation drastically changed in January 2019, when Maduro was sworn in for a new six-year term following a rigged election. The illegitimacy of his extended rule, along with the collapse of the economy and the ensuing humanitarian crisis, broadened and inflamed the political opposition. Hundreds of thousands of irate Venezuelans poured into the streets of Caracas and other cities to demand the resignation of Maduro and to support the head of the duly elected National Assembly, Juan Guaidó, who assumed temporarily the presidency of the country pending free elections, as called for by the country's constitution.

The United States, Canada, and over fifty Latin American and European countries withdrew their support of the "usurper" (Maduro) and recognized Guaidó as the sole legitimate caretaker president of Venezuela. Although the armed forces so far have backed Maduro, their unified front could eventually splinter or crumble.

The expectation has been that by offering amnesty to army officers who flip, coupled with massive anti-Maduro rallies and diplomatic and economic sanctions (such as cutting off Maduro from Venezuela's largest foreign revenue stream—US oil sales), a democratic transition under Guaidó could be achieved without bloodshed.

But on April 30, 2019, the opposition to Maduro suffered a major setback when a planned uprising fizzled out for lack of support of several key government officials and army generals who apparently were involved in the plot. This mishap emboldened Maduro, who intensified repression and arrested the vice president of the National Assembly and other democratic leaders.

Meanwhile, Russia, with military personnel on the ground, continues to support Maduro (as does China, financially). But that is not all. As recently denounced by Elliott Abrams, the State Department's special envoy for Venezuela, Russian companies are now handling seventy percent of Venezuela's oil to evade US sanctions. "They market it, they finance it, they hide it, ship to ship transfers, changing the name of boats, turning off transponders." (*Washington Post*, 1/7/2020).

Moreover, Cuban officers effectively control Maduro's Special Action Forces involved in torture and killings. As reported by United

Nations human rights commissioner, Michelle Bachelet, those forces
in Venezuela ("death squads") have carried out several thousand extrajudicial killings in the last two years to spread terror and neutralize
political opposition. [16]

To complicate matters, Venezuela and Cuba apparently played a
role in the recent riots that shook Bolivia after Evo Morales resigned
under pressure as president, as well as Ecuador, Chile and Colombia.
In each case the protests, including acts of vandalism, required curfews
and the deployment of the armed forces. Although economic and social
issues may have been the root causes of the breakdowns of law and
order, the organization displayed and the sophisticated explosives used
suggest subversive intent with external support, especially in Chile.
Agents from Venezuela and Cuba, along with radical followers of the
Sao Paulo Forum, reportedly fanned the flames of rebellion in those
countries." [17]

It should be noted that the incoming government of Bolivia demanded that the Cuban medical mission leave the country after some
of its members were caught funding activists to spread violence. And
the government of Ecuador sent the Cuban doctors home when agents
embedded in the medical mission were found inciting turmoil.

Given these troubling developments, largely emanating from the
Venezuelan quagmire, the United States and other countries backing
Guaidó plan to intensify pressure to seek the departure of Maduro and
his narco-criminal cohorts, the restoration of law and order under an
interim government of national unity headed by Guaidó, and free and
fair elections. Despite the failed Oslo-led mediation and Maduro's latest ploy to strip his opposition of control over the National Assembly
through force and fraud, negotiations with the Venezuelan dictator will
likely be renewed.

But what if Maduro and his clique block again a peaceful democratic transition, even a reasonable compromise solution? Would military action continue to be ruled out to end what some experts have

called "the worst collapse of a nation outside of war in decades," along with mounting crimes against humanity?

What we know so far is that Washington conducts frequent air reconnaissance over Venezuela. Moreover, ten countries of the Americas, led by the United States and Brazil, held in August 2019 a twelve-day naval exercise near the coast of Río de Janeiro with a multinational force of close to four thousand marines. Admiral Craig Faller, head of US Southern Command, oversaw the display of force and the exercise. After warning against Venezuela's formidable weapons system and denouncing the support provided by Cuba, Russia and China to the Maduro regime, Faller declared that the purpose of the mobilization was to prepare for "the day after" the departure of Maduro. [18]

But what about preparation for the "day before," if needed as a last resort to push Maduro out? Under what circumstances would it be warranted and legal to take military action? If the Maduro dictatorship and the countries intervening in Venezuela (namely Cuba, Russia and China) pose a clear and present danger to the peace and security of the region, the Inter-American Treaty of Reciprocal Assistance (Rio Treaty) could be invoked and applied with two-thirds majority vote to address the emergency. This would enable signatory countries to adopt the collective measures prescribed by the treaty, including the use of force, to restore peace.

As of now, however, most of the countries supporting Guaidó seem to reject military action and bet on negotiations, coupled with diplomatic and economic sanctions, to seek a peaceful way out of the crisis. Let us hope that this is not just wishful thinking.

The Tehran Connection

Venezuela is not the only looming threat in the Caribbean. The Castro regime's close relationship with Iran, reinforced by former president Ahmadinejad's visit to the island in January 2012 and subsequently by the visits of other senior Iranian government officials, includes intelligence and military cooperation. This disturbing development, however, did not seem to have been raised as a serious issue by the Obama administration in its negotiations with Iran and Cuba.

It has been reported that the Castro brothers were instrumental in cementing the Caracas-Tehran strategic pact that has enabled Iran to mine, and potentially enrich, uranium in Venezuela, use the country's banking facilities, and amass a large number of Venezuelan passports. Iran has liberally compensated the Castro regime for its solidarity and services to the Islamic Republic. Since 2005, Cuba has received from Tehran the equivalent of over one billion euros in credits.[19]

Cuba's close alliance with Iran—the most powerful and active state sponsor of terrorism—dates back to 1979, when Fidel Castro became one of the first heads of state to recognize the Islamic Republic of the ayatollahs. Then, in the 1990s, Cuba sold to Iran dual-use biotechnologies that could be used both for medicinal purposes and as lethal bioweapons agents.

Cuba's dual-use biotechnology capability was disclosed in May 1998 by William Cohen, secretary of defense under President Clinton. In his report to Congress titled "The Cuban Threat to US National Security," Cohen stated that "Cuba's current scientific facilities and expertise could support an offensive BW [bioweapon] program in at least the research and development stage. Cuba's biotechnology industry is one of the most advanced in emerging countries and would be capable of producing bioweapons."

In March 2002, Carl Ford, assistant secretary of state for intelligence and research under President George W. Bush, reported to Congress that Cuba had at least limited offensive biological warfare research and developmental capability, and confirmed that it had "provided dual-use biotechnology to rogue states." This report, expanded by Undersecretary of State for Arms Control and International Security John Bolton just before former president Carter's trip to Cuba, became an explosive political issue.

Partisanship notwithstanding, how accurate are these reports? Are they credible? Yes, said a key witness, Ken Alibek (formerly Kanatjan Alibehov), who from 1987 to 1992 was the first deputy chief of research and production of Biopreparat, the Soviet Union's clandestine biological weapons program. Alibek defected in October 1992 and relocated to the United States a few months later.

In his book *Biohazard*, published by Random House in 1998, Alibek recounts how the Soviet Union helped Cuba develop its biotechnology program following Fidel's 1981 meeting with Leonid Brezhnev in Moscow. "Within a few years," wrote Alibek, "Cuba had one of the most sophisticated genetic engineering labs in the world—capable of the kind of advanced weapons research we were doing in our own." According to Alibek, his boss, Major General Yury Kalinin, returned from a 1990 visit to the biocomplex in Havana "convinced that Cuba had an active biological weapons program."[20]

Among Cuban defectors, the one who seemed most knowledgeable on this matter was José de la Fuente, former director of research and development at the Center for Genetic Engineering and Biotechnology (CIGB) in Havana from 1990 to 1998. He disclosed that the Castro regime had invested more than $1 billion in the various centers of the biotechnology complex. The CIGB alone had eleven hundred employees with more than two hundred scientists in R & D working on a pipeline of one hundred twelve products.

Despite this huge investment, the entire Cuban pharmaceutical-biotechnology industry only exported $50 million per year during the period 1995–1999. So how could the Castro regime keep this costly venture afloat, particularly after losing Moscow's massive aid?

De la Fuente offers a plausible answer: The regime developed other sources of income, such as the sale of dual-use biotechnologies to Iran (and other countries). Specifically, Havana provided Tehran with recombinant protein production technologies in yeast and *E. coli*, which could be used both for medicinal purposes and as lethal bioweapons agents to produce anthrax bacteria or smallpox virus.[21]

There are strong indications that Castro's motivation was not only commercial but also strategic, meaning anti–United States. This was borne out when Fidel visited Tehran in May 2001 to extoll what was vaunted as the spectacular creation of a Cuba-Iran joint venture—the largest center of genetic engineering and biotechnology in the region.

He arrived there with the swagger of a conquistador and brazenly declared that "Iran and Cuba, in cooperation with each other, can bring America to its knees."[22] Always prepared for an encore, Fidel followed up in Havana with this veiled threat: "Today this country has more options than ever, is stronger than ever, and has more weapons than ever to wage the ideological battle—and let's not forget the other weapons we have stored away and the very clear idea on how we'd use them. So we are calm."[23]

How did Washington react to these troubling developments? US officials cast a skeptical eye on the allegations that Cuba had been developing biological weapons. This is how they parsed words in crafting their ambiguous June 1999 statement: "Cuba certainly has the know-how and capability to brew terrorism-sized batches of deadly agents, but there has been no proof that it has methodically produced military-grade agents or munitions."[24]

Since the Castro regime will not allow an independent inspection of the secluded sections of its biotechnology center, it is not surprising that no hard evidence of biological weapons has been produced so far. Nevertheless, there is enough smoke if not to cry fire, then at least to continue probing and remain vigilant.

Sponsor of Terrorism

It is well-known and well-documented that since coming to power in 1959, the Castro regime has trained thousands of guerrillas and terrorists from around the world. Its grand design was to subvert most countries in this hemisphere, as well as in Africa and the Near East, inciting and supporting Marxist insurgencies. The well-coordinated forays, aided and abetted by the Soviet Union, wreaked havoc and caused innumerable deaths.

The United States, which has ample evidence of these atrocities, finally in 1982 decided to add Cuba to the list of state sponsors of terrorism, also graced today by Iran, Syria, and Sudan. Apart from the stigma attached to the list, the designation triggered a number of export and financial sanctions and restrictions.

Raúl Castro took advantage of President Obama's interest in seeking a rapprochement with Cuba and made it very clear that he (Castro) would not agree to restore US-Cuba diplomatic relations unless and until the island nation was removed from the terrorism sponsor list. Obama caved following a perfunctory investigation that gave a pass to the Castro regime.

Despite this unilateral concession, Castro's Cuba remains a sanctuary for dozens of fugitives and terrorists from the United States and other countries and refuses to extradite them. Among the US fugitives is JoAnne Chesimard, alias Assata Shakur, a member of the Black Liberation Army. One of the FBI's "Most Wanted Terrorists," she was convicted of first-degree murder for the execution-style killing of a New Jersey state trooper. Chesimard received a life sentence but escaped prison and made her way to Cuba.

William Morales, leader and chief bomb maker for the terrorist organization FALN, also was granted safe harbor in Cuba. He committed numerous terrorist attacks on US soil in 1977, killing five people and injuring sixty others.

The Castro regime granted refuge to terrorists from Colombia's Revolutionary Armed Forces (FARC) prior to the peace agreement Bogotá signed with them in 2016, and currently provides an operational base for Colombian narco-guerrillas from the National Liberation Army (NLA). This was described in an article—"Waging War in Colombia, via Havana"—carried by the *New York Times* on August 25, 2018.

Also harbored in Cuba are terrorists from Spain's Basque separatist group ETA, responsible for the death of more than eight hundred people.[25] It should be noted that prior to the removal of Cuba from the list of state sponsors of terrorism, Spain asked the United States to use its overture to Havana to obtain the extradition of two ETA fugitives, but to no avail.[26]

To support Nicaragua's current reign of terror, the Castro regime (along with Russia) has reportedly been providing military and intelligence assistance to the Ortega regime as it tries to quash the growing prodemocracy opposition led by students. If the bloody repression continues to escalate, it could well lead to another Venezuela-type quagmire in Latin America.

Castro has also been involved in trafficking arms and drugs. In July 2013, Cuba colluded with North Korea to smuggle through the Panama Canal 240 metric tons of heavy weapons, which included MiG jets, missile batteries, and explosives. This contraband, hidden under tons of sugar, reportedly constituted the then largest violation of United Nations Security Council sanctions against North Korea. Yet the Castro regime emerged from this flagrant transgression unrepentant and unscathed.[27]

Then in February 2015, Colombian authorities intercepted in the port of Cartagena a Chinese-flagged ship headed for Cuba with a weapons cache hidden as grain products. The unregistered cache consisted of one hundred tons of gunpowder, almost three million detonators, and some three thousand cannon shells. As reported by the *Wall Street Journal* editor and columnist Mary O'Grady, mounting evidence suggests that the secret arms shipment was destined for the FARC terrorist group in Colombia with the Castro regime acting as go-between. Further probing of the regime's suspected complicity was halted or silenced, presumably for political considerations. Informed sources believe that Washington did not wish to hamper the removal of Cuba from the US list of state sponsors of terrorism.[28]

Two months later, in April, Panamanian authorities uncovered an illegal shipment from Cuba. This time it was not arms but drugs, and it was hidden under not sugar or grain but molasses. Panamanian newspapers reported that in an operation dubbed "Caña Brava" (Fiery Cane), local police intercepted over four hundred kilos of cocaine in a shipment from Cuba en route to Belgium. The cocaine was found in Colón, about fifty miles north of Panama City, under a container camouflaged with molasses tanks. Yet again Washington seemed unperturbed.[29]

A few days after the drug contraband from Cuba was uncovered, the admiral then in charge of the US Southern Command invited a delegation of Cuban government security officials to tour the Pentagon's counterdrug center in Key West. Apparently, Washington felt that the Castro regime could be trusted as a partner in cracking down on illegal trafficking in the Caribbean.[30]

The Obama administration expected that in return for the removal of Cuba from the list of state sponsors of terrorism and other US unilateral concessions, the Castro regime would stop its subversive activities and conform to basic international norms. Washington seemed confident that Raúl Castro could at least be swayed to withdraw the thousands of Cuban military and intelligence officers deployed to Venezuela to "Cubanize" the country and buttress the Maduro dictatorial government.

The Cuban ruler, however, was not prepared to distance himself from his Caribbean confreres. This is how he publicly responded to Washington's entreaty: "The United States should understand once and for all that it is impossible to seduce or buy Cuba or intimidate Venezuela. Our unity is indestructible."[31]

China's Push into Latin America

While the United States for the past decade or more took for granted its historic leadership position in Latin America and focused elsewhere, China seized the opportunity to move into the region with an ambitious long-range plan.

Trade between China and countries in Latin America and the

Caribbean reached $244 billion in 2017, twice what it was a decade earlier. Since 2015, China has been South America's top trading partner, surpassing the United States.[32]

Eager to lock up vast amounts of resources and enhance its influence and power in the region, Beijing issued billions of dollars in commodities-backed loans, mainly to leftist authoritarian governments, and made major infrastructure investments. This falls within its "Belt and Road Initiative," designed to create economic dependence on China. Some have called this stratagem the "diplomacy of debt," involving predatory loans difficult to pay back.

That's what occurred in Ecuador under its previous radical president, Rafael Correa. As reported by the *New York Times* [33], China lent Ecuador $19 billion to build a gigantic dam, as well as bridges, highways, irrigation systems, schools, and clinics. This major project has become part of a national scandal, engulfing the small South American country in widespread corruption and a huge amount of debt. To settle the bill, Beijing gets to keep 80 percent of Ecuador's most valuable export—oil—thereby largely controlling the economy of the country and influencing the political arena.

China also has tried to gain a strategic foothold in tiny, impoverished El Salvador. Presenting itself as a partner offering "shared opportunities [and a] shared future," a state-owned Chinese company requested a hundred-year lease of the isle of Perico to create a global trade hub that would enable Beijing to develop an alternative route to the Panama Canal. According to US officials, the special zone "would also give China a valuable perch to expand its military and intelligence capabilities in Washington's vicinity." The United States finally woke up and helped to thwart the deal, at least for the time being. [34]

Beijing took a big bet with Venezuela, which has received an estimated $62 billion, mainly as oil-backed loans. But as noted by the Washington-based Center for Strategic and International Studies, even if Venezuela comes apart at the seams (or its government is overthrown), China could end up grabbing a major part of the national resources of

Venezuela—a country that has the largest proven oil reserves in the world.[35] Time will tell.

According to the US Southern Command, "17 out of 31 Latin American nations have joined China's Belt and Road Initiative; meanwhile 23 host Chinese infrastructure projects, including 56 ports across the region." [36]

China's interest in Latin America is broader than commodities and trade. It includes strategic and military clout. With that in mind, Beijing organized joint military training exercises, including naval missions, off the Brazilian coast in 2013 and the Chilean coast in 2014. And in October 2015, China's defense minister hosted officials from eleven countries in Latin America for a ten-day forum on military logistics.[37]

But what particularly concerned Admiral Tidd, head of the US Southern Command, is China's "telecommunications and space ventures with dual-use potential, which could facilitate intelligence collection, compromise communication networks, and ultimately constrain our ability to work with our partners." He was presumably referring to the $50 million satellite and space mission control station built by the Chinese military in Patagonia, following secret negotiations with Argentina's previous leftist government, which included a $10.2 billion currency swap deal to help stabilize the Argentine peso.[38]

Closer to our shores, in Cuba, a brand-new electronic installation suggests augmented cyberwarfare capabilities for potential signals interception and disruption from satellites servicing the entire eastern United States. As reported in June 2018 by the Asia-Pacific current affairs magazine *The Diplomat*, this signals intelligence facility, with a new steerable parabolic antenna and its spherical enclosure (together called a radome), was recently erected on a site adjacent to the Bejucal spy base just south of Havana.

The functions of the new antenna are not clearly discernible from the satellite images obtained by *The Diplomat*, but similar antennas have been employed for signals interception, missile tracking, satellite uplinks and downlinks, and radio communications, and in some cases to disrupt satellite communications.[39]

It is not clear who provided the financing for the new facility. What is known is that Beijing's intelligence officers have been using the adjacent Bejucal spy base since 2001, and that China—now Cuba's largest international trading partner—has shown a keen interest in expanding its cyber capability on the island, particularly after its prime minister Li Keqiang visited Havana in 2016 and signed twenty cooperation agreements with Raúl Castro.

China's geostrategic interest in Cuba is further evidenced by the fact that the island has been the largest single beneficiary of Beijing's debt forgiveness over the last eighteen years—$6 billion in debt canceled in 2011. [40]

The Havana-Moscow Axis

Even more worrisome in the short term is another potential security threat looming in the Caribbean with geostrategic ramifications: the expanded intelligence and military cooperation between Castro's Cuba and Putin's Russia. Since early 2013, telling developments point to a new strategic partnership between the two countries ominously aimed at the United States.

It all started to gain prominence when Russian prime minister Dmitry Medvedev visited Cuba in February 2013 and announced that Moscow intended to forgive most of Cuba's Soviet-era debt. Moscow's largesse was not one-sided as became apparent in the following months.

When Russian chief of staff General Valery Gerasimov arrived in Cuba in April, he visited several strategic sites and indicated that Moscow wanted to step up its military and intelligence presence on the island. Word then spread that Russia was considering reopening, with updated technology, the former Soviet electronic spying base in Lourdes, near Havana, as well as considering using Cuban ports to resupply Russian naval task forces and local air bases to refuel strategic aircraft.[41]

The rumors soon started gaining credibility. In August 2013, Russia dispatched to Havana the *Moskva* guided-missile warship—the flagship of the Russian Black Sea Fleet—accompanied by the Udalog-class destroyer from the Northern Fleet and a large seagoing tanker.

Then in February 2014, just when Russia was taking over Crimea, the Russian intelligence-gathering ship *Viktor Leonov* docked in Havana, and Russian defense minister Sergey Shoigu announced that Moscow intended to establish permanent bases in several countries, including Cuba.[42] The *Viktor Leonov* has since visited the island several times.

To formalize a major strategic agreement, Alejandro Castro Espín, Raúl Castro's son who headed the Commission of Defense and National Security, led a Cuban delegation to Moscow in March 2014 and signed with Russia's Security Council secretary Nikolai Patrushev a memorandum on interaction to increase intelligence cooperation.[43]

Also in March, concern about the expanding Moscow-Havana military connection was likely raised in the Pentagon in the context of a potential cruise missile threat to the United States from the Gulf of Mexico. In his Senate testimony, US Northern Command head General Charles Jacoby declared that the 2014 defense authorization bill mandated a US focus on "ballistic missiles that could be launched from vessels on the seas around the United States, including the Gulf of Mexico."

Jacoby acknowledged that the Pentagon has "some significant challenges" in countering this type of missile, more so, it should be added, if Cuba—the Gibraltar of the Gulf—were to serve as a base or refueling center.[44]

In June 2014, Moscow found a way to get its foot in the door to North America by installing the Global Satellite Navigation System (GLONASS) in Cuba. The space cooperation agreement that Russia signed with Cuba added a new dimension to the strategic partnership. As noted in the *Moscow Times*, "If Russia is ever to bring GLONASS up to snuff with the US-owned and -operated global positioning system, or GPS, which Moscow needs to do to effectively utilize GLONASS for military and economic purposes, it must have a truly global network of tracking stations. In this regard, Cuba is a beachhead for Russia's satellite technology in North America."[45] After four years in the planning stage, a GLONASS station in Cuba, under the Russian Ministry of Defense, is expected to be operational soon.

The various agreements between Moscow and Havana that laid the groundwork for their new strategic entente climaxed on July 11, 2014, when Putin visited Cuba and met with Fidel and Raúl Castro. The Russian leader officially wrote off $32 billion of bad Cuban debt and signed about a dozen accords, which included the modernization of the maritime port of Mariel and the construction of a modern airport.[46]

But what grabbed worldwide attention was the report carried by the Russian newspaper *Kommersant* on July 16 stating that Moscow had decided to reopen the Lourdes electronic eavesdropping base in Cuba. Putin denied that an agreement had been reached to reopen the base, but according to a *New York Times* report posted in Moscow on July 17, "members of the Russian Parliament appeared to confirm the report in public statements, praising what seemed to be a step by Russia toward reestablishing a military presence in Cuba."[47]

Doubling down on Moscow's decision to increase its military and intelligence involvement in the Caribbean, using Cuba as a base, Russian defense minister Sergey Shoigu stated in Moscow in November 2014 that Russia will extend the aerial missions of its long-range bombers "as far as the Gulf of Mexico and the Caribbean."[48]

One need not be a conspiracy theorist to surmise that Moscow and Havana are colluding to undermine and possibly threaten the security of the United States and the region. Obama and his foreign policy team, however, did not seem overly concerned since they believed that the Castro regime, intent on reaping the benefits of normalizing relations with the United States, would not cross the line.

But in October 2015, less than one year after Obama announced the new Cuba policy, an alarming report involving Moscow and Havana raised serious questions, at least in the Pentagon. As disclosed by the *New York Times*, "Russian submarines and spy ships were aggressively operating near the vital undersea cables that carry almost all global Internet communications, raising concerns among some American military and intelligence officials that the Russians might be planning to attack those lines in times of tension or conflict."

The *Times* further reported that the United States had been monitoring significantly increased Russian activity, even in waters close to American shores, along the routes of the cables that carry "the lifeblood of global electronic communications and commerce." Clearly, Moscow was enhancing its cyberwarfare capability within the defensive perimeter of the United States. "Just last month," added the *Times*, "the Russian spy ship *Yantar*, equipped with two self-propelled deep-sea submersible craft, cruised slowly off the East Coast of the United States on its way to Cuba—where a major cable lands near the American naval station at Guantanamo Bay."[49]

Russia has modernized its once-decrepit Soviet-era fleet of submarines and dramatically stepped up its activity around undersea data cables throughout the Atlantic. This recently led NATO ministers to revive a Cold War command that is expected to be embedded inside the US Fleet Forces Command in Norfolk, Virginia.[50]

As if this sequence of troubling episodes were not enough to bear out the potential threat in the Caribbean, we learned in January 2016 that a US Hellfire missile sent to Europe for a NATO exercise "inadvertently" landed in Cuba. Washington reportedly became aware of it in June 2014. This laser-guided air-to-surface missile, which can be launched from a helicopter, a drone, or a plane, is a highly sensitive military technology that has become an important part of the US government's antiterrorism effort. Was this a shipping error or a deliberate diversion concocted by Castro? To our knowledge, no one has been held accountable.

What is even more intriguing is that the Obama administration allowed the Castro regime to keep the Hellfire for about two years before returning it to the United States, while the rapprochement with Communist Cuba was being negotiated. It's no stretch to suspect that during that period Castro shared the sophisticated technology with his rogue friends Russia, Iran, and North Korea—a likely outcome feared by defense experts.[51]

Another project that remains pending involves nuclear cooperation with Cuba. In July 2016, the news agency TASS reported that Russia's Council of Ministers had decided to renew nuclear cooperation with Cuba, purportedly to address the island's energy needs. The announcement did not indicate whether the agreement would call for the completion of the Soviet-funded power plant in the southern Cuban town of Juraguá, which was abandoned when money from Moscow dried up in 1992. The United States then viewed the potential risk posed by a Russian nuclear station close to Florida's Key West as a threat to national security.[52]

Also significant is the expected Russian takeover of Venezuela's 49 percent stake in Cuba's refinery in the city of Cienfuegos, in the southern part of the island. Igor Sechin, head of Russia's state-owned Rosneft oil company, signed the deal with Raúl Castro shortly after Venezuela awarded Sechin two gas exploration contracts.[53]

In the coming months, Putin will likely determine how far he is willing to go in leveraging Russia's strategic partnerships with Cuba, Venezuela, and Nicaragua—the "Troika of Tyranny" in the words of Trump's former national security adviser John Bolton.

This is how Admiral Tidd broadly defined the troika's threat in his February 15, 2018, report to the Senate Armed Services Committee referred to earlier: "Expanded port and logistic access in Cuba, Nicaragua, and Venezuela provide Russia with persistent, pernicious presence, including more frequent maritime intelligence collection and visible force projection in the Western Hemisphere. The sanctuary of robust relationships with these three countries provides Russia with a regional platform to target US and partner nation facilities and assets, exert negative influence over undemocratic governments, and employ strategic options in the event of global contingency.

"Left unchecked," the admiral warned, "Russian access and placement could eventually transition from a regional spoiler to a critical threat to US homeland."

Given the abundant evidence of Russia's stepped-up strategic engagement with Cuba and other Latin American countries in recent years, that warning is well-grounded.

Relying on the Castro regime's control of Venezuela's repressive and counterintelligence agencies and paramilitary forces, Moscow decided to provide yet more support to the embattled Maduro dictatorship. As a show of force in 2018, Putin deployed in Venezuela two of its nuclear-capable bombers to carry out drills over the Caribbean Sea, but reportedly put on hold the possible use of a forward outpost (air base) on the Venezuelan island of La Orchila in the Caribbean Sea.

Yet on March 23, 2019, two Russian military planes landed in broad daylight at the international airport in Caracas, carrying about one hundred military "advisers" and supplies. The *New York Times* flagged that "the arrival of the advisers came as Venezuela activated Russian-made S-300 air defense systems." It is still unclear whether, and to what extent, the United States will counter any further Russian provocation.

Regarding Nicaragua, the *Washington Post* reported on April 8, 2017, that three decades after Nicaragua became a major Cold War battleground, it is now the site of a new Russian-Cuban buildup. It involves a Russian GLONASS satellite system with potential capability for electronic espionage aimed at the United States. The buildup also includes the supply of Moscow armored personnel carriers, aircraft, mobile rocket launchers, and tanks; the visit of Russia's warships; and the presence of some 250 Russian military experts and trainers.

The Castro regime is also involved in Nicaragua, providing intelligence and military support to the Ortega dictatorship to quell major protests against arbitrary policies, government corruption, and blatant violations of human rights. Over three hundred student activists were killed in 2018 by Ortega thugs.

A recent Russian show of force in the Caribbean was the arrival in Havana on June 26, 2019, of a detachment of Russian naval warships, including one of its advanced frigates, the *Admiral Gorshkov*. Although described as a routine port visit, this display of power coincided with Moscow's warning against the planned US deployment of a missile defense system in eastern Europe. "We could find ourselves in a situation where we have a rocket crisis close not just to the crisis of the 1980s, but close to the Cuban Missile Crisis," Russian deputy foreign minister Sergei Ryabkov reportedly declared, according to Reuters.

———

In sum, Admiral Tidd's clarion call was very timely. The menace posed by Castro's Cuba, in collusion with Russia, China, and rogue states, is real and should not be underestimated. It calls for a well-thought-out strategy that draws on sixty years of painful and eye-opening experiences in dealing with the Castro regime and its powerful allies.

To avoid the delusions and miscalculations that dotted those experiences, we need to probe and learn from the past. Hence the relevance of the next section of *Why Cuba Matters*.

SECTION II

The Daunting Past

CHAPTER 2

How Democracy Died in Cuba: From Batista to Castro (1952–58)

▌Batista and His Infamous Coup

It was March 10, 1952, close to 2:00 a.m., when a heavily armed convoy of three Buick sedans and five police cars stealthily approached gate no. 4 of army headquarters in Havana. Seated in the front car, wearing a plain white shirt and a tan zip-up jacket, was the leader of a military coup in the making—the fifty-one-year-old sturdy retired general Fulgencio Batista.

The officer in charge of the military camp that day, who was a party to the conspiracy, rushed to the gate to ensure safe passage. Except for a few minor glitches, the carefully choreographed coup was consummated with lightning speed, encountering little resistance. Most of the armed forces backed the coup or remained neutral, and the cordial Democratic president of Cuba, Carlos Prío, who was caught off guard, could not rally enough support and sought diplomatic asylum at the Mexican Embassy.[1]

My father, then Senate majority whip, had met with Prío the evening before the coup at his private home La Chata in the outskirts of Havana. He told me that the president seemed unaware or unconcerned of Batista's plot. All they had discussed that evening were issues related to the upcoming general elections.

Surely there was no justification for the coup, which disrupted the constitutional process just three months prior to the scheduled multiparty elections. But the nation was tired of violent political feuds and corruption.

Prío's presidency, though respectful of human rights and fruitful from a legislative standpoint, had been weakened by its own scandals and by the incessant tirades of the opposition. Those tirades were inflamed by a populist leader, Senator Eduardo Chibás, who had launched an implacable campaign against graft, bribes, and shady deals in the government under the slogan of "Honor vs. Money" (Vergüenza contra Dinero). The symbol used was a broom to sweep away corruption. Chibás became Cuba's Cato the Censor, with unfortunate excesses.

During one of his top-rated Sunday radio broadcasts in 1951, Chibás was unable to substantiate a wild accusation against an honest cabinet minister. At the end of his harangue, thinking he was still on air, he took out his gun and shot himself as he shouted: "This is my last clarion call!" (¡Mi último aldabonazo!)

Chibás's scorched-earth campaign and tragic death, sublimated by a sensationalist and highly politicized media, further eroded the institutional underpinnings of Cuba's fragile democracy.

Batista, who was running for president anew without any chance of winning, took advantage of his army contacts and of the mood of the country—the people yearning for stability and order—to perpetrate his coup. The staging was relatively easy, but the consequences were disastrous for the nation.

Lust for Power and Money

Before the coup, Batista could boast a salient place in history, albeit with stains on his record. Coming from a humble family with European, African, and Indian roots, he'd earned a living as a laborer in cane fields, docks, and railroads in the far-eastern province of Oriente.

In 1921, at twenty, he joined the Cuban army as a private, and in 1933, following the overthrow of the Machado dictatorship, he led the Sergeants' Revolt that catapulted him as "the Strongman of Cuba."

Then in 1940, after paving the way for an exemplary constitutional convention with broad multiparty representation, Batista shed his military uniform and was elected president.

Batista's 1940–44 democratic government, though marred by graft and sporadic heavy-handedness, deftly tackled the war challenges aligned with the United States, hastened the recovery of the economy, and ended the term on a high note. Batista held free and transparent elections, won by the opposition; transferred power to the new president—his archrival Ramón Grau San Martín—and took up residence in Daytona Beach, Florida.

After his having won plaudits for his overall performance as president, why did Batista stage a military coup and become a dictator eight years later? From his self-imposed exile in Daytona Beach, Batista, still in his forties, missed the limelight and hungered for power. And along with power, he lusted for money to replenish his coffers, partially depleted by his lifestyle and his divorce.

So after running for senator and winning the election in absentia, he returned to Cuba in 1948 with a single objective in mind: the presidency—by ballots or bullets. Since he didn't have the votes to win (he was running a distant third), he stealthily seized the ship of state on March 10, 1952.

Batista's Paradoxes and Miscalculations

Batista was not the traditional Latin American dictator. Rarely seen in public with the military, always donning a civilian's neatly pressed white linen suit, he invited some prestigious public figures to join his cabinet and Consultative Council, and became initially a part-time dictator, or a dictator with a democratic complex. Interspersed throughout his rule were periods of free press and assembly.

Eager to gain a patina of legitimacy, he ran for president in 1954, but the elections were boycotted by most of the opposition leaders for lack of adequate guarantees. He ostensibly welcomed mediation efforts to resolve the political crisis but refused to shorten his four-year term and cede power to an interim government of national unity.

Batista was ruthless when provoked by acts of terror and aggression. The reprisals were indeed brutal, particularly when his head of military intelligence and his chief of police were gunned down in Havana by the revolutionaries and when he barely survived an assault on the presidential palace.

During some of the clashes that bloodied the island, two of Cuba's young resistance trailblazers—José Antonio Echeverría, twenty-five, president of the Federation of University Students, and Frank País, twenty-two, underground rebel chief, were killed by Batista's police. This was a tragic loss to the cause of freedom since these two promising leaders, with strong democratic and Christian principles, would have bravely opposed the Castro-Communist takeover of Cuba. Yet when two of Cuba's most prominent political heavyweights (former president Carlos Prío and former prime minister Manuel Antonio "Tony" Varona) were directly involved in military attempts to overthrow him, Batista allowed them to leave the island without putting their lives, safety, and/ or properties at risk. But the most glaring of Batista's paradoxes was his soft, lackadaisical attitude toward Fidel Castro, a young man who, according to the government's own sources, had a record of violent crimes and Communist ties, and who, thanks in part to Batista's short-sightedness, became the key driver of an insurgence that eventually toppled him.

After Castro led a bloody attack against the Moncada garrison in 1953, Batista spared his life, pardoned him after less than two years in prison, where Fidel had enjoyed privileged treatment, and allowed him to leave for Mexico. From there, Fidel and eighty-one of his comrades (including his brother Raúl and Ernesto "Che" Guevara) launched a military expedition against the Batista dictatorship and landed on the southeastern coast of Cuba, near the steep forested cordillera of the Sierra Maestra, on December 2, 1956.

When Batista was informed of the landing, he was placidly playing canasta—a frequent pastime that he relished—at a friend's house. As revealed by Francisco "Silito" Tabernilla, a brigadier general and son of the commander in chief of the armed forces, this is what happened. Batista told Silito: "Let's discuss [this] later; I don't want Martica [Batista's wife, who was nearby] to know, because she gets very nervous."

A few hours later, after the canasta game was over, Batista stepped into a separate room, asked to see a map of the region, and said: "Let's send forty men to get them." Silito, somewhat startled by Batista's nonchalant attitude, respectfully countered: "If you allow me, Mr. President, what I would do is to send two thousand men to [comb the area], corner them against the sea, and wipe them out or force them to surrender." Batista retorted: "Silito, are you crazy? What we need to do is drive them into the Sierra Maestra. Don't you know that *there*, nobody can survive?"[2]

Batista not only underestimated the threat, but he also micromanaged the military operation without any knowledge of guerrilla warfare and without ever having visited the combat zone. He thought he could isolate the small group of rebels without having to snuff them out.

A state of pseudowar suited Batista's plans. It afforded him the pretext to suspend constitutional guarantees as he saw fit and find new ways to enrich himself, through kickbacks from public works and development projects.

He also felt he was secure in power, owing to several factors. The first of these was public fear of a Communist takeover if Castro's insurgents were to prevail (a delusion, since not many then believed that he had Communist ties or inclinations). The second was a booming economy fueled by foreign investors, including notorious mobsters who were allowed to control the leading casinos in Havana and several hotels in exchange for payoffs. To tourists, Cuba was an idyllic playground, offering sun-drenched days on the beaches and starlight evenings at the cabarets featuring such top artists as Edith Piaf, Nat King Cole, Maurice Chevalier, and Frank Sinatra. And the third was that Batista believed he could rely on the continued support of the US government—an assumption that proved fatal as Washington's Cuba policy during the civil strife veered from neutral, to anti-Batista to, indirectly, pro-Castro.

Clearly those factors did not enable Batista to win over most Cubans. University students and young professionals, primarily from the middle and upper-middle classes, were unhappy with the state of affairs. They voiced their protest against dictatorial rule and corruption; supported the resistance movement, which at times proved to be more powerful in the cities than in the mountains; and helped turn the tide against Batista.

After the United States decreed an arms embargo on Cuba in March 1958, the already demoralized army realized that Batista's days in power were numbered. And when Washington gave Batista an ultimatum in December to leave the country, the plots against him (some in concert with Castro) reached the highest echelons of the army.

Even his old friend the commander in chief of the armed forces Francisco "Pancho" Tabernilla-Dolz met with the US ambassador Earl E. T. Smith in December without Batista's knowledge and proposed an interim military junta to replace him. When Batista learned about this, he had his "Et tu, Brute?" encounter with his friend. "Pancho, why did you do it without my authorization?" Batista asked him point-blank.

"I tried to find a national solution, which you, yourself, had asked us to look for," explained Tabernilla.

"You were staging a coup d'état against me," rejoined Batista.

"What I did was in good faith," Tabernilla curtly replied.[3]

This incident strained their long-standing relations but did not sever them. They were both in the same boat—a sinking boat.

By the end of 1958, Batista knew full well that he could no longer cling to power. He had myopically foreclosed the last opportunity for a political solution by rigging the November general elections.

On the military front, Batista's final, ill-conceived offensive, involving an armored train, miserably collapsed. The situation was indeed hopeless for the besieged dictator—opposed by most of his people and hard-pressed by Washington to leave. So he finally decided to exit, not honorably with a well-planned transition in place, but disgracefully, leaving a power vacuum behind.

In the early hours of January 1, 1959, Batista, his family, and high-level government officials secretly fled the island on three planes and headed to the Dominican Republic. A desperate but belated effort to pursue an orderly succession under the most senior Supreme Court justice (Dr. Carlos M. Piedra) was attempted, as prescribed by the constitution in the absence of elected leaders.

My maternal grandfather, José Manuel Cortina, former secretary of state, was involved in this last-minute undertaking to avoid the collapse of the republic. He joined other retired senior statesmen, including the grandfather of my wife-to-be, Dr. Raúl de Cárdenas, former constitutional vice president of Cuba.

The acting army chief of staff, General Cantillo, summoned them to the presidential palace to form an interim government presided by Justice Piedra with the objective of pacifying the country and holding free elections as soon as possible. Unfortunately, the majority of the Supreme Court justices did not consent to the constitutionally prescribed succession, alleging, to their later regret, that the revolution (meaning Fidel Castro) was the fountain of legitimacy and the source of law.

When my grandfather left the presidential palace and met with the family, his face was grim. According to the notes I kept, he told us about the belated attempt to find a constitutional solution and added with a tone of sadness, not characteristic of him, "Seven years of corrupt dictatorship have gravely weakened the fabric of the republic and sapped its political and moral defenses. This is like a case of severe immune breakdown. Cuba lacks the vital antibodies to protect itself. It has fallen into the hands of Castro, and there is nothing solid in sight to limit his power or contain his influence. Who knows what the future will bring?"

The fate was sealed. Accelerating the demise of the beleaguered republic, the rudderless forty-thousand-strong army, betrayed by its chiefs who had escaped, unconditionally surrendered to Castro and his rebel forces. Batista, bitter and dejected, didn't seem to care. Was he thinking of the apocalyptic phrase of Louis XV, "After me, the deluge"? Perhaps, but with a twist. He was most likely telling Washington and his Cuban opponents, "You forced me out. Now just wait and see what's coming to you."

The Splintered Democratic Opposition

During the early stages of the insurgence against the Batista dictatorship, Fidel Castro was not a key or even a respected player. There were other, weightier political leaders in the mix who had formed a united front, known as the "Montreal Pact," to oppose the military coup. Soon, however, a divergence of strategies and tactics, coupled with conflicting personal ambitions, splintered the coalition. Some of the leaders tried to find a peaceful electoral solution to the national crisis, but most either abstained (lacking confidence or courage to get involved) or became insurrectionists (at least in name), postulating that military action was the only effective way to get rid of Batista.

After five attempts to overthrow the dictator without Castro's involvement, most of the insurrectionists joined forces with Fidel, thinking naively that they could control or guide him.

It Was Not the Economy, Pundits

Contrary to the opinion of many historians, the peasants were not a significant factor in Castro's rise. They did not swarm to Fidel's camp while he was holed up in the mountains. According to one of the leaders of Castro's 26th of July Movement, "To attract peasants it was necessary to pay double the value of everything that was bought from them."[4]

Nor were the workers interested in backing the revolution. Although they certainly welcomed further improvements in their quality of life, most were generally satisfied with the growth of the economy and with the labor and social benefits accorded by the 1940 constitution and respected by Batista.

Those benefits included relatively high salaries for workers. According to the International Labor Organization, the average daily industrial wage in Cuba in 1958 placed the island in the company of some of the most developed countries—even ahead of Australia and England.

Cuba's workforce before Castro could exercise the right to collective bargaining and to strike and enjoyed social security and health-care coverage. As reported by the United Nations Department of Economic and Social Affairs, Cuba had 1.01 physicians per 1,000 inhabitants in the 1950s, which placed the country ahead of Norway, Spain, and Sweden.

Moreover, the 1940 constitution granted employees what was then unheard of in most countries—one month of yearly vacation with pay. Not surprisingly, the national revolutionary strike that was launched against Batista in April 1958 lacked labor support and failed.

Economic factors, though important, were not the key drivers of the revolution against Batista. Despite cyclical unemployment during the "dead season" following the sugar harvest, and glaring (but narrowing) inequities between urban and rural areas, Cuba in 1958 topped most Latin American countries in standards of living.

The island ranked third in national income per capita. Globally, Cuba's was almost as high as Italy's and considerably higher than Spain's and Japan's. Close to 80 percent of the population was literate (only surpassed in Latin America by Argentina, Chile, and Costa Rica, per the United Nations Statistical Yearbook), and its growing and enterprising middle class was injecting vitality into the economy, which actually peaked in the late 1950s.[5]

Nor was there any widespread sentiment against US investors or, for that matter, "Yankee imperialism." That is why Castro did not publicly express his animus toward the United States and capitalism at that time. In an article he published in *Coronet* magazine in February

1958, titled "Why We Fight," he denied having plans to expropriate or nationalize foreign companies. "I personally have come to feel," he wrote, "that nationalization is, at best, a cumbersome instrument. It does not seem to make the state any stronger, yet it enfeebles private enterprise." He then reiterated, "Foreign investment will always be welcome and secure here."

The underlying cause of the unrest was primarily political, and the prevailing feeling that galvanized large swaths of the population was anti-Batista and not in favor of anyone in particular. However, through masterful propaganda spread by foreign reporters, the bearded warrior eventually turned the Batista enmity into Castro fervor.

Most of the activists did not join the guerrillas in the mountains but stayed in Havana and other cities and worked part time in the underground in what was called "civic resistance," raising funds and smuggling arms. They largely fought for democracy and honesty in government under the 1940 constitution, which Castro himself ostensibly supported, and not for a radical revolution. Castro publicly revealed his Marxist-Leninist design only when he was firmly entrenched in power in the last quarter of 1961.

The other important element of civil society—the business community—was somewhat divided. Although most of the leaders publicly advocated a peaceful resolution of the national crisis, some of them, to protect their business interests or out of hatred of Batista, paid a "revolutionary tax" (euphemism for extortion) on sugar mills, cattle ranches, and coffee and cocoa plantations. In the specific case of the sugar industry, the levy drew 15 cents on each 250-pound bag of sugar produced in the mills.[6]

One of the prominent contributors was Julio Lobo, known as the "sugar king" of Cuba. Echoing a sentiment that pervaded large segments of the population, Lobo reportedly said, "We didn't care who overthrew Batista, so long as someone did."[7] Others phrased it differently: "Nothing could be worse than Batista."

The business group that possibly became the revolution's strongest backer was the highly regarded Bacardi family, led by Pepin Bosch, Daniel Bacardi, and Victor Schueg. They supported Castro in the belief that he would, as promised, restore democracy and implement the social reforms prescribed by the 1940 constitution with due respect for private property and human rights.

Not only did they funnel significant financial contributions to the revolution, but they also arranged critical meetings between leaders of Castro's 26th of July Movement and US government officials. One of these was CIA Inspector General Lyman Kirkpatrick, who made a fact-finding visit to Santiago de Cuba in the spring of 1957. He was assured that Castro and his followers were not Communists and that they were only working for "what you Americans have: clean politics and a clean police system."[8] These platitudes seem to have tranquilized the not too perspicacious inspector general.

Castro, of course, never acknowledged how much assistance he and his movement got from the very businessmen whose properties he later seized. That would have marred his anticapitalist credentials when he later disclosed his allegiance to Marxism-Leninism. As he advised two of his confidantes: "Lots of smiles and glad-handing for everyone. … There will be time enough to smash those roaches all at the same time."[9]

Several attempts were made to settle the strife, including the 1956 "Civic Dialogue," led by the Cuban War of Independence patriot Cosme de la Torriente, and the March 1958 Catholic Church mediation, but these efforts were either called off or aborted. The situation was too polarized to forge a compromise with broad-based consensus.

The Failed Third Force

Despite the odds against a peaceful electoral solution (even though Batista was not running for reelection), a last-ditch effort was made to create a political force that would challenge the dictator's intended successor and his other candidates in the rescheduled November 1958 elections and offer a democratic alternative to Castro and his revolutionary allies.

This effort was led by Dr. Carlos Márquez-Sterling, a talented and prestigious statesman who had presided over the 1940 Constitutional Assembly and who was supported by several former senators and congressmen, including my father, who was elected vice president of the newly formed Free People's Party (FPP).

I temporarily left the family law firm where I was working to join my father in the campaign. My main tasks were to write speeches for him, coordinate his agenda, and make sure he did not start smoking again since he was convalescing from a severe heart attack. Security was also an issue since we were exposed to attacks from two fronts: the Batista hard-liners, called *tanquistas*, and the Castro terrorists opposed to elections. However, my father refused to be armed or to enlist the services of private security guards. We were lucky to elude aggression.

Although Batista repeatedly assured the heads of the FPP that he would abide by the results of the elections, they did not blindly rely on Batista's word. To broaden public backing for his candidacy (thereby making government fraud more difficult), Márquez-Sterling pledged, if elected, to form a government of national unity and, in two years, hold general elections in which he would not run. He also made overtures to democratic leaders who were abstaining or had joined forces with Castro, but without much success.

Even those who were aware of Castro's background and radical tendencies were dulled by the so-called "ninety-mile syndrome"—the belief that a Communist regime couldn't be established, much less endure, ninety miles off the US coast. This belief, which turned out to be a myth, seemed to assuage the concerns of seasoned political leaders like former president Prío, who had provided financial assistance to Castro.

When Márquez-Sterling raised the issue of a possible Communist infiltration or takeover through Castro, he told us that Prío had dismissed that as unlikely, adding, "In any case, the United States would not tolerate it."

"What if they do?" insisted Márquez-Sterling.

"Then we're screwed!" retorted Prío.[10]

Despite the snub of numerous democratic leaders of the opposition, Márquez-Sterling's candidacy started to gain traction, but not enough to overcome the terrorist attacks unleashed by Castro to intimidate the candidates and the voters and disrupt the elections. As a result, many stayed home and didn't cast their votes. The coup de grâce was delivered by Batista, who orchestrated a massive fraud to ensure the "victory" of his presidential candidate, Andrés Rivero-Agüero, and of his followers.

As Brigadier General Silito Tabernilla revealed in his memoirs, forged ballots, which had been secretly printed and marked in one of the houses at army headquarters (Camp Columbia), were stuffed in the ballot boxes across the island to consummate the fraud. According to Tabernilla, "If the fraud had not been perpetrated, Dr. Carlos Márquez-Sterling would have been the winner. The political picture would have radically changed. Fidel Castro would have had no alternative but to negotiate or lay down the arms and pursue political avenues if he aspired to be president."[11]

US ambassador Smith, who wanted to weigh in publicly in support of free and honest elections, was barred by Washington from doing so. He later wrote: "If Dr. Márquez-Sterling had won the elections, it would have removed from Castro his alleged goal to rid Cuba of Batista."[12]

Castro was well aware of that. In 1959, after Batista had fled and the republic had collapsed, and Fidel reigned supreme, Castro confided to the Argentine ambassador Julio Amoedo: "Márquez-Sterling was the one we feared the most. Had he won the elections, I would not be here today."[13]

▌Fidel's Histrionics, Violence, and Duplicity

Fidel Castro's meteoric rise was powered by a confluence of internal and external factors, but the main driving force was Castro himself—a phenomenon in the annals of totalitarian deception and prolonged domination. Although he was in the limelight longer than all post–World War II revolutionary icons and has been the subject of many probing books, his multilayered personality, scheming, and duplicity have confounded savvy historians, as well as relatives and colleagues who thought they knew him well.

There is no consensus of opinion as to Castro's proclivities, ideology, and early ties, but most experts on Cuba at least agree that his illegitimacy and dysfunctional family had a traumatic impact on his psyche and conduct.

Fidel was one of seven children born out of wedlock. His father, entangled in a contentious and protracted divorce, sent him, at the age of four, along with two of his elder siblings, to Santiago de Cuba under the guardianship of the consul of Haiti. While attending Catholic schools in Santiago, Fidel was tormented by two stigmas: he was the son of a Spanish soldier who had fought against the Cuban patriots during the war of independence, and he was a bastard who was legitimized by his father only when he was seventeen.

Fidel's rebelliousness surfaced while he was still in elementary school. Once reprimanded by a teacher for not doing his homework, he disrupted the classroom, turning tables upside down, and asked his classmates to join him in protest.[14]

His unabashed boldness and interest in public affairs also sprouted early on. In November 1940, when Fidel was fourteen, he penned a personal letter to President Franklin D. Roosevelt, in faulty English, congratulating him on his reelection and asking him for a ten-dollar bill. In his postscript, he told the president that if he wanted iron ore to build boats, he (Fidel) could show him the best mines located in Mayari, Oriente. Fidel proudly displayed the pro forma thank-you note he received from the White House (even though it was not signed by the president) but felt slighted for not having received a ten-dollar bill.[15]

In 1941, Fidel was admitted to a renowned Jesuit school (Belén) in the outskirts of Havana, the same school where several members of my family studied. There, Castro distinguished himself as a bright but undisciplined student with a prodigious memory and a knack for letters, and as a tall and agile all-around athlete.

Oratory was one of Fidel's high priorities at school, but he, who years later felt at ease at the podium delivering endless speeches, had to conquer paralyzing stage fright. To be admitted to the exclusive literary and debating society at Belén (Academia Literaria Avellaneda), students had to speak for ten minutes without notes about a subject given an hour in advance. After failing three times, Fidel mustered enough courage to pass. A teacher who saw him suffering at the podium reportedly quipped: "If you put bells on his knees, he could give us a concert."[16]

Bizarre episodes laden with histrionics marked Fidel's record at Belén and landed him a nickname that would haunt him for years: "el loco." Several of his classmates told me that one of the episodes was the five-dollar bet he'd made with another student who dared him to throw himself headfirst from a moving bicycle, at full speed, against a wall on the school's hallway. Fidel won the bet but ended up unconscious in the clinic.

Fidel's deep-seated violence, which became a constant in his adult life, flared up at school. One day when he was chatting with some girls (a strain for him given his social awkwardness and shyness), a fellow student jokingly called him "el loco." A fistfight ensued and Fidel was knocked down. He then ran to his room and returned with a pistol, which he menacingly brandished until a shocked priest intervened and disarmed him.[17]

In 1945, Fidel enrolled in the University of Havana to study law. There, he led a double life. Privately he immersed himself in the study of populist and totalitarian systems but mainly focused on Marxism-Leninism and developed ties with young Communists and fellow travelers, which he kept under wraps. What became more visible was his public persona, embroiled in volatile student politics, spiked by quasi gangster groups. In that violent environment, which aroused him, Fidel was implicated in two murders and an attempt on the life of a third rival, but he was not indicted, mainly because of political influence.

In 1948, Fidel, who remained shy with girls and who was not prone to socializing, proposed matrimony to Mirta Díaz-Balart, a sweet, green-eyed young woman who came from a well-heeled Cuban family who lived near the Castro hacienda in the far-eastern province of Oriente. Those close to Fidel felt that he was truly smitten with Mirta, but his first marriage was to be only a brief interlude in his tumultuous life.

Living a conventional life did not appeal to Fidel, and practicing law was of little interest. In fact, he had no desire or need to earn a living since he could count on the financial support of his father, who had become wealthy as a landowner in Oriente. The rugged but cunning Spaniard, who had worked hard for the United Fruit Company, expanded the neighboring land he acquired reportedly by moving fences at night and paying off the Rural Guard to quash complaints.

Revolution was Fidel's passion, and power, absolute power, his aphrodisiac. He did enjoy affairs, including an early one with a voluptuous socialite (Natty Revuelta), which wrecked his marriage and led to a messy divorce seven years later. However, his romances were mostly fleeting experiences, and sex never seemed to be more than a sideshow.

Fidel thrived on military adventurism. Apart from his university forays, he trained for an invasion against the Dominican dictator Rafael Trujillo, which was aborted at the last minute by the Cuban government, and he later participated in a Communist-inspired uprising in Bogotá, Colombia. But his goal was Cuba, and the seizure of power his obsession, preferably taking shortcuts and resorting to violent means.

A bizarre episode prior to Batista's coup is particularly revealing. In 1945, following a student demonstration against the democratically elected president Ramón Grau-San Martín for having increased the bus fares, a student delegation, which included Castro, was invited to confer with Grau at the presidential palace. Since it was a very warm day, the students were escorted in the course of the discussion to the balcony on the third floor.

While they were waiting for the president to rejoin them, Fidel whispered to his colleagues: "When the old man [Grau] returns, let's pick him up, the four of us, and throw him off the balcony. Once the president is dead, we'll proclaim the triumph of the student revolution." The leader of the delegation nixed Fidel's macabre plan, saying, "We came here to ask for a lowering of the fares of the buses, not to commit an assassination."[18]

Logic in His Madness

As could be expected, following this and other similar episodes, Fidel was again branded with the appellation of "el loco." But was he really crazy? Perhaps the most illuminating early analysis of Castro's complex personality and outlandish conduct that I have researched was published by Bohemia Libre in 1961, without much fanfare, by Dr. Oscar Sagredo-Acebal, the then exiled former president of the Cuban Society of Psychoanalysis and of the Cuban Society of Psychotherapy.[19] His article was missed by Castro biographers and historians and was possibly overlooked by CIA psycho-profilers.

To introduce his theme in plain, not professorial, language, Sagredo refers to a joke that circulated in Cuba in late 1959. A group of psychiatrists had been asked to analyze Fidel Castro. After listening to him on radio, watching him carefully on television, and interviewing him personally, the psychiatrists concluded: "When he's mad, he's paranoiac; when he's lucid, he's a Communist."

Turning serious, Sagredo affirms that Fidel is not a typical psychotic (or madman in the vernacular). His deftness to outmaneuver his rivals and deceive even his followers, and his methodical coldness to vivisect his country as he gradually laid the foundations of the Communist regime, do not characterize a psychotic. There is logic in his madness, albeit totalitarian logic. Although abnormal in several ways, he is conscious of, and responsible for, his own acts, but is not pained by guilt.

According to Sagredo, Fidel is a psychopath with a paranoid disorder. (The terminology used these days to diagnose his pathology is most likely narcissistic personality disorder, which can coexist with a paranoid or schizoid condition.) The Cuban psychiatrist highlights Fidel's persecution mania as well as his delusions of grandeur—the insatiable need for attention and recognition—which manifests itself in the cult of personality that he fosters, the many titles that he collects, even the two watches he used to carry. These things all reflect basic insecurity tempered by the reassurance of applause. As Sagredo points out, Fidel does not shine as a speaker; in fact he turns pale and starts to stutter when confronted by unexpected face-to-face challenges, such as the Spanish ambassador's irate rebuttal many of us watched on TV in early 1960.

Another of Castro's traits analyzed by Sagredo is his dirtiness (at school he was called "bola de churre" or greaseball). Habitual dirtiness is generally a symptom of severance from or aggression toward the outside world. In Castro's case, the breaking of ties with values, traditions, family, and society at large was probably motivated by the scorn that he suffered as an illegitimate boy. His lack of empathy—indeed his ruthlessness and cruelty—has been one of his hallmarks.

Not even his elder son, Sagredo reminds us, was spared from Fidel's heartlessness. During one of Castro's TV appearances shortly after taking power, he was informed that Fidelito, gravely wounded in a car accident, was about to undergo delicate surgery. Instead of rushing to the hospital, Fidel impassively continued pontificating for two more hours.

His exiled sister, Juanita, also attests to Fidel's lack of family attachment and his disdain for tenderness and compassion, which he views as signs of weakness. According to Juanita, Fidel stated when the revolution had triumphed that "all family ties are produced by virtue of purely animal instinct."[20] She also recounts in her published memoirs that when their father, Angel, died in October 1956, Fidel rebuked his brother Raúl, who was deeply distressed, saying, "There is no time for grief; we must prepare for worse things."[21]

Sagredo refers to Castro's two faces as expressions of his dual personality: the soiled, tired, bearded face with a distrustful and paranoiac look, like that of an animal that expects an attack, and the placid, boyish-looking face with an aura of candor that projects charisma. The psychiatrist believes that the two distinct facial expressions, which reflect lack of integration of personality caused by defective identification with his father and mother, enabled Fidel to develop his histrionics and uncanny ability to spin half-truths, myths, and outright lies.

No other demagogue or tyrant in modern times has matched Castro's infamous record of deception. When he declared in December 1961 that he had been a Marxist-Leninist since his university days, he offered no apology or explanation for his concealment except to say, with undisguised cynicism, that had he then revealed his ideology, he would not have been able to descend from the Sierra Maestra and carry out his socialist design.

This is how Sagredo summarizes Fidel's diagnosis: "psychopathic paranoid personality with basic insecurity, affective coldness, defective identification, histrionics, symbolic satisfaction of oral needs, and anal aggressiveness." Since his prognosis was incurable, the suggested treatment transcended psychiatry: "surgical removal of the patient in the interest of hemispheric prophylaxis." Judging from history, this was a sharp and portentous assessment.

Castro's Communist Connection Dismissed by Washington

The State Department and the CIA knew there were Communists in the highest echelons of the 26th of July Movement, but lulled by Fidel's prodemocracy siren song and by his repeated denials of any Communist allegiance, they naively believed that he would fend off the radicals and even oppose them.

Although Castro was not a card-carrying member of the Cuban Communist Party—an unreliable and often misleading litmus test to detect Communist fealty—there was credible intelligence of his Red ties before he took power.

Why then did Washington, which had ample opportunity to investigate Fidel's background and follow his footprints, misread his revolutionary goals, underestimate his threat, and abet his takeover? Was it Castro's genius to deceive or Washington's failure to discern? Or was it a combination of both?

The United States had access to the files on Fidel and Raúl Castro and their coconspirators held by BRAC, the Cuban counterintelligence bureau tracking Communist infiltration and subversion, which was set up by Batista and US ambassador Arthur Gardner and was upgraded by Lyman Kirkpatrick of the CIA.[22]

The BRAC files reportedly contained detailed information of Fidel's activities at the university, where he left a trail not only as a rambunctious, trigger-happy activist vying for student leadership but also as a secretive student of Marxism-Leninism who had forged close ties with a network of both registered and nonparty Communists. Among these were Leonel Soto, Alfredo Guevara (no relation to Che), and the two heads of the Cuban Socialist Youth organization, Flavio Bravo and Luis Mas Martín.

The intermittent mastermind of that network was the pint-sized sinister Pole Yunger Samjovich, known as Fabio Grobart—one of the founders of the Cuban Communist Party in the mid-1920s who served on and off as éminence grise in Cuba for the Comintern, an organization promoting world communism. Over the years, he was expelled several times from the island but returned when the political climate was propitious. Fidel Castro, after his ascent, honored Grobart as a true hero of the Cuban Revolution and continued to seek his guidance.

Castro was so concerned that the BRAC intelligence records of his Communist ties would prematurely leak out that a few days after he grabbed the reins of power, he instructed his henchmen to seize and destroy the files. Not content with that, he ordered the arrest of then acting director of BRAC, Captain José de Jesús Castaño, a nonpolitical, well-educated professional who spoke four languages and was not involved in any malfeasance.

Castaño was subjected to a denigrating mock trial on fabricated charges of rape. The alleged victim was a Communist stooge who, according to one observer, easily qualified as one of the ugliest and most despicable women in Cuba.[23] Despite the plea made by several ambassadors who knew Castaño well and vouched for his professionalism and integrity, he was condemned to death and executed.

The other copious files on Castro, containing incriminating evidence of his early Communist connection, were held by Salvador Díaz-Versón, a distinguished Cuban journalist and intelligence officer who devoted twenty years of his life to the study of Communist penetration in Cuba and the rest of Latin America. Díaz-Versón served as director of Cuban military intelligence during the constitutional government of Carlos Prío and as president of the Inter-American Organization of Anti-Communist Journalists.

When Fidel learned of the wealth of information that Díaz-Versón had gathered over the years on Communist agents, including a full dossier on him (A-943), which reportedly ran to 264 pages, he ordered the seizure and destruction of the files on January 26, 1959, less than a month after he took power.

Díaz-Versón was luckier than Captain Castaño. He was able to elude arrest and execution and fled the island in March 1959. While in exile in Miami, he tried hard to reconstruct some of the intelligence he had amassed on Fidel Castro. Although the information he later put out was incomplete and lacked corroboration in several areas, it carried the weight of a responsible professional with many years of experience.

According to Díaz-Versón,[24] the plot started in 1943, shortly after Cuba established diplomatic relations with the USSR. Evidence of the importance that Moscow ascribed to the island as a potential strategic base of operation in Latin America was the direct involvement in

Cuba of two of the Kremlin's heavyweight envoys to Washington: Ambassador Maxim Litvinov and his successor, Andrei Gromyko, who later became Russian foreign minister.

When these envoys started to lay the foundations of a major Soviet subversive apparatus in Havana with a staff of over 150 agents, Spruille Braden, the feisty US ambassador to Cuba who described Gromyko as having the "coldest eye I have ever seen in a human being,"[25] sounded a warning in Washington, but without eliciting much attention.

Among the Soviet officers who came to Cuba, recounts Díaz-Versón, was Gumer W. Bashirov, who during the Spanish Civil War had acted as an agent to recruit and train receptive Spaniards. Fluent in Spanish, Bashirov's assignment in Havana, in concert with, but separate from, the Soviet Embassy, was to engage young, non–Communist Party intellectuals, students, artists, and activists who could carry out important tasks without arousing suspicion.

Díaz-Versón monitored some twenty Cuban youngsters who assiduously visited Bashirov's Miramar residence in the outskirts of Havana and received a monthly stipend, including the geographer Antonio Núñez Jimenez, the ballet dancer Alicia Alonso, and the university student Fidel Castro.

The Díaz-Versón files seized by Castro's minions reportedly contained photographs of those entering and leaving Bashirov's residence, details of counterfeit passports, and photocopies of intercepted letters. One of these letters, addressed in Spanish by Fidel to Abelardo Adam García, a companion receiving special training in Prague, read in part: "Our friend [Bashirov] has told me that he is keeping me in reserve for greater endeavors and that I should not get 'burned' by traveling [to Eastern Europe] now. They have a plan in which I will be the axis that will be implemented very soon."

From the "Bogotazo" to the Moncada Assault

A prelude to that plan, which served as a rehearsal for Castro, was the 1948 uprising in Bogotá, Colombia, known as the "Bogotazo." This occurred during the Ninth International Conference of American States attended by secretaries of state, including General George C. Marshall representing the United States

To disrupt the conference, the Soviets concocted a student and labor union subversive plan supported by Latin American leftist leaders who were keen on taking a stand against "American imperialism" and British "colonial" vestiges in Latin America (the Falkland Islands or Malvinas). The plan began with the murder of Jorge Elías Gaitán, the popular firebrand of the Colombian Liberal Party. The killing, falsely attributed to the conservative government, triggered one of the bloodiest political riots in the hemisphere.

Among the identified foreign ringleaders in the uprising was Fidel Castro. Prior to the outbreak, the Colombian police had detained and interrogated him for distributing subversive leaflets printed in Havana and giving a lecture to Communist activists on the technique of a coup d'état. He met Gaitán and his killer shortly before the assassination and was spotted near the scene of the crime in the company of well-known Communists.

As soon as Gaitán was shot dead, a team of radical agitators, including Castro, started to distribute arms, inciting the masses to loot, burn, and destroy and march on the presidential palace.

William D. Pawley, former US ambassador to Brazil and Peru, who had been asked by Secretary Marshall to help organize the conference, testified under oath at a US Senate Committee hearing that "the day that this happened General Marshall was at our house. ... Walter Donnelly, then ambassador to Venezuela ... was also with us, and when General Marshall left, Walter and I started down to the headquarters in our car, and on the radio I heard a voice saying: 'This is Fidel Castro from Cuba. This is a Communist revolution. The president has been killed. All the military establishments are now in our hands. The navy has capitulated to us, and this revolution has been a success.'"[26]

Castro's statement was, of course, untrue, but it was not all that wild. The uprising, which had unleashed a bacchanalia of blood, could have swept the government had not President Ospina Pérez joined forces with the Liberal Party and firmly resisted the palace siege until army reinforcements arrived from the interior.

The Colombian secret police, which had incriminating evidence of Castro's participation in the revolt, tried to arrest him, but he and other Cuban students were shielded by the head of Cuba's delegation to the conference and flown back to Havana.

Castro's conspicuous involvement in this tragic episode, which was well-documented in the BRAC and Díaz-Versón's files, as well as in the Colombian police records, was discounted by the State Department, the CIA, and many historians. To them it was just another manifestation of Fidel's zest for notoriety and adventure, devoid of any shred of Communist conspiracy.

Back in Cuba, Fidel and close associates deepened their Marxist-Leninist studies, focusing on Lenin's *The State and Revolution*, which, as Castro later commented, "clarified for us the role of the State as an instrument to dominate the oppressive classes, and [showed] the need to create a revolutionary power to crush the resistance of the exploiters."[27]

Fidel's journey in pursuit of his then far-fetched Leninist goal started to gather steam in 1952, courtesy of Batista's military coup, which quashed Castro's candidacy for congressman but opened for him the insurrectionary arena—a milieu that played into his hands.

As he plotted his first move against Batista (the Moncada garrison assault of July 26, 1953), he wanted to make sure that his trusted younger brother and deputy Raúl was well trained and ideologically aligned. So he encouraged him to study Marxism-Leninism (he gave him some of his books on Marx) and to travel behind the Iron Curtain to train and develop relationships there. (Eastern Europe remained off-limits to Fidel lest he undermine his democratic, nonaligned facade.)

Raúl went to Vienna to attend an international youth conference sponsored by the Kremlin. Afterward, he spent a month receiving Communist training in Romania and visited Budapest and Prague. On his way back to Havana on the Italian liner *Andrea Gritti*, he struck up a relationship with the Soviet agent Nikolai Leonov, who later became the KGB's top intelligence officer for Latin America. This relationship was cemented by Fidel and Che Guevara in Mexico while they were preparing to launch their military expedition against Batista.[28]

When Raúl returned to Havana, he was detained by security police officers, who confiscated his travel diary and the Communist propaganda he was carrying and kept him behind bars for three days. Soon after he was released, Raúl took up formal membership in the youth wing of Cuba's Communist Party and participated in the ill-fated Moncada garrison assault led by his brother.

That operation was a dismal failure, but it gave Fidel the national publicity he yearned for as an idealistic, if unhinged, young man willing to risk his life to overthrow the Batista dictatorship. The fact is that he stayed outside the garrison when his comrades barged in, did not take part in the bloody struggle, and left the scene as the army soldiers quashed the assault and started to restore order.

When Castro and other survivors gave themselves up, under the protection of the archbishop of Santiago de Cuba, the police found in their possession a book by Lenin. Fidel was quick to dismiss any ideological implication, declaring, "Yes, that was our book, and anyone who does not read those books is an ignoramus."[29]

The leaders of the Cuban Communist Party, who had gathered the day before the assault in Santiago de Cuba, ostensibly to celebrate the birthday of their secretary-general, immediately repudiated the failed assault (standard procedure known as plausible denial), calling it a "putschist" method peculiar to bourgeois factions.

During the highly publicized trial, Fidel lambasted the Batista regime in his self-defense oration and spelled out his alleged democratic goals, which were later expanded and published in a widely distributed pamphlet titled *History Will Absolve Me*. He was sentenced to fifteen years in prison, but having been granted amnesty by Batista, he actually served less than two.

Except for a brief period of solitary confinement, prison for Fidel was hardly an ordeal. He read a lot, but what he enjoyed the most were the works of Marx and Lenin. In one of his private letters, he wrote: "After breaking my head on Kant for a good while, Marx seems easier to me than saying an Our Father. He, like Lenin, had a terrific appetite for polemic, and I really enjoy myself and laugh as I read them. They [Marx and Lenin] were implacable and terrifying to their enemies—two real revolutionary prototypes."[30]

When Batista, pressed by public opinion, asked the Cuban Congress to pardon Fidel and the others involved in the Moncada assault, there was one notable government congressman who vigorously opposed the amnesty and described in a prophetic speech what would ensue by setting them free. This congressman, Rafael Díaz-Balart, who had been Fidel's brother-in-law and university classmate, knew him well and was privy to many of his secrets.

As Rafael later testified at US Senate hearings, Fidel had told him that "he was going with the Communists because that was the best way [to go] for a young leader who was thinking in the future to promote himself to the highest rank." With that in mind, he became, according to Díaz-Balart, a non-card-holding member of the Kremlin's "Third International."[31]

In Rafael's speech opposing the amnesty, he described Castro as a power-hungry "psychopath [determined] to install the most cruel, barbarous tyranny ... a totalitarian regime ... that would be very difficult to overthrow in at least twenty years." He then pointed out, "With the backing of the forces of international communism [which Fidel would seek], the spiritual, historic, moral, and legal heritage of the republic would be destroyed."

Díaz-Balart ended his impassioned discourse with these words: "I believe that the amnesty, so imprudently approved, will bring ... many

days of mourning, sorrow, blood, and misery to the Cuban people. ...
I pray to God that I am wrong."[32] But, alas, he wasn't.

Rafael Díaz-Balart pursued his anti-Castro crusade in exile, and
two of his sons, Lincoln and Mario, who were elected to the US House
of Representatives, pressed for strong sanctions against the Castro-
Communist regime.

Determined to become the leader of the revolution to topple Batista
(as a first step), Fidel left the island and established his temporary operational base in Mexico. There, he and his recruits received guerrilla
training at the Santa Rosa farm under the leftist Alberto Bayo, a former
colonel of the Spanish army who had sided with the Soviet-backed
Spanish Republic during the civil war.

Among the trainees was a twenty-six-year-old Argentine medical
graduate, Ernesto "Che" Guevara, who would soon become one of the
leaders of the Cuban Revolution under Fidel. Che, a sharp, ruthless
tactician, was not a card-carrying Communist Party member, but he
had been involved with the Argentine Communist youth organization
and later, while in Guatemala, had vigorously opposed the CIA-backed
overthrow of the leftist president Jacobo Árbenz.

The image that Che Guevara projected was that of a freewheeling,
do-good bohemian, but his allegiance and beliefs, not publicized at
that stage, were clearly defined in a private letter sent to a Cuban underground chief on December 15, 1957. Che wrote: "I belong, because
of my ideological background, to that group which believes that the
solution of the world's problems lies behind the Iron Curtain, and I
understand this [Cuban] movement as one of the many provoked by
the desire of the bourgeoisie to free itself from the economic chains of
[Yankee] imperialism."[33]

As Fidel prepared to launch the expedition against Batista, he had
to overcome a number of challenges and setbacks. In June 1956, the
Mexican police raided the Santa Rosa farm and another hideout, where
they found large quantities of arms, Marxist books, and subversive
material. Twenty of the revolutionaries were arrested, including the

Castro brothers and Che Guevara. They were released and not de-
ported thanks to the intervention of Mexico's radical labor strongman
Lombardo Toledano and the former leftist president of Mexico Lázaro
Cárdenas, who weighed in at the request of the leaders of the Cuban
Communist Party.

Fidel was secretly in touch with Nikolai Leonev, the KGB officer in
Mexico with whom Raúl had forged a close relationship. The Kremlin,
however, was very cautious, wanting to make sure that the planned,
high-risk guerrilla operation to be headed by the charismatic but as yet
untested Fidel Castro had a reasonably good chance of winning.[34]

To ward off the specter of communism that Batista continued to
raise, Fidel enlisted former Cuban president Carlos Prío to support the
expedition, bankrolling the purchase of the sixty-two-foot diesel-engine
boat (Granma) that landed eighty-two young revolutionaries on the
southern coast of Oriente province, close to the imposing Sierra Maestra
cordillera.

The expeditionary force was encircled and crushed by the Batista
army in early December 1956, and the government promptly announced
that Fidel had been killed in battle and that the mini-insurgence was
over. In reality, Castro and eighteen of the revolutionaries had managed to scramble and survive, but they had to hide in the mountains,
ill-equipped, ill fed, and with dim prospects of success.

Fidel believed that the best chance he had to overcome his desperate situation was to be interviewed by a prestigious and gullible
journalist, preferably from the United States, one who would not only
tell the world that he was very much alive but also build his romantic
image and spin the myths of the democratic ideals that he stood for, of
the hordes of guerrilla fighters who had joined him, and of the many
battles he had won.

As Castro later declared, a well-placed article playing up his almost
dead-on-arrival revolution was more important than a military victory.
Prescient words of a master of psychological warfare.

The Malleable Media

To kick off the propaganda campaign that created the legend of the Robin Hood of the Sierra Maestra, Fidel could not have found a more influential journalist-cum-partner than Herbert Matthews. A tall, graying, fifty-seven-year-old senior editor of the *New York Times* experienced in Latin American affairs, Matthews had extensively covered the Spanish Civil War and other international conflicts. Well aware of the need to bedazzle and dupe the reporter during the arranged interview, Fidel gave one of his best theatrical performances as a virtuoso in the art of seduction and deception.

To trick Matthews into believing that his insurgent force was larger than it really was, Castro had a handful of guerrillas repeatedly march around him during Matthews's interview with different reporting men. The ruse worked, and Castro later publicly bragged about it, to Matthews's distress.

Matthews's story, elevating Fidel to Olympian heights and assuring the world there was no communism to speak of in the rebel movement, was not brushed aside as the tendentious opinion of an impressionable journalist. After all, it carried the imprimatur of the world's most respected and powerful newspaper. The credence of the report was therefore guaranteed, and its impact was tremendous.

Matthews was not overly hyperbolic in his claim that the articles on Fidel Castro and the Cuban Revolution he wrote in February 1957 "have literally altered the course of Cuban history."[35] And William Buckley's *National Review* was not too flippant when it printed a cartoon in 1960 showing a happy-go-lucky Fidel Castro sitting astride a map of Cuba that carried below the famous advertising tagline: "I got my job through the *New York Times*."

Matthews, of course, was not the only American reporter who flocked to Cuba and extolled Fidel. Robert Taber of CBS, the news photographer Andrew St. George, who wrote for *Coronet*, and TV host Ed Sullivan, among others, joined the pro-Castro media frenzy.

But what set Matthews apart from other Castro sympathizers was the unsurpassed clout that he wielded as both a reporter and editorial writer for the *New York Times*. This unorthodox dual role, which reportedly created strain within the *Times* establishment, enabled Matthews to influence the newspaper's position during the Cuban Revolution, which generally evinced an anti-Batista tilt and a pro-Castro bent.[36]

Matthews's bias was not confined to journalism; it spilled into the political arena, where he acted as a fervent Castro proselytizer. This fact became evident when he visited Dr. Carlos Márquez-Sterling, the Cuban leader who had denounced the Castro-Communist threat and was running for president against Batista's candidate.

As Márquez-Sterling's son Manuel told me, Matthews went to see Carlos in early 1958, purportedly to interview him. After some perfunctory remarks, Matthews lavished praise on Márquez-Sterling's patriotic ancestors and then bluntly asked him, "How come *you* are not with Castro?" Somewhat taken aback, Márquez-Sterling deflected the impertinent question, pointing out that his ancestors had nothing to do with the present Cuban situation.

Whereupon the journalist whipped out a twenty-two-point Castro manifesto calling for a general strike in April and threatening those who did not honor it. He handed it to Márquez-Sterling. After reading it carefully, the distinguished parliamentarian, visibly disturbed by Matthews's meddling in Cuba's internal political affairs, did not hold back his temper. "Mr. Matthews," he said, "you have no right to do what you are doing. You are a foreign journalist, not a Cuban militant. ... Acting as a Castro supporter and coming to my home to invite me to support [him] is something I won't permit. I thought you had come to interview me."

Standing up, Matthews haughtily retrieved the document, which he was sharing with other personalities in Havana, and said, "I would like to leave." Without hesitation, Márquez-Sterling replied: "As soon as possible, please." When the US ambassador called him a little later to inquire what had happened with Matthews, Márquez-Sterling matter-of-factly said, "Nothing, Mr. Ambassador. I just finished talking to a Castro partisan disguised as an American reporter."[37]

US Policy Makers

While most of the US mainstream media was spinning the legend of the indomitable guerrilla liberator, the Eisenhower administration was struggling to formulate its own policy toward Cuba.

Several factors may explain the lack of high-level focus on the island during the insurgence. For one, Eisenhower and Secretary of State John Foster Dulles had an abundance of big, thorny issues to address—from the cease-fire in Korea to the fall of Dien Bien Phu in Vietnam; from Egypt's seizure of the Suez Canal to the Soviet invasion of Hungary. And, of course, Berlin continued to fester.

Adding to Dulles's heavy burden, he was diagnosed in 1956 with advanced-stage colon cancer, which could not be contained for long, even with multiple surgeries and radiation. His health sharply declined, and he died in 1959.

Given the circumstances, the main responsibility for Cuba policy fell mostly on a dysfunctional and often feuding trio composed of two midlevel officers on the fourth floor of the old State Department building, Roy Rubottom and William Wieland, and the newly appointed US ambassador to Cuba, Earl E. T. Smith. Since Rubottom's and Wieland's immediate superiors were not too familiar with, or interested in, the Cuba situation, these two officers exercised unusual power with little oversight and no qualified referee to settle their frequent disputes with Ambassador Smith.

Roy Rubottom, assistant secretary of state for Western Hemisphere affairs, was an urbane diplomat who started his career as second secretary at the US Embassy in Bogotá, Colombia, in 1947, one year before the Communist-inspired uprising that featured Fidel Castro as one of its ringleaders. He was later transferred to the US Embassy in Spain. When he was promoted to assistant secretary of state, he seemed, in the words of a desk officer who worked there, "pretty much out of his depth."[38]

His detractors say that, having been an eyewitness to Fidel's subversive activities during the "Bogotazo," he did not raise enough red flags when the guerrilla leader started to gain traction in Cuba. His defense rests on the allegation that Ambassador Smith was too close to Batista and never came up with a solution to avert the Castro takeover. What is indisputable, though, is that Rubottom, on matters pertaining to Cuba, relied heavily on the recommendations of his controversial subordinate William Wieland.

Wieland was director of the Office of Caribbean and Mexican Affairs and, as such, was the State Department's point person for Cuba. This fifty-year-old, dark-haired officer with bushy eyebrows and pencil-thin mustache had a shadowy background and scant diplomatic experience. He partly grew up in Cuba under the alias of Guillermo Arturo Montenegro (the name of his Venezuelan American stepfather), dropped out of school, and was reportedly fired as a reporter from the *Havana Post* for pirating stories.

In 1948, he was stationed in the US Embassy in Brazil as press officer, but then ambassador William D. Pawley had him removed because of his strange far left ideas. Wieland subsequently became a foreign service officer and, in 1957, landed the job of director of Caribbean and Mexican affairs.

Some of those who worked with Wieland deny that he was a Castro sympathizer. In fact, they argue that, to avert a Fidel takeover, he strongly recommended that a "middle ground" (without Batista and Castro) be sought.[39]

Yet it was Wieland who arranged for Ambassador Smith to be briefed, before assuming his post in Havana, by none other than Herbert Matthews, Castro's chief media trumpeter. And it was Wieland who recommended the arms embargo against Batista, which gave a critical boost to Castro's insurgence, and who wrote a memorandum to Rubottom on February 19, 1959, stating that Fidel Castro was geared "toward moderation and the establishment of a prosperous, democratic Cuba with honest government."[40]

But what really cast serious doubts, if not suspicions, on Wieland was his untoward conduct in August 1959 when the US Embassy in Mexico briefed Dr. Milton Eisenhower, the president's brother and unofficial foreign affairs adviser, on the Communist threat posed by the already entrenched Castro regime.

As testified by the then US ambassador to Mexico Robert C. Hill, "When the briefing started, it was opposed by Mr. Wieland because he gave the impression that we were misrepresenting the situation in Cuba. ... Each time that communism ... and its control of the situation in Cuba ... was mentioned, it was discounted by Mr. Wieland. An argument ensued [over the June 1959 intelligence report on Cuba being presented to Dr. Eisenhower]. Colonel Glawe [the embassy's air attaché who was disturbed by Wieland's constant denial of any Castro-Communist connection] referred to [him] as either a damn fool or a Communist, and, of course, it caused tempers to flare and Dr. Eisenhower said he did not want to hear any more about the situation."[41]

Wieland was subsequently cleared of the security-risk charge leveled against him, but doubts remained, at least about his judgment. He retired a few years later, resentful and in disgrace.

The other member of the discordant Cuba trio (viewed by the Fourth Floor as the odd man out) was Ambassador Earl E. T. Smith, a six-and-a-half-foot-tall former Yale heavyweight boxing champion and successful investment broker who had served as chairman of the finance committee of the Republican Party in Florida. This elegant, Palm Beach–based political appointee, married to a former model, was sent to Cuba in 1957, amid the strife that was engulfing the island, without any prior diplomatic experience and no knowledge of Spanish.

Despite these major handicaps, Smith proved to be more adept at discerning the Communist danger than his colleagues on the Fourth Floor and most of the staff at the embassy. In sworn testimony before a

Senate committee in 1960, he declared that even his chief of the Political Section and the chief of the CIA Section were Castro sympathizers.[42]

It is true that Smith was unable to broker a deal between Batista and the opposition to usher in a democratic transition, but was it because the ambassador was in the bag of the dictator, as the Fourth Floor suggested, or because he was barred by them from trying to catalyze a peaceful electoral solution, as Smith contended?

The record shows that when in March 1958 the Cuban bishops and the papal nuncio called for the formation of a government of national unity and the cessation of sabotage and terrorism, asking the ambassador to take a public stand in support of their initiative, he had to decline because Washington barred him from "intervening" in the internal affairs of Cuba.

And yet despite the ostensibly neutral noninterventionist US policy, several pilots flying a Cessna 99, a Beechcraft, and a Lockheed PB-2 Lodestar repeatedly managed to take off from an abandoned airfield in Florida to transport arms to Castro and his followers in the Sierra Maestra. More than twenty such missions were reportedly completed during the first half of 1958.[43]

According to Paul Bethel, US press attaché at the embassy, the US naval base of Guantánamo rescued American pilot Charles Hormel, involved in airlifting arms to Castro, when his plane crashed in the bay. His wounds were healed in Havana, and embassy staff spirited him off to the United States.[44]

As disclosed by a Cuban underground leader, the equipment required to install Castro's most effective weapon, Radio Rebelde, was secretly brought into the country thanks to the personal intervention of the US consul in Santiago de Cuba. This was not an isolated episode. Robert D. Wiecha, a CIA case officer attached to the US Consulate in Santiago, confided to Georgie Anne Geyer in 1987, repentant and forlorn, that "they were all pro-Castro ... all. And so was everybody in State, except [Ambassador] Earl Smith."[45]

The anti-Batista and pro-Castro bias continued even after

forty-seven Americans, including twenty-seven marines and sailors stationed at the US base of Guantánamo, were kidnapped in June–July 1958 by Raúl Castro. Rubottom vetoed the recommendation of the Navy Department, the embassy, and top officials in Washington to land the marines to rescue the hostages. As a result, the negotiations dragged on for more than a month, paralyzing Batista's half-hearted "summer offensive" and facilitating rebel advances in several areas.

Washington "absolved" Fidel Castro of any direct responsibility since the Fourth Floor and the CIA apparently fell for the canard that he was incensed with Raúl for having ordered the kidnapping without his authorization.

In the meantime, the Cuban Communist Party, which had tactically distanced itself from Fidel in the early stages of the revolution, sent off to the Sierra several of its leaders loaded with cash. Raúl Castro, who had opened a new front in Sierra Cristal, organized Marxist orientation courses for officers and new recruits.

According to declassified KGB records, the Kremlin authorized the Czech Embassy in Mexico to send rifles and mortars to the Castro forces through a shady Costa Rican trading company with the express proviso that "no Soviet-made weapons could be sent."[46]

At long last, in November 1958 an intelligence section of the State Department issued a warning, albeit somewhat vague, in an "Estimate Regarding the Communist Danger in Cuba." According to Ambassador Smith, "this report conceded that [Castro's] 26th of July Movement was open to Communist exploitation and admitted the existence of Communist infiltration ... and control of the revolutionary movement, but claimed they did not have sufficient evidence to determine the degree of control."[47]

Former US ambassador to Brazil William D. Pawley, who had business interests in Cuba and knew Batista well, was alarmed by the Communist threat and volunteered in Washington to meet with Batista to try to persuade him to cede the helm to an independent caretaker government that would hold free elections and preempt a Castro takeover.

The State Department authorized the meeting, which took place in Havana on December 9, 1958, but prohibited Pawley from saying that the proposal, which offered Batista the possibility of residing in Florida, was blessed by Washington. Since US approval was the essential condition that could have induced Batista to accept, as Pawley testified, the mission failed.[48]

Less than a week later, on December 14, the State Department (namely, Rubottom and Wieland), which had been reluctant to sponsor or publicly support any democratic alternative to Batista and Castro, alleging that it would smack of intervention, instructed Ambassador Smith to inform Batista that the United States would not support his government or that of his successor, and that it would be advisable for him to leave Cuba.[49]

This pointed message—an ultimatum couched in diplomatic language—was not the sole cause of the downfall of the corrupt Batista regime, but it certainly precipitated the flight of the dictator, the heads of the armed forces, and other key government officials in the early hours of January 1, 1959. The resulting collapse of the regime created a power vacuum that Castro and his cohorts were ready to fill.

CHAPTER 3

The Vatican Mystified, and the White House in the Dark (End of 1958)

Father Llorente's Daring Mission

Among the firsthand accounts of Castro's gigantic fraud during the insurgency, one of the most credible and insightful is the testimony of Fidel's former Belén school mentor, the pious and keen-minded Jesuit priest Amando Llorente. At the behest of the then papal nuncio in Cuba, Monsignor Luigi Centoz, he went to see Fidel at the Sierra Maestra hideout and stayed with him three days in November 1958, less than two months prior to Fidel's rise to power.

Llorente was informed that the Vatican needed an objective evaluation of what was going on up there because some of the reports that the Holy See was getting depicted Castro's revolution as just, even Christian, whereas others depicted it as Marxist.

The priest had become very fond of Fidel during his school years and predicted in the 1945 Belén yearbook that his life would be filled with brilliant pages and that the actor in him would not be lacking. Years later, the Jesuit sharply commented that there were two Fidels at school: the engaged Cuban (who saved Llorente when he was drowning during an excursion in the countryside) and the callous Gallego who'd inherited the cruelty prevalent in the north of Spain.[1]

Llorente told the nuncio that his concerns about Castro had increased during the insurgence since he felt that Fidel's rejection of all mediation efforts suggested that he wanted "to grab power all for himself—total, absolute, and despotic [power], which is consistent with his character ...; and I know him very well."

The priest agreed to undertake the dangerous mission, deep into the war zone, on the condition that if he were killed in the endeavor, it be said that "he did not go to the Sierra Maestra as a *fidelista*, or for political purposes, but only to render a service to the Catholic Church and to the Vatican."

In 2008, two years prior to his passing in Miami, Llorente decided to record the astonishing findings of his journey in a notarized document that up to then remained unpublished.[2] The notary public, Dr. Agustín de Goytisolo, a devout follower of the Jesuit and a close friend of mine, gave me a copy of the text on one condition set by the priest: that I would not publish it or disclose its contents until Castro and Llorente had passed away. I honored that commitment despite my eagerness to publish it earlier.

I had never met Father Llorente, but he knew members of my family who had studied at Belén. And when he read a presentation I had given in New York on the church in Cuba, he sent me this uplifting and generous note: "I hope and pray to God that men like Néstor Carbonell can return to Cuba the soul that Marxism has tried to kill without success."

Llorente recounts in his testimony how he evaded on horseback most of the army's checkpoints with the help of trusted farmers who knew the area. If stopped by Batista soldiers, he would say that he was a Chilean investor interested in buying cattle from some of the nearby ranches. After three days of travel, he finally reached Fidel's hideout high in the Sierra Maestra, near the Charco Redondo mines. In this makeshift camp, commanded by Castro himself, Llorente counted only twenty-eight mostly ragtag guerrillas who comprised the so-called vanguard of *Column No. 2 José Martí*.

Fidel, who reportedly slept on a hammock in the forest with a case of Marqués de Riscal wine at hand, did not appear until the following day, so the priest was able to chat privately with some of the rebels he knew and gauge the situation.

The conversation with Humberto Sorí Marín, a Catholic attorney who had been with Fidel in the mountains for eight months and had been appointed auditor-general of the rebel forces, was particularly worrisome. He confided his concerns about Fidel's autocratic leadership and his detachment from the rest of the group for fear of being killed by his own comrades. With a sense of foreboding, he told Llorente, "We need him for now; we'll see what we do [with him] later in Havana."

(Sorí Marín served as minister of agriculture in the early stages of the revolutionary government. When he realized that it was Communist-controlled, he broke off with Fidel and became one of the leaders of the resistance movement. Shortly before the Bay of Pigs operation, he was arrested by Castro's police and, following a kangaroo trial, was executed on April 20, 1961, a day after Fidel Castro had personally assured Sorí Marín's mother that the life of her son would be spared.)

Fidel appeared the next morning with a thick beard, rumpled olive-green uniform, and his trademark rifle with telescopic lens. He knew of Llorente's trip and greeted him very warmly. They chatted almost nonstop for two days, Fidel at ease without much to do.

There were several startling comments made by him, which Llorente highlighted in his notarized document. When the priest asked him how he planned to win the war with the scant forces that he had, Castro calmly replied, "Father, I fight not only with what I have, but with what people believe I have"—the candid confession of a sly propagandist.

He took great pleasure in recounting the stories that were circulating (mostly planted by him) about the legions of militant fighters—the so-called "rebel army"—that he supposedly led. Eager to preserve the myth, he beseeched his former mentor not to disclose that his column was comprised of only twenty-eight tattered guerrillas.

Llorente was up front about the Vatican mission entrusted to him and, in that context, asked Fidel directly whether he was a Communist. Castro, the foxy dialectician who had learned the ropes with the Jesuits, replied with a question: "From whom am I going to draw communism? My father is a franquista [supporter of Spain's ultra-right-wing ruler Francisco Franco], even more so than you!"

Shifting gears, Fidel then said, "The only problem here are the Americans." (This pointed remark jibes with what he had written to his confidante Celia Sánchez on June 5, 1958: "When this war is over, I shall begin a longer and greater war—the war I'll wage against them [the United States]. I realize that this is my true destiny." Castro's hatred of Yankee imperialism was both ideological and ingrained, and it was not mitigated by Washington's March 1958 arms embargo against Batista—a game changer in Fidel's favor.)

When Llorente asked Castro how he expected the insurgence to play out, he responded, "Well, I would say that, within six months, Santiago [the capital of the far-eastern province of Oriente] will fall." (Fidel did not tell the priest that his bullishness was based on the fact that Batista's army chiefs in Oriente had already conveyed their interest in striking a deal with him.)

"Well," interjected Llorente, "but after that, what, Fidel?" The rebel leader was not too sanguine about a total victory in the near term. He mused about a possible stalemate, perhaps for several years. "We won't be able to overthrow Batista," Castro said, "but neither will he be able to beat us, so perhaps the island will be split for some time." (He did not anticipate that Batista would flee in a few weeks, pushed by the very Americans that he, Fidel, detested.)

Llorente needled Castro about his dearth of competent human resources. "With these people," the priest pointed out, "you won't be able to govern."

"But nobody wants to come [here]," Fidel defensively responded.

Llorente rejoined, "I know some who would come. After all," he facetiously added, "in Havana today there is more danger than here."

Toward the end of Llorente's stay at the camp, his conversation with Fidel veered to religion. Sorí Marín had told Llorente, "There is a chaplain with us [Father Sardiña] who in the eight months I have been with Fidel has not even said an Our Father." Llorente surmised that the presence of the chaplain was sheer propaganda to counter the accusation of communism in their midst.

When the Jesuit admonished Castro for not having a practicing priest, Fidel replied, "Why don't you stay?" knowing full well that it was not in the cards. Then he solemnly added, "Father, I have to tell you something that will be painful to you: I have lost my faith."

Llorente, who never minced words with Fidel, said to him, "One thing is to lose your faith and another, your verguenza" (the term in Spanish is a cross between *honor* and *shame*).

"No, Father," emphasized Fidel, "*that* I have not lost."

Just before Llorente's departure, the judge anointed by Castro as the provisional president of Cuba post-Batista, Manuel Urrutia, arrived at the camp. He had flown on a small plane from Venezuela carrying arms and funds. Llorente observed that Fidel did not pay much attention to the president-designate; in fact, he humiliated him as if to stress that there was only one boss calling the shots. (Following Batista's flight, Urrutia served as provisional president of the revolutionary government for about seven months, but when he publicly raised the issue of Communist infiltration, Fidel forced him to resign, seek diplomatic asylum, and leave the country. He died in exile in the United States several years later.)

The other personality who approached Llorente before he departed was José Pardo-Llada, a popular *ortodoxo* politician and radio commentator with a stentorian voice who opposed Batista and felt that military action was the only effective solution to get rid of him. In his private conversation with the priest, he was highly critical of Castro. Since Pardo-Llada had a more prominent national standing at the time than Fidel, he was miffed for having been marginalized in the mountains by the bearded leader.

He gave Llorente a personal letter for delivery to his wife in Havana and allowed the Jesuit to read it. In his missive, he referred to Castro's megalomania—"his [grandiose] complex as sole chief." (Despite his misgivings, Pardo-Llada became a rabid supporter of Castro in the early stages of the revolutionary government, but later opposed his totalitarian grip and sought refuge in Colombia, where he died.)

Llorente returned to Havana heavyhearted, alarmed by what he had seen and heard. Although the priest could not then categorically affirm that Castro was a Communist, he harbored gnawing suspicions. Fidel's denial did not tranquilize him since he knew that his former student was adept at lying with a straight face and even believing his own lies. What he definitely discerned during his trip was Castro's overpowering sway—egocentric and dictatorial.

Thinking that perhaps there was still time to check or counterbalance Fidel's authoritarianism, Llorente sent off to the Sierra Maestra a couple of young, truly democratic Catholic activists with leadership potential in the hope that they might influence decisions at the top. This proved to be a noble but futile effort.

The insurgence gained momentum after Llorente left the Sierra. In a matter of weeks, several factors propelled Castro's rise to power. Confident that triumph was near, the Cuban Communist Party no longer kept a low profile. Several of its leaders, laden with cash, made the pilgrimage to Fidel's and Raúl's hideouts.

Arms shipments from the United States, Venezuela, and Costa Rica to the rebel forces rapidly increased. The plots against Batista reached the highest levels of the demoralized army, particularly after the word spread that Washington wanted him out.

The columns headed by Che Guevara and Camilo Cienfuegos advanced from the far-eastern province of Oriente to the central province of Las Villas. The heralded feat, however, was not accomplished by fighting the government forces head-on but mainly by skirting their military outposts or paying them off along the way.

The Batista dictatorship was crumbling. The end was near.

Eisenhower's Belated Awakening

When President Eisenhower was informed of the Communist danger in Cuba just days before the flight of Batista, he was "provoked," as he put it in his memoir, that the warning had not been given earlier.[3] To assess the implications of the report and determine next steps, a meeting of the National Security Council was held at the White House on December 23, 1958. The declassified Memorandum of Discussion—overlooked or glossed over by most historians—is perhaps the most telling evidence of how unaware the president was of what would soon occur: the Castro-Communist takeover that he wanted to prevent and that others in his government had unwittingly abetted.

As recorded in the memorandum,[4] not as direct quotes, Allen Dulles, the CIA director, defined the danger in these terms: "The situation in Cuba was worsening. Batista was unlikely to take any action to remedy conditions, short of a desperate military move for which the army does not appear to have the stomach. The Communists appear to have penetrated the Castro movement, despite some effort by Fidel to keep them out." (Even the director of the CIA had bought the story that Castro would try to keep the Communists at bay because he was not one of them.) But Dulles did end his opening statement with this sobering warning: "If Castro takes over Cuba, Communist elements can be expected to participate in the government."

When the president heard this, he asked "whether the Department of State had requested the Department of Defense to study military action which might be necessary in Cuba." Acting Secretary of State Christian Herter, standing in for John Foster Dulles, who was gravely ill, replied that "he did not know of any study of military action ... [just] State/Defense conversations ... centering on the possibility of evacuation." (In other words, there was no contingency plan other than a possible rescue operation.)

Deputy Secretary of Defense Donald Quarles then jumped in, asserting that "Castro was the greater of the two evils represented by

Castro and Batista ... and, therefore, [we] should move against the bases in the US which support Castro."

Attorney General William P. Rogers "reported that arrests of Castro partisans in the US were being made when the statutes were violated." (Rogers did not seem to be aware that, despite some arrests, the clandestine shipments of arms from Florida to the Sierra Maestra had continued, and no one referred at the meeting to the US arms embargo against Batista, which had tipped the balance in favor of the Castro forces.)

When the CIA director unequivocally stated "that we ought to prevent a Castro victory," the president, flashing his vexation, deliberately punctuated, "This is the first time that statement has been made in the National Security Council." Vice President Nixon cautioned, with fine political instinct, that "we could not support Batista in order to defeat Castro."

George Allen, director of US Information Agency, seemingly oblivious to the seriousness of the situation, wondered why the United States should prevent a Castro victory. Allen Dulles reminded him that "extremely radical elements" were backing Fidel, and Nixon pointed out that "it would be undesirable to take a chance on Communist domination of Cuba, which had one the largest Communist parties in the hemisphere in proportion to population."

Secretary Herter, unprepared to make any meaningful contribution, simply observed that "opinion as to the undesirability of the Castro regime appeared to be unanimous ... and a contingency paper was needed."

The president, expecting more than a paper to tackle the threat, stated that "the US should take a position [on Cuba] progressives could support." When Quarles opined, with a dash of skepticism, that "there was no 'third force' [i.e., a force other than Batista or Castro] to support," the president demurred, saying that "he saw hope of a 'third force' growing in strength and influence if it were organized around an able man and provided with money and arms." (Eisenhower seemed unaware that the State Department [Fourth Floor], which had been re-luctant to foster or back a third force, had already given an ultimatum to Batista to leave.)

Following the president's recommendation, which was really an admonition, State, Defense, and the CIA hurriedly started discussing contingency plans and exploring the possible support of a third force to avert a Castro takeover—definitely the right move, but way too late. In just a few days, Castro was in control of Cuba.

According to Ambassador Smith, "When timing was propitious and opportunities were available for a solution without Batista or Castro, our Department of State refused to lend its support. The refusal was based on the grounds that the United States would be accused of in-tervening in the internal affairs of Cuba. Yet, eventually, the State Department did advise Batista that the time had come for him to absent himself from his country. This was positive intervention on behalf of Castro."[5] Five other US ambassadors familiar with Cuba essentially concurred with that assessment when they testified at Senate hearings under oath.[6]

It would be wrong and unfair to impute the fall of Cuba solely or mainly to Washington's blindsided facilitation of the Communist take-over. There were other, weightier factors that contributed to the woeful outcome. But it is hard to dispute what actually ensued: that Castro and his 26th of July Movement served as the Trojan horse that enabled the Soviet Union to jump the Atlantic, penetrate the defensive perimeter of the United States, and establish and retain for several decades a strategic military and subversive base that threatened the peace and security of the Americas and other regions of the world.

CHAPTER 4

In the Eye of the Storm: Denouncing the Takeover (1959–Mid-1960)

The Joyful Dawn (January 1959)

The end of Batista's dictatorship gave rise to euphoric celebrations. It seemed that liberty had finally dawned on the beleaguered island and that violence had given way to civility and reconciliation. The majority of the impressionable Cuban people, prone to political messianism, began to revere the towering figure credited with the triumph: Fidel Castro. He was embraced as a savior, not bound to the "vested interests of the corrupt past," but able to usher in a just and flourishing new era. That's what many thought at the time.

My family and I were happy that Batista had left, but most of us were wary of the future with an idolized Castro at the helm. Glued to the TV, we watched the spectacular show he was mounting and wondered how radical or autocratic he might be without checks and balances.

Fidel's arrival in Havana on January 8, 1959, was viewed as the apotheosis of a heroic guerrilla fighter who had alighted victorious from the mountains. Riding in a tank with olive-green combat fatigues, a rifle slung over his broad shoulder, and dark horn-rimmed glasses perched over his aquiline nose, Fidel appeared the ideal liberator.

The welcome he received was rapturous, if not entirely spontaneous. Castro's propaganda machine provided posters that were hung on the doors of many houses with these inscriptions: "Gracias, Fidel"

(Thank you, Fidel) and "Esta es tu casa" (This is your home). The cult of Castro's personality took off, powered by rousing rhetoric and catchy slogans.

The adulation was not limited to Cubans. Among the fawning descriptions of the Maximum Leader, Norman Mailer's portrayal ranks high in the annals of hagiography. "It was as if the ghost of Cortés had appeared in our century riding Zapata's white horse," he wrote. "You [Fidel] were the first and greatest hero to appear in the world since the Second [World] War. ... The answer to the argument of commissars and statesmen that revolutions cannot last, that they turn corrupt or total or eat their own."

Castro took almost a week to complete his victory lap across the island, which was virtually paralyzed by the national strike he had decreed. Showing no apparent urgency to grab the reins of power, Fidel wallowed in the exultation. But the hiatus was not solely for hero worship. Fidel wanted to make sure that before he arrived in Havana the armed forces serving under Batista had unconditionally surrendered and all the key government posts had been vacated. Fidel and his 26th of July Movement saw those as essential preconditions for a total takeover. Having thoroughly studied Lenin's "all power to the Soviets," Castro pretty much followed that same strategy.

To allay the lingering fear of communism lurking in the shadows of the revolution, Castro and his bearded guerrilla fighters paraded like biblical prophets in a procession, displaying rosaries, scapulars, and other religious badges supplied by Castro cohorts near Havana. Fidel himself, who had confided to his mentor, Father Llorente, that he had lost his religious faith, carried on a chain around his neck a medallion of Cuba's patron saint, the Lady of Charity, clearly visible under his open-collar shirt.

The spiritual imagery climaxed during Castro's first major speech in Havana at Camp Columbia, which many of us watched on TV. As he started to warm up on stage, one of the tamed white doves released by his assistants perched "by chance" on his shoulder. To many, this was the Holy Spirit descending on Cuba's redeemer. The crowd went wild.

To soothe the skeptics and buy some time, Castro shrewdly put together a short-lived, Kerensky-type transitional government, mostly composed of respected personalities with democratic credentials. The anointed provisional president was Manuel Urrutia, a modest but principled judge who had acquitted some of Castro's rebels during the insurgence, invoking their constitutional right to fight against oppression. And the designated prime minister was José Miró-Cardona, former president of the Cuban Bar Association who had led the civic institutions that opposed the Batista dictatorship. That gave many of us some peace of mind.

Castro astutely assigned low-profile posts to Raúl Castro and Che Guevara, the two revolutionary leaders who were perceived as radicals, if not Reds. Raúl remained for a while as head of the military in Santiago de Cuba, and Che oversaw the early execution of hundreds of so-called Batista war criminals at the Havana fortress of La Cabaña, a function he seemed to relish.

A former Castro ambassador and distinguished psychiatrist told me that during a private meeting he had with Guevara at his office in La Cabaña, Che removed a curtain to watch, with a broad smile, one of those executions by firing squad.

Mass Manipulation

As commander in chief with no official executive power, Fidel was supposed to focus solely on his self-imposed task of "restructuring" the armed forces, but in fact he exercised control over everything, while keeping the population in a state of frenzy. Having studied at length the French Revolution and the Jacobins' White Terror, as well as the orchestrated rallies that fueled the onslaughts of Lenin, Mussolini, and Hitler, Castro relied on mass mobilization and inflammatory speeches to arouse, indoctrinate, and subdue the population.

He leveraged to the hilt a technology that the earlier totalitarians lacked, the power of television, to drill his daily messages—this in a country that ranked first in television sets per inhabitant in Latin America. The irony is that Cuba's advanced broadcast technology, which served Castro so well, was courtesy of the capitalist system he abhorred and would soon destroy.

Turning the population into a gigantic mob—a technique brilliantly described by the French social psychologist Gustave Le Bon—enabled Castro to mesmerize, numb rationality, and heighten the susceptibility to manipulation. He knew that crowd behavior, stirred with mass rallies and spread live through the airwaves, was so emotionally contagious that it could induce individuals to sacrifice their personal interests and beliefs for the grandiose revolutionary goals set from above.

The challenge, however, was not only to ignite the dynamism of the pliable masses but also to steer and sustain it. Castro achieved this objective with his brand of "direct democracy," inciting from his pulpit the lower passions of the crowds and conditioning them to obey his command. Pavlov would have been very proud of his Cuban devotee.

Fidel's power to manipulate was evident at a huge rally I watched on January 21, 1959, attended by the entire diplomatic corps and about four hundred foreign reporters visiting the island. First he aroused the anger of the crowd by repeatedly declaring that Batista's war criminals had massacred twenty thousand rebels and innocent citizens—a Goebbels-like mendacity, since the actual number of all those killed by *both* sides during the seven-year struggle did not exceed fifteen hundred—still, of course, too many. Then Castro asked the incensed multitude to raise their hands if they were in favor of executing the vicious war criminals. They did so like robots, in unison, whereupon Fidel proudly proclaimed: "One million have voted [yes]. This *is* democracy!"

Castro repeated his theatrical performance at another mass rally on April 9, this time raising the issue of elections. With the cold-blooded skill of a matador, he killed the idea of early elections (repeatedly promised by him before assuming power) by posing this captious question to the crowd: "Do you want elections to stymie the revolution and bring back fraud, corruption, cronyism, and the vested interests of the oligarchy?" As expected, the response was a resounding no.

Not many in Cuba were alarmed by this trend. Even savvy observers opined that the early excesses of the Castro regime did not reflect an ominous pattern. They felt it was nothing but the meandering process of a high-minded revolution that just needed time to find its way. The elders in my family, however, did not buy this rosy story. They clearly saw disturbing demagogic and autocratic tendencies, but there was not much they could do about it.

My maternal grandfather, Cortina, who had intervened as a moderating voice in quite a few of Cuba's past crises, was now too old and too frail to enter the turbulent civic arena. And my father, who had been ostracized and placed under surveillance by the regime for having been one of the leaders of a third force (against both Batista and Castro), was battling serious cardiac problems.

Under those circumstances, I felt the mantle had been passed. It was my turn to speak out on major national issues. Several of my cousins joined me in that endeavor. As a twenty-three-year-old budding attorney, I was short on experience and gravitas but reasonably well versed in political science and constitutional law. I had also studied in depth major world revolutions, particularly the French and the Russian. In any case, I did not have the luxury of waiting for maturity to catch up. There was just too much at stake. Caution, of course, was necessary because under the prevailing environment, it was risky to challenge or even question the course of the Cuban Revolution.

A few weeks after Castro's ascent, interpreting the feelings of so many Cubans, I expressed in a newspaper article my hope that he would fulfill his professed democratic goals and foster a new peaceful and prosperous era That hope was soon dashed by his continuous hate-spewing invectives, purges, and executions, as well as by several radical constitutional reforms that seemed to be edging the country toward a reign of terror and oppression.

One reform empowered revolutionary courts to summarily try and execute not only the so-called Batista war criminals but also anyone deemed to be a "counterrevolutionary" or accused of subverting the public order or the national economy. Another reform enabled the regime to confiscate the properties of all those suspected to have collaborated with the Batista regime or charged with illicit enrichment or counterrevolutionary acts.

In the absence of an independent judiciary with ample authority to safeguard individual rights, these and other related reforms would lead, I believed, to the criminalization of political dissent. Life, liberty, and property would hang on the whim of an omnipotent ruler.

The 1959 "case of the airmen" was particularly shocking. Forty-four members of Batista's air force, accused of war crimes, were brought to trial. When the tribunal acquitted them, a furious Castro ordered a retrial with a second, handpicked tribunal, which delivered thirty-year sentences. The defense counsel was dismissed from his post and disappeared, several witnesses were arrested, and the president of the first tribunal, who had fought with Castro in the Sierra Maestra and dared acquit the pilots, was found dead in his car with a .45-caliber bullet in his heart. To close this woeful chapter, Castro proclaimed, "Revolutionary justice is based not on legal precepts, but on moral conviction."

Deeply concerned by these developments, which were dismissed or downplayed by most of the enraptured population, I wrote an article on March 8, 1959, titled "The New Republic." I called for the rule of law and for the full reinstatement of Cuba's democratic 1940 constitution as Castro had pledged during the struggle against Batista. The article was carried by one of the few newspapers that dared to voice dissent (*Diario de la Marina*), headed by José Ignacio Rivero.

To my great surprise, Castro not only read my article but also rebutted its salient points in a speech he gave five days later—fortunately without mentioning my name. He certainly didn't want to give me any standing in the debate, for which I was grateful. Fidel said, "There are those who call for the rule of law. But which law? The old law passed by the vested interests or the new revolutionary law that we are going to make? For the old law, no respect; for the new law, all our respect." (I later traced Castro's dialectical response, including his choice of words, to Marx's defense in 1849 when he was indicted for inciting armed resistance against the Prussian tax authority.)

As to my call for the full reinstatement of the 1940 constitution, Castro asserted that the constitutional power was now vested in the Revolutionary Council of Ministers (which he controlled) and that if any article of the constitution was "inoperative or too old ... the [Council of Ministers] would modify ... or replace it."

Class Warfare and Agrarian Reform

The message could not be clearer to me: the law of the land was Fidel's will. Dictatorships under military chiefs or *caudillos* who ruled with an iron fist were not alien to Cuba and Latin America. But this one seemed to be different (certainly from Batista's). It went beyond political censorship, coercion, and control and started to impinge on culture, traditions, economy, and business. I sensed a totalitarian bent in both sway and scope.

To neutralize resistance, particularly from the bourgeoisie, Castro unleashed, with volcanic intensity, class warfare—the most effective tool prescribed by Lenin to split, subvert, and subdue a nation from within.

Castro pursued this endeavor with bravura and gusto. To pave the way for the so-called agrarian reform, the first major step to controlling the economy and abolishing private property, he pitted the poor peasants and small farmers, to whom he promised the title to the land they tilled, against the sugar growers and cattle ranchers, who were vilified as a class. No distinction was made between the ravenous and the socially responsible entrepreneurs, between the absentee landowners and the hands-on producers.

The Agrarian Reform Law that was published in May 1959 was not the largely balanced and harmonious law proposed by Castro's minister of agriculture, which would have boosted productivity, ensured a fair and orderly land adjustment process, and obtained the support of the business community. The promulgated law was drafted, we later learned, by a "shadow government" created by Fidel comprised of trusted Communists who were charting the course of the revolution. Their objective was not socioeconomic development following liberal tenets but a phased Marxist-Leninist systemic change disguised as "humanism."

On May 24, 1959, the National Cattle Ranchers Association held a major conference in Havana to discuss the implications of the law and agree on next steps. I attended the conference, representing my grandfather Cortina, former president of the association, who was ill. Although I had thoroughly studied the law in the light of other revolutionary precedents, I was not planning to address the assembly. I changed my mind when I realized that the speakers, whether by fear or confusion, were dodging the core issue. They focused on isolated articles of the law and not on the collectivist mold on which it was cast.

In my impromptu speech, I zeroed in on the so-called National Institute of Agrarian Reform, a gigantic state agency with unlimited power to control and strangle the agro-industrial private sector. Following an analysis of the law, including what it didn't explicitly say but implied, I warned the cattle ranchers that under the newly created superagency, they would not really have rights to their businesses but only revocable concessions.

I pointed out that the land they would be allowed to keep would eventually be grabbed by the state without recourse. As to the government bonds that were promised as compensation for the expropriated land, I said they would be worthless if issued (and they were not ever issued). Finally I argued that the proclaimed beneficiaries of the law—the peasants and small farmers—would be dragged into state cooperatives or communes and never receive the title to the apportioned land. (Sadly, my grim forecast turned out to be true.)

Stressing that the Agrarian Reform Law, if not substantially modified, would deal a death blow to private property and free enterprise and would place Cuba on the path to serfdom, I ended my remarks with this plea: "Cattlemen of Cuba, I urge you to join forces with the other economic and business sectors to defend the democratic principles and liberal traditions that this law would destroy. Cattlemen of Cuba, stand up and be counted, for if you do not rise, you will be crushed by the uncontainable avalanche of state interventionism!"

I received a standing ovation. Still, some subsequent speakers sniped at me, dismissing my warning as juvenile, rash, and unfounded. They thought that the government would soften the law or grant sweet deals to those who quietly genuflected. As I saw it, the blind and the spineless—enablers of tyranny throughout history—were unwittingly nailing their own coffins. Other organizations and institutions also had their share of shortsighted sycophants.

The president of the Cattle Ranchers' Association, Armando Caíñas-Milanés, and other prominent cattle ranchers, however, did not side with the appeasers. They realized that the central issue was not acres of land, more or less, but free enterprise. The threat we faced was a gargantuan state not bound by law that would constantly expand its sphere of control.

Unable to stem the interventionist tide sweeping away individual rights, Caíñas-Milanés became one of the leaders of the first major conspiracy against the regime, which was aborted in mid-August 1959 and landed he and his coconspirators in jail.

I was not involved in the conspiracy, but given my speech, my articles, and my relationships with some of the plotters (including my twenty-eight-year-old cousin, former city councilman Eddy Arango), I was detained and taken to army headquarters. I barely escaped arrest, possibly because the captain who interrogated me was not a hard-liner and had bigger fish to fry. Still, it was a close call, one that prompted me to lower my profile and leave no trail. I knew I would be closely watched.

The situation in Cuba had become very dangerous for any dissenter, particularly after two of the revolution's hierarchs dared to raise the issue of Communist infiltration. The first one was Castro's chief of the air force, Major Pedro Luis Díaz-Lanz. He defected in June 1959, escaped to the United States, and denounced Castro's Red plot when he testified at a Senate subcommittee hearing.

The second was Cuba's president Manuel Urrutia, having expressed in a couple of interviews his opposition to communism. In July, he was forced to resign and seek diplomatic asylum following a ferocious attack by Castro on television—perhaps the first known case of a TV coup d'état.

Fidel, who in February had assumed the role of prime minister with unlimited power, replaced Urrutia with a trusted Marxist, Osvaldo Dorticós.

Marxist-Leninist Trend

Despite these alarming developments, many still fell for Castro's charade: although he was not a Communist, he claimed, he could not allow "counterrevolutionary traitors" to raise the specter of communism to justify US aggression. Even well-educated compatriots did not yet discern the Marxist-Leninist trend of Castro's revolution.

To open their eyes, I wrote in mid-1959 a sixty-page paper titled "Where Are We Headed?" It pierced the veil of Fidel's deception and brought to light the stark similarity between the steps prescribed by Marx and Lenin for a Communist takeover and the pivotal measures adopted by Castro during the first eight months of his regime.

The side-by-side comparison first pointed to the concentration of power (single party headed by an absolute ruler) and the progressive curtailment of individual rights by fiat and diffuse terror. The comparative analysis then turned to class warfare, pitting the underprivileged and resentful against the well-off to split the nation and cripple resistance. Then came collectivization of the economy through confiscatory taxes, staged labor unrest, and expropriations without compensation—all aimed at controlling and eventually abolishing private property and free enterprise.

Finally the analysis covered the conditioning of minds and hearts through orchestrated mass rallies, incessant propaganda with catchy slogans, Marxist indoctrination (subtle at first), and a permanent state of emergency to fend off the "vile [American] imperialists" and justify the regimentation of society.

Fragments of this paper were published without my name in *Diario de la Marina*, which waged a courageous anti-Communist campaign until it was assaulted and closed by the government several months later. I distributed copies of the document to select members of the emerging resistance movement, and a friend delivered an English version to the US Embassy. I was hoping it might awaken Washington to the threat posed by the Castro regime and induce the State Department to change the Cuba policy of patience and forbearance.

Little did I know that the architect of that policy was the US ambassador in Havana, who was not particularly concerned about Fidel. He actually stated in an August 2, 1959, cable to the State Department that the Castro regime "is, in many respects, the most hopeful ... Cuba has ever had."[1]

Why did this viewpoint prevail in Washington during most of 1959, while Castro was laying the foundations of his Marxist-Leninist regime and systematically excoriating the United States? And what accounted for the policy change in early 1960 that led to the Bay of Pigs? Fresh or previously glossed-over information has shed light on these perplexing questions.

US Policy of Patience and Forbearance

Bowing to the larger-than-life bearded leader (despite the alarming issues raised at President Eisenhower's December 23, 1958, summit on Cuba), the State Department rushed to recognize the Cuban revolutionary government on January 7, 1959, even before it was duly constituted. And to please the new ruler, Washington promptly replaced Ambassador Earl E. T. Smith, who had repeatedly warned of the Communist threat posed by a Castro takeover.

The new appointee, viewed by some as an exemplar of courtliness and soft diplomacy, was Philip W. Bonsal, a tall, polished, fifty-six-year-old foreign service veteran with a liberal reputation and a sedate personality. Early in his career he had spent some time in Cuba working for a US company and later as an embassy staffer. He also was fluent in Spanish.

Confident after his first meeting with Castro that he could work with him if Washington did not interfere with his popular revolution, Bonsal strongly advocated "continuance of the US policy of hopeful and watchful wait and see."[2]

His recommendation was upheld at the State Department regional meeting with US ambassadors in El Salvador, beginning April 8. Not everyone at this important conference embraced that policy. The clear-eyed US ambassador to Mexico, Robert C. Hill, very familiar with Castro's background and trajectory, argued forcefully that there was enough intelligence on Castro's Communist entanglement to alert Latin American governments to the looming danger and jointly take appropriate action to forestall it.

When Hill indicated that he would not go along with a communiqué that whitewashed Castro, Bonsal haughtily remarked, "If you cannot be a team player, why not resign?" Hill fired back: "It [is] not up to Mr. Bonsal to deal with my resignation [but] up to the president and the secretary of state."[3]

The only other ambassador who dared to support Hill's position was Whiting Willauer, US envoy to Costa Rica. Though assigned to a small country, he was no lightweight. Packing impressive academic credentials (Exeter, Princeton, and Harvard Law), fluency in four languages, and vast experience in legal, diplomatic, and Cold War affairs,

Willauer was deeply worried about the progressive Castro-Communist control of Cuba. He viewed it as a clear and present danger.[4]

On January 26, 1959, he had shared his concern with his friend José Figueres Ferrer, the short but gutsy former president of Costa Rica who had supported the Castro insurgency with arms and ammunitions, and urged him to weigh in, along with other leaders of the "Democratic Left" who also had helped to put Fidel in power. Willauer was referring to the newly elected president of Venezuela, Rómulo Betancourt, and the governor of Puerto Rico at that time, Luis Muñoz Marín.

After consulting with his Latin American confreres, Figueres agreed to approach Castro at the earliest opportunity. Invited by Fidel to attend a major labor rally in late March, Figueres flew to Havana and tried to meet with him beforehand, but the Maximum Leader had no time for him. Figueres did not take that as a snub. In the spirit of camaraderie, he arrived at the rally clad in his revolutionary attire—the overseas cap, khaki shirt, and trousers he had worn to fight the forces of tyranny in his country—and was greeted by the crowd with an ovation.

The climate changed dramatically, however, when in the course of his laudatory speech Figueres broached a delicate but, in his mind, defining issue. He essentially framed it this way: "Whatever you may feel about liberalism or communism, there is a Cold War going on, and Latin America must be on the side of the US and against Russia in a showdown between those two sides."

Pandemonium broke out when he uttered those words. I watched the televised rally in astonishment as the Cuban labor chief, David Salvador, grabbed the microphone away from Figueres and blasted him. Then Fidel took over and humiliated the former Costa Rican president, accusing him of being a reactionary and a false friend with intolerable imperialist tendencies. Relentless in gushing vitriol, he then thrashed US corporations, which in their greed, he claimed, had killed more Cubans than had Batista.[5]

Upon his return to San José, Figueres commented to Willauer: "We have no doubt that this matter [the Castro revolution] is a Communist matter ...; if it is not already, it is about to be." Ambassador Bonsal did not see it that way. He attributed the serious incident not to ideology or allegiance but simply to Fidel's "extreme sensitivity to advice even from a friendly source."[6]

Castro's Trip to the United States (April 1959)

Nothing that Castro did or said during the first four months of his sweeping revolution seemed to have marred his visit to the United States, which he adroitly turned into a charm offensive. Invited by the American Society of Newspaper Editors to deliver a keynote address, he arrived in Washington donning his signature olive-green fatigues and high black boots, and was besieged by photographers and reporters and hailed by his ecstatic admirers.

He told the Society of Newspaper Editors and other audiences in Washington and New York basically what they wanted to hear: that he was not a Communist; that his revolution was "humanistic"; that he welcomed foreign investments and would not confiscate American properties; and that he would respect the freedom of the press—"the first enemy of dictatorships," he proclaimed—and hold open elections.

Even though Castro arrived with his entire economic team, he left with empty pockets. Had the US government turned its back on him, offering no financial assistance to the revolution? And was this seeming rebuff, as many "blame America" observers alleged, one of the main reasons why Castro turned to the Soviets for support? Rufo López-Fresquet, Cuba's minister of finance who accompanied Fidel during the trip, put this myth to rest when he defected two years later.

López-Fresquet disclosed what actually happened: "[Fidel] warned me as we left Havana not to take up Cuban economic matters with the [US] authorities. ... At various times during the trip, he repeated the warning. That is why, when I visited the then secretary of the Treasury, Robert B. Anderson, I did not respond to the American official's indications that the United States was favorably disposed toward aiding our country.

"Also, for this reason," continued López-Fresquet, "when I exchanged views with Assistant Secretary of State for Latin American Affairs Roy Rubottom, I feigned polite aloofness to his concrete statement that the US Government wished to know how and in what form it could cooperate with the Cuban Government in the solution of the most pressing economic needs."[7]

López-Fresquet explained why Castro did not seek, or accept, US aid. "If the US had helped Cuba, he could never have presented the Americans as enemies of the revolution." Felipe Pazos, president of the National Bank of Cuba, who also accompanied Fidel and was barred by him from pursuing the International Monetary Fund's overtures, concurred with López-Fresquet's views.

During the trip, not everyone was totally convinced that Castro and his revolution was not Communist. One of those who harbored some doubts was Vice President Richard Nixon, who privately met with Fidel in Washington for more than two hours. According to a summary of the conversation filed by the State Department (April 1959), Nixon noted that "Castro was either incredibly naive about communism or under Communist discipline." His guess, however, was the former. In any case, he concluded, "We have no choice but at least to try to orient him in the right direction."

A high-level CIA official who secretly met with Fidel in New York did not share Nixon's ambivalence. The official was the German-born CIA veteran Gerry Droller (alias Frank Bender), who later formed part of the task force that spearheaded the Bay of Pigs operation. After Droller's three-hour meeting with Castro, arranged by Rufo López-Fresquet, Droller went to Rufo's hotel suite "in a state of euphoria. He asked for a drink, and with great relief exclaimed: 'Castro is not only *not* a Communist, but he is a strong anti-Communist fighter.'"[8]

It seems that Droller bought Fidel's spiel (the same that had bewitched Rufo): "I am letting the Communists stick their head out so I will know who they are. And when I know them all, I'll do away with them, with one sweep of my hat."

Castro's Shadow Government

The contention that Castro did not have a Communist game plan when he visited the United States, which most historians still hold, is contradicted by reliable testimonies. Juan Vivés (a nom de guerre), a well-informed Castro secret service defector now residing in France, wrote: "On March 3, 1959, at the offices Che Guevara had at La Cabaña [fortress], Fidel Castro held a private meeting with Fabio Grobart, the Comintern's secret envoy to Cuba since 1927. ... This truly secret conference went on from 2:45 to 5:30 in the morning. I recall the date and time because that day I was on duty and I recorded all those details on the registry. The next morning, Che tore the page with the annotations and told me not to make any comments."[9] Vivés further disclosed that following this meeting, five Cuban Communist leaders left for the Soviet Union and Red China on a secret government mission.

The most startling revelation, however, was that, unbeknownst even to his own Council of Ministers, Castro had operated a shadow or parallel government with the Communists from the time he took power—an undercover scheme akin to his ideology and duplicitous personality. As confirmed by Fidel's biographer Tad Szulc, based on extensive interviews in Cuba, this secret network functioned on two levels simultaneously.

On one level were the old Communist hierarchs (including the wily Fabio Grobart) who dealt primarily with the phased and bumpy integration of Castro's 26th of July Movement and the Socialist Popular (Communist) Party. The process, which gave rise to purges, clashes, and defections along the way, reached its first official milestone in 1961 with the formation of the Integrated Revolutionary Organizations.

Blas Roca, the historic leader of the Socialist Popular (Communist) Party, commented to Szulc that when they secretly met with Castro to design the strategy in early 1959, Fidel laughingly exclaimed as he took a puff on his cigar, "Shit, now we are the government and still we have to go on meeting illegally."[10]

On the other level was a separate task force, carrying as a cover the innocuous name of the Office of Revolutionary Plans and Coordination, which was composed of young Marxist leaders of the 26th of July Movement (including Raúl Castro and Che Guevara). They met at Che's beach resort in Tarará, some ten miles east of Havana, and later at Fidel's nearby villa in Cojímar—both spacious properties confiscated by the "austere" regime.

Among the foreign Communists who joined the Tarará group was Angel Ciutah, a veteran of the Spanish Civil War who was close to Ramón Mercader, the Catalán who murdered Leon Trotsky in Mexico. The Kremlin reportedly sent Ciutah to Havana, along with Luis Alberto Lavandeira, to help the Castro regime set up a police state backed by a G2 repressive body modeled on the Cheka, the Soviet organization charged with rooting out counterrevolutionary activities.[11]

Che Guevara took charge of G6, the agency that oversaw the Communist indoctrination of the officers of the rebel army, which Raúl Castro had started during the insurgence in Sierra Cristal.[12]

Among the other Leninist initiatives pursued by the Tarará group, the most salient ones were the Agrarian Reform Law and the revolutionary militias charged at the outset with the enforcement of that law. Their main task was to "intervene" (euphemism for seize) the private farms that were to be converted into state cooperatives à la Chinese communes.

Castro's Failed International Forays (April–August 1959)

As Castro rolled out his broad-scale domestic agenda, he did not forgo his far-reaching international goals. Since he took power, he was determined to export his revolution or, as he later put it, turn the Andes into the Sierra Maestra of Latin America. To do that, he needed more arms, so the first thing he asked his newly appointed minister of finance, Rufo López-Fresquet, in January 1959, was to use the $5.3 million left by the Batista regime in European banks to purchase automatic FAL rifles, ammunitions, and grenades from Belgium.[13] This, less than two weeks after Fidel had delivered his "Arms for What?" inaugural speech at Camp Columbia, chastising the members of the Revolutionary Student Directorate for not disarming.

A little later, the Castro regime provided refuge and military training to young leftist rebels from several Latin American countries. Some of them secretly trained in the hacienda of my grandfather Cortina in the far-western province of Pinar del Río, without his knowledge.[14] Between April and August 1959, four small armed expeditions were launched from Cuba to overthrow or destabilize the governments of Panama, Nicaragua, Haiti, and the Dominican Republic.

The US ambassador did not attach much importance to these flagrant acts of intervention, confirmed by an OAS investigative committee. He apparently did not realize that these amateurish and failed attempts to export the Cuban Revolution were but a prelude to the major Castro-led subversive campaign that would rock the continent for more than three decades.

The First Major Conspiracy against the Castro Regime (August 1959)

Anti-Castro Cubans who maintained close relations with US Embassy staffers were generally aware that Ambassador Bonsal—a keen practitioner of constructive engagement—opposed taking a firm stand against the Castro regime, but they never imagined that he would be a whistle-blower. Declassified State Department documents suggest that the ambassador conveyed to Cuban authorities confidential information on the first major conspiracy against the Castro regime, which was foiled in early August 1959.

Led on the civilian side by a former labor minister, Arturo Hernández Tellaeche, and by the president of the National Cattle Ranchers Association, Armando Caíñas-Milanés, the planned uprising was backed by several former officers of Cuba's standing army (pre-Castro), as well as by two chiefs of the rebel army, Eloy Gutiérrez Menoyo and an American adventurer with a shady background, William Morgan. The "Americano," as Morgan was called, fought against the Batista forces in the Second Front of the Escambray Mountains and rose to the highest rank of comandante.

Key units of the aviation and tank divisions were reportedly involved in the plot, which received military aid from Trujillo, the Dominican ruler. This was his way of reciprocating Castro's sponsorship of the recent foray on Santo Domingo.

According to declassified State Department documents, Ambassador Bonsal informed Washington on August 3 that he had advised Castro's foreign minister, Raúl Roa, of the planned uprising and of Morgan's involvement, based on an FBI report. Bonsal further stated that "on August 4, [he] called on Roa at the latter's request. Roa said that he had conveyed the information on Morgan to President Dorticós, who was 'highly alarmed.' Apparently, Castro has not yet been given the information, according to Roa."[15]

In his memoir, Bonsal explains that his tip-off was prompted by his "worries ... for the safety of resident Americans because of the possible impact of the Castro tirades about the evil intentions of the United States."[16] He also wrote that an attempt was made to induce a young embassy official to meet with some of the conspirators before they were caught, but no such meeting took place. This assertion is flatly contradicted not only by several cattle ranchers who reportedly shared information on the plot with embassy officers, but also by Paul Bethel, the ambassador's own press attaché.

As related in his book *The Losers*,[17] Bethel received in late June a mysterious call from Morgan, who whispered on the phone, "Come to my house early tomorrow morning." Bethel had met Morgan and Menoyo when they both visited the embassy a few months earlier and provided details on the progressive Communist takeover of the Castro regime.

Given the urgency of the message, Bethel went to see Morgan at the mansion given to him by the revolutionary government in the swank residential section of Miramar. Dressed in his rebel army uniform, bearing the one-star rank of comandante, the tough, squat, blue-eyed "Americano" greeted Bethel like a "long-lost brother."

As they walked in the garden, Morgan suddenly turned to Bethel and said: "I have five thousand men, willing and able to fight against communism ... Castro is a Communist, see, and we don't like Communists. I told you about this before. Well, we've been working to get our people into strategic spots." He then ticked off several "comandantes" and captains who "are with us."

After answering a few probing questions posed by Bethel, Morgan became a little nervous, wondering whether he had been wise to divulge "all this information" to him. Bethel assured him, as he swiftly left the house through the garden, that "embassy officers had no obligation to become a source of intelligence for the Cuban government." It didn't cross Bethel's mind that the gist of the long memorandum of the conversation that he wrote and gave to the deputy chief of the CIA in Havana would later be leaked by the ambassador to the Castro regime.

It is still an open question whether Morgan acted as a double agent throughout the process or only when Castro confronted him with general foreknowledge of the conspiracy. On the basis of all the evidence gathered by the embassy, Bethel wrote, Morgan was indeed plotting against Castro. But when Morgan learned that certain of his conspiratorial activities had been brought to the attention of the Maximum Leader, he spilled the beans to save his skin and told Fidel that he had been acting as a double agent to gather as much information as he could on the plotters. As a result of these developments, the planned uprising was quashed. More than one thousand conspirators were rounded up and imprisoned.

Morgan and Menoyo (who also flipped over) were declared heroes for having helped to uncover a "treasonous plot" supported by the Dominican dictator Trujillo. But Morgan was not considered trustworthy by the revolutionary elite, particularly after this episode. So, a few months later, he was assigned to a frog farm near the Escambray Mountains to develop several products from frog skins. There he remained vocal about his opposition to the Communist inroads into the revolution. It seems that he also started to amass arms and to enlist disaffected members of the rebel army for a possible revolt. But Fidel was quicker on the draw and arrested him in October 1960.

Morgan's mettle and disciplined comportment in the dreaded La Cabaña prison, putting himself through a daily routine of calisthenics as if he were in a military camp, was vividly described by fellow American inmate John Martino in his book *I Was Castro's Prisoner.* But what has not been published is this startling episode recounted by another inmate, Ramón "Rino" Puig, married to my cousin Ileana Arango Puig, who showed the valor of her husband in her stance against the Communist regime.

Rino, a twenty-nine-year-old former Olympic rower who worked for Bacardi, had been sentenced to fifteen years for his involvement in an anti-Communist conspiracy. Although his plot had nothing to do with Morgan, they struck up a relationship behind bars.

According to Rino, Morgan was congenial and upbeat during his stay in La Cabaña. He would say, "Not to worry, Rino. We will soon be out of here." When he told Rino that embassy officers would soon visit him with good news, Rino dismissed that as pure fantasy and said, "The US has revoked your citizenship and wouldn't allow any emissary to come close to you. You must be delusional!"

To Rino's astonishment, a few days later he was summoned to a small visitors' room close to the office of La Cabaña. There was Morgan with a big smile surrounded by three embassy officers (presumably from the CIA). The conversation was animated and jovial—kind of odd for a prison. Rino recalled that one of the officers, without making any reference to the US-backed military operation against Castro that was being planned (the Bay of Pigs landing), whispered to both of them, "You will be free in six months."

Morgan was so excited that, on the way back to their cells, he took out a pack of Kent cigarettes and said to Rino, "Since we don't have champagne to celebrate, let's at least take a puff."

Morgan's elation was short-lived. On March 9, 1961, the once-hero of the revolution was accused of treason during summary court proceedings and sentenced to death. It was reported that he marched to his trial singing "As the Caissons Go Rolling Along." On March 11, he was executed along with another young comandante of the rebel army close to him, Jesús Carrera.

Morgan's Cuban wife served twelve years in prison, and his comrade-in-arms-and-conspiracies, Menoyo, managed to escape to the United States. But when he returned to the island to launch a guerrilla operation, he was caught and condemned to death. His sentence was subsequently commuted to twenty-two years in prison, which he served with long periods of solitary confinement and forced labor.

Bonsal's Appeasement Backfired (September–October 1959)

If Ambassador Bonsal's tip-off was intended to improve US-Cuba diplomatic relations, he didn't get much, if anything, out of it. After waiting three months to see Fidel Castro, Bonsal finally got to meet with him on September 3 for several hours.

As reported by the ambassador, Castro continued to denounce the alleged anti-Cuban media campaign launched by US opinion leaders. He failed to give any assurance that the harassment of the US telephone and electric companies in Cuba would stop, and he justified his support of local Communists because, he said, it helped him politically and in labor circles.[18]

Nonetheless, Bonsal felt that he had been given "a hearing by a responsible person interested in what I had to say and with sufficient consideration for my country, my government, and myself."[19]

The ambassador's advocacy of "understanding and sympathy with the broad aspirations of the Cuban Revolution," as reiterated in his memorandum to the State Department in late September,[20] was seriously undermined by a string of events during the period October–November.

In early October, the Castro regime seized the records of all foreign companies that had been prospecting for oil and took steps to reduce Cuban dependence on imports from the United States.[21]

On October 19, Comandante Huber Matos, military governor of Camagüey province and one of the top Sierra Maestra military chiefs, resigned over the issue of the rapidly spreading Communist infiltration of the armed forces. Although Matos continued to defend the revolution, Castro vilified him and ordered his arrest. Raising the specter of communism, Fidel claimed, "bordered on treason." Following summary court proceedings, Matos was sentenced to twenty years in prison.

Then, on October 21, Castro's former air force chief who had defected to the United States in June, Pedro Luis Díaz-Lanz, flew over Havana and dropped a large quantity of leaflets accusing Castro of betraying the revolution and turning it over to the Communists. Although the antiaircraft fire from Cuban military and naval installations was the cause of several deaths and injuries, Castro brazenly accused the United States of instigating the "bombardment" of Havana, an action allegedly similar to the attack of the Japanese on Pearl Harbor.[22]

A few days later, a twenty-seven-year-old comandante, Camilo Cienfuegos, who was rising in popularity, reportedly died when his twin-engine Cessna flying from the cities of Camagüey to Havana crashed into the ocean. Suspicions abound because the plane mysteriously disappeared and not a single trace was found.

More Radicals in Key Posts (October–November 1959)

Of more portentous significance than Castro's anti-US fulminations were the government appointments announced in the last quarter of 1959. In late October, Raúl Castro was named minister of the consolidated armed forces. Reporting to him as head of the military intelligence and secret police was the hard-liner Ramiro Valdés, assisted by Manuel Piñeiro Losada, the red-bearded ideologue. These appointments denoted Fidel's determination to place the levers of totalitarian power in trusted hands.

Raúl was generally viewed as a rather sinister individual, even by those who were not aware of his ruthlessness and Communist background as a member of the youth organization of the Socialist Popular (Communist) Party who had trained behind the Iron Curtain. Squint-eyed (he looked more Asian than Cuban) with a slight physique and a dour personality, he was overshadowed by his imposing and charismatic brother.

Raúl's extremism had been intentionally brought up by Fidel to spread the myth that he (Fidel) was moderate compared with Raúl and other leaders of the revolution. In his January 21, 1959, speech, two weeks after he had seized power, he warned his enemies that if something were to happen to him, they would get Raúl. He backed his words by nominating his brother then and there as second-in-command of the 26th of July Movement, thereby laying the groundwork early on for dynastic succession.

Born in 1931 out of wedlock, like Fidel, Raúl shares his brother's ruthlessness and violent history. Both are responsible for numerous cold-blooded executions, torture, and the largest exodus of political refugees in the history of the Americas (prior to Venezuela). But Raúl differs from Fidel in many ways. Raúl lacks Fidel's magnetism, audacity, and histrionics, as well as his physical stature. More level-headed and structured than his brother, he shows a collegial side to loyalists and a closer attachment to his family.

While Fidel captivated the Cubans with his bold and brawny leadership and incendiary speeches—he was both the absolute CEO and PR supremo of the revolution—Raúl served as his opaque but effective chief operating officer, quietly laying the underpinnings of Cuba's totalitarian edifice with Soviet assistance. This is a man so low-key that for years only those close to him knew of his long battle with alcoholism.

If Fidel was the rambunctious Marxist-Leninist firebrand, then Raúl is the methodical Communist apparatchik—a role he began playing in his twenties when he joined the youth organization of Cuba's Socialist Popular (Communist) Party. Traveling behind the Iron Curtain for training, he developed warm relations with Soviet bloc officials who later helped the revolution to gain and retain unlimited power.

Raúl liked the Russians, and the Russians reciprocated. According to the Romanian general Ion Mihai Pacepa, one of the highest-ranking officers to have defected from the Soviet bloc, Raúl was always under the influence of alcohol and self-importance and found a kindred spirit in Soviet prime minister Nikita Khrushchev. Khrushchev trusted Raúl and had some misgivings about the unruly Fidel.

As revealed by Pacepa, General Aleksandr Sakharovsky, who created Communist Romania's intelligence structure and then rose to head the KGB's First Chief Directorate, secretly brought Raúl to Moscow the first time. "Both Nikita and Raúl loved vodka," Sakharovsky reportedly told Pacepa. "Both were fascinated with Marxism [and] hated school, religion, and discipline. Both considered themselves military experts. Both were obsessed with espionage and counterespionage. And both liked to sleep with their boots on."

Indeed, Sakharovsky maintained that had it not been for the closeness of the two men, Khrushchev would never have "thrown himself entirely into the Cuban Revolution."[23]

Che Guevara and the Path to Collectivization

To spur the collectivization of the economy and the confiscation of assets and personal properties, two moderate ministers were replaced with radical revolutionaries on November 26. The remaining one, Rufo López-Fresquet, minister of finance, resigned a few weeks later. But what really stunned the alert segments of the population was the appointment of the most vocal of the radical leaders, the Argentine swashbuckler Che Guevara, as president of the National Bank of Cuba. He succeeded the last of the free market reformists, Felipe Pazos.

A few days after the appointment, Fidel reportedly said that "he was astonished to see people who had money take it out of the bank." That didn't really matter, he sardonically added, "because we are going to print new money." And print they did, gracing the currency with the signature "Che."

The Cubans, even in times of great distress, don't lose their sense of humor. I well remember a joke that circulated shortly after the appointment of Che Guevara as czar of the economy. It went like this: Castro had assembled all the senior members of his government and said, "I need an economist to head the National Bank," whereupon Guevara raised his hand and got the job. Later, when Fidel and Che were alone, Castro expressed his surprise: "Che, I didn't know you were an economist." "Economist?" exclaimed Guevara. "I thought you said Communist."

Joke aside, by the end of 1959, there was growing concern about the radical direction of the revolution, but few dared to demonstrate against the Castro regime. Political parties had been banned, except for the 26th of July Movement and the Socialist Popular (Communist) Party, which had not yet coalesced at the base. The few privately owned newspapers and radio and television stations that had survived the initial government purge were constantly harassed, and the streets were controlled by Castro mobs.

The Church Weighs In (Late November 1959)

There was only one independent institution that remained standing, one that had not yet been besmirched and pummeled by the regime: the Catholic Church. Although most of the clergy and parishioners had hailed the revolution, the church had become increasingly alarmed by the fracturing of the nation with class warfare and hatred, by the systematic suppression of the right to dissent, and by the undeterred momentum of Communist penetration.

To counter this trend and uphold the threatened Christian values, the church decided to convene in late November a two-day national congress, starting with an open-air torchlight procession and Pontifical Mass.

The congress was featured as a purely religious event, but it definitely had political, anti-Communist overtones. Capitalizing on growing unrest and discontent, the church, which lacked the prestige and clout of its counterparts in other, more religious Latin American countries, was able to gather close to one million Cubans from all the provinces and all walks of life.

It was a moving experience that I shall never forget. Braving inclement weather conditions, the multitude marched in orderly fashion, carrying candles and waving white handkerchiefs. Choruses of "Caridad" (referring to the Virgen de la Caridad del Cobre, Cuba's patron Virgin of Charity) were heard in the same staccato rhythm as the revolutionary slogan "Paredón" ("To the firing wall") that was chanted at Castro's rallies. It was the Catholics' response to the regime's extremism and violence. Toward the end of the ceremony, the crowd burst into a cry that reverberated through the streets of Havana like a stirring echo of defiance: "Cuba, sí. Rusia, no!"

Fearing the contagious spread of opposition under the cloak of religion, Fidel Castro, who had attended the Mass-turned-protest, prohibited any similar event and soon unleashed relentless attacks on the church, which culminated in the forced exodus of hundreds of priests and nuns in 1961.

Washington's Ambivalence toward Castro (November–December 1959)

Meanwhile, Washington had started to shift its policy toward Cuba from patience and forbearance to a slightly more robust opposition to the "extremist, anti-American course of the Castro regime." But the November 5 policy guidance stipulated: "In achieving this objective, the United States should avoid giving the impression of direct pressure of intervention against Castro, except where defense of legitimate United States interest is involved."[24]

Although US policy makers were losing patience with the Castro regime, there were still those in Washington, even in the upper echelons of the intelligence community, who did not view Fidel as a dangerous and intransigent ideologue. They tended to believe that he was an impetuous nationalist, not wedded to the Communists, who cleverly used them for self-serving purposes.

As expounded by General C. P. Cabell, deputy director of the CIA, at a November 5 hearing before a Senate subcommittee, "Our conclusion … is that Fidel Castro is not a Communist. … It is questionable whether the Communists desire to recruit Castro into the Communist Party, that they could do so if they wished, or that he would be susceptible to Communist discipline if he joined."[25]

The perceptive and well-informed Cardinal Richard Cushing of Boston did not share Cabell's wishy-washy position on Castro. When asked by the press at the time if he thought that Fidel was a Communist, the cardinal replied, "When I see a bird that walks like a duck and swims like a duck and quacks like a duck, I call that bird a duck."

Cabell seems to have overlooked the Leninist path that Castro had taken since he seized power—adapted, of course, to Cuba's circumstances and to his own idiosyncrasy. He also apparently ignored or dismissed Moscow's growing but still covert involvement in Cuba as evidenced by the visits in May and October of Vadim Vadimovitch Listov, reported to be a high-ranking Soviet intelligence operative, and of Aleksandr Alexeyev, who posed as a TASS news agency correspondent and would later become the second Soviet ambassador to Cuba. Around this time, four top Cuban pilots had gone secretly to Czechoslovakia to lay the groundwork for a MiG jet training program.[26]

Ambassador Bonsal, for his part, reluctantly conceded on December 2, eleven months after his arrival, that "the efforts of our government to create an atmosphere of goodwill and good faith [in our relations with Cuba] have certainly not found an echo."[27] But even as 1959 gave way to 1960, he insisted there was no evidence "that either the Cuban or the Russian Communists were plotting with Castro behind the backs of the Cuban people to suppress [their] liberties."[28] Still hopeful for a rapprochement with the Castro regime, the US Embassy backed the mediation pursued by the Argentine ambassador Julio Amoedo in early 1960.

The Argentine Ambassador's Mediation (January–February 1960)

Amoedo was an engaging ambassador with a keen political instinct and a penchant for diplomatic intrigue and dealmaking. My parents and I got to know him well after he rented our house on the outskirts of Havana for his official residence. Amoedo had developed a good rapport with Fidel Castro, so we were not surprised when he told us in late January that he was privately acting as a mediator in an effort to overcome the festering US-Cuba stalemate.

Relations had sharply deteriorated following the most recent of Castro's tirades against the United States. As a result, Ambassador Bonsal was recalled to Washington and the Cuba situation was reassessed by President Eisenhower and his National Security Council. Although expectations of reaching a meaningful and lasting accord with Castro were low, the president decided to take another crack at constructive engagement.

On January 26, 1960, Eisenhower issued a conciliatory statement in which he reiterated the US policy of nonintervention in Cuban affairs, recognized the Cuban government's right to undertake reforms with due regard for international law, and expressed a desire to seek resolution of disagreements through diplomatic negotiations.

It was then that the US chargé d'affaires in Havana, Dan Braddock, gave Amoedo the green light to explore an understanding with Castro along these lines: (1) the slanderous campaign against the United States must stop; (2) Castro should receive Bonsal to address and resolve outstanding issues; and (3) the US government would consider providing financial assistance to support the agrarian reform and other initiatives. (This last point was later disputed by US Embassy officials who were fearful of being accused of appeasing or bribing Castro.)[29]

Amoedo promptly located Fidel and had a four-hour meeting with him at the house of his confidante Celia Sánchez. The ambassador recounts that Fidel was lying down, reviewing some papers. When he heard what had prompted Amoedo's visit, Castro reacted very negatively. He read to the ambassador the papers he was holding in his hand, which turned out to be the editorial that would be published in the government newspaper *Revolución*. That editorial thrashed Eisenhower's statement and leveled grave charges against the United States.

Following a long and heated discussion, Fidel remained adamant, and Amoedo felt that it was useless to continue arguing with him. "As I was … leaving," recalled the ambassador, "Castro stopped me … and said there was nothing to lose by hearing what the Yankees want."[30]

As agreed with Amoedo, Castro ordered that the blistering editorial not be published and that all attacks against the United States be stopped. Fidel also agreed to discuss the differences with the United States and indicated that President Dorticós would make a statement to that effect. These seemingly positive developments gave rise to considerable optimism.

Then, on February 4, Soviet deputy premier Anastas Mikoyan arrived in Cuba with a large delegation and stayed there for ten days. Under the trade agreement that was signed prior to Mikoyan's departure, the Soviet Union would buy from Cuba one million tons of sugar per annum for five years—about one-sixth of the total crop—and extend $100 million in trade credits at a low interest rate. Moscow also agreed to provide technicians, who turned out to be experts in "disinformation and agitation."[31]

No public reference was made to the supply of Soviet arms, but when Mikoyan in a speech at a rice cooperative talked about agrarian assistance, the crowd shouted, "And guns and planes too." Mikoyan then repeated, "And guns and planes too."[32]

It was only on February 22 that an official reply was delivered by Castro's foreign minister, Raúl Roa, to the proposal that Amoedo had relayed. It basically said that the revolutionary government was prepared to initiate negotiations provided that both the executive branch and the Congress of the United States refrain from adopting any measure that Cuba might consider prejudicial to the diplomatic parley. When Washington explained that it was not constitutionally possible to accept that proviso, the mediation abruptly ended.

Amoedo later acknowledged that he had been taken for a ride. He wrote: "In my opinion, the Castro regime accepted my efforts at mediation as a dilatory tactic to diminish tension between Cuba and the US while awaiting Mikoyan's arrival. ... From the moment [of his arrival], the Castro regime virtually paralyzed the negotiations with various excuses and evasions, which were designed to gain time until the Cuban-Soviet pact was signed on February 13." The ambassador concluded: "The insincerity of the Castro regime is evident in the Roa statement of February 22, with its impossible condition."[33]

Despite Amoedo's objective testimony, some historians and pundits have asserted that had the United States been more flexible and forthcoming with Castro, Washington could have preempted the Havana-Moscow alliance. This observation fails to take into account the repeated efforts made by the United States to seek an understanding with the Castro regime—efforts not reciprocated by Havana.

The respected journalist Arthur Krock, who judiciously researched this matter, held that Washington was not guilty of alienating Castro and pushing him into the Soviet camp. He wrote in the *New York Times*: "From the time Castro assumed power until May 17, 1960, the United States made nine formal and sixteen informal offers to negotiate all differences with Cuba. ... On February 22, 1960, Castro did propose ... to negotiate with the United States. ... However, his conditions were that during the negotiation the United States should bind both the Executive and Congress to refrain from any action which Cuba would consider to affect its interests, while he remained free to negotiate or procrastinate as he chose—conditions obviously unacceptable and, so far as Congress was concerned, constitutionally impossible."[34]

The collapse of the last-ditch mediation effort undertaken by Amoedo and the formalization of the Havana-Moscow pact in February 1960 reached a turning point in US-Cuba relations. CIA director Allen Dulles's report to the National Security Council that "Mikoyan's visit had marked the definite espousal of Castro by the USSR" laid to rest the failed US policy of patience and forbearance and set in motion the Program of Covert Action Against the Castro Regime.[35]

To complicate matters, on March 4, 1960, the French freighter *La Coubre* exploded in the harbor of Havana while it was unloading seventy-six tons of munitions ordered by Castro. Casualties may have been as high as one hundred. Unloading explosives directly onto the dock in Havana was forbidden by port regulations. Still, without any evidence, Castro accused the United States of sabotage—a charge vehemently denied by Washington—and linked the explosion to the sinking of the US battleship *Maine* in 1898. Availing himself of this pretext, the Cuban ruler proceeded to confiscate American properties on the island and intensify his anti-US tirades.

CHAPTER 5

The Cloak and the Dagger—Joining the Exile Front (Mid-1960)

For many of us on the island, Soviet deputy premier Anastas Mikoyan's visit to Cuba in February 1960 had ominous implications. It signaled the Kremlin's direct involvement in our struggle—on Castro's side. About a hundred anti-Communist students—vanguard of the emerging resistance movement—staged a strong protest in Havana, chanting, "*Cuba, sí. Rusia, no.*" And a courageous journalist confronted Mikoyan on television and raised the specter of the Soviet invasion in Hungary.

Following these developments, the big question outstanding was: Will the United States weigh in to counter the looming Soviet threat and help Castro's opponents recover Cuba's freedom?

The US Program of Covert Action against the Castro Regime

The Havana-Moscow entente, brought to light during Mikoyan's sojourn, only showed the commercial trade component (Cuban sugar in exchange for Russian oil). It was Chairman Nikita Khrushchev who later disclosed, with his customary bombastic style, the geopolitical and potential military elements of the pact.

On July 9, 1960, Khrushchev made the following remarks: "It is clear to everyone that the economic blockade of the American monopolies may prove to be the beginning of preparations for intervention against Cuba. We must therefore raise our voice in Cuba's defense and give notice ... that we for our part shall do everything to support Cuba and its courageous people in the struggle for freedom and national independence."

Then the Soviet premier laid down the gauntlet: "It should not be forgotten that the United States is not so inaccessibly distant from the Soviet Union as it used to be. Figuratively speaking, in case of need, Soviet artillerymen can support the Cuban people with their rocket fire if the aggressive forces in the Pentagon dare to launch an intervention against Cuba."

Khrushchev's provocation—half serious, half bluster—lit the fuse of Eisenhower's quick temper. Although the president had been rather circumspect in his public statements on Cuba, trying not to foil Washington's numerous attempts to seek a rapprochement with Castro, he now had no choice but to respond to Khrushchev's challenge in unequivocal terms. That same day, the president issued this press release from Newport, Rhode Island: "The statement which has just been made by Mr. Khrushchev ... shows the clear intention to establish Cuba in a role serving Soviet purposes in this hemisphere." Then, invoking the Rio Treaty of the Inter-American System, which directs its members to fend off any extracontinental intervention, the president added: "I affirm in the most emphatic terms that the United States will not be deterred from its responsibilities by the threats Mr. Khrushchev is making. Nor will the United States, in conformity with its treaty obligations, permit the establishment of a regime dominated by international communism in the Western Hemisphere."[1]

On July 12, Khrushchev, always eager to have the last word, asserted that the 1823 Monroe Doctrine (which states that "the American Continents ... are henceforth not to be considered as subjects for future colonization by any European powers") "had died ... and should best be buried."

Was he right? Only in part. Although the Monroe Doctrine "died" as a US *unilateral* responsibility, it was "resurrected" as a *multilateral* commitment adopted by the members of the Organization of American States (OAS).

Eisenhower didn't see the need to prolong the debate with another rejoinder. He quietly opted to back his stern warning with something more effective than words: the Program of Covert Action against the Castro Regime.

This program, developed by the Special Group of the National Security Council (the supersecret Committee 5412), was presented to the president by CIA director Allen Dulles at an Oval Office meeting on March 17, 1960, attended by Vice President Richard Nixon, Admiral Arleigh Burke, and other high-level government officials. It outlined four courses of action:

1. create a responsible, appealing, and unified Cuban opposition to the Castro regime, located outside of Cuba;
2. launch a powerful propaganda offensive in the name of the declared opposition (long wave and shortwave gray broadcasting facility to be located on Swan Island off the coast of Honduras);
3. build a covert intelligence and action organization (underground movement) within Cuba responsive to the Cuban opposition in exile; and
4. develop a paramilitary force outside of Cuba and provide logistics support to operate on the island. (No full-fledged invasion was then envisaged, just the training and infiltration of about three hundred guerrilla fighters. Initially based in the United States and the Panama Canal Zone, the training shifted in June to a makeshift camp in the mountains of Guatemala after an accord was reached with President Miguel Ydígoras.)

Eisenhower said at the meeting that "he knows of no better plan for dealing with this situation ... and told Dulles he thought he should go ahead." He wanted to know at the next meeting what was the sequence of events, and asked that contingency plans be developed to address all likely Cuban reactions. He instructed the State Department to obtain OAS support for anti-Castro collective action but recognized that some of the shaky governments in Latin America may be reluctant to take a firm stand against Castro for fear of a populist backlash.

Finally, the president cautioned that "our hand should not show in anything that is done," and to ensure plausible deniability by the White House, he specifically stipulated, "Everyone must be prepared to swear that he [Eisenhower] has not heard of it [the plan]."[2]

Given Washington's paramount objective during the Cold War to thwart or oppose Communist expansion by all possible means, this cloak-and-dagger plan didn't seem all that outlandish. It was viewed as a sequel to the two covert operations authorized by Eisenhower and successfully carried out by the CIA against Mohammad Mosaddegh in Iran (AJAX, 1953) and against Árbenz in Guatemala (PBSUCCESS, 1954). These spectacular feats—not exempt from controversy—gave impetus and validity to the Cuba plan.

The CIA Team and the Template

Drawing on the Guatemala experience, the CIA put together a team to implement the covert program headed by Richard Bissell, deputy director for plan—the overlord of the agency's vast underground network—who had played a coordinating role in Operation Success (Guatemala). A towering figure with a six-foot-four frame, Bissell, fifty, had impressive academic credentials—Groton, Yale, and the London School of Economics. After the war, he served as assistant deputy administrator of the Economic Administration, responsible for allocating the resources of the Marshall Plan. This was his first major opportunity to exert influence in the international arena—albeit through the power of the purse—and he relished it. Following some freelance advisory work for the CIA, he was appointed special assistant to Allen Dulles and gained kudos and fame developing the top secret high-altitude reconnaissance aircraft that revolutionized photographic surveillance—the U-2.

With an aura of grandeur and wielding considerable clout, Bissell became the leader of the covert operation that resulted in the Bay of Pigs invasion.[3] He was brilliant and bold, cerebral and action-oriented, but his judgment was clouded by hubris and ambition. He yearned for Dulles's job as director of the CIA, and in his dealings with the White House he seemed reluctant to do or say anything that could jeopardize his aspiration. Within the agency, Bissell wanted to control the Bay of Pigs operation without interference, and Allen Dulles apparently obliged. The day of the landing, Dulles was in Puerto Rico delivering a speech.

Bissell was joined, initially as second-in-command, by his old friend from Groton and Yale, the charismatic and debonair Tracy Barnes, a CIA senior field officer who oversaw the psychological warfare side of Operation Success in Guatemala. But the record suggests that during the implementation of the Cuba covert plan, he acted more as an adviser to Bissell than as second-in-command.[4]

Bissell's key operations director was Jacob Esterline, then CIA station chief in Caracas. Working for the Office of Strategic Services (OSS) in World War II, he was parachuted into Burma behind enemy lines in 1944. He joined the CIA in 1950 and later participated in the Guatemala paramilitary operation.

Also reporting to Bissell were two military officers on loan to the CIA: Colonel Jack Hawkins, who took the lead in military planning in September 1960 (when the Cuba plan changed from infiltration to amphibious and airborne assault), and Colonel Stanley Beerli, in charge of air operations.

The delicate political task of selecting and interacting with the Cuban opposition leaders who would receive US support was assigned to an unlikely CIA operator, the German-born Gerry Droller, who had worked for the OSS during the war and later joined the agency as a Swiss desk officer. The slight, balding, cigar-chomping Droller (known as Frank Bender or Mr. B.) was the same person who, duped by Fidel

Castro during his 1959 visit to the United States, opined that the bearded chief was not radical and would eventually banish the Communists.

What impaired Droller's effectiveness in his new assignment was not his early flawed assessment of Fidel but his inability to speak Spanish (not a word) and his dearth of cultural sensitivity and diplomatic finesse to deal with the mercurial Cuban exile leaders. To offset those deficiencies, the CIA brought in two Spanish-speaking and more congenial operatives: Howard Hunt (a.k.a. Eduardo), who years later masterminded the infamous Watergate break-in, and Bernard Barker (code-named "Macho"), a Cuban American agent who served in the US Air Force and later became a CIA informer in Havana. This duo managed to keep the haughty Mr. B. as far away from Miami as possible, and they patiently coped with the squabbles that often erupted within the anti-Castro coalition—squabbles the duo sometimes provoked or exacerbated by playing favorites with CIA funds.

Their covert activities called for so many smoke-filled, hush-hush meetings at Hunt's residence in Brickell Point Apartments in Miami that his neighbors believed he was a bookie. When he later moved to an ample house in Coconut Grove, the nocturnal visits of male agents generated further speculation. Hunt's nearest Grove neighbor—a widow with a gorgeous blonde daughter who modeled in TV commercials—thought he was a homosexual. Hunt proved her wrong when he went out with her daughter. Put to the test, the CIA he-man reportedly performed with flying colors.[5]

The fundamental problem with the Cuba Covert Program, as originally conceived, was not the CIA team assigned to it (warts and all) but the template from which it was cast—the Guatemala PBSUCCESS operation.

The Cuban scenario was markedly different from the Guatemalan, starting with geography. Guatemala had neighboring countries that served as CIA bases to train and arm soldiers and infiltrate the liberation forces, whereas Cuba was surrounded by water. Guatemala had a swayable standing army that had not yet been significantly purged by the pro-Communist government. In Cuba, Castro had disbanded the army. He filled the key posts of the reconstituted forces with loyal cohorts, established ideological indoctrination, and created the so-called people's militia, which subjected large swaths of the population to military discipline.

Another key point of difference was the degree of Moscow's involvement in these two potential Latin American client states—much less in Guatemala than in the strategic island of Cuba, which in 1960 started to receive sizable quantities of arms and personnel from the USSR and its satellites. As disclosed by Richard Bissell at a Senate hearing on April 28, 1961, at the time of the Bay of Pigs invasion the Soviet bloc already had in Cuba fifteen hundred to two thousand personnel, including several hundred military experts.[6]

Finally, Guatemala had a weak leader (President Jacobo Árbenz), who was easily toppled by a colonel (Carlos Castillo Armas), backed by a small-scale CIA paramilitary operation that included a few acts of sabotage, limited strafing, and psychological warfare. Cuba, on the other hand, had Fidel Castro, a bold, charismatic, and wily revolutionary commander who, despite the erosion of his popularity brought about by his despotic rule, could still mobilize large segments of the population and counter any halfhearted attack that gave him latitude to maneuver.

CIA historian Jack Pfeiffer found an undated and unsigned confidential memorandum on file that warned that Cuba was no Guatemala and pointed out some of the differences and risks.[7] If the paper was ever read, it did not temper the enthusiasm of the drivers of the Cuba covert plan. Those who had worked with Eisenhower on the Guatemala operation were confident that the World War II leader and strategist would not allow this new CIA program, or any variant, to fail.

The Guatemala veterans recalled that just before Colonel Castillo Armas and his forces crossed the border from Honduras to strike, President Eisenhower met with CIA director Allen Dulles; his brother John Foster Dulles, secretary of state; the Joints Chiefs of Staff; and other senior government officials.

"Are you sure this is going to succeed?" queried Eisenhower. The men around the table assured him it would. "I'm prepared to take any steps that are necessary to see that it succeeds," the president said. "If it succeeds, it's the people of Guatemala throwing off the yoke of communism. If it fails, the flag of the United States has failed."[8] Unfortunately, Eisenhower's successor did not follow this guiding principle in Cuba.

The Cuban Anti-Castro Team

The anti-Castro torchbearers invited by the CIA to form a coalition were invigorated by the prospects of an alliance with the United States to overthrow the Castro-Communist regime. The coalition was composed of middle-of-the-road political and civic leaders who had opposed Batista and of non-Marxist members of the Castro regime who had defected.

Forming the initial nucleus were Manuel Antonio "Tony" Varona, the fiery and honest politician who had served as president of the senate and prime minister during the last constitutional government of Cuba under President Carlos Prío; Aureliano Sánchez Arango, an articulate and combative former revolutionary who had been minister of education and minister of foreign relations in Prío's cabinets; Justo Carrillo, a seasoned professional with revolutionary credentials who had ably presided over the Agricultural and Industrial Development Bank under both Prío and Castro; José Ignacio Rasco, a talented and amiable professor, former classmate of Fidel Castro, and founder of the newly-formed Christian Democratic Movement along with Laureano Batista-Falla and other compatriots; and Manuel Artime, a young, impassioned physician and former captain of the rebel army who had bravely denounced Castro's Communist plot in late 1959.

None of these leaders was a caudillo who could rival Castro's magnetism and riveting histrionics. But tapping a non-Communist replica of Fidel—if one even existed—was no solution for a country that needed to anchor its future to the rule of law. Better to rely on the selected leaders who, though short on flair, were true Democrats with sound

principles and growing appeal. Mindful of the nation's woeful experience with rabble-rousing and deception, they offered a refreshing contrast pitting integrity against demagoguery, institutions against the cult
of personality, and individual freedom against government oppression.
One big handicap: none of them was fluent in English.

Having left the island to spur the liberation of Cuba with US backing, they held a secret meeting on May 12–13, 1960, at the New York
Bar Association's office with CIA's point man Frank Bender (whose
real name was Jerry Droller). According to the confidential notes of the
meeting taken by Dr. Pedro Martínez-Fraga, former Cuban ambassador
to Washington, Bender advised the group of the three conditions laid
out by Washington for US support:

1. The US government had empowered the CIA, represented by
    Mr. B., to provide assistance to anti-Castro revolutionaries in
    their struggle for freedom. Maximum discretion was urged. If
    asked, Washington would officially deny the entente.
2. The Cuban revolutionaries, through a central committee,
    would prepare, direct, and wage war against Castro. All major
    anti-Communist groups would be invited to join the front,
    except those connected with Batista.
3. The CIA would make available and manage the funds required
    to organize and prosecute the struggle. The expense budget
    would be monitored and approved by the CIA, operating as
    Bender Associates (Group B).[9]

After considerable debate, the Cuban leaders acceded to the so-
called Gentlemen's Agreement, but with serious misgivings. They were
expecting a full and open alliance with the US government and not a
clandestine and subordinate relationship with a midlevel CIA officer.
They had requested a war loan to be repaid by the government of a free
Cuba and not discretionary grants or handouts managed by the CIA.
But given their lack of resources and the magnitude of the struggle,

which was not against a local dictatorship like Batista's but against a Soviet-backed totalitarian regime, they reluctantly accepted the unilateral terms and implicit dependency conveyed by Bender.

In reality, they didn't have much choice. There was no other country in the hemisphere prepared to shelter thousands of Cuban refugees and embrace and finance their freedom cause. So, with a leap of faith, they swallowed their pride, shook hands with Bender, and forged ahead.

Shortly after the New York meeting, the Cuban anti-Castro coalition formed the Revolutionary Democratic Front (the "Front") headquartered in Miami, and Tony Varona emerged as the "coordinator." To achieve consensus, no president was named, but Varona was clearly the head.

Once installed, Tony sent me a message to join him in Miami as his executive assistant. My father and Varona were close friends since their days in the Senate, and following Castro's rise to power, I had developed a personal relationship with Tony that bridged the generational gap (I was then twenty-four and he fifty-two). At his behest, I had drafted a statement of principles denouncing Castro's betrayal of the democratic revolution he had promised. Varona honored me by incorporating parts of my statement in his call-to-arms manifesto.

Varona's new request had far-reaching implications for me. It meant leaving behind my family and friends, and the country I loved, to embark on a risky venture, carrying only one suitcase (the maximum allowed) and a few dollars in my pocket. But it was no ordinary venture. I viewed it as a crusade to help rescue my homeland from an alien tyranny.

After consulting with my parents, I decided to go. The farewell was painful, but my hopes were high. I left the island on June 17, 1960—a splendid sunny day etched in my memory—confident that I would soon return to a free Cuba.

My first mission upon arrival in Miami was to spell out in a pamphlet what the Front stood for—its purpose and its mission. Varona also asked me to work with the planning committee, which had been tasked with drafting interim legislation for the post-Castro transitional government, based on Cuba's democratic 1940 constitution.

The committee was like a minicongress composed of a select but diverse group of Cuban exiles—revolutionaries and politicians, businessmen and labor leaders, attorneys and former judges, professors and young graduates. Thanks to the able stewardship of the chairman, Ambassador Pedro Martínez-Fraga, an experienced parliamentarian and diplomat, we accomplished our mission in good time. When Don Pedro felt that we were enmeshed in long-winded, byzantine discussions (a notable Cuban propensity), he would ceremoniously remove his glasses and admonish us with an impish smile: "Stop splitting hairs and move on, lest our impatient friends on the banks of the Potomac present us with their own drafts ... in English!"

The OAS San José Conference

In mid-August 1960, Varona, who was mainly focused on beefing up the underground movement in Cuba and seeking recruits for military training in Guatemala, asked me and a few other Front colleagues to attend the OAS Conference of Foreign Ministers in San José, Costa Rica. This high-level meeting was scheduled to address the threat of Soviet intervention in this hemisphere (meaning Cuba without naming it).

Given the highly polarized environment in Latin America, Washington thought that by taking a back seat (or "leading from behind" as pundits would say these days) and having another country (Peru) sponsor the OAS meeting, the United States would not be accused of bullying Castro—a puerile delusion as was soon borne out.

Our Front delegation, armed with journalist credentials, left Miami on a direct LACSA flight to San José. Our mission was to counter the myths and lies of the Castro revolution and point to the Communist threat it posed to the rest of the hemisphere. Upon our arrival, a pro-Castro security officer at the airport with a bushy mustache and an icy gaze subjected us to hostile interrogation. Alleging that we were going to incite disturbances, he ordered us to return to Miami on the same flight that had brought us to San José.

As the plane was preparing to take off, the order was countermanded thanks to the personal intervention of the director of the leading newspaper in Costa Rica and we were allowed to stay. We had no idea that on the way back to Miami the plane was scheduled to stop in Havana.

The following day the *Miami Herald* headlined our saga: "Exiles Have Close Call." The story began: "Three exiled Cuban journalists, all known foes of the Fidel Castro regime, almost got sent to Havana by Costa Rican officials."[10]

As we had anticipated, Castro's minister of foreign relations, Raúl Roa, a sardonic intellectual and consummate showman, said that Cuba had come to the meeting not as the defendant but as the prosecutor. Displaying pungent dialectics and wit, he charged the United States with more than fifty acts of aggression and intervention in Latin America since the start of the century, which he theatrically recited one by one. Then he argued that Washington had no legal or moral basis to indict Cuba for reserving its right to receive Soviet military support in the event of US aggression.

The United States was represented by Secretary of State Christian Herter, a tall, polished diplomat with a soothing voice and avuncular manner. His mission was to rally Latin American support to condemn the Soviet-backed Castro regime and provide a patina of legitimacy to the military action envisaged by President Eisenhower. Secretary John Foster Dulles accomplished something similar with the Declaration of Caracas passed by the OAS in 1954, just before the CIA launched its operation in Guatemala to overthrow Marxist president Árbenz. But Herter was no John Foster Dulles, an unabashed and muscular practitioner of carrot-and-stick diplomacy, nor had he prepared the terrain for a meaningful OAS resolution.

Herter tried to center the debate on the key issue of the communization of Cuba and its hemispheric implications. His speech was a well-documented but lifeless brief lacking keen-edge arguments and rhetorical flourishes to rouse the Latins. It censured Castro but did not outline a convincing course of action to address the looming Soviet intervention in Cuba.

It was clear to the Front delegation that Herter had not impressed, must less swayed, the majority of the foreign ministers. We did our best to respond to Roa's tirades in full-page ads carried by local newspapers, but this was not enough to turn the tide in our favor. What was most disconcerting was that the foreign minister of Peru—the very same country beckoned by the United States to request the OAS meeting— was only recommending mediation between the United States and Cuba as if the crisis had sprung from bilateral issues.

To complicate matters, the influential Venezuelan foreign minister (a vocal Castro sympathizer) was sponsoring, with considerable backing, a resolution that would warn the United States and the Soviet Union not to intervene in Cuba. The not too subtle inference was that both were equally at fault.

Absent strong US leadership, we felt, the situation would get out of hand. Finally Washington woke up and decided to flex its muscle. The presidents of Peru and Venezuela were pressed to remove their wayward foreign ministers on the spot (they did), and the United States was able to muster the necessary votes to pass a tepid resolution declaring that the acceptance by any American state of a potential extracontinental intervention threatened the security of the hemisphere and would oblige the OAS to oppose it.

Even though the resolution, known as the Declaration of San José, had no teeth and didn't even mention Cuba, Castro's foreign minister, Roa, refused to sign it and decided to walk out. As he and his aides abruptly left the conference chanting anti-US slogans, a stirring shout of "Cuba, *sí*. Comunismo, *no*" rocked the theater. It was our group responding to Roa's diatribes and waving a large Cuban flag from one of the balconies. We wanted to show, at least symbolically, that the Castro delegation did not represent freedom-loving Cubans.

Castro's Game Plan

The pusillanimity of the foreign ministers in Costa Rica, who only obliquely touched on the Cuba-Soviet issue, further emboldened Fidel Castro. At a huge mass rally in Havana, he heaped scorn on the OAS—dubbed the "Ministry of Colonies of the United States"—tore up the insipid Declaration of San José, and issued his own Declaration of Havana, ratifying Cuba's acceptance of Soviet military support.

As a wily manipulator of public opinion, Castro's strategy was simple but very effective. He constantly provoked, vilified, and abused the United States, and when Washington responded to his egregious challenges, he would play the role of David seemingly victimized by the implacable Goliath of the North.

As noted by writer and historian Theodore Draper, "By waiting for the opportune occasion, every aggressive action can be made to appear in a defensive light." He added, "Fidel Castro and his inner circle have never been innocent victims of circumstances; they have always been the engine of this revolution in perpetual motion; they have leaped at one pretext or another to do what they wanted to do; they have incessantly increased their power by taking the initiative against their enemies and relentlessly pressing the advantage."[11]

Here's an example of Castro's technique of deliberately jabbing the United States and then yelling foul play or aggression when Washington reacted to defend its interests:

On June 11, 1960, Castro demanded that three US- and British-owned oil refineries in Cuba process two barge loads of Soviet crude oil—this after piling up a large overdue debt of $16 million for previous oil imports from other sources and $60 million for refining. When the three companies refused to take Russian oil, the Castro regime seized their assets.

Then on July 6, when Washington, in retaliation, partially cut Cuba's three-million-ton US sugar quota by seven hundred thousand tons—about the same amount that Moscow had agreed to buy from

Cuba at prices well below those obtained by the United States—Castro accused Washington of economic aggression aimed at destroying the Cuban Revolution. To compensate for the losses brought about by the alleged aggression, he confiscated in early August a large number of US businesses including thirty-six sugar mills. (This was but the first wave of confiscations of US properties in Cuba with an estimated present value of $8 billion.)

Castro set off the US-Cuban feud and kept it going for several reasons. First, it served as a pretext to align Cuba with the Soviet bloc and Red China and to receive large quantities of arms and military experts. The alignment was formalized with close to seventy economic, political, cultural, and strategic agreements during the period 1960–61.

The feud also enabled Castro to maintain a virtual state of emergency in Cuba to guard against the purported perennial threat of US aggression. The siege mentality that he instilled in the population facilitated the regimentation of life under stringent totalitarian rule.

Finally, battling the United States, fearless and unbowed, gave Castro the heroic anti-imperialist mantra to fire up the radicals throughout the continent and spread his revolution. During the first half of 1960, some fifteen members of Castro's foreign service were accused of intervening in the internal affairs of various Latin American republics and declared personae non grata. In most cases, they used the Cuban embassies as centers for Marxist propaganda, espionage, and subversion.

The August 18 White House Meeting on Cuba

The purpose of the meeting was to update the president on the Cuba covert plan. In attendance were Allan Dulles and Richard Bissell of the CIA, the national security adviser, the secretaries of Defense, State, and Treasury, and several generals from the Pentagon.

The review touched on the Front anti-Castro leaders. Although Dulles called them "prima donnas" without having met them, he assured the president that all of them were "favorably known in Cuba" and "were non-Batista-ites." Regarding the proposed paramilitary operation, Dulles reported that the training of twenty or thirty instructor cadres had been finished in the Panama Canal Zone, and they would now go to Guatemala to instruct about five hundred Cubans. "He indicated there will be a need for some air force trainers and logistic support people. These would be [US] military personnel [fifteen or twenty in all] under cover."

Bissell intimated that a standby force, preferably of non-Americans, may be required for the later action phase. He also advised the group that if local resistance (the anti-Castro US-trained force) was unable to accomplish the mission, there may be a need for air action and the possible occupation of the Isle of Pines in Cuba for a base of operations.

When the secretary of defense Thomas Gates asked whether US officers and men would be involved in the backup force, Dulles dodged the query and missed a great opportunity to discuss that likely contingency. He insisted that a decision on the backup force be deferred.

The national security adviser Gordon Gray, sensing reluctance to face up to this critical issue, "pointed out that it would be unwise to mount any kind of an operation without the determination to see it through, and that an abortive effort would be worse than no effort at all."

President Eisenhower was even more emphatic. He said that he "would go along [with any proposed plan] so long as the Joint Chiefs, Defense, State, and the CIA think we have a good chance of being successful." Regarding the need to increase the budget for the operation, he indicated that "he wouldn't care much about the kind of cost; indeed, … he would defend this kind of action against all comers, and that if we could be sure of freeing the Cubans from this incubus [less than one line declassified], it might be a small price to pay."[12]

Anti-Castro Guerrillas in Cuba

Inside the island, Fidel Castro's popularity was rapidly declining as a result of his draconian measures, from massive confiscations to the obliteration of the free press to arbitrary executions and arrests. Widespread discontent was compounded by the manifold disruptions produced by Fidel's totalitarian reengineering of society. The government-support programs designed to alleviate the crisis while creating state dependency (food supply, housing, health care, and education) had not yet been fully implemented. In that chaotic environment, nothing seemed to work other than propaganda, which was relentless; spying, which was pervasive, and military training, which was mandatory.

Still, the Castro regime, though vulnerable, was not in danger of unraveling or of being toppled from within. According to the US Embassy in Cuba, Castro could at least count on the hard-core support of 15 percent to 25 percent of the population.[13] This segment comprised not only the registered Communists and the direct beneficiaries of the regime's perks (the so-called "New Class") but also militant youngsters inflamed by the revolution; pliant intellectuals; and regimented workers. With the additional backing of his reconstituted army and newly formed people's militias, Fidel was not too concerned about the growing underground movement engaged in sabotage. Nor was he particularly alarmed by the anti-Communist guerrillas who were springing up in the mountains, mainly in the Escambray cordillera, in the south central region of Cuba.

Those freedom fighters were a mix of purged officers of the pre-Castro army, local farmers whose properties had been confiscated, and former guerrillas who had fought alongside Castro and who now opposed the Communist takeover.

Although the insurgents (about a thousand during the last quarter of 1960) lacked unified command and arms, they knew the area well and were backed by the largely sympathetic *guajiros* (peasants). Castro initially underestimated their staying power and potential to grow, dubbed them "bandits," and only threw against the insurgents' unseasoned militias with not many soldiers to round them up. They failed and had to be replaced with a much larger, experienced contingent.

The CIA strategists correctly surmised that they only had a window of a few months to bolster the insurgents before Castro mobilized overwhelming forces against them. Sure enough, with the guidance of about four hundred Soviet military and KGB experts stationed in the nearby military compound of El Condado, Castro launched in early 1961 a scorched-earth offensive against the rebels, who had soared to over three thousand guerrillas, backed by several thousand active supporters.[14] Other estimates were higher. To cut off their supply lines, the regime uprooted most of the peasant families living in the area and dragged them into concentration camps. Many of the guerrilla prisoners were tortured and executed.

Given these developments inside Cuba, the CIA rapidly built two bases in Guatemala. One of them, called "Trax," was located on a coffee plantation surrounded by steep mountains not far from the western town of Retalhuleu. It served for guerrilla and later infantry training. The other, "Rayo," an air force base constructed on flat terrain with a forty-eight-hundred-foot asphalt runway, was thirty-three miles from the Pacific coast of Guatemala, very close to Retalhuleu. Both bases were under CIA command, assisted by US military officers on loan.

While Trax trained what eventually became the invasion brigade, Rayo focused initially on preparing some fifty-eight Cuban pilots to drop weapons and ammunitions to the anti-Castro guerrillas operating in the Escambray Mountains. By the end of September 1960, the C-46 and C-54 transport squadrons at Rayo were ready for action. But they faced enormous hurdles.

As described by Captain Edward B. Ferrer, one of the Cuban pilots involved in the operation, they had to fly "over the mountains of Guatemala, the highest peaks in Central America at over 13,000 feet, in antique, World War II, unpressurized, propeller-driven aircraft, at night, fully loaded, with no … sophisticated navigational system [or reliable radio beacons]." The round trip of sixteen hundred to eighteen hundred nautical miles took from eleven to fourteen hours depending on the type of aircraft and weather conditions.[15]

Worse still, there was no direct communication between the

guerrillas and the Rayo air force base. As noted by Ferrer, "When the guerrillas requested an airdrop, they used an intelligence network operating between Cuba and the United States. The agents in the United States would then inform the advisers at Rayo of the date, time, and place of the scheduled drop. If for any reason the guerrillas had to move, there was no way for us to know." Not surprisingly, most of the supply airdrops did not reach the guerrillas.[16]

This awkward, inefficient method of operation was the outgrowth of the delusion that primitive facilities and flawed execution would serve to mask Washington's involvement. The unrealistic US goal of plausible deniability would hang like an albatross around the neck of CIA planners throughout the various phases of the Cuba covert operation.

But in the case of the Escambray episode, a most disturbing factor may also have accounted for the lack of full and sustained support of the anti-Castro guerrillas. According to Colonel Fred D. Stevens, who was US air attaché at the embassy in Havana until diplomatic relations were severed in January 1961, Washington key players let the Escambray dry up because they had no control of the insurgents and questioned their ideology and political allegiance. In Colonel Stevens's opinion, the abandonment of the guerrillas was a shortsighted and heartless decision with grave consequences for the cause of a free Cuba.[17]

Some have challenged this serious charge, but what is unquestionable is that by November 1960, when the besieged insurgents were being assailed by Castro forces and the Soviet Union had increased its arms shipments to Cuba, the CIA covert operation shifted from infiltrating teams geared for guerrilla warfare to launching an amphibious and airborne assault.

The Politicization of the Cuba Issue

During the 1960 presidential campaign, there were two hot foreign policy issues: the so-called "missile gap" with the Soviet Union (the reverse was actually the case) and the rising threat of a Communist Cuba buttressed by the Soviet bloc. The Castro-Khrushchev public embrace in New York during the September UN General Assembly, and their synchronized vitriolic speeches against the United States, underscored the danger posed by their sinister alliance.

Senator John F. Kennedy, running for president against Vice President Richard Nixon, took advantage of the inflammatory Cuba issue to accuse the Eisenhower administration of dereliction of its responsibilities for "permitting a Communist satellite only ninety miles from the shores of the United States." Even though CIA director Dulles had twice briefed Kennedy on the overall strategy and ongoing plans to overthrow the Castro regime, the young Democratic candidate taunted Nixon: "Those who say they will stand up to Khrushchev have demonstrated no ability to stand up to Castro."

Kennedy later doubled down with this statement: "We must attempt to strengthen the non-Batista democratic anti-Castro forces in exile, and in Cuba itself, who offer eventual hope of overthrowing Castro. Thus far these fighters for freedom have had virtually no support from our government."

Nixon was infuriated by Kennedy's foul play, which put him in a bind. He was unable to defend the Eisenhower administration—and himself—without revealing the anti-Castro plans that were, in fact, under way. To safeguard the covert operation, he rejected Kennedy's "irresponsible and reckless" proposal that would be condemned by the UN and invite Khrushchev's intervention in Cuba. To address the Castro threat, Nixon could only point to the Eisenhower administration's limited trade embargo, ridiculed by Kennedy "as too little, too late."[18]

Nixon's perceived weakness on Castro, despite having championed the paramilitary plan to topple him, may have cost him the election. And Kennedy's opportunistic bravado, publicly advocating US support to overthrow the Cuban dictator, came back to haunt him shortly after he became president. Such are the startling ironies of history.

▌The November 29 White House Meeting on Cuba

Although the anti-Castro covert plan had already shifted from the infiltration of guerrilla-trained Cuban exiles to the launch of a combat-ready expeditionary force,[19] President Eisenhower was critical of the slow progress that had been made. He echoed the concerns conveyed to him by his good friend, former ambassador William D. Pawley, namely, that the "500 [Cuban exiles] now in training should be increased to at least 2,000" and that the disjointed committee overseeing the covert operation "should have a strong Executive."

The president agreed that it was impossible to train the force in the United States with any hope of keeping it under wraps and felt that it was not feasible at the time to recognize a Cuban government in exile, but he dismissed the State Department's worry about "shooting from the hip." In fact, he thought that "we should be prepared to take more chances and be more aggressive."

There were two points that Eisenhower stressed at the meeting. First, given the impending transfer of the executive responsibilities to President-Elect Kennedy, he said that "we would not want to be in a position of turning over the government in the midst of a developing emergency." Hence his desire to be bolder and nimbler in recasting and advancing the operation, which he planned to review with Kennedy on December 6.

The second point Eisenhower underscored was the need to select immediately a very senior government official who would coordinate all aspects of the larger-scale operation—intelligence, military, and diplomatic relations with the Front—and report to the president.[20]

The "coordinating chief," subsequently appointed as deputy to Assistant Secretary of State for Inter-American Affairs Thomas Mann, was Whiting Willauer, US ambassador to Costa Rica and, previously, to Honduras. Apart from his diplomatic background, Willauer had gained considerable air force logistics experience during World War II as assistant to the president and executive secretary of China defense supplies, which became the principal backstopping agency for General Claire Chennault's Flying Tiger operation during the war. Willauer later played a key role in supporting the CIA-led Guatemala paramilitary action against President Árbenz.

Tony Varona's November 29 Meeting at the State Department

The very same day that President Eisenhower reviewed the anti-Castro operation at the White House, Tony Varona, head of the Front, was received at the State Department. He had requested a meeting with Assistant Secretary of State Thomas Mann but was granted an audience with midlevel officials empowered only to listen, raise questions, and take notes.

Varona, although miffed by the apparent snub, decided to go on with the meeting. There were more important issues to air than title and rank. Not known for diplomatic niceties, Tony was very direct, if not blunt, in stating his position on the Cuba situation and on discussing what the Front expected of the US government to address the Castro-Communist threat and hasten the liberation of Cuba.

During the meeting, which lasted two hours and twenty minutes, Varona covered a lot of ground. The declassified minutes summarize his views but do not record any comments or observations made by the impassive officials.

Varona made several key points. Given the ongoing training of Castro's armed forces and militias—which training was progressively raising their level of discipline and efficiency—and the increasing shipments to Cuba of Soviet arms and military personnel, Varona said, "It is essential that the opposition forces mount their attacks at the earliest possible moment. ... Time is running against us, and it is an illusion to believe that economic hardship will ever, by itself, achieve the objective which is sought."

He shrugged off as impractical the idea considered by the CIA of launching an invasion to take the Isle of Pines, an area reportedly defended by twenty-five hundred Castro fighting men. Varona correctly pointed out that "after seizing the island, presumably at a heavy cost, the invading forces would still be faced with the major task of launching still another invasion against the mainland of Cuba."

As a better alternative, the exile leader outlined his proposed plan: "A force of 2,000–3,000 men [US-trained Cuban brigade along with the Front heads] should be put ashore in Cuba, should take control of an area, consolidate their hold over it, and declare themselves the new government of Cuba. The existence of such a controlled area, in the nature of a safe haven, would ipso facto encourage large-scale defections of Castro's forces." With his customary emphatic style, Varona added, "It would then be incumbent upon the United States to recognize the newly established government and actively and effectively support it."

When asked if he meant by this the actual dispatch of United States troops or just equipment, Varona didn't mince words. He explicitly responded that he meant both. Near the end of the conversation or quasi monologue, "he repeated his personal conviction that Castro [would] be overthrown only by a major military effort, and that armed intervention by the United States with men and equipment would prove unavoidable." No one at the meeting contradicted Varona or disabused him of that expectation.[21]

The Eisenhower–Kennedy Transition (January 3–19, 1961)

At the start of 1961, Castro yet again brazenly provoked Washington. On January 3, at 1:20 a.m., the Cuban Ministry of Foreign Relations in Havana sent a telegram to the chargé d'affaires at the US Embassy informing him that the total number of personnel at the US Embassy and Consulate must not be more than eleven persons. The telegram further stipulated that the personnel exceeding that limit had to leave the island within forty-eight hours.

Eisenhower did not delay his response to that riling diktat. After telling his advisers at an emergency meeting that morning that the United States "should not tolerate being kicked around," he proceeded to break diplomatic relations with Cuba. The president, however, wanted to go beyond that. He was eager to finish the job of helping to overthrow the Castro-Communist regime before leaving office on January 20. But since not enough Cuban exiles had yet been recruited and trained to launch the planned assault, he was prepared to intervene unilaterally if the Cuban regime provided him a really good excuse. Failing that, the president said, perhaps the United States "could think of manufacturing something that would be generally acceptable."[22]

In the end, the president agreed that the ongoing CIA operation was the best course, and he instructed Dulles and Bissell to increase with a sense of urgency the size of the force being trained in Guatemala.

In the meantime, Ambassador Whiting Willauer, who had been appointed as coordinator in chief of the operation, held an interdepartmental meeting on January 11 at the office of the chief of naval operations to assess the plan developed by the CIA for an invasion of Cuba. This was the first time that the plan had been reviewed by working-level officers of the Joint Chiefs of Staff.

For seven days—from the January 11 to January 18—the Interdepartmental Working Group on Cuba, representing the CIA, the State Department, Defense, and the Joint Chiefs of Staff (JCS), reviewed the plan and produced several papers that summarized the discussions, posed questions, and formulated recommendations. Although there was not enough time before the Kennedy inaugural on the twentieth to blend the respective views of the CIA and the Defense Department and incorporate them into a single document, there seems to have been general concurrence at least on the following key points:[23]

1. Timing

The CIA reported that "while the support of the Castro government by the Cuban population is deteriorating rapidly and time is working in our favor in that sense, it is working to our disadvantage in a military sense." According to US intelligence, as many as one hundred Castro pilots were undergoing jet flight training in Czechoslovakia, and the appearance of modern radar throughout Cuba indicated a strong possibility that Castro would soon have an all-weather jet intercept capability. Further, the Soviet bloc was shipping to the island vast quantities of military equipment, including medium and heavy tanks, field artillery, heavy mortars, and antiaircraft artillery, along with military experts and trainers. MiG fighter planes were expected to arrive shortly.

Based on that report, the Interdepartmental Working Group believed that it was not realistic or advisable to postpone the operation, say, for seven months, in order to recruit and train a much larger force of Cuban exiles and possibly Latin American volunteers (five thousand to ten thousand strong). The rationale: it would be very difficult to unseat a Soviet-backed Communist regime, once consolidated, without a major US military intervention.

2.   Invasion

An amphibious-airborne force of Cuban exiles trained in Guatemala (seven hundred fifty men at the time, increasing to about fourteen hundred by D-Day) would seize and defend a small lodgment on Cuban soil near a terrain propitious for guerrilla warfare in case the landing failed to ignite a sizable uprising.

3.   Air cover

Control of air lanes and sea-lanes in the landing area was viewed by the group as an absolute requirement. "The Cuban Air Force and naval vessels capable of opposing our landing must be knocked out or neutralized before our amphibious shipping makes its final run into the beach. If this is not done—the Group emphasized—we will be courting disaster."

The group also noted that "the idea of air strikes beginning three days before D-Day has been killed [as that would give Castro too much advance notice of the invasion], and a strike beginning the day before D-Day has now been accepted [by the group]."

It was pointed out, particularly by Willauer, that there was a need for US jet fighters to provide top-level air cover for the low-level strafing by the B-26 bombers that were assigned to secure the beachhead.[24]

4. US military support

The lodgment seized by the invasion force would be used as the site for the establishment of a Free Cuba provisional government, which would be promptly recognized by the United States and several Latin American states and given overt military assistance. The prevailing view of the group was that US support (at least logistics) shortly after the landing was necessary to break out of the beachhead, stimulate an uprising, and topple the regime. At that stage, the command of the operation would shift from the CIA to CINCLANT (commander in chief of the US Atlantic Fleet).

As we shall see, these plausible recommendations, which may have averted the Bay of Pigs disaster, were not heeded by the incoming administration.

▮ Eisenhower's Parting Counsel

On January 19, the day before Kennedy's inaugural, Eisenhower met with him at the White House together with their principal advisers. When the issue of Cuba came up, Eisenhower stressed that the United States must not allow the Castro-Communist regime to continue to exist in Cuba. He counseled that the training of anti-Castro forces in Guatemala be continued and accelerated, and urged the Kennedy administration to "help such forces to the utmost."[25]

CHAPTER 6

Inside a Doomed Expedition: The Bay of Pigs (January–April 1961)

Shortly after Kennedy took office, his New Frontier executive team proceeded to reassess the proposed Cuba paramilitary plan. The key players were Robert McNamara, secretary of defense; McGeorge Bundy, national security adviser; Dean Rusk, secretary of state; Chester Bowles, undersecretary of state; Thomas Mann, assistant secretary of state for inter-American affairs; Adolf A. Berle, chief of Department of State Latin American Task Force; and Arthur Schlesinger, special assistant to the president. Kennedy also invited Senator William Fulbright, chairman of the Committee on Foreign Relations, to join the team and express his views at a crucial meeting.

The Interdepartmental Working Group on Cuba that Ambassador Willauer had put together, with State, Defense, CIA, and Joint Chiefs of Staff (JCS) representatives, was disbanded. As a result, there was a break in the continuity of the development of the Cuba paramilitary plan. Willauer was first marginalized and subsequently eased out with no formal notice of termination. As he testified in Senate hearings: "I kept trying to get an appointment [with Secretary of State Rusk]. I tried for thirty days straight. I saw him once in the hall. He said: 'I am awfully busy. I will see you later.' I just got a general runaround. The thing that amazed me most was that I was never debriefed."[1]

The official records clearly show that Kennedy's executive team was not sanguine about the covert paramilitary plan. Most of the advisers, particularly Bowles, Mann, and Schlesinger, plus Fulbright, strongly opposed it for moral, legal, and political reasons. They apparently disregarded the possibility of recognizing a Free Cuba provisional government concurrently with the landing of the strike force, which could have legitimized US overt support and paved the way for collective action by the OAS under the Rio Treaty.

Arguing that the operation was out of proportion to the alleged Communist threat, Fulbright said famously that "the Castro regime is a thorn in the flesh, but is not a dagger in the heart." (The senator had to eat those words the following year, when the Soviet Union established a strategic base in Cuba with a nuclear dagger pointed at the heart of the United States.)

In a memorandum to the president advocating cancellation of the invasion, Schlesinger wrote that the risks of the operation outweighed the risks of abandonment. Carried away by wishful thinking, he mused, "We might ... be able to make some diplomatic capital out of the abandonment. We might have [Ambassador] Thompson say to Khrushchev, for example, that we have discouraged an invasion of Cuba; that this shows our genuine desire to compose differences; that K. should tell his friend [Castro] to behave."[2] It's hard to imagine how this transparent ploy would have induced the hard-boiled comrades Khrushchev and Castro to "behave."

When the momentum in Washington finally tilted toward a downsized military action against Castro, most of the Kennedy advisers who had been against it withheld their opposition and jumped on the bandwagon. But they seemed more interested in protecting the president politically in case of failure than in bolstering the operation militarily to ensure success. As reported and endorsed by Schlesinger, Secretary of State Rusk suggested that "someone other than the president make the final decision [to launch the invasion] and to do so in his absence—someone whose head can later be placed on the block if things go terribly wrong."[3] Not precisely the kind of leadership that the president extolled in his book *Profiles in Courage*.

Kennedy's Moment of Truth

Kennedy's eloquent inaugural address—masterly delivered on a cold, blustery day in January—positioned him as a gallant and unflinching leader of the free world, prepared to "pay any price, bear any burden, ... oppose any foe to [en]sure the survival and success of liberty."

In an oblique warning to both Castro and the Soviet Union, he postulated, "Let all our neighbors know that we shall join with them to oppose aggression or subversion anywhere in the Americas. ... And let every other power know that this hemisphere intends to remain the master of its own destiny." The words were just right to rally the allies and forewarn the foes. The big question: Would the president's actions match his stirring rhetoric?

Having barely settled down in the White House, Kennedy had to face his moment of truth on Cuba. The issue was too compelling to be shrugged off or held in abeyance. It required a prompt and clear-eyed decision on whether to proceed with the plans to topple the Castro regime and, if so, under what conditions.

The president had been briefed three times on Cuba (twice during the presidential campaign). But then he didn't own the issue and could exploit it, as he unabashedly did to his advantage, pummeling Nixon for being "soft" on communism in Cuba. Now, however, he was in the driver's seat. The issue was his—to resolve or to botch.

Troves of declassified documents and personal records point to a dithering president with no executive or international experience who was not sold on the covert plan to overthrow the Castro regime. But instead of canceling it altogether, given his concerns and doubts, he micromanaged and eviscerated the risky operation and doomed it to failure with not enough pushback from the CIA and the Joint Chiefs of Staff.

Following is an unvarnished recount of the ill-advised decisions that led to the disaster of the Bay of Pigs and its portentous consequences:

February 8—a Preview of the Operation at the White House

The meeting with the president opened with a brief overview by Richard Bissell of the CIA's proposed plan for launching an expeditionary force against Castro with the Cuban troops trained in Guatemala. He reported that after careful evaluation, the Joint Chiefs of Staff believed that the plan had "a fair chance of success." By success they meant ability to survive, hold ground, and attract growing support from Cubans. At worst, the invaders would fight their way to the nearby mountains and go into guerrilla action (even though most of them had not been trained for guerrilla warfare).

The president pressed for alternatives to a full-fledged "invasion" supported by planes, ships, and supplies provided by the United States. He envisaged "a force that would land gradually and quietly and make its first major military efforts from the mountains." The CIA expressed reservations about a quiet, piecemeal operation but agreed that the matter should be carefully studied.

The president also intruded in the restructuring of the Front, which was being enlarged and subsumed by the newly formed Cuban Revolutionary Council. The White House's position was that the council should have a "strong left-of-center balance."[4]

March 11—Presentation to Kennedy of the Trinidad Plan

The option recommended by the CIA and the JCS to the president was an amphibious-airborne assault carried out by the Cuban brigade trained in Guatemala (close to fourteen hundred strong) with concurrent (but no prior) tactical air support. The brigade was to seize a beachhead in the south central part of Cuba near the town of Trinidad. This was an optimal location that had access to a port (Casilda) and an airfield, and was close to the Escambray Mountains, where anti-Castro guerrillas were valiantly resisting the regime's onslaught.

The leaders of the Cuban Revolutionary Council in Miami would land as soon as the beachhead had been secured and establish a Free Cuba provisional government-in-arms. If initial operations were successful and if there was evidence of rebellion against the Castro regime, the provisional government could be recognized and a legal basis provided for US logistics support.

The president rejected the well-thought-out Trinidad plan because he said that it would "put us so openly in view of the world. ... He directed the development of a plan where US assistance would be less obvious, and [said he] would like to meet again within the next few days."[5]

Kennedy specifically indicated that "an acceptable plan should provide for a quiet landing, preferably at night, without having the appearance of a World War II–type amphibious assault."[6]

As the president continued to emasculate the operation in the interest of non-US attribution, the chance of success progressively dimmed.

▌March 15—Presentation of the Substitute Zapata Plan[7]

To satisfy the president, the CIA and the JCS worked feverishly to reframe the landing plan in seventy-two hours. Three options were presented, none of which, according to the JCS, was "considered as feasible and likely to accomplish the objective as the basic paramilitary plan [Trinidad plan]." Nevertheless, the president was inclined to go along with one of the options, which, as noted by Admiral Arleigh Burke, had only a 50 percent chance of success: the Zapata plan, which called for the landing of the Cuban brigade at the Bay of Pigs, on the Zapata Peninsula, south of Cuba.

The beachhead had an airstrip that could accommodate the brigade's B-26 bombers, and its few access roads would make it difficult for Castro to deploy his troops. Those were some of the reported advantages of the Bay of Pigs location. But there were also major disadvantages that were flagged to the president: resupply, including food, would have to come from outside Cuba; exits from the beachhead could be sealed off by Castro forces; and no sizable local support could be expected since the Bay of Pigs area was largely uninhabited.

It was wrongly assumed that if the landing forces could not hold their positions, they would "melt" into the mountains and become guerrillas. That would have been feasible in Trinidad but not in the Bay of Pigs, which was surrounded by alligator-infested swamps with no mountain hideouts within reach.

General Máximo Gómez, the renowned master of guerrilla warfare during Cuba's long quest for independence, expressly avoided the Zapata Peninsula as a "geographical and military trap."[8] Of course, we can't blame the US strategists for failing Cuban history. But flunking geography? That's another story.

The president did not like the idea of the dawn landing and felt that to make this appear as an inside guerrilla-type operation, the troops with all their equipment should disembark at night and the ships should be clear of the area by dawn. This was a tall order for an amphibious operation with few successful wartime night precedents to draw on.

To meet the president's directive that the initial landing be as unspectacular as possible, the immediately prior and concurrent tactical air support—the air cover deemed critical by the CIA and the JCS to protect the landing—was reluctantly dropped. As a compromise, a plan was to be devised to make a few strafing runs by fake defectors against the Castro air force several days before the landing. The downside was that this would alert the Cuban regime to the imminent invasion and expose the landing forces to relentless bombing if Castro's fighter planes were not all knocked out ahead of time—which is exactly what happened.

In the course of the meeting, "the president also inquired what would happen if it developed after the invasion that the Cuban exile force were pinned down and being slaughtered on the beaches." After further discussion, "it was decided they would not be re-embarked because there was no place to go. Once they were landed, they were there."

March 31

On March 31, Undersecretary of State Chester Bowles, who opposed the invasion, wrote Secretary Rusk that "those most familiar with the Cuban operation [the Zapata plan as curtailed and weakened] seem to agree that ... the chances of success are not greater than one-out-of-three. ... The one way we can reduce the risk [of failure] is by a sharply increased commitment of direct American support. In talking to Bob McNamara and Ros Gilpatric at lunch Tuesday at the Pentagon, I gathered that this is precisely what the military people feel we should do."[9]

April 4[10]

On April 4, President Kennedy held a meeting at the State Department with high-ranking members of the JCS and the CIA, and with his executive team, to review the scaled-down Zapata plan and agree on next steps. The president was still hesitant about the plan and again indicated his preference for an operation that would infiltrate the force in units of two hundred to two hundred fifty and then develop them through a buildup.

Colonel Jack Hawkins, chief of the CIA paramilitary section on loan from the US Marine Corps, took exception to Kennedy's recommendation. Armed with vast experience acquired in the invasions of Corregidor in the Philippines, Okinawa Island southwest of Japan, and Inchon in Korea, the colonel explained to the president "that landing small groups would merely serve to alert Castro, and they would be eliminated one by one. He indicated that a group of 200 was below the critical number able to defend themselves."

Senator Fulbright, who had been invited by the president to attend the meeting, thrashed the invasion plan, calling it immoral, illegal, and absurd. By lambasting the plan in such a sweeping and high-handed manner, he implicitly condemned and irked all those in attendance who for more than two months had been grappling with the operation. Fulbright's haughty sermon (coming from an "outsider") only served to galvanize the esprit de corps of the group and to draw sharp rebuttals and criticism. Except for Rusk, no one spoke against the Zapata plan, not even those who had serious reservations about it.

Indeed, when Kennedy went around the table and asked for their verdicts, they cast their votes in favor. The sentiment of the group was captured by Adolf Berle, who, when pressed by the president to cut short his long-winded speech and vote, blurted out: "Let 'er rip."

Kennedy adjourned the meeting with no final decision, saying, "We'd better sleep on it." The clock was ticking, but the wavering persisted.[11]

April 5–17

During the twelve days prior to the launch of the pared-down invasion, the president reiterated to the CIA and the JCS that no US troops would be involved, and he rejected the so-called "Nestor plan" (no relation to the author) that called for US paramilitary support. The only hope of averting disaster rested on the air supremacy of the brigade, but this critical condition was effectively thwarted by fatal decisions.

The original plan recommended by the CIA and the JCS to President Kennedy envisaged all-out air strikes not prior to D-1, so as not to alert the Castro forces prematurely. But since the president had rejected a massive air attack as too "spectacular," it was decided as a compromise to go to limited air strikes starting on D-2 with the objective of destroying Castro's attack planes on the ground. The strikes were to be carried out by brigade pilots posing as defectors from the Castro air force.

This convoluted scheme was intended to back up the fiction that air support for the invasion force was coming from within Cuba. The

CIA and the JCS reluctantly went along with this plan upon the understanding that full air cover would be provided at the crack of dawn on D-Day.[12]

On April 14, the president, intent on further playing down the magnitude of the imminent invasion, instructed Bissell to cut the size of the air strike scheduled for D-2 (April 15) from sixteen aircraft to eight. Bissell's impression was that "Kennedy issued this instruction without consulting the JCS or the secretary of defense."[13] Owing primarily to the cutback, about half of Castro's offensive air capability, including the deadly T-33 jet fighters, was not destroyed or neutralized during the April 15 air raids.

Then the White House proceeded to cancel the air strikes that were planned for D-1 and for early morning of D-Day. McGeorge Bundy notified General Charles Cabell, deputy director of the CIA, that no further air strikes would be permitted until the landing force had secured an airstrip within the beachhead. He also curtly told Cabell that any further discussion on the matter should be with Secretary of State Dean Rusk.

Cabell and Bissell immediately went to see Rusk, who explained that the decision had been made by the president for "political considerations." Castro's secretary of state had accused the United States at the UN Security Council of masterminding the bombing conducted by fake defectors, and Ambassador Adlai Stevenson—furious for not having been forewarned of the ploy—insisted that any further air strikes would make the US position untenable.

Cabell and Bissell, deeply distressed, argued that the strikes were essential to protect the brigade, and they informed Rusk that it was too late to stop the overall landing operation as the convoy was just beginning to put the first boat ashore. To drive the message home, they warned that failure to proceed with the planned air strikes against Cuban airfields, a harbor, and a radio broadcasting station, and to control the air at dawn on D-Day, "would clearly be disastrous." Rusk did not budge. He confirmed that the White House's decision to cancel the air strikes would stand, and Cabell and Bissell saw no point in appealing directly to the president.

To compensate for the lack of the vital air strikes, Cabell called Secretary Rusk at his home at 4:30 a.m., April 17 (D-Day), and requested that the US Navy in the area provide air protection to the invasion ships as they withdrew from the beachhead. Rusk telephoned the president and allowed Cabell to make his case directly to him. Kennedy's response was unequivocal: "Request for [navy] air cover disapproved."[14]

The upshot of these last-minute decisions spelled doom, but the brigade commanders, unaware of what was going on in Washington, proceeded in high spirits with the landing. As described by the *Miami Herald* (April 20, 2006), "Eduardo Zayas-Bazán fired the first shots at the Bay of Pigs as he sneaked on shore with five other men as part of an underwater demolition team. As the inflatable boat was nearing the beach, a Cuban army jeep heard a noise and was turning its headlights toward the water. Grayston Lynch, an American [CIA case officer] who joined the brigade, gave the order to fire, and they did, destroying the jeep." That went fine, but huge problems soon arose.

First was the inability to effectuate a diversionary landing in the far-eastern province of Oriente just prior to D-Day. The operation was to be carried out by a group of about 168 Cuban combatants, trained by the CIA in New Orleans and led by Nino Díaz, who had fought alongside Raúl Castro in the Sierra Maestra. Their reconnaissance platoons reportedly saw many armed militias surrounding the area where they were supposed to land. Thinking that it was a trap, Díaz decided not to land.

But the worst news came from the Bay of Pigs. Unable to complete the unloading before dawn, two of the old freighter ships used for the landings were sunk or grounded by unopposed Castro fighter planes. As a result, the ten-day reserves of ammunition on board, as well as food, hospital equipment, and gasoline, were lost. Two of the other freighter ships had to put out to sea without unloading all the war matériel. The fifth one, the *Lake Charles*, carrying reinforcements, including my Operation 40 unit and a medical team with outstanding Cuban doctors who had been promised a hospital ship that never appeared, was ordered to remain on standby off Cuban territorial waters because of the continuous attack by Castro's fighter planes. That order from the command ship not to land infuriated us at the time but possibly saved our lives.

Major General George Reid Doster, who had been recruited by the CIA to train and direct the brigade's pilots, foresaw what would happen as a result of the cancellation of the D-1 air strikes and the early morning D-Day air cover. When informed of that critical decision at the rear base in Puerto Cabezas, Nicaragua, he threw his cap to the ground and yelled, fuming in anguish, "There goes the fuckin' war!"[15] Sadly, his presage proved to be right.

What Went Wrong, and Why?

The whats are, to some extent, well-known, but the whys remain cloudy. The purpose of delving into the causes of the failure of the invasion, including the motives that drove the fateful decisions, is not to point fingers and apportion blame but to extract from the disaster some useful lessons. With that in mind, we'll focus on those who played, or should have played, a key role in the final stages of the operation: President Kennedy, the CIA, the JCS, and the Cuban exile and resistance leaders.

President Kennedy

Historians, analysts, and psychologists still ponder what accounted for Kennedy's strange conduct throughout this process, particularly his indecisiveness (he gave his reluctant go-ahead only twenty-four hours before the landing) and his micromanagement of the operation, whittling it down to bare bones and condemning it to failure. Was it the poor advice he got from the "experts"—the CIA and the JCS—as he claimed, or was it that he simply was unprepared to tackle this complex and contentious issue so early in his presidency? To what extent did the president's Addison's disease and persistent back pain, alleviated by extra doses of cortisone, synthetic hormones, and painkillers, affect his judgment and willpower? Was he held back by the fear of Soviet retaliation in Berlin or by the futile attempt to conceal the widely known or presumed US involvement in the invasion?

Perhaps all those factors influenced his performance. But still the crucial question remains: Why, instead of emasculating the operation, did Kennedy not simply cancel it? This is where the political side of the story comes in. As Allen Dulles reminded the president, there was "the disposal problem": what to do with the brigade if the invasion were canceled. How to deal with the expected outcry of the US-trained Cuban freedom fighters, who would feel double-crossed by the White House?

McGeorge Bundy foresaw the political consequences of calling off the invasion. He commented, "The Republicans would have said: 'We were all set to beat Castro, and this chicken, this antsy-pantsy bunch of liberals.' ... There would have been a political risk in not going through with the operation. Saying no would have brought all the hawks out of the woodwork."[16]

The "disposal problem" and its potential reverberations certainly weighed heavily in the president's ultimate decision. He pondered the pros and cons of canceling versus going ahead with the pared-down operation and concluded that the cost of abandonment outweighed the political risk of defeat. With that in mind, he confided to Schlesinger: "If we have to get rid of these eight hundred men [the brigade fighters], it is much better to dump them in Cuba than in the United States, especially if that is where they want to go."[17]

One could argue that the president didn't really mean what his callous words implied. But what is indisputable is that the young Cuban patriots, who in good faith relied on the support of the United States, were indeed dumped in Cuba with scant chance of success.

▌The CIA and the Joint Chiefs of Staff

The record shows that the CIA and the JCS recommended to President Kennedy the Trinidad plan as the most favorable course of action under the circumstances. They raised serious issues and concerns when Kennedy rejected Trinidad, pressed for a "less noisy" alternative (the Zapata plan), and then canceled half the air strikes prior to D-Day and the vital air cover during the landings.

Yet, despite their caveats, why did the CIA and JCS ultimately go along with the president and not vigorously push back or urge him to call off the invasion? Was it because they (particularly the CIA chiefs) were too emotionally committed to the invasion? Perhaps, but not to the point of embarking on such a risky venture without having a card up their sleeves. Was it that they were counting on the elimination of Castro entrusted to mobsters Johnny Roselli, Salvatore "Sam" Giancana, and Santo Trafficante?

Circumstantial evidence suggests that both President Eisenhower and President Kennedy were aware of the assassination plot, which envisaged poisoning Castro with botulinum toxin just prior to the invasion.[18]

As early as February 17, 1960, President Eisenhower had questioned why the secret 5412 Cuba Group was not trying to identify alternative approaches to the Castro problem, "including even possible things that might be drastic." He added that "he didn't mind making the study of possible courses, but he wanted to make it clear that this action is forbidden until the Group has fully reviewed it, and if they think we should go ahead, he would like to be involved."[19]

As for President Kennedy, he reportedly told his old friend and confidant Senator George Smathers of Florida that the CIA had led him to believe Castro would be assassinated before the invasion.[20]

The bizarre plot, however, was not a crucial element of the overall Cuba plan. So when it failed to materialize, no one in Washington viewed the foul-up as a major setback warranting the cancellation or postponement of the operation.

What most likely led the CIA and the JCS to support the pared-down Zapata plan was the expectation that Kennedy would not allow it to fail. If things didn't work out as planned, they likely thought, the president would change his mind and authorize US military support to ensure success.

The Pentagon was certainly prepared for that contingency with standby forces in Florida and the isle of Vieques, off Puerto Rico, and with an imposing armada assembled near the Bay of Pigs. Admiral Arleigh Burke, chief of naval operations, reportedly placed twenty-two warships in the area. They included "a submarine, the aircraft carrier USS *Essex* with its jet fighters, the helicopter carrier USS *Boxer*, which carried a complement of two thousand combat-ready Marines, and twelve destroyers."[21]

Since the fleet of warships was not stationed close to the battle zone just to watch impassively how the Castro forces crushed the brigade, Admiral Burke and others in the Pentagon and the CIA believed (or hoped) that President Kennedy would relent and authorize them to use some of the available US assets if urgently needed to turn the tide.

The admiral did his best to stave off the ensuing debacle. This is what transpired of the historic Burke–Kennedy exchange when the brigade, short on ammunition and under incessant attack by Castro jets and heavy tanks, was desperately struggling to survive:

It was close to midnight, April 19 (D+2). The president, dressed in white tie and tails, had just wrapped up his first gala event at the White House (the traditional congressional reception). He walked to the mansion of the West Wing to review the grim Bay of Pigs situation. Admiral Burke did not beat around the bush.

"Let me take two jets and shoot down those enemy aircraft," he asked the president.

"No," Kennedy replied, "I don't want to get the United States in-volved in this."

"Hell, Mr. President," Burke retorted, "we *are* involved!" Burke didn't give up. "Can I not send in an air strike?"

"No."

"Can we send in a few planes?"

"No, because they could be identified as United States."

"Can we paint out their numbers?" insisted Burke.

"No," the president firmly replied.

"One destroyer, Mr. President?"

Kennedy remained adamant. "No" was his unequivocal answer.[22]

It was close to 2:00 a.m. when the president, still in white tie and tails but visibly distraught, finally relented—but not much. He authorized six unmarked US jets to fly over the beaches, for one hour only, to provide cover for a squadron of the brigade's B-26 bombers that remained operational (most had been shot down or severely damaged, mainly by Castro's T-33 jets). The limited "umbrella" would also enable the brigade ships in the area (including the *Lake Charles*, where I was) to unload ammunition and reinforcements.

Unfortunately, this tardy and half-hearted attempt to salvage the besieged brigade went awry. Owing to a timing mix-up, the US Skyhawks arrived too late to provide the brief air cover. Two of the brigade's bombers flying from the Nicaragua rear base were shot down by Castro's jets, killing four American trainers who had gallantly volunteered to fill in for some of the exhausted and dispirited Cuban pilots. And the brigade ships that tried to unload the desperately needed supplies and reinforcements were unable to accomplish their mission.

The outcome could not have been worse for the cause of freedom. Close to fourteen hundred Cuban patriots, trained, armed, and steered by the United States, were abandoned to their fate; the Pentagon's armada—so close to the Bay of Pigs—was barred from lending a hand to the freedom fighters, even when they ran out of ammunition and urgently asked for help; US honor and credibility were stained; and Castro and the Communists emerged victorious, boasting "the first great defeat of Yankee imperialism."

Cuban Exile and Resistance Leaders

The big remaining question: What role did the Cuban exile and resistance leaders play in the Bay of Pigs saga? Were they kept in the dark by the CIA and the White House, or did they fail to see or react to troubling signs? Were they misled, or did they delude themselves with a dose of wishful thinking?

Following are salient episodes of their story, ignored or glossed over by most historians:

It was late January 1961, less than three months prior to the Bay of Pigs invasion, and Tony Varona, the head of the leading anti-Castro organization backed by the United States (the "Front"), still had not been allowed by the CIA to visit the Trax training camp in Guatemala. The CIA did not want the "politicians" to meddle in military affairs. Varona's controlled anger turned to rage when he learned that a major dispute at the camp threatened to fracture, if not dissolve, the brigade.

Under considerable pressure from Varona, the CIA finally permitted him and two other Front leaders to visit the camp. Although Tony faced a tense situation on arrival, inflamed by leadership issues, he deftly settled the dispute and uplifted the morale of the troops.

Before returning to the United States, Varona had a private conversation with Lieutenant Colonel Frank Egan, who was in charge of training the Cuban recruits at camp Trax, including Tony's son, a brother, and a nephew who had enlisted. When Varona questioned whether the brigade could stand up against the thousands of armed men Castro would mobilize, Egan responded with a reassuring smile: "Don't worry, Dr. Varona, we will have complete control of the air, and Castro won't be able to move a single car or truck any place in Cuba." The colonel also promised to discuss the invasion plan with Varona before D-Day.[23]

The recruitment drive was stepped up, and word spread that the planned assault would soon be launched. Despite the excitement that this generated within the Cuban community in Florida, Eduardo Martín-Elena, the titular head of the Front's military affairs based in

Miami, was not happy. Martín-Elena, a former colonel of the Cuban army who had given up his regimental command in protest over Batista's 1952 coup, was highly respected as a competent officer and a man of integrity. But his dry, humorless personality and rigidity (not particularly simpatico) did not endear him to the younger brigade officers in Guatemala, who viewed him as passé. His other handicap perhaps was that he was not willing to bow to the CIA.

The colonel felt that he was marginalized and kept in the dark about the invasion by the CIA, so he decided to voice his complaint to Howard Hunt, one of the key CIA operatives who liaised with the Front in Miami. Hunt did not attempt to sugarcoat his reply, because he believed that Martín-Elena needed to face up to reality. He basically told him that the United States was the sole provider of the resources for the invasion, including the expertise required for a complex amphibious-airborne assault. The words carried two subtle messages: first, he who pays, rules, and second, the operation was "too intricate ... to be left to Cuban generalship."

As Hunt recounted: "Martín-Elena listened with increasing depression, and when I concluded, said: 'When will I be allowed to see the invasion plans?'"

"I don't think you will be," Hunt told him.

"Then I must resign," the colonel replied. And resign he did, quietly, without venting any anger or resentment, like a patriot.[24]

It is true that Martín-Elena was not qualified to spearhead the type of invasion that was being planned. But had he been consulted, he would have at least warned the CIA and the Pentagon that the site they had finally chosen for the landings—the Bay of Pigs—was an alligator-infested swampy trap that would make it impossible for the brigade to "melt into the mountains" if besieged by Castro forces.

The Front's exile leaders were disappointed but not alarmed by Martín-Elena's resignation, thinking that a suitable replacement (which was not found) would resolve the incident. They did not realize that the issue that had prompted the colonel's decision—the exclusion from any participation in the planning of the invasion—would haunt them as well.

The Underground in the Dark

The instruction not to inform the exile leaders of the invasion ahead of time came from the president himself and had grave consequences.[25] It hampered the vital coordination of plans with the underground in Cuba, which may have contributed to the arrest of the five resistance chiefs who were in the dark twenty-nine days before the landings. Had they been advised that the invasion was imminent, they most likely would not have held the secret March 19 meeting in Havana where they were caught by Castro's secret police.

Among those arrested was Manuel "Ñongo" Puig, a tall, thirty-six-year-old, congenial former Olympic rower and hardworking distributor of wines and spirits. He was married to my cousin Ofelia, a convent-educated statuesque brunette with striking blue eyes. Theirs was a sunny love story eclipsed by tragedy.

Happily married with four children and a prosperous business, they were lured by the lofty ideals proclaimed by Castro in the Sierra Maestra and decided to support his revolution against the Batista dictatorship. When they became aware of Castro's Communist design after he took power, Ñongo joined the underground. He narrowly escaped arrest in late 1960 after his brother Rino was caught conspiring, and fled to the United States. The CIA provided paramilitary training in Guatemala and Panama and arranged to infiltrate Ñongo into Cuba in March 1961. His shipmate on the way back was Humberto Sorí Marín, a former Castro "comandante" and minister of agriculture, who had emerged as the pivotal leader of the resistance movement. During the voyage, Sorí Marín struck a rapport with Ñongo and took him under his wing.

Their mission was to join forces with the other underground chiefs and organize an uprising that would coincide with the invasion. Owing to the president's order not to inform them of the military plans and the timeline for the landings, they were unaware that the invasion would soon be launched and decided to hold an ultrasecret coordination meeting on March 19 at a safe residence in Havana's Siboney suburb.[26]

Extreme precautions were taken. The venue was disclosed to the participants only one hour before the start of the meeting. The brave Ofelia drove Sorí Marín and Ñongo to their destination. Both were armed and visibly tense. Fearing recognition, Sorí Marín held a handkerchief close to his face and told Ofelia, "Don't drive alongside other cars. Avoid red lights. If stopped, we'll shoot."

All of the five conspirators safely reached the meeting place. While Ofelia and two other young women played cards in the living room to allay suspicion, the underground chiefs gathered in the back of the house around a heavy table covered with street maps. In the course of their discussion, a purely accidental chain of events occurred. When Castro's secret police, looking for a suspect, stormed a house adjoining the resistance leader's meeting place, the young housewife who opened the door panicked and ran to her neighbor's house, unaware of the crucial summit that was being held there.

In a matter of seconds, heavily armed guards barged into the house and caught everyone by surprise. One of the officers immediately recognized Sorí Marín and exclaimed: "Look who is here, the big fish, and we never suspected it!" While the plotters were being searched, the agile Sorí Marín dashed like a hounded deer through a partly opened door and tried to flee.

The guards, who carried snub-nosed Czech machine guns, wounded him and foiled the desperate escape. He and the other resistance chiefs, along with Ofelia and the other two young woman, were arrested, subjected to torturous interrogation, and imprisoned pending summary trial.[27]

The terrible news jolted the exile community (particularly my family) but did not dishearten us. We believed that the second tier of underground leaders would be able to rise against the Communist regime during the invasion and set free their jailed compatriots. We were confident that with the support and unparalleled experience of our US allies, we would prevail in our liberation efforts. If the United States had succeeded in Normandy, how could they fail in Cuba?

With that positive frame of mind, I decided in March to join the brigade in Guatemala as a private. Tony Varona, the head of the Front, tried to persuade me to remain with him at the Miami headquarters, arguing that my intellectual skills would be more useful to the cause than my insignificant military abilities. I felt, however, that my time had come to practice what I preached, so I proceeded to enlist.

Just before departing for Guatemala, I was invited to join a newly formed unit—Operation 40—which was to be integrated into the brigade and charged with the occupation and temporary administration of liberated territories.

After a brief but intense training program in Miami, we underwent polygraph tests. Then, packed into army trucks with rear canvas flaps pulled down, we were driven in total darkness to the abandoned air base in Opa-locka, Florida. Soon we were airborne inside an old C-54 military transport with metal seats placed along the fuselage and windows painted black and covered with masking tape. Although I felt somewhat claustrophobic and apprehensive, the security measures taken by the US officers handling logistics put me at ease. My sense was that we were in good hands.

It was a long and arduous journey to Trax in Guatemala, a rustic training camp that had been built in the heights of cloud-shrouded mountains surrounded by thick vegetation. I was very happy to see my nineteen-year-old cousin Humberto Cortina, who had become a deft radio operator, and to meet many old friends and make new acquaintances. I saw Cubans from all social classes and ethnic backgrounds— scions of families that used to be symbols of wealth and power marching side by side with men of humble origin, like the lanky and good-hearted Francisco Guerra, who used to be my father's chauffeur.

But what impressed me the most was the discipline of the various battalions of the brigade, the military prowess they displayed, and above all their esprit de corps. But my impression carried no weight. After all, I was a novice in military affairs with no voice or rank. But Colonel Jack Hawkins, the experienced marine who had devised the paramilitary plan for the invasion, certainly had the qualifications and standing to evaluate the combat-readiness of the brigade. This is the last report he submitted to his superiors in Washington after visiting the camp:

"My observations the last few days have increased my confidence in the ability of this force to accomplish not only initial combat missions but also the ultimate objective of Castro's overthrow. ... These officers are young, vigorous, intelligent, and motivated with a fanatical urge to begin battle for which most of them have supreme confidence they will win all engagements against the best Castro has to offer. I share their confidence."[28]

This buoyant report assumed, of course, that the two essential conditions spelled out in the invasion blueprint would be met: control of the air and US recognition of, and overt support to, a Free Cuba government-in-arms established on the beachhead held by the brigade.

While I was training in Guatemala, the White House instructed the CIA to broaden the exile representation by persuading—nay, compelling—the Front to join forces with the MRP (Movimiento Revolucionario de Pueblo) dissident group headed by Manuel Ray, a young liberal engineer who had been Castro's minister of public works before defecting. The Front, led by Tony Varona, resisted Washington's intrusion and perceived leftist tilt but finally relented under pressure. What helped settle the controversy was the selection of a moderate leader accepted by all—Dr. José Miró-Cardona, a talented and mild-mannered criminal lawyer and university professor who had served as Castro's prime minister during the first six weeks of his regime. Miró-Cardona became president of the enlarged exile coalition, the Cuban Revolutionary Council (the Council), which subsumed Varona's Front and Ray's MRP.

In early April, about two weeks before the brigade was flown to a military base in Puerto Cabezas, Nicaragua, to board the ships for the invasion, Miró-Cardona and his executive committee visited Trax camp in Guatemala. He addressed the troops, pledged that he would join them on the battleground, and ended his peroration with this moving statement: "I leave with you what I treasure the most—my son and the memory of my father, who fought for the independence of our homeland." The assembled brigade, no longer harboring petty rivalries or dissensions, gave him an ovation.

On our way to the chapel, I had a brief conversation with Miró-Cardona, who knew my parents well and had earlier sought my confidence and assistance in Miami. When I voiced my apprehension about the insufficient troops available in Guatemala to launch an all-out invasion, he told me, "I'm also concerned, but Colonel Frank [Egan] has just assured me that we will be able to count on thirty thousand US soldiers, including those stationed on the island of Vieques, plus the backing of three Latin American countries and complete control of the air." Not really knowing whether the colonel was well-informed enough and authorized to make that promise (which went beyond the assurance he had previously given Varona), Miró-Cardona added, "In the next few days I will go to Washington to seek confirmation."[29]

According to Miró-Cardona's notes, shared with me after his passing by his son, the meeting he had requested to discuss US plans on Cuba was held at the State Department on April 5. Chairing the meeting was Adolf Berle, appointed by President Kennedy as head of the Latin American Task Force at State. Berle, a prominent lawyer, educator, author, and diplomat with a baronial bearing, had served under President Franklin D. Roosevelt as a member of his "brain trust" and as assistant secretary of state for Latin American affairs. Also in attendance were Philip Bonsal, the last US ambassador to Cuba; William Bowdler, a State Department official; and Arthur Schlesinger, special assistant to the president, representing the White House.

At the outset, Berle asked Miró-Cardona point-blank whether he was an advocate of the Left. That question, which jibed with Berle's background as founding member and chairman of the New York Liberal Party, seemed to be a password for New Frontier support. Miró-Cardona did not answer directly, but he expounded his views on the Cuba of the future. When Berle complimented him on his "socially advanced vision," Miró-Cardona told him that he was simply enunciating the principles embodied in Cuba's progressive 1940 constitution, which he planned to restore.

As the Cuban leader started to raise the military issues that concerned him, Berle remarked that they were not in a position to discuss them, but he added with great aplomb: "We're not deaf. We will listen." Miró-Cardona then referred to the assurances Colonel Frank Egan had given him in Guatemala and requested confirmation since, he emphasized, he was "assuming a tremendous responsibility toward [his] compatriots." There was no further discussion, but Miró-Cardona was told that someone would get back to him shortly.[30]

The following day, April 6, William Carr of the CIA informed Miró-Cardona that Berle was ready to see him at his Georgetown residence, preferably alone. There was no need for an interpreter since Berle was fluent in Spanish. Ernesto Rojas, a perceptive and discreet Cuban attorney based in Washington, drove Miró-Cardona to Berle's house and waited in the car.

According to the Cuban leader's notes, Berle told him that the military plan was proceeding very well, that the invasion forces would have "control of the air," and that they would be supported by fifteen thousand additional troops. When Miró-Cardona pointed out that Colonel Frank Egan had promised thirty thousand, Berle responded firmly that a reinforcement of fifteen thousand men would suffice. (Miró-Cardona assumed that they would come from the United States, but Berle did not explicitly say so.)

When the Council president asked for a more concrete guarantee, Berle pointed out that the United States could not enter into a formal alliance, but he gave Miró-Cardona his word of honor (*parole d'honneur* was the term he used). He added: "The United States cannot admit that it is backing the invasion, but it will have our total support." Before the meeting ended, Berle stated that several Latin American republics were willing to support the invasion and that the United States was prepared to provide substantial economic aid to a post-Castro Cuba.[31]

Although there were still troubling signs and open questions, Miró-Cardona left the meeting very satisfied with Berle's assurances, coming as they had not from a midlevel military officer in Guatemala or a CIA spook but from a very senior and prestigious US government official. Rojas, who drove Miró-Cardona back to the hotel, confirmed to me that the exile leader waxed euphoric as he recited Berle's assurances.

There does not seem to be any official record of Berle's affirming or denying meeting privately with Miró-Cardona and making the alleged commitments. However, the Council president did refer to the meeting with Berle and to his assurances in general terms in the testimony he gave the board of inquiry on the Bay of Pigs (Taylor Committee).[32]

Kennedy's Shocking Statement

Six days later, on April 12, came the shocker. President Kennedy stated in a press conference, "There will not be, under any conditions, an intervention in Cuba by the United States Armed Forces. ... The basic issue in Cuba is not one between the United States and Cuba. It is between the Cubans themselves. I intend to see that we adhere to that principle and as I understand it this administration's attitude is so understood and shared by the anti-Castro exiles from Cuba in this country."

Miró-Cardona was surprised by the president's categorical pronouncement, which contradicted the assurances that Berle had just given him, but he was not particularly alarmed. He thought that perhaps Kennedy with his disclaimer was playing to the gallery or trying to confound Castro. Dr. Arturo Mañas, a prominent Cuban attorney and sugar expert, much more experienced than Miró-Cardona in international affairs, urged him to request immediately a meeting with Berle and seek clarification. The exile leader heeded his advice.

The lunch meeting took place the next day, April 13, at the Century Club in New York, with Berle, Schlesinger, and John Plank, a specialist on Latin America from Harvard, who had been designated Miró-Cardona's liaison with Washington. Following are the contrasting versions of the momentous discussion—Schlesinger's and Miró-Cardona's—not fully covered by historians and analysts:

According to Schlesinger's account, highlighted in his book *A Thousand Days: John F. Kennedy in the White House*, Miró-Cardona "was much irritated because CIA had not cut him in on the invasion. ... His particular concern ... was the question of the United States military support. ... He displayed resistance and incredulity at the statement that no United States troops would be used."

Berle told him, according to Schlesinger, "We'll take you to the beaches," but this did not satisfy him. "Berle then said that it [the invasion] could not succeed without an internal uprising, and that, if one came, we would provide the democratic Cubans with the things necessary to make it successful. Once the provisional government was established on the beachhead, we would offer all aid short of United States troops."

Miró-Cardona "went on to tell us," Schlesinger wrote, "that, if the provisional government was established and things then began to go badly, he planned to call for help from all the nations of the hemisphere—including the United States. He said with solemnity, 'This help must come.'"

Schlesinger further stated in his book, "I returned to Washington considerably depressed. Whatever Miró was told [implying that someone may have assured him that US troops would be available], it was evident he simply would not believe he could not count on US military support. He is a serious person, I reported to the president, and will not be easily moved from his present position."[33]

Miró-Cardona's version differs sharply from Schlesinger's.

According to his notes, Berle informed him at the outset that "the Soviet embassy in Washington had privately expressed some interest in exploring with them a peaceful solution to the Cuban problem which would enable the exiles, including the Council leaders, to return to the Island." When Miró-Cardona flatly rejected the proposal as a Castro-Soviet diversionist ploy, Berle told him, "We just wanted to hear your views on the subject, but please keep this in confidence."

Schlesinger did disclose in his book that George Kornienko, the counselor of the Soviet Embassy in Washington, had approached him on April 12 (one day before the Century Club meeting with Miró-Cardona) to explore a possible deal with the United States on Cuba. According to the historian, neither Kennedy nor Rusk saw much in this trial balloon and dismissed it. If that was the case, why then was this reportedly dead issue raised with Miró-Cardona and silenced by Schlesinger in the latter's recount of the meeting? Was the White House hoping that the Council leader would agree to a possible rapprochement with Castro and thereby provide the president with political cover to call off the invasion? Intriguing questions that remain unanswered.

Miró-Cardona then turned to the central issue of United States military support. He wrote in his notes: "When I expressed concern about the president's statement, Berle explained that for the very same reason that I [Miró-Cardona] proclaim that the invasion will be Cuban, the president has to deny US participation. But, Berle stressed, our agreement stands—'nuestros pactos quedan en pie' were the exact words he used." This, Miró-Cardona interpreted to mean that the agreement reached at Berle's home on April 6 regarding the additional fifteen thousand troops remained in effect.[34]

Why didn't Miró-Cardona probe further? Was he reading too much into Berle's vague response in Spanish? Or was it, as suggested by Schlesinger, that the exile leader, "as a driven man, probably heard what he desperately wanted to hear"? There may have been some wishful thinking on the part of Miró-Cardona, prompted by his strong belief that the United States had too much at stake to allow the invasion to fail. But regardless of Miró-Cardona's interpretation, it is hard to fathom why President Kennedy's decision not to provide US military support to the invasion was only discussed with the head of the Cuban Revolutionary Council when the brigade, geared for battle, was already on its way to Cuba.

Before the Century Club lunch ended, Miró-Cardona told Berle that he could not continue in the dark as far as the invasion plans were concerned and requested that a high-level military liaison be designated to brief him. Berle promised to fulfill his request.

The following day, April 14, US general Barley met with Miró-Cardona and Tony Varona at the Blackstone Hotel in New York. It turned out to be a courtesy visit with virtually no briefing. The general listened to Varona's recommendation that the brigade land in Trinidad but did not disclose that the Trinidad plan was precisely what the CIA and the JCS had proposed to President Kennedy, who vetoed it as too spectacular and only accepted the whittled-down Bay of Pigs alternative. To fend off any questions, Barley gravely intoned that "in times of war the civilian leadership must yield to the military." Before leaving, he did mention, in broad terms, that some raids on Castro's airfields would take place the following morning (April 15).

The Council leaders would only learn, after the fact, that the D-2 raids, carried out by brigade pilots posing as defectors, were cut in half by the president and later suspended. This enabled the Castro regime to retain enough T-33 jets and Sea Fury fighters to sink or severely damage several of the defenseless brigade ships on D-Day.

Realizing that the April 15 raids were but a prelude to the invasion, Castro had enough breathing space to ward off any attempt by the underground to ignite an uprising. In an unprecedented wave of arrests across the island, as many as one hundred fifty thousand to two hundred thousand suspects were packed into stadiums, theaters, and music halls. Among those detained were key activists of the resistance movement who had not been apprised of the imminent invasion.

One of the freedom fighters, José Basulto, a member of the brigade infiltration team operating on the island, managed to avoid arrest. When he received a belated CIA coded message to rise and blow bridges, he wired back with a mix of distress and stinging sarcasm: "Impossible to rise. Most patriots in jail. Thanks for your damned invitation. Closing transmission."[35]

Having crippled the resistance movement and overcome the limited air strikes, Castro threw down the gauntlet. On April 16, the day after the strikes, in a staged event reminiscent of Adolf Hitler's rallies, Fidel gave a stirring speech, ostensibly to honor seven Cubans killed in the raids. But the speech was much more than a eulogy or even a morale booster. It was a message to Washington, one of defiance and glee. With his strident voice and fiery gaze, a stabbing finger pointed north, Castro thundered: "What they [the imperialists] cannot forgive is that we have made a socialist revolution right under the very nose of the United States!"

This was the first time Castro publicly admitted that the revolution he had spawned was socialist. Not the silken socialism of Scandinavia, but the harsh Stalinist version of Marxism-Leninism, spewing anti-US venom and spurring Moscow's expansionist design.

The invasion went ahead on the seventeenth with virtually no support from the underground, hamstrung by mass arrests, and with no air cover to protect the ships and the troops during the landings. In the letter that accompanied the Bay of Pigs plan, Colonel Hawkings had issued this stern warning: "This is a marginal plan. It will succeed only if all elements of the plan are left intact. Also, all of Castro's fighters must be destroyed on the ground prior to the landings. If only one of his fighters is left intact, the invasion forces must withdraw at once. Otherwise, this operation will result in a complete disaster."[36]

The brigade's old B-26 medium-range bombers were no match for the enemy's T-33 jets, Sea Fury fighters, and B-26 bombers that remained operational after the curtailed July 15 raids (a total of seven planes). The tail gun turrets of the brigade's bombers had been removed to reduce weight and allow the mounting of two droppable fuel tanks on the wings. The extra fuel was necessary for the long flight from the Puerto Cabezas, Nicaragua, rear air base to Cuba. The planes required nine hours to turn around for a second mission from Nicaragua.

Despite their vulnerability, no fighter escort was provided to protect the bombers, particularly from the feared T-33's. These small jet trainer/fighter planes were much faster than the brigade's bombers. They carried rockets under their wings and two .50-caliber machine guns with a lethal velocity of seventeen hundred rounds per minute.

From April 15 to April 19 the brigade flew thirty-six missions over Cuba. Eight of its planes were downed and fourteen pilots were killed, four of them Americans.[37]

Still, against all odds, the brigade's infantry battalions and paratroopers were able to seize early on a beachhead forty-two miles long and twenty miles deep. But lack of ammunition made it impossible for them to hold their tenuous positions. They had spent most of their ammunition the first day, and the resupply had either gone down with the two bombed ships or was out at sea aboard the other defenseless vessels and landing crafts that could not return to offload their cargoes.

Even with scarce ammunition, and under heavy bombing, the brigade troops fought with remarkable resilience and courage, as evidenced in the battle of La Rotonda, a strategic intersection near Playa Larga where combat raged for more than six hours. Erneido Oliva, the wiry and magnetic former officer of the Cuban army and second-in-command of the brigade, took a firm stand with three hundred seventy men and three tanks. They stymied the advance of over twenty-one hundred soldiers and more than twenty tanks and inflicted heavy casualties on Castro's forces: five hundred dead and one thousand wounded. Oliva had twenty dead and fifty wounded.[38]

At dawn on April 18, after the first wave of Castro's forces had withdrawn, one of their heavy Stalin tanks suddenly approached La Rotonda. The brigade soldiers in that area were exhausted and nearly out of ammunition. Some had started to head toward the beaches. To set the example, Oliva placed a 57 mm cannon in the middle of the road, knelt down, and faced the enemy tank. Luckily for Oliva, the tank stopped, the hatch opened, and the driver got out and approached him.

"Are you the commander of these men?" he asked Oliva.

"Yes," he replied.

"I congratulate you because these men are heroes. I would like to fight with you."[39]

This is a testament to the bravery and military deftness of the brigade officers and soldiers. It is also a hint of what they could have achieved had they ruled the air, as planned, and had had enough ammunition to hold the beachhead and enable the Council leaders to form a government-in-arms and secure international recognition and support. If those two conditions had been met, the outcome of the Bay of Pigs could have been starkly different. This, of course, is conjecture, but highly plausible. What we do know for certain is that absent air cover to obtain vital resupply and reinforcement, the brigade was encircled by Castro's troops on D+2 and forced to retreat to the beaches.

The last messages sent by the military chief of the brigade, José "Pepe" San Román, reflect the mettle of this stalwart commander in the face of disaster. The dispatches were recorded by Grayston "Gray" L. Lynch, the US Army captain and CIA officer who went ashore at the Bay of Pigs with the brigade's frogmen to mark the landing areas and subsequently handled communications from the command ship *Barbara J.*

Well aware of the desperate situation of the brigade and of President Kennedy's decision not to provide US military support, Lynch told San Román, "Remember, Pepe, that if things get too bad, we will come in and bring you out."

Pepe: "No, Gray, we will not leave this island. We will fight to the end here if we have to. Thank you, but we will not evacuate."

Pepe (later): "Tanks closing on Blue Beach from north and east. They are firing directly at our headquarters." Then: "Fighting on beach. Send all available aircraft now!" And: "In water, out of ammunition. Enemy closing in. Help must arrive in next hour."

Pepe's last words: "I can't wait any longer. I am destroying my radio now." The radio went silent. It was over.

As Grayston Lynch poignantly wrote, "The brigade's fight was ended. Its men were not defeated in battle, nor did they surrender. They simply ran out of ammunition, and the fighting slowly died away. ... Many have called the Bay of Pigs invasion a fiasco. It was not a fiasco—it was a tragedy. For the first time in my thirty-seven years [of service], I was ashamed of my country." This from a decorated army officer who had been wounded at Normandy, at the Battle of the Bulge, and at Heartbreak Ridge in Korea; had served with the Special Forces in Laos; and had received three Purple Hearts, two Silver Stars, and one Bronze Star with a V for valor.

After the fall of the beachhead, some of the brigade fighters tried to hide in the wooded marshland. In their desperate effort to survive, they had to eat grass and lizards and lick the dew off leaves in the mornings. Others tried to escape, heading for the open sea in any sailboat or floating device they could find. They were hopeful that US destroyers in the area would come to their rescue, but very few evacuation attempts were made—hardly a Dunkirk. Sadly, most of those who drifted in the Gulf died of thirst, hunger, and exposure to the sweltering heat.

Following the end of hostilities, one of the Castro regime's many crimes against humanity occurred inside a truck trailer known as La Rastra de la Muerte (the Truck of Death). As described in my book *And the Russians Stayed: The Sovietization of Cuba* and in other Bay of Pigs publications, 135 brigade prisoners were forced into an airtight meat truck trailer and ordered to pile in until the truck was packed with bodies.

Before the heavy doors to the sealed and insulated cargo space were locked shut, Osmany Cienfuegos, a loyal Castro commander, minister of construction, charged with the transportation of the prisoners to Havana, was warned not to cram so many of them into the paneled truck because they could die. Several of the prisoners heard Cienfuegos reply in a loud voice: "Let them die. ... It will save us from shooting them."

The nonstop trip to Havana took eight hours. When the doors of the truck were unbolted, nine of the men lay lifeless on the floor, asphyxiated. Others survived because, in their frantic quest for air, they were able to scratch holes through the truck's aluminum walls with their belt buckles.

During the brigade's three-day incessant combat at the Bay of Pigs, which resulted in close to twelve hundred of its men captured by Castro with one hundred fourteen dead and sixty seriously wounded, the CIA kept the Council leaders incommunicado in heavily guarded shabby barracks at Opa-locka, Florida. They learned of the landing and ensuing battles when they turned on a portable radio they had found in one of the rooms. They were incensed for having been held in confinement and not allowed to join the brigade at the beachhead as planned.

At President Kennedy's behest, Adolf Berle and Arthur Schlesinger flew to Opa-locka on April 19 to tranquilize the Council chiefs. Miró-Cardona, somber and dignified, argued that with more planes the battle could still be won. The feisty Tony Varona was more blunt and pugnacious. Clenching his fists, he told the Washington emissaries that the Council leaders would no longer tolerate being kept secluded and incommunicado. "We don't know whether we are your allies or your prisoners," he averred, and then defiantly added: "I plan to leave the barracks at noon to hold a press conference in Miami. Let them shoot me down if they dare."[40]

Faced with this explosive situation, Kennedy invited the Council chiefs to the White House that afternoon. Looking "exceptionally drawn and tired," the president preempted all recriminations by assuming responsibility for the failed invasion. He shared their grief as a man who had seen combat and lost a brother and a brother-in-law in the war, and he reaffirmed the US commitment to Cuba's freedom.

The gloom that hung over the White House contrasted with the glee that permeated Castro's headquarters in Havana. He boasted that

he had defeated Yankee imperialism. Not content with having defied
the hated Goliath, which served to fuel subversive activities throughout
Latin America, Fidel wrung ransom from Washington for most of the
brigade prisoners.

Fidel did not release or spare the lives of other political prisoners.
Among those executed were the five leaders of the underground, including Manuel "Ñongo" Puig, my cousin Ofelia's husband who had
been arrested a few weeks prior to the Bay of Pigs invasion. Thanks
to Ofelia, who was also taken prisoner with them, we learned of the
charade of trial to which they were all subjected.

The prosecutor, whose record of performance had earned him the
appellation "Bloodbath," accused the prisoners, without a shred of evidence, of plotting to assassinate Castro. He demanded the death penalty
for the five underground chiefs (plus two others who were added) and
thirty years' imprisonment for Ofelia and other female defendants.

Through the twelve-hour proceedings, the comportment of the five
members of the military tribunal clearly showed that the defense was
futile. When they were not delivering acrimonious tirades, applauded
by the militiamen watching the spectacle, they would chat among
themselves with their feet perched atop the table. Occasionally they
would play games with paper balls and laugh heartily.

When the president of the tribunal pronounced the death penalty
for Ñongo and the other male defendants, Ofelia, sitting near him,
cried out in desperation: "Ñongo, if they're going to do something to
you, defend yourself. Don't let them hurt you!" Looking at Ofelia with
unbelievable serenity, he gently whispered: "Ofelia, to die is nothing.
We all have to die—a little sooner or a little later. At least I know what
I die for. My death has meaning. Don't worry, Ofelia. I'll be all right."

Following the denial of an appeal by another kangaroo court whose
president collapsed drunk on the table after ratifying the death penalty,
Ñongo and the other valiant resistance leaders were led, one by one, to
a wooden stake before a wall of sandbags. With spotlights trained on

them amid a murmur of prayers coming from the prison cells above La Cabaña fortress, they were shot at around 2:00 a.m., April 20.

A few hours later, at the Guanabacoa penitentiary where she was held, Ofelia heard on a hidden portable radio the dreaded government announcement naming those who had just been executed—among them her beloved husband. For several days, she stayed in a state of shock, tearless and immovable, sleepless in bed. Released with a broken heart, she sought refuge in the United States with her four children. Although scarred for life, she raised her family, pursued a career as a psychologist, and remained true to the memory of Ñongo and to the cause of Cuba's freedom for which he had died. She passed away in Miami in 2010 and was buried on the very same month and day that her husband was executed—April 20.[41] I delivered her eulogy, barely containing my grief.

The Aftermath

How did Kennedy react to the Bay of Pigs debacle? Did he fully gauge its far-reaching consequences?

On April 18, after the president had reaffirmed his position not to provide US military support to save the operation, the journalist James "Scotty" Reston asked him if he thought defeat in Cuba would hurt American prestige. "No doubt we will be kicked in the ass for the next couple of weeks," said Kennedy, "but that won't affect the main business." This flippant and seemingly heartless comment did not reflect his sentiment, since he truly grieved for the brigade's dead and wounded and for the plight of the prisoners. His brother Robert, the attorney general, said that he had never seen the president so distraught. "He kept shaking his head, rubbing his hands over his eyes."[42]

Domestically, the great majority of the people rallied to the president's side when he publicly assumed responsibility for the defeat (while privately blaming and subsequently sacking the upper echelons of the CIA). Shortly after he wistfully invoked the old saying that "victory has a hundred fathers, and defeat is an orphan," Kennedy's approval rating hit a peak of 83 percent.

Internationally, however, the president did not fare well. Arthur Schlesinger wrote in his journal while traveling in Europe immediately following the invasion, "We not only look like imperialists; we look like ineffectual imperialists, which is worse; and we look like stupid, ineffectual imperialists, which is worst of all."[43] But it was Kennedy's predecessor, Dwight D. Eisenhower, who most insightfully predicted how the Soviets would respond to Kennedy's perceived ineptitude and weakness.

After President Kennedy took office and grappled with the Cuban conundrum, he did not seek the advice of the hero of Normandy, veteran of the paramilitary operations in Iran and Guatemala, and architect of the initial blueprint for the Cuban operation. It was only on April 22, 1961, three days after the Bay of Pigs disaster, that Kennedy invited Eisenhower to Camp David to review the situation.

It was not a cordial meeting. There was no love lost between the two of them. Kennedy felt that Eisenhower had handed him a burning issue (Cuba) and a reckless plan to resolve it (the invasion). For his part, Eisenhower blamed his young, inexperienced successor for condemning the invasion to failure without foreseeing its ominous consequences.

According to Eisenhower's recollection of the discussion, shared with his biographer Stephen Ambrose, the former president peppered Kennedy with pointed questions. Why on earth hadn't he provided the exiles with air cover? Kennedy said he had feared the Soviets "would be very apt to cause trouble in Berlin."

Eisenhower's quick response was in essence an admonition, if not a rebuke for Kennedy's naivete: "That is exactly the *opposite* of what would really happen. The Soviets follow their own plans, and if they see us show any weakness, then is when they press us the hardest. ... The failure of the Bay of Pigs will embolden the Soviets to do something that they would not do otherwise."

Kennedy tried to justify his decision by saying that "my advice was that we must try to keep our hands from showing in the affair." Eisenhower pulled no punches in his retort: "How could you expect the world to believe we had nothing to do with it? Where did these people get the ships to go from Central America to Cuba? Where did they get the weapons? ... I believe there is only one thing to do when you go into this kind of thing: it must be a success."[44]

Eisenhower could not have been more clairvoyant on the consequences of the Bay of Pigs. Sensing that Kennedy was an immature pushover and that the United States was too flaccid and complacent to fight, Khrushchev clobbered the president at their June 1961 summit meeting in Vienna, built the Berlin Wall, and provoked a nuclear confrontation by installing strategic missiles on the island of Cuba.

CHAPTER 7

The Battle of the OAS and the Mongoose Plots (Mid-1961—Early 1962)

The Bay of Pigs Fallout (April–May 1961)

On April 21, 1961, Secretary of Defense Robert McNamara met with the Joint Chiefs of Staff to assess the impact of the Bay of Pigs failure. He urged them to accept appropriate responsibility and avoid backbiting. He also disclosed that the president was going to establish a high-level committee to reexamine the entire operation and make recommendations.[1] This committee, known as the Cuba Study Group, was chaired by General Maxwell D. Taylor.

Attorney General Robert Kennedy didn't wait for the formation of Maxwell Taylor's committee, which he joined, to express his strong views on the ill-fated invasion and its fallout. Not having been directly involved in the Bay of Pigs operation, he did not want to remain on the sidelines on matters pertaining to Cuba and national security.

On April 19, the same day the Bay of Pigs brigade, encircled by Castro's tanks and abandoned by the United States, fired its last shots, the attorney general wrote a memorandum to the president calling for a new muscular policy toward Communist Cuba. He stressed that "the immediate failure of the rebels' activities in Cuba does not permit us … to return to the status quo with our policy toward Cuba being one of waiting and hoping for good luck."

In light of the failed invasion, Robert Kennedy argued that "Castro will be even more bombastic, will be more and more closely tied to communism, will be better armed, and will be operating an even more tightly held state than if these events had not transpired." To address the looming danger, the attorney general mentioned possible actions, from a US armed intervention in Cuba (which had been ruled out) to a military blockade of the island, preferably in concert with other members of the OAS.

The memorandum ended with this prescient warning: "The time has come for a showdown, for in a year or two years the situation will be vastly worse. If we don't want Russia to set up missile bases in Cuba, we had better decide now what we are willing to do to stop it."[2]

Robert Kennedy's assessment of the Castro-Communist imbroglio (after the United States had missed a great opportunity to end it) was prompted by genuine concern. But it also reflected anger over the humiliation the Bay of Pigs disaster had brought to his brother. He described it in his memorandum as an affront to the nation: "the US having been beaten off with her tail between her legs."[3]

The following day (April 20), the cabinet meeting convened by the visibly shattered president turned out to be a painful and rather chaotic postmortem of the Bay of Pigs—everyone jumping on everyone else. The attorney general was the toughest in his comments, mostly directed at the State Department. When Undersecretary of State Chester Bowles, sitting in for Secretary Dean Rusk, took exception to Robert Kennedy's stinging reproach, the attorney general turned "savagely" on him.

The liberal undersecretary, a Yale graduate who had made a fortune in advertising and later served as governor of Connecticut, congressman, and ambassador to India, did not take Robert Kennedy's zinger lightly. With a condescending tone, he characterized the attorney general and Vice President Lyndon Johnson in his notes on the cabinet meeting as newcomers "with no experience in foreign affairs, ... involving complex politics, economics, and social questions that require both understanding of history and various cultures." And yet, according to Bowles, both were "determined to be experts at it."[4]

The undersecretary of state would soon be eased out of his job, whereas Robert Kennedy became his brother's closest confidant, adviser, and partner, wielding considerable clout in foreign affairs, particularly on Cuba. He is believed to have been one of the instigators of the president's directive to the Defense Department "to develop a plan for the overthrow of the Castro regime by the application of US military force."

The plan, as summarized in Secretary McNamara's April 20 memorandum, was to include, among other things, an appraisal of the Cuban military forces; an analysis of alternative programs for accomplishing the objective, for example, a complete naval and air blockade versus an armed invasion; and a detailed statement of the US forces required. As a safeguard, the memorandum pointed out that "the request for this study should not be interpreted as an indication that US military action against Cuba is probable."[5]

The president seemed interested in pursuing this matter, and on April 29 he met with Admiral Arleigh Burke and Secretary of Defense McNamara to review Contingency Plan I for the Invasion of Cuba by US troops. The plan envisioned a first wave of approximately sixty thousand troops, excluding naval and air units, and required twenty-five days of preparation from date of decision to D-Day. Complete control of the island would take about eight days, save for some anticipated guerrilla resistance in the mountains. The president concurred in the general outline and asked to prepare the detailed instructions necessary to implement the plan.[6]

Then, in less than a week, the president shifted gears. At the meeting of the National Security Council held on May 5, he put on hold all the military plans against the Castro regime and decided to pursue a nonconfrontational policy recommended by the State Department. The new Cuba policy called for intelligence gathering, propaganda (but no electronic warfare), censure and isolation of the Castro regime by the OAS, and economic aid to Latin America through the Alliance for Progress to contain the spread of Castro communism.

To placate the Cuban exiles, who blamed Washington for the Bay of Pigs disaster, it was agreed that US relations with the Cuban Revolutionary Council—the leading anti-Castro organization headed by José Miró-Cardona—should be improved and made more open but without recognizing the Council as a government-in-exile. It was also agreed that Cuban Americans should be encouraged to enlist in the US Army, but a separate Cuban military force was ruled out.[7]

The declassified State Department documents make no reference to two meetings with exile leaders that likely accounted for the inclusion of the Council-related items in the new Cuba policy. Thanks to the notes taken by Ernesto "Bebo" Aragón, Miró-Cardona's executive assistant and interpreter who attended both meetings, we learned what happened.

According to Aragón's records, handed to me prior to his passing, after Miró-Cardona and other Council leaders had rounded up the Bay of Pigs survivors in Central America and the island of Vieques, they were summoned to Washington for a high-level parley with US government officials. The meeting was held on May 2 in a private conference room at the Park Sheraton Hotel. Representing President Kennedy were Paul Nitze, then assistant secretary of defense, and Richard Goodwin, a thirty-year-old Harvard Law School graduate who had started with Kennedy as a speechwriter and soon became a special presidential assistant in charge of the task force on Cuba. (His purview was later expanded to cover Latin America.)

The exile leaders thought that the main purpose of the May 2 meeting was to discuss new plans for the liberation of Cuba. The president's emissaries, however, had a different agenda. Goodwin stated that he and Nitze were there at Kennedy's request to discuss the fate of the brigade prisoners and survivors, and the assistance to the families of the deceased. That was well received. But when Goodwin indicated that the agenda also included the relocation of Cuban refugees based in Miami—a sensitive issue perceived as a deliberate attempt to disperse and weaken the exile community—the Cuban leaders exploded in anger.

Before the interpreter could translate, the Council representatives fired a string of rebukes in Spanish at their befuddled interlocutors: "We didn't come here for this. We've been duped again. ... It's another betrayal. ... We want military support, not relocation!"

Miró-Cardona managed to restore order and asked Goodwin to convey to the president that the Cuban Revolutionary Council was prepared to discuss the items on his agenda, but only after the liberation plans had been mapped out. Thereupon, he tersely ended the discussion and told the president's envoys that he and his colleagues would return to Miami the following day.

Kennedy feared that the rift would flare up in public if not promptly and diplomatically defused. Two hours after the rowdy meeting had concluded, Goodwin called to inform Miró-Cardona that the president wanted to see him alone, but that Miró could bring his own interpreter if he wished.

The confidential meeting took place at the Oval Office on May 4. Accompanying Miró-Cardona was Aragón, who acted as interpreter for both his boss and Kennedy. According to Aragón's notes shared with me, the president, all by himself at the Oval Office, greeted the exile leader warmly and sat in the rocking chair he used to ease his back problem, flanked by two small sofas occupied by his guests. He calmly lit a Havana cigar and commented that he was running out of them. Without missing a beat, Aragón said: "Mr. President, with all due respect, I hope you will exhaust your supply of Cuban cigars soon so that we can help you get some more." Kennedy laughed heartily.

At the president's request, Miró-Cardona ticked off the salient points covered in a memorandum in Spanish he handed to Kennedy: recognition of the Council as a Cuban government-in-exile; economic, technical, and military support to continue the struggle; reinvigoration of the underground movement; and recruitment and training of Cuban military units to serve as the vanguard of a future liberation force.

The president listened carefully and promised to review Miró-Cardona's aide-mémoire. He did advance, however, some pertinent observations. Kennedy explained why the United States could not recognize a government-in-exile, which, lacking territory and coercive power, could not exercise authority or command respect. He promised instead to back the Cuban Revolutionary Council and raise its profile in Washington.

To ensure good communications, the president told Miró-Cardona, "You and I should each designate a representative to discuss specific issues, forge consensus, and implement decisions. If our delegates fail to reach an accord, we should meet again." The president designated Richard Goodwin as his representative.

Kennedy agreed to proceed with the recruitment and training of Cuban military units but within the Armed Forces of the United States. He also favored revitalizing the Cuban underground and suggested that the details of the program and of the financial and technical assistance to the Council be discussed by their respective representatives.

The president ended the fifty-minute discussion by reiterating his full support for the Council. He expressed the hope that the new entente would further the cause of a free Cuba. Miró-Cardona thanked the president and, escorted by Goodwin, left the White House with a much-needed boost to face the disgruntled exile community, which had not yet recovered from the Bay of Pigs shock. Although he left the Oval Office with only vague promises, Miró-Cardona felt he had developed a good rapport with the president and could reach out to him if things didn't work out as planned.[8]

The Thrashing of JFK in Vienna (June 1961)

JFK hoped that the specter of the Bay of Pigs would not haunt him at the June 3–5, 1961, summit meeting in Vienna with Nikita Khrushchev or prevent a relaxation of tensions over Berlin. But that was not to be.

Cuba became a central issue, and the Soviet prime minister used it to lecture and hector the president and place him on the defensive.

Khrushchev derided Kennedy for attempting to halt the "unstoppable" spread of communism and for fearing Fidel Castro. "Can six million people really be a threat to the mighty US?" Kennedy, who meekly conceded that he had made a mistake with the Bay of Pigs, told aides at the end of the first day of the summit, "He [Khrushchev] treated me like a little boy."[9]

Having vowed to render the Castro regime all necessary help to repel any armed attack on Cuba, Khrushchev told Kennedy that he was planning to sign a treaty with East Germany that could effectively block access by the West to Berlin. To play up his threat, he cockily remarked, "If the US wants to start a war over Berlin, let it be so."[10]

Kennedy was taken aback by Khrushchev's hostile rhetoric. Instead of warning the Soviet premier that the United States had the power (indeed the nuclear superiority) and the unflinching resolve to counter any threat to its security and international alliances, he nervously sought to avoid a confrontation. This hesitancy to take a stand, perceived as weakness, emboldened the Soviet ruler not only to clobber the president in Vienna but also to confront him later with a wall in Berlin and offensive missiles in Cuba.

When *New York Times* writer James Reston asked Kennedy in Vienna how it had gone with the Soviet premier, the president candidly replied: "Worst thing in my life. ... He savaged me." Then he added: "Because of the Bay of Pigs, Khrushchev thought that anyone who was so young and inexperienced as to get into that mess could be taken. And anyone who got into it and didn't see it through had no guts. So he just beat the hell out of me. ... I've got a terrible problem."[11]

What accounted for Kennedy's pitiful performance in Vienna? As Frederick Kempe explains in his book *Berlin 1961*, the president ignored the advice of foreign policy experts and fell for the ploy of a Soviet spy, Georgi Bolshakov, who had "sold" to Bobby Kennedy his closeness to Khrushchev and lied about Moscow's intent and game plan.

Bolshakov, a congenial bon vivant with a trace of black hair, piercing blue eyes, and strong Russian accent, had penetrated Washington's social circles and gained the confidence of the attorney general prior to the Vienna meeting. Relying on Georgi's good faith and trying to avoid misunderstandings during the summit, Bobby candidly relayed to the spy what the president wanted to avoid, namely, being viewed as spineless after the Bay of Pigs and being drawn into a heated discussion of Berlin's status and what he desired to achieve—a nuclear test ban deal. With this valuable information, the Soviet leader was well prepared to pound the president where he was most vulnerable.

Kennedy's stress, and its likely impact on emotion and judgment, was heightened by his severe back pain and battery of medications to alleviate it. The pain, intensified by an injury suffered during a tree-planting ceremony in Canada, forced him to use crutches, wear a back brace, and bring along to Europe not only his personal physician but also an unconventional medic, known as "Dr. Feelgood," who lost his medical license years later. These two men administered to the president anesthetic procaine for his back, cortisone for his Addison's disease, and a cocktail of vitamins, enzymes, hormones, and amphetamines. Between doses, Kennedy's mood and demeanor swung from a high of overconfidence to a low of depression.

Bouts of despondency hit Kennedy hard in Vienna. When his secretary, Evelyn Lincoln, was filing the classified documents of the summit, she found a slip of paper on which the president had written these two lines: "I know there is a God—and I see a storm coming. If He has a place for me, I believe I am ready."[12]

The Alliance for Progress and Che Guevara's Gambit (July–August 1961)

After his return from Vienna, Kennedy tried to turn the Bay of Pigs page and deemphasize the Cuban situation. After all, the island was not the center of the universe, and the president had other, more important and more pressing issues to address. Yet the Castro regime remained a festering problem, and Moscow's increasing involvement in Cuba was a cause for concern.

On July 11, an ad hoc committee of the United States Intelligence Board issued a detailed report on the arms buildup in Cuba, flagging that "the Soviet bloc continues to extend considerable military assistance to Cuba in the form of military equipment, training, and technicians and advisers." The equipment included MiG aircraft and heavy tanks, and there were indications that the Castro regime would also receive Soviet jet bombers.

According to the intelligence report, the major Soviet military buildup in Cuba was designed to hasten the consolidation of the Communist regime "through the regimentation of the Cuban people under a police state" and to establish "a secure base of operations for furthering their aims throughout Latin America."[13]

This report troubled the president and prompted him to pose pertinent questions to someone he respected for his straightforwardness and clear-eyed assessment of the Cuba situation: Admiral Arleigh Burke. Kennedy invited Burke to the White House on July 26, just before the admiral's retirement, and they talked about Cuba. This is how Burke summarized the conversation in a memorandum for the record: "He [the president] asked me if I thought we would have to go into Cuba. I said yes. He asked would Castro get stronger. I said yes. Castro would increase his power over his people. He asked whether we could take Cuba easily. I said yes, but it was getting more and more difficult. He asked what did I think would happen if we attacked. I said all hell would break loose, but that someday we would have to do it."[14]

Despite Burke's advice, the president ruled out drastic action in Cuba and attempted to isolate the Castro regime and neutralize its destabilizing activities by promoting economic development and social reforms elsewhere in the hemisphere. The vehicle used was the Alliance for Progress, and the strategy pursued was to "avoid other

Cubas by attacking the root causes of communism: poverty, hunger, and social injustices."

Although these were not the main causes that had catapulted Castro into power, few would quarrel with the lofty goals of the Alliance for Progress, which was to be fueled by $20 billion in US foreign aid over ten years. There was a problem, however, with this long-term development program that required business confidence and political stability to stimulate investments. The hitch was that if the Castro-Communist regime—promoter of subversion throughout the continent with Soviet backing—was not first eliminated, the alliance would degenerate into a futile race to see whether dollars poured in by the United States could outpace dollars taken out by frightened Latin Americans.

As a representative of the Cuban Revolutionary Council, I stressed to several US senators and congressmen the need to link the Alliance for Progress to an Alliance for Freedom. For if economic aid was not tied to a collective commitment to excise the Castro-Communist cancer, the leftist governments and demagogues in Latin America would most likely "court the radicals, take the dollars, and thank Fidel."[15]

Still, the Kennedy administration went ahead with the formal launch of the Alliance for Progress at an inter-American conference held in Punta del Este, Uruguay, in August 1961. Cuba was represented by none other than Ernesto "Che" Guevara, who seemed to have undergone an ideological metamorphosis. Instead of spewing radical epithets, he sedated the conclave with the soothing bromide of peaceful coexistence.

Had the Marxist firebrand really changed, or was this a show, orchestrated by Castro, to dupe their enemies, lower their guard, and buy some time? Guevara's record speaks for itself. During the insurgency against the Batista dictatorship, Guevara wrote to a Cuban underground chief, "I belong, because of my ideological background, to that group which believes that the solution of the world's problem lies behind the Iron Curtain."[16]

During the first five months of the Castro regime, while Guevara was in charge of La Cabaña fortress in Havana, then used as a prison, he supervised and, according to witnesses, often watched with delight the execution without fair trial of several hundred alleged "traitors to the revolution" and "war criminals."

When Guevara addressed the United Nations in 1964, he proudly defended the executions and offered this definition of peaceful coexistence: "As Marxists, we have maintained that peaceful coexistence among nations does not encompass coexistence between the exploiters and the exploited, between the oppressors and the oppressed." Then he proceeded to denounce the United States as "the perpetrator of exploitation and oppression against the peoples of the world and against a large part of its own population."

Perhaps the statement that more faithfully captures Guevara's steadfast conviction can be found in the message he sent to the Tri-Continental Solidarity Congress held in Havana in 1966. As recorded in the Guevara internet archive, he asserted that hatred, relentless hatred, was an essential element of the struggle, and added that a true revolutionary had to be "an effective, violent, cold killing machine."

Given Che Guevara's core beliefs and trajectory, his conciliatory message in Punta del Este was simply a ruse. Some of the Latin American delegates were instrumental in toning down references to representative democracy, elections, private property, and free enterprise so that the Castro regime could join the Alliance for Progress. So encouraged was Guevara that in the final session of the conference, he declared that the alliance charter recognized and included a nation with different characteristics from the rest. He was, of course, referring to socialist Cuba.

Douglas Dillon, head of the US delegation, felt that, if left unchallenged, Guevara's audacious claim would nullify Washington's policy of isolating Castro. Dillon's reply left no room for ambiguity. He categorically stated that the United States did not, and would not, recognize the permanence of the current regime in Cuba. To do so, he emphasized, would be to betray the thousands of Cuban patriots who were still waiting and fighting for the freedom of their country.

Dillon's firm statement, endorsed by the majority of the delegates with prolonged applause, was unfortunately undermined when the word leaked out that Richard Goodwin, the White House's special assistant on Latin America attending the conference, had privately met with Che Guevara in what was described as a "chance encounter" at a birthday party in Montevideo. Goodwin later acknowledged that had he been "wiser and more experienced," he probably would have left the apartment when Guevara walked in, accompanied by two bodyguards, wearing his olive-drab combat fatigues. But the temptation to chat with the "romantic figure of the revolution" was too intense, so Goodwin decided not only to stay but also to converse with Guevara until 6:00 a.m.

It was clear to Goodwin that Che had appeared at the private party for the sole purpose of talking with him. So while a few couples danced to Latin music, the two of them moved to a quiet sitting room, accompanied by a Brazilian and an Argentine—both government officials—who alternated as interpreters. At the outset, the iconic revolutionary, displaying an ironic smile, thanked the White House emissary for the Bay of Pigs, which, he claimed, had helped them consolidate their regime. He asserted that the Cuban Revolution was irreversible, and he warned the United States not to try to "rescue Cuba from the claws of communism."

He also told Goodwin, "You should not believe that Fidel is a moderate surrounded by a bunch of fanatic and aggressive men, and might conceivably be moved over to the Western side. He is one of us and always has been."

With that as a preamble, articulated with glacial calmness, Guevara proceeded to convey his core message: "We don't want a true understanding with the US," he said, only a "modus vivendi." The terms he spelled out included: no return of confiscated properties, only payment "in trade"; elections eventually, but with a "one-party system"; close ties with the Soviet Union but no (formal) military alliance; and agreement to "limit" the activities of the Cuban Revolution in other countries, signaling, however, that its growing "impact" would possibly spawn a socialist revolution in the Americas.

In exchange for this "grand" overture, the Castro regime expected from the United States a free flow of goods, services, and credits to Cuba (i.e., no economic embargo) and an undertaking to stop any attempt to overthrow the Cuban government.[17]

Goodwin told Guevara that he had no authority to negotiate with him, but upon his return to Washington he recommended to the president to "seek some way of continuing the belowground dialogue which Che had begun. We can thus make it clear that we want to help Cuba and would help Cuba if it would sever Communist ties and begin democratization."[18]

It seems that Goodwin didn't quite get Guevara's message, perhaps because it wasn't as explicit as the one he conveyed to the president of Argentina, Arturo Frondizi, on August 18, immediately after the Goodwin parley.

Frondizi was one of the "doves" in Latin America who advocated a rapprochement with the Castro regime and who opposed any attempt to isolate Cuba. He thus decided to have a secret meeting with Guevara, Argentina's bête noire. Without revealing to his military aide the name of the mysterious individual he was supposed to greet at the airport, the president said, "You will see someone descend from the plane who you are going to recognize. Escort him to your car and bring him to Olivos [the presidential residence]. That man must talk to no one."[19]

Needless to say, despite all these precautions, the ultrasecret meeting soon became public, to Frondizi's regret.

According to the record of Frondizi's mediation efforts, the Argentine president met with the guerrilla leader for more than an hour. During their amicable conversation over a succulent *bife* lunch, Frondizi informed Guevara that he was advocating a comprehensive understanding between Latin America and the United States without excluding or isolating Cuba. And he stressed that only through social, economic, and cultural development, and not through violence, could Latin America resolve its problems.

Guevara, without raising his voice or gesticulating, drew an "explosive" picture of Latin America and predicted that it would soon become "another Vietnam." Only through "armed struggle," he postulated, "could the countries in this hemisphere liberate themselves from imperialistic influence." While Cuba wished to remain within the Inter-American System, he reiterated that small and poor countries could not eschew the "path of violence."[20] (Such was the harmonious modus vivendi that Guevara and the Castro brothers had in mind.)

Following his meeting with Frondizi, Guevara left for Brazil, where he was solemnly decorated by President Jânio Quadros. When the guerrilla maverick arrived in Havana, he declared, beaming with joy, that with the support of leading Latin American governments, efforts to isolate the Cuban regime would be quashed.

Turmoil in the Exile Community, and Reign of Terror in Cuba

Guevara's triumphal Latin American tour, hyped by the media, enraged the Cuban exiles in Miami and heaped further strain on the embattled president of the Revolutionary Council, Miró-Cardona. His prestige had been severely tarnished by the Bay of Pigs tragedy, and five months later he couldn't really show that Washington was earnestly supporting the liberation of Cuba beyond empty promises and best wishes. The only thing that appeared to be on Kennedy's agenda was the Alliance for Progress, which most exiles dismissed as a delusion or a distraction.

Meanwhile in Cuba, Castro was tightening the screws on the captive population. Executions of opponents continued apace. These included Catholic students and young graduates—vanguard of the harassed resistance movement—who bravely defied the firing squads with a stirring cry: "Viva Cuba Libre. Viva Cristo Rey!"

By the end of 1960 and early 1961, all independent newspapers had been closed, and all radio and television stations were under state control. The government took over private schools and universities, and Raúl Castro became the chief of the purged armed forces. On the political front, steps were taken to integrate the revolutionary organizations, paving the way for a one-party (Communist) state under Fidel Castro's omnipotent rule. To intensify surveillance and strengthen its totalitarian grip, the regime created the Committees for the Defense of the Revolution (CDRs), which monitored the movement of individuals in virtually every block.

Against this background, Miró-Cardona felt compelled to raise troubling issues in Washington without holding back his grievances and concerns. At a meeting held at the White House with Richard Goodwin and Robert Woodward, assistant secretary of state for Latin America, he complained that the CIA made his task of enlarging the Council very difficult, if not impossible, by financing behind his back groups of Cuban exiles who wished to pursue a competing or independent course. That only weakened the resistance to the Castro regime.

Miró-Cardona also referred to the Cubans who, at his behest, were joining the US Army. "The question in his mind was whether he was simply encouraging them to become professional soldiers or whether they were equipping themselves for an invasion of Cuba." Miró-Cardona recognized that a US unilateral invasion of the island was likely out of the question, but he needed to be reassured that the Cubans were being recruited into the US Army for an eventual joint action with other compatriots and friendly nations to overthrow the Castro-Communist regime.

At the end of the meeting, not having received a satisfactory response to his issues and concerns, he told Goodwin and Woodward that he would retire to Baltimore for a couple of days to reflect on the course of action he would likely take.[21]

Miró-Cardona, son of a hero of Cuba's war of independence against Spain and father of a Bay of Pigs combatant who was taken prisoner, was a man of honor. Mild-mannered and professorial in his comportment, he tried to skirt futile controversies and seek honorable compromises. Within the exile community, he was criticized, however, for lack of decisiveness and a proneness to wishful thinking. His boundless patience was attributed by some to a deficit of leadership steel. But now that patience had reached the limit of his endurance. Even his health was at risk. His shortness of breath and the deep rings under his bloodshot eyes worried his doctors.

Having thought long and hard about his predicament, Miró-Cardona tendered his resignation as president of the Cuban Revolutionary Council on September 11, but he averred that he would continue the struggle as an adviser and foot soldier of the resistance movement. That same day, he wrote a letter to President Kennedy to apprise him of his decision. With due respect and aplomb, he referred to the issues that prompted his resignation, thanked the president for his courtesies, and urged him to support the liberation of Cuba.

The president, surmising the implications—and embarrassment—of losing the only Cuban exile leader semiofficially recognized by the White House, sent Miró-Cardona this letter dated September 14:

> Dear Dr. Miró-Cardona:
>
> I write to express my confidence in your leadership of the Cuban Revolutionary Council. The United States Government deeply admires the distinguished service you have already rendered to the cause of a free Cuba; and I hope you will continue to lead this fight until your country is liberated from the tyranny which has been imposed on it. I am sure that any problem arising from your relationship with the United States can be worked out in the spirit of mutual cooperation and common aspirations which lie behind all our efforts.
>
> Sincerely,
>
> John F. Kennedy[22]

Following the president's instructions, an agreement was reached with Miró-Cardona to bolster his leadership position, increase the funds allocated to the Cuban Revolutionary Council for propaganda and underground activities, and keep him abreast of any US support provided to anti-Castro groups not connected with the Council. A CIA officer was assigned to Miró-Cardona, and the door was left open for such meetings with the president as may be urgently required to further the cause.

Having made meaningful progress to strengthen the alliance, albeit without an explicit US commitment of military action against the Castro regime, the exile leader withdrew his resignation and resumed his post.

The Battle of the OAS (September 1961–January 1962)

The Miró-Cardona crisis had been averted, but another, bigger challenge lay ahead for the Cuban Revolutionary Council. It seemed to the exile chiefs that unless the Organization of American States (OAS) condemned and ostracized the Castro regime, the White House would not seriously consider any military action in Cuba (beyond contingency planning). But standing in the way of OAS sanctions were the appeasers of Latin America—primarily the leaders of Argentina, Brazil, Chile, and Mexico—who, out of sympathy for the Cuban Revolution or fear, wanted to accommodate Castro.

The leader of the appeasers or conciliators, as they preferred to be called, was the president of Argentina, Arturo Frondizi, who, even after listening to Che Guevara's ode to violence in this hemisphere, felt that a deal could be worked out with the Cuban regime. This was implied by Frondizi during his September 26 meeting with Kennedy in New York City. The Argentine president opposed any new attempt to overthrow the Castro regime and was not keen about sanctioning or isolating Cuba. He emphasized "that the solution to the problem must be found within the framework of the OAS" (Cuba included). From his perspective, the priority was to proceed vigorously with the Alliance for Progress and postpone any OAS Meeting of Consultation to address the Cuban situation.

Although Kennedy voiced the need to isolate Cuba, he reiterated that "any action taken by the United States had to have the support of Argentina."[23] So, in essence, the president granted a veto power to Frondizi and his gang of appeasers to block any effective OAS action against the Castro regime.

That's the issue I faced when the Cuban Revolutionary Council appointed me as its special representative to the OAS. My mission was clear: overcome the opposition of the self-styled "Big Powers" of Latin America to any Castro sanctions, knowing that Washington was reluctant to weigh in and counter their resistance.

We needed a strong Latin American leader who would reject appeasement and champion our cause. That leader, we believed, was the democratically elected president of Peru Manuel Prado, who came from a distinguished family of statesmen who had supported Cuba in its wars of independence against Spain. He was well aware of the threat posed by Castro-Communism and had severed diplomatic relations with Cuba. I met him in September at the airport in Miami, on his way to Washington on a state visit, and handed him a personal letter from my grandfather Cortina, who had honored him in Havana years back. Attached to the letter was a brief outline of our position, calling for collective action against the Castro regime under the Rio Treaty and recognition of our belligerence.

Prado was very warm and receptive and needed no prodding. He went to Capitol Hill and stated before a joint session of Congress: "The moment is of utmost gravity. Grave moments call for grave decisions— bold action, courage, and faith. ... Communism is the negation of the Americas, of its traditions and of its mission in the future. It must be expelled from the Americas."[24]

The White House and the State Department were uneasy with Prado's hard line. They cautioned him not to recognize a Cuban government-in-exile or press for collective action against Castro since that could split the OAS. Prado was not dissuaded by Washington's wait-and-see attitude and instructed his OAS ambassador, Juan Bautista de Lavalle, to file a formal petition to start the process to indict Castro.

To secure as much support as possible for the Peruvian petition, I met with most of the OAS ambassadors. Even though I did not represent an established government and, at age twenty-five, did not have the gravitas or experience of a seasoned diplomat, my surnames helped to open doors since many of the ambassadors had met or heard of my forebears. I also drew on the experience and contacts of two former Cuban ambassadors to Washington and the United Nations, Dr. Guillermo Belt and Dr. Emilio Núñez-Portuondo, and joined forces with the representatives of other anti-Castro groups in Washington and Miami.[25]

We put together a solid bloc of countries buffeted by Castro-Communist subversion (Guatemala, Honduras, El Salvador, Nicaragua, Costa Rica, Panama, and Venezuela), but it was not enough to activate Peru's motion. To break the impasse, we convinced the Peruvian ambassador to merge his initiative with Colombia's anti-Castro proposal, which carried the added weight of its president, Alberto Lleras-Camargo, an illustrious statesman who was the first secretary-general of the OAS. Another plus was Colombia's foreign minister, José Joaquín Caicedo-Castilla, a renowned jurist and foremost authority on OAS affairs.

In an unprecedented move, the Inter-American Peace Committee of the OAS, which was laying the groundwork for the possible indictment of the Castro regime, invited us and two other anti-Castro organizations to appear before its members and present evidence of Cuba's violations of human rights, interventions in the internal affairs of other countries, and subservience to the Soviet bloc.

Our file was replete with incriminating facts, but what really bolstered our case was the unexpected testimony of Fidel Castro himself. In his stunning speech in Havana on December 1, 1961, he claimed that he had been a Marxist-Leninist since his student days and that he had concealed his ideology to enlist the support of the Cuban people and take power. He climaxed his speech with a defiant cry: "I am a Marxist-Leninist, and I will be a Marxist-Leninist until the last days of my life."

Castro's cynical confession did not change the appeasers' stance against holding an OAS Meeting of Foreign Ministers under the Rio Treaty, which could judge and condemn the Castro regime. But it did tilt to our side the position of the ambassador of Uruguay, Carlos Clulow. Although he was instructed by his neutralist government to abstain, he followed the dictates of his conscience. He cast the critical vote in favor of the Meeting of Foreign Ministers and then resigned.

When I went to see the ambassador to thank him for his support, he greeted me with open arms and said, "I receive you as the legitimate representative of the Cuban people, betrayed by Castro and oppressed by communism." Apart from those kind words, he gave me a letter of introduction addressed to Uruguay's foreign minister Homero Martínez. "Since Uruguay will be hosting the Conference of Foreign Ministers on Cuba," he added, "this letter might be useful to you." It certainly was.

I attended as an observer the OAS conference (Eighth Meeting of Consultation) held in Punta del Este, Uruguay, on January 22–31, 1962, along with Miró-Cardona and a few other exile leaders and activists. My task was to help secure the votes necessary to condemn and sanction the Castro regime.

The US delegation, headed by Secretary Dean Rusk, focused on a resolution declaring that Cuba's Marxist-Leninist regime was incompatible with the Inter-American System. Rusk was satisfied because it was unanimously approved. We were not, because it was toothless. It didn't sanction the Castro regime or stop Brazil and other doves from attempting to grant Communist Cuba a "special statute"—a pass to be left alone for the sake of peaceful coexistence.

The hawks, headed by Colombia, supported our demand for something stronger—at least to expel the Castro regime from the OAS and deprive it of all the attendant protections and prerogatives. We were, however, short one vote to garner the supermajority (two-thirds) required to pass the resolution. Uruguay's uncommitted vote was again pivotal.

Carrying Clulow's letter of introduction, I managed to meet Uruguay's foreign minister Homero Martínez, a short but upright former naval officer. The dialogue was brief and tense because the minister was facing a crisis of confidence that could well force him to resign. He told me that he would be pleased to see Miró-Cardona and me if the crisis was resolved. It was, and he kept his word.

Arrangements were made for a meeting shrouded in secrecy. To our surprise, the venue finally selected by the minister was my tiny bedroom at the Hotel Lancaster in Montevideo—so tiny that it had only one chair, which was, of course, ceded to our guest. Miró-Cardona and I sat on my bed.

The minister came alone, carrying the memorandum I had handed him earlier. He agreed that the Castro-Communist regime posed a threat to the hemisphere and indicated that he was prepared to back our position since we were calling for collective (not US unilateral) action under the Rio Treaty as a prelude to liberation. He told us that we could count on his support, but he asked us to meet with two powerful members of his government to reinforce his stance and provide political cover. The mission was accomplished, and with the backing of another Cuban exile leader, Luis Conte Agüero, who gave a rousing speech at the influential Ateneo forum in Montevideo, we were able to clinch the decisive vote of Uruguay.

Crunch time came to decide: sanction or no sanction against the Castro regime. Secretary Dean Rusk devoted most of his speech to extolling the Alliance for Progress. He did not endorse the severance of diplomatic and economic relations with Cuba because that would have created a schism within the OAS, we were told. He supported the expulsion of the Castro regime from the Inter-American System (labeled "exclusion" to be politically correct) but recommended to defer execution pending confirmation by the OAS council that the ministers were empowered to adopt such a measure. Since the Colombian foreign minister Caicedo-Castilla, leader of the hard-liners, felt that Rusk's proposal was unnecessarily dilatory, indeed a cop-out to satisfy the doves, the United States delegation put a lot of pressure on him to relent. As requested by Rusk, Kennedy asked Colombia's president Lleras Camargo to impress upon Caicedo-Castilla the need for more flexibility.

I saw Caicedo-Castilla as he left one of his private meetings with Rusk and his aides. He looked tired but composed. When I asked him how things were going, he discreetly pointed toward the US diplomats leaving the meeting rooms and said with a placid smile, "They leave me alone; they leave me alone. But I am made of iron." And thanks mainly to this "Iron Chancellor," as he was called at the conference, we managed to line up the two-thirds majority of fourteen (including Rusk's last-minute assenting vote) to condemn and expel the Castro regime from the OAS as a pariah and threat to the Americas.

In addition, a resolution was adopted urging the member states "to take those steps that they may consider appropriate for their individual or collective self-defense and ... to counteract threats or acts of aggression, subversion or other dangers to peace and security resulting from the continued intervention in this Hemisphere of the Sino-Soviet powers."

Buoyed by the results achieved at the conference, Miró-Cardona and I left Punta del Este with renewed energy to forge ahead. We had defeated the advocates of coexistence with Castro and had secured a platform that legitimized self-defense against the danger posed by the Soviet-backed, heavily armed, and unabatedly subversive Cuban regime. But our enthusiasm was tempered by the fact that we still had to persuade Washington to act before the threat escalated and turned into a dreadful international confrontation.

Operation Mongoose (January–March 1962)

Unbeknown to the council, on January 19, 1962, Robert Kennedy held a meeting with US government officials from several agencies (members of an augmented Cuba task force) to impart a sense of urgency to a program code-named Operation Mongoose authorized by the president on November 3, 1961. The attorney general vehemently stated that a solution to the Cuban problem today carried "the top priority in the United States Government. All else is secondary—no time, money, effort, or manpower is to be spared." He echoed the president's comment that "the final chapter on Cuba has not been written" and emphatically added, "It's got to be done and will be done."[26]

The president's idea behind Mongoose, as expressed by him at a November 3, 1961, meeting and summarized in writing by the attorney general, was to "stir things up on the island with espionage, sabotage, [and] general disorder, run and operated by Cubans themselves with every group but Batistaites and Communists. Do not know if we will be successful in overthrowing Castro, but we have nothing to lose in our estimate."[27]

Overall control of the operation was entrusted to a Special Group (Augmented) with senior representatives of key agencies, including CIA, Defense, and State. General Edward Lansdale, experienced in counterinsurgency in the Philippines and Vietnam, was appointed chief of operations overseeing CIA implementation, and General Maxwell Taylor was designated chairman of the group.

The real "chief executive," however, who carried no official title but in fact steered Mongoose with the full backing of the president, was Attorney General Robert Kennedy. An operational force of some four hundred CIA agents headquartered in Miami, perhaps the largest of its kind at the time, was allocated to Mongoose.

Lansdale, having no prior knowledge of the Cuban situation, assigned thirty-two tasks to the agencies involved in the operation (which some believed was a huge bureaucratic or theoretical exercise). The objective was to assess US capabilities to carry out a comprehensive action plan that would include intelligence collection, recruitment and training of infiltration teams, diplomatic initiatives, propaganda and psychological warfare, economic pressure, sabotage, and paramilitary activities.

Lansdale subsequently detailed a six-phase schedule for Mongoose designed to culminate in October 1962 with an open revolt and overthrow of the Communist regime and the establishment of a government with which the United States could live in peace.[28]

The CIA cautioned that it would be very difficult for the Cuban people on their own, without the support of overt US military operations, to revolt and bring down the totalitarian regime. Cuba was already a police state. Moreover, the underground groups that remained active after the Bay of Pigs debacle were, in the main, disjointed and dispirited and had largely lost their faith in the United States. The anti-Castro guerrillas in the Escambray Mountains were being encircled and pounded by Castro forces with the involvement of Soviet experts in counterinsurgency.

Given the steep hurdles that Mongoose would face to revive the resistance movement in Cuba, the CIA alerted Defense that it would require considerable covert military support, including "two submarines, PT boats, Coast Guard–type cutters, Special Forces trainers, C-54 aircraft, F-86 aircraft, amphibian aircraft, Helio Couriers, army leaflet battalion, and [the use of] Guantánamo as a base for submarine operation." This request, which exceeded the scope of the presidential Mongoose directive, was denied.[29]

The Kennedy brothers were enraged by the CIA's skeptical attitude toward the practicality of Mongoose. They railed at the agency for not promptly implementing its assigned tasks. Richard Bissell, who remained active in the CIA until February 1962, was again the target of the Kennedy ire.[30] He dismissed the criticism with sardonic detachment: "I never lost sight of the irony that the same president who had canceled the air strikes and ruled out open intervention [during the Bay of Pigs invasion] was now having his brother put tremendous pressure on the Agency to accomplish even more."[31]

Then in March 1962, the Cuba strategy was again changed in Washington. The Special Group (Augmented), marshaled by the attorney general, ordered General Lansdale to cut back the Mongoose plan drastically and focus primarily on intelligence collection. Covert activities undertaken concurrently with intelligence collection were to be inconspicuous and "short of those reasonably calculated to inspire a revolt within the target area, or other development which would require US armed intervention."[32] As a result of the new directive, the sabotage activities carried out in 1962 were few and inconsequential, and the support for the underground and the Escambray guerrillas was scant and ineffective.

There was, however, a subchapter of Mongoose that was not canceled or curtailed, an ultrasecret and sordid subchapter euphemistically called "Executive Action Capability." Its foremost objective: the assassination of Fidel Castro. The failed efforts to take down the Cuban leader surfaced during the 1975 US Senate Investigation on Alleged Assassination Plots Involving Foreign Leaders, led by Idaho Democrat Frank Church.

The investigation of the so-called Church Committee revealed that the CIA had indeed arranged or encouraged a few attempts on the life of Castro, using poison pills, toxic cigars, exploding mollusks, and a bacteria-loaded skin diving suit. But most of the outlandish ideas had not made it beyond the drawing board or the feverish imagination of the conspirators. This, of course, did not deter Fidel Castro from boasting that he had survived more than six hundred CIA plots to kill him.

In the course of the investigation to determine whether the president and the attorney general had expressly or tacitly authorized the assassination attempts, or were aware of them, some suspicious pieces of information were brought to light. However, despite the potentially incriminating testimonies and records that surfaced, both men emerged virtually unscathed.

The April 1962 Miró-Cardona–JFK Meeting

The Cuban Revolutionary Council was not fully aware of the Mongoose Operation, as originally conceived in November 1961, or of the fact that it was defanged in March 1962 and turned primarily into an intelligence-collection enterprise. But the Council leaders felt that plans for the overthrow of the Castro regime had been shelved, if not canceled.

Washington instituted on February 3, 1962, a trade embargo on Cuba but took no action and sounded no warning to stop the continued Soviet military buildup on the island. On March 27, the United States simply declared that the Soviet bloc had furnished about $100 million worth of military equipment and technical services to Cuba and that several hundred Cuban military personnel had received training in the bloc. (According to Soviet records, Moscow had delivered to the island from 1960 to the spring of 1962 more than $250 million worth of weapons systems, not counting Eastern Bloc military assistance. The shipments included close to four hundred tanks and self-propelled weapons and forty-one military planes, mainly MiG-15's and MiG-19's.)[33]

What accounted for Washington's impassive attitude toward this ominous trend? The answer lies not only on the White House's tendency to dither on Cuba but also on intelligence reports that minimized the potential threat. The first of four 1962 pre–Missile Crisis Intelligence Estimates, released on January 17 (SNIE 80-62), considered it very likely that communism across the region would grow in size during the coming decade, but concluded that the establishment of Soviet bases (missile, submarine, or air bases) was unlikely because "their military and psychological value, in Soviet eyes, would probably not be great enough to override the risks involved."[34]

The second 1962 Intelligence Estimate, released on March 21 (NIE 85-62), stated that the considerable Soviet military assistance provided to the island was essentially "defensive." And although the estimate did not preclude the liberal provision of bloc advisers and surface-to-air missiles and radar, or the improvement of Cuban naval and air facilities, it again tranquilized Washington by concluding that the "USSR would almost certainly not intervene directly with its own forces ... and hazard its own safety for the sake of Cuba."[35]

Miró-Cardona, under great pressure from Council board members to produce results, met in Washington with National Security Adviser McGeorge Bundy on March 29 and told him that "present US policy drastically limited the Council's sphere of activity." He then stated that the "Council would either have to be permitted to organize and conduct commando raids, sabotage operations, or similar activities, or disband." Bundy responded that "he was not in a position to decide this question, but that the matter would be carefully studied and Dr. Miró given a reply reasonably soon."[36]

Realizing that a meaningful reply could come only from the Oval Office, Miró-Cardona requested an urgent meeting with President Kennedy. It was to be their fourth in less than twelve months. In anticipation of the discussion, I drafted an aide-mémoire for the Cuban exile leader. Arguing that diplomatic and economic isolation was not enough to topple a police state that was sustained and armed by the Soviets, I stressed the need to prepare for military action against the Castro regime, preceded by sabotage and other underground operations.

The memorandum emphasized the importance of accelerating the recruitment and training of Cuban exile units in the US Armed Forces, a program designed to form the front line of a potential joint liberation force that had been bogged down in bureaucratic details. Finally the paper called for the formalization of the de facto alliance between Washington and the Council to facilitate the coordination of war efforts and the unification of exile and resistance groups.

The meeting with the president took place at the White House on April 10, 1962. Miró-Cardona was accompanied by Ernesto Aragón, his executive assistant and interpreter. Also present were Attorney General Robert Kennedy and the presidential aide overseeing Cuban and Latin American affairs, Richard Goodwin. The documents declassified by the State Department made no reference to this meeting, but Aragón shared his notes with me.

Miró-Cardona touched on the points covered in my aide-mémoire, starting with the obstacles facing the service of Cuban exile volunteers in the US Armed Forces. The program, approved by the president on June 26, 1961, was to be implemented by the Department of Defense in coordination with the Department of Health, Education, and Welfare and the US Selective Service System. Although it was not positioned as a new invasion force, quite a few Cuban exiles tried to enlist, but most of the volunteers did not qualify. Given the excessively high standards that were applied, we wondered if the recruiters were expecting West Point–caliber candidates.

The president, who appeared very disappointed to learn that the program he had blessed had not really taken off, instructed Goodwin to step up the recruitment and training of Cuban exiles, obviating unrealistic requirements. As to the point raised by Miró-Cardona that only through armed action could the Castro regime be overthrown, the president said that "the Cuban problem was essentially military—of six divisions," and the Council would be expected to contribute as many combatants as possible. He assured Miró-Cardona that any military action against Castro would be a joint effort, "not unilateral."

Kennedy, however, did not deem it necessary to formalize the embryonic alliance with the Council at that time. Alluding to pressures and difficulties that Miró-Cardona was facing with his board and with the exile community at large, he told him with a reassuring smile at the end of the meeting, "Your fate is to suffer. Do not flag or waver. You have my support."[37]

That evening I joined Miró-Cardona and Aragón at the Manger Annapolis Hotel in Washington, where they were staying. They were reasonably satisfied with the outcome of the discussion with the president. Kennedy's reference to a military solution to Cuba's problem did not seem to them a mere option but a necessary course of action.

CHAPTER 8

Unheeded Warnings: The Looming Missile Crisis (August–October 1962)

▌Khrushchev's Nuclear Decision (April–June 1962)

On April 12, the Kremlin authorized a significant increase in the shipments of military equipment to Cuba, this time including SA-2 surface-to-air missiles (four divisions of antiaircraft launchers with one hundred eighty missiles for them), ten IL-28 bombers, and four R-15 cruise missile launchers. In addition, a six-hundred-fifty-man contingent of Soviet military personnel was sent to the island to train the Cubans in using the advanced weapons system.[1]

Later in April, during a trip to Crimea, Defense Minister Rodion Malinovsky drew Khrushchev's attention to the US Jupiter missile bases just over the horizon of the Black Sea in Turkey. He reportedly told Khrushchev that while the US missiles in Turkey could hit the Soviet Union in ten minutes, Soviet missiles required twenty-five minutes to strike the United States. Khrushchev then pondered whether the Soviet Union shouldn't do the same thing in Cuba, just ninety miles off the US coast.[2]

The Soviet nuclear inferiority went beyond the strike time. As Malinovsky reported to the Kremlin, the United States had four times as many intercontinental ballistic missiles as the Soviet Union, and they were more advanced. Although the Soviet premier recognized in his memoirs, *Khrushchev Remembers*, that having medium- and intermediate-range missiles in Cuba would have redressed the strategic imbalance, he stressed that what prompted him to install the nuclear weapons on the island was the need to deter the United States from taking military action against the Castro regime.

Khrushchev's alleged fear of losing Cuba is questionable. It is true that the Kennedy administration had developed contingency plans for possible armed intervention in Cuba, under certain circumstances, and was conducting a series of large-scale military exercises in the Caribbean. But the president had shied away from proposals to attack or invade Cuba and had even whittled down Mongoose's covert operations. He certainly was not keen on rocking the boat before the November congressional elections. Moscow was aware of that.[3]

Regardless of the Soviet premier's motive or motives, he pressed forward with his Cuba nuclear plan despite the initial objections raised by Mikoyan that Castro would not accept the installation of offensive missiles on the island and that it could not be kept secret from the United States.

Before the Soviet delegation departed for Cuba to seek Castro's approval, Khrushchev on May 27 gave a farewell party to his envoys at one of his opulent dachas in the presence of all of the members of the Presidium. To put to rest the notion that he was irrational or reckless, Khrushchev reportedly emphasized that the Soviet missiles in Cuba would "not in any case" be used. "Every idiot can start a war, but it is impossible to win this war. ... Therefore, the missiles have one purpose—to scare them [the Americans], to restrain them so that they have appreciated this business." In short, "to give them back some of their own medicine."

Khrushchev also stated that it was very important that the Soviet plan not be disclosed before November 6, the day of the US congressional elections. He planned to present Kennedy with a fait accompli, leaving him no alternative to accepting the missiles. Khrushchev informed the envoys that he intended to visit Cuba between November 25 and November 27 and sign a treaty with Castro. "Tell him," he added, "that we will do all that is necessary to guarantee him the maintenance of forces, rockets, and equipment." But in the event that Castro did not agree, "we will help in other ways."[4]

Castro, of course, did agree. After consulting with his inner circle on May 30, he welcomed the Soviet nuclear missiles. But to save face, he accepted them as a gesture to bolster the strategic position of the socialist camp in the international arena, not as a desperate attempt to forestall a US attack on the island. Fidel told the Soviet delegation that Raúl would visit Moscow in early July to work out the details of the formal agreement.[5]

Having received a favorable response from Fidel Castro, the Presidium voted unanimously to adopt the plan of deploying nuclear weapons to Cuba outlined by Defense Minister Malinovsky on June 10. The deployment included 24 medium-range ballistic missiles (MRBM), which had a range of 1,050 miles, and 16 intermediate-range ballistic missiles (IRBM), which could fly twice as far. Both carried nuclear warheads. Once installed in Cuba, they would double the number of Soviet nuclear missiles that could reach the US mainland.

In addition, the Soviets agreed to send to the island forty-two MiG-21 fighter planes, forty-two IL-28 bombers, twenty-four advanced SA-2 surface-to-air missile (SAM) batteries, twelve Komar-class missile defense boats, and a total force of about fifty thousand military personnel. The plan also envisaged the construction of a submarine base in Cuba capable of servicing the USSR's new ballistic missile submarines.

Fidel Castro was delighted to receive Khrushchev's letter, hand-delivered by Soviet Major General Dementyev, confirming Moscow's approval of the missile plan to "protect Cuba ... [and] improve the strategic position of the USSR," as well as confirming its readiness to proceed immediately with the implementation stage. The Cuban leader conveyed his eagerness to start working on the preparations with Soviet experts as soon as possible. His brother Raúl Castro, head of the Revolutionary Armed Forces, was even more enthusiastic. As reported by Dementyev, he "hugged me and kissed me, expressing joy at the contents of the letter."[6]

The Clueless CIA (May–June 1962)

While these portentous developments were unfolding, the CIA analysts (not the director and high-level officers) did not seem particularly perturbed, contending that the Soviet Union was having second thoughts about its entente with the Castro regime.

As revealed in recently declassified CIA documents, the spy agency believed that Castro's purge of old, historic Communist Party leaders had created a rift between Moscow and Havana. Based on that flawed assessment, the CIA reported to President Kennedy on May 21, 1962, "We are seeing more and more signs that Castro's current moves against veteran Communists may lead to serious problems with the USSR."

A few days later, after Khrushchev's military delegation had reached the crucial understanding with Castro that cleared the path to the deployment of Soviet strategic missiles in Cuba, the CIA analysts informed the president, "We suspect that Moscow has decided it was time for a searching review of Soviet program in Cuba. … Another sign of the USSR's displeasure and intent to tighten its political and economic reins."[7]

Launch of Moscow's Anadyr Covert Operation (July 1962)

The Soviet planners employed both secrecy and deception to launch this huge and complex operation—Moscow's first attempt to deploy ballistic missiles outside the Soviet Union. They code-named it "Anadyr"—the name of a town and river in northeastern Siberia—and told those involved in the expedition that they were going to a very cold region. To support the Arctic cover story, Soviet trains carried carloads of winter clothes, including boots, fur hats, and even skis, to the loading docks.

According to Soviet vice premier Mikoyan's son Sergo, "A large number of ships had to be modified to carry large loads. The parts of decks that could be seen aerially were crammed with fertilizer packages, agricultural machinery, and other innocent types of cargo. ... IL-28 bombers and MiG-21 fighters were disassembled and shipped in crates."[8]

Probably the fear of leaks prompted Khrushchev to defer the execution of a mutual defense agreement with Cuba. During Raúl Castro's two-week stay in Moscow in early July, discussions went very smoothly, but the Castro brothers didn't get the signed agreement they wanted to have up front, rather than after November.

Still, Khrushchev was aware of the vulnerability of the Anadyr operation. He knew he couldn't prevent Kennedy from eventually sending U-2 reconnaissance planes over Cuba, but he might get him to stop photographing, at least temporarily, the cargo on the ships making their way to Cuba. In their thorough review of Soviet declassified documents, writers Aleksandr Fursenko and Timothy Naftali uncovered Khrushchev's ploy.

Alleging that the US overhead reconnaissance in international waters was "harassment," Khrushchev sent a request to President Kennedy in July 1962 that, for the sake of better relations, these flights be stopped. The messenger was Georgi Bolshakov—the Soviet back channel whom the attorney general frequently used in Washington. Although Bolshakov had misled him with false expectations of the June 1961 Vienna summit, Robert Kennedy felt comfortable with the engaging Soviet manipulator and had even invited him to spend a Sunday at his family home in Virginia.

The president tried to turn Khrushchev's request to his advantage. Since Berlin, not Cuba, was Kennedy's foremost concern in July 1962, he agreed to halt US reconnaissance over open waters and asked in exchange that the Soviets put, in his words, the Berlin issue "on ice." Khrushchev thanked the president through Bolshakov for grounding the U-2 but made no firm commitment on Berlin as he needed to understand what Kennedy really meant by "placing the Berlin question on ice." The ploy seemed to work—at least for a while.[9]

Washington in Denial (August 1962)

In late July and early August, US intelligence noted a sudden rise in the level of Soviet military aid to Cuba. The average of Soviet dry-cargo ships per month increased from fifteen for the first half of 1962 to thirty-seven. Many of the ships were unloaded at night with non-Soviet personnel excluded from the dock areas. It was also reported that some of the arriving personnel were young, trim, physically fit, formed in ranks of four on the docks and moved out in truck convoys, carrying heavy weaponry covered with canvas.[10]

Still, the National Intelligence Estimate of August 1, 1962 (NIE 85-2-62), again stated that "it is unlikely that the Bloc will provide Cuba with the capability to undertake major independent military operations" or that "the Bloc will station in Cuba Bloc combat units of any description, at least for the period of this Estimate." Erroneously deducing that Raúl Castro's July military mission to Moscow had failed because no public communiqué was issued, the Estimate concluded that Moscow would not be inclined to take major risks to protect and defend the Castro regime.

Indeed, the CIA communicated that Raúl Castro's trip had been a failure as evidenced by this report: "Raúl Castro is back in Havana after two weeks in Moscow, where we believe he was seeking more and better military equipment. The red carpet was out for him when he arrived in Moscow, but he left unheralded, a pretty good sign that the visit was unproductive."[11]

Even on September 19, after a stream of intelligence had reported further acceleration of the Soviet arms buildup in Cuba, National Intelligence Estimate SNIE-85-3-62 yet again asserted that "the establishment on Cuban soil of Soviet nuclear striking forces which could be used against the US would be incompatible with Soviet policy as we presently estimate it."

The flawed evaluation and assessment of the massive intelligence data—largely attributed to miscalculation of Soviet intentions, systematic dismissal of refugee reports, and an overriding focus on Berlin—did not convince or blindside the director of the CIA John McCone. On the contrary, it spurred him to sound off repeated warnings and to call for effective action to address the ominous threat.

McCone, a bright entrepreneurial mechanical engineer, had developed flourishing businesses in steel, construction, shipping, shipbuilding, and aircraft production. He served as undersecretary of the air force in 1950 and subsequently as chairman of the Atomic Energy Commission under Eisenhower. In 1961, President Kennedy appointed him director of the CIA, replacing Allen Dulles after the Bay of Pigs debacle.

Although McCone had not previously held any intelligence position, his innate skepticism of Soviet intentions, indeed his visceral mistrust of the Kremlin's promises, plus his engineering background, served him well as the head of the CIA at that time. Although a registered Republican, his firm stance during the looming Missile Crisis was not prompted by politics but by genuine national security concerns.

On August 10, 1962, at a meeting of the Special (Cuba) Group Augmented, chaired by State Secretary Dean Rusk and attended by Secretary of Defense McNamara, McCone maintained that "the Soviet Union will not let Cuba fail." After examining reports on the movement of cargo ships from the Black and Baltic Seas to Cuba, McCone expected that Moscow would supplement economic, technical, and conventional military aid with medium-range ballistic missiles. (CIA analysts took exception to the director's inference, alleging that he did not have hard evidence to back up his suspicions.)[12]

Secretaries Rusk and McNamara also disagreed with McCone's warning of the potential threat posed by strategic missiles in Cuba, arguing that the Soviet buildup was purely defensive. So, the director of the CIA, who continued to sound the alarm during his honeymoon in Europe, decided to submit a memorandum to the president dated August 21, 1962.

In the light of additional intelligence on the shipments of concealed weapons and equipment to Cuba, and of the arrival of four thousand to five thousand Soviet/Bloc technicians and possibly military personnel, McCone contended that a Soviet-controlled Cuba would not only be used as a springboard for subversion in Central and South America but would also serve as a possible location for medium-range ballistic missiles and for COMINT (communications intelligence) and ELINT (electronic intelligence) facilities targeted against the United States.

Since the sharply curtailed Mongoose program (even if reenergized and expanded) would not, by itself, stop the ongoing Soviet military buildup in Cuba, the CIA director recommended that a multipronged plan be carried out before Moscow could turn the island into a menacing, missile-poised strategic base.

McCone urged the president to alert the Latin American republics and leaders of the free world to the impending threat. And he called for intensified covert operations and for the "simultaneous commitment of sufficient armed forces to occupy the country [Cuba], destroy the regime, free the people, and establish in Cuba a peaceful country which will be a member of the community of American states."[13]

On August 23, the president convened a meeting of the National Security Council to air McCone's concerns and determine what actions should be taken in light of the stepped-up Soviet bloc military activities in Cuba. The "actions" authorized by Kennedy were more studies, six of them. They included an analysis of the probable military, political, and psychological impact of the establishment in Cuba of either surface-to-air missiles or surface-to-surface missiles and a study of the advantages and disadvantages of warning against the deployment to the island of military forces, which might launch a nuclear attack against the United States.[14]

On August 31, one week after the president ordered the new studies, he was confronted for the first time with U-2 photographic evidence that eight surface-to-air missile sites were under construction in Cuba and would soon be operational. At least the entire western third of the island would be defended in a matter of days. Fragmentary evidence suggested that the Soviets were building another sixteen surface-to-air missile sites on the rest of the island.

McCone was quick to point out that, in his view, those emplacements were designed to protect strategic nuclear missiles. The president was worried that the information would leak and force his hand. He instructed CIA deputy director Marshall Carter to severely limit access to the evidence, saying, "Put it back in the box and nail it tight."[15]

The Council Goes Public (August 15–31, 1962)

Washington's toleration of the Soviet military buildup in Cuba alarmed the Cuban Revolutionary Council in Miami, and its disregard of the underground and refugee reports puzzled and disturbed us. It is true that those reports were mostly raw and unfiltered and were at times magnified by alarmists on the island and abroad. But, on the whole, they were directionally more accurate than the polished but shortsighted and slanted National Intelligence Estimates.

Apart from the copious flow of data we were getting on nighttime convoys carrying large cylindrical weapons covered with canvas, we started to receive startling information on mysterious work going on at a feverish pace where some of Cuba's vast caves were located. The sites were cordoned off, and many trucks were seen bringing building material. To allay suspicions, the Castro regime had earlier announced that many of the caves and caverns that dot the island would be spruced up to promote tourism. However, what the regime was actually doing in mid-1962, with the guidance of Soviet experts, was conditioning some of them for military use.

The Castro regime was well prepared to select the most suitable caves for military use, adding steel reinforcements and refrigeration equipment. Cuba's most renowned speleologist, the geographer and Communist leader Antonio Núñez Jimenez, had personally explored and mapped out those caves which could best serve as bomb shelter, as underground storage of military equipment, and even as silos for

aircraft and rockets. As we later found out, the sites that had been selected to install most of the Soviet strategic missiles were located near
the caves where burrowing and tunneling had been reported.

Most troubling in August 1962 was the flash we got from the island
regarding the arrival of about five thousand Soviet soldiers and military
personnel. Other exile groups and activists had received similar information, and the *Miami Daily News* carried the story, quoting unidenti-
fied sources (presumably from the US intelligence community). Still,
before going public, the Council needed further verification.

A couple of disgruntled CIA agents we knew in Miami had also
heard through their channels of the Soviet military contingent in
Cuba. But the one who gave us more reliable information was Massimo
Muratori, an official of the Italian Embassy in Havana, who carried
diplomatic credentials as a cover for intelligence missions.

A burly and balding Italian with a ruddy complexion and a zestful
personality, Muratori had frequently flown to Miami via Mexico to
meet with US intelligence officers, share information, and receive special training on the use of ultramodern electronic gadgets, including
infrared cameras and underwater equipment. There were other intelligence officers of NATO allies based in Cuba who also worked closely
with the United States.

In one of his trips to Miami, Muratori met my parents, and they
struck a rapport that led to a close friendship. During a dinner at our
home in mid-August, I had an aside with Massimo to discuss the Soviet
military buildup in Cuba. He confirmed the arrival of some five thousand Soviet elite troops and added with visible concern, "I am afraid that
that is only the first wave." He also indicated that Moscow's surface-to-
air missiles had been brought to the island and would soon be operational. This, he suspected, was the forerunner of strategic installations.

With Muratori's validation, the Cuban Revolutionary Council publicly denounced on August 20 the onset of what we called "the Soviet
invasion of Cuba" with several thousand soldiers and large concealed
arms—all with the consent and encouragement of the Castro brothers.

We also called for hemispheric action to repel the Soviet intervention forbidden by the inter-American treaties.

A US State Department spokesman ridiculed the report and said that the troops "were more likely four hundred or five hundred agricultural and industrial advisers." Then the president, in his August 29 press conference, stated, "In response to your specific question, we do not have information that [Soviet] troops have come into Cuba, number one. Number two, that main [Soviet] thrust, of course, is assistance because of the mismanagement of the Cuban economy which had brought widespread dissatisfaction, economic slowdown, [and] agricultural failures, which have been so typical of the Communist regimes in so many parts of the world. So that I think the situation was critical enough that they needed to be bolstered up."

To our utter dismay at the Council, the president had not only denied any knowledge of Soviet troops in Cuba (despite McCone's August 21 memorandum alluding to them) but also had in effect publicly justified Moscow's military buildup in Cuba by implying that it was just assistance to prop up the island's failing economy.

Congressional Pressure (September 1962)

The Council and other exile groups were not the only ones challenging the White House's laissez-faire attitude toward the Soviet intervention in Cuba. US senators and congressmen also voiced their alarm and called for immediate action. Some of them echoed our findings; others relied on leaks from US government sources. Among this latter group was Senator Strom Thurmond (then a Democrat from South Carolina). As a prominent member of the Armed Services Committee with excellent antennas, he had gathered enough intelligence to announce on September 3, 1962, that the Soviets were building bases for strategic ballistic missiles in Cuba.

But it was New York's Republican senator Kenneth B. Keating who was most vocal in flagging the threat. From August 31 to October 12,

1962, he made ten Senate speeches and fourteen other public statements revealing alarming aspects of the Soviet military buildup in Cuba. In his first major speech on August 31, he signaled that Moscow had sent some twelve hundred soldiers to the island and was building missile bases there.

The president was under increasing pressure to be up front about the Soviet military involvement in Cuba and its national security implications. To quell the unrest, Kennedy invited on September 4 leading Democrats and Republicans from Congress to a special meeting on Cuba. After providing an intelligence briefing, he stressed that Khrushchev was building up defensive capability on the island and nothing else. And then he added, to our dismay, that this did not violate the Monroe Doctrine. If anything, it reflected the weakness of Castro's state socialist model.[16]

That evening, the president acknowledged during his press conference that the Soviets had deployed to Cuba a number of antiaircraft defense missiles with a short range, as well as some thirty-five hundred technicians. (They were in fact Soviet troops belonging to four elite armored brigades.) To tranquilize the nation, he emphasized that there was no evidence of any organized Soviet bloc combat forces in Cuba; or of the presence of offensive ground-to-ground missiles; or of other significant offensive capability. Were it otherwise, he warned, grave issues would arise.

At his September 13 news conference, Kennedy again denied the presence of Soviet offensive missiles or troops. He also reiterated that if Cuba should ever "attempt to export its aggressive purposes by force … or become an offensive military base of significant capacity for the Soviet Union, then this country will do whatever must be done to protect its own security and that of its allies."

The Ominous Photo Gap (September 10)

To assure Congress that he was taking all the steps necessary to prepare for any eventuality in Cuba, the president announced through the
White House Press Office on September 7 that he had requested that
one hundred fifty thousand men in the US Ready Reserve be ordered
to active duty for twelve months. In addition, US war exercises in the
region continued apace, and military contingency plans involving a
possible blockade and/or invasion of Cuba were updated.

Following those sensible measures to enhance preparedness, an
ill-advised decision nearly crippled the ability of the United States to
detect the installation of Soviet strategic surface-to-surface missiles in
Cuba before they became fully operational. This is what happened:

On September 10, a meeting was held at the White House office of
National Security Director McGeorge Bundy to discuss CIA director
McCone's request to extend overflights. The objective was to photo-
graph those areas of Cuba known to have Soviet surface-to-air missiles
(SAMs) that had not been covered in previous missions. McCone, rep-
resented at the meeting by CIA deputy director Lieutenant General
Marshall "Pat" Carter, suspected that those SAMs had been emplaced
to protect medium-range surface-to-surface missile bases.

Secretary of State Dean Rusk strongly objected to the overflights
in view of two recent U-2 incidents: the straying of a U-2 over Sakhalin,
Russia, on August 30 and the loss of a Chinese Nationalist U-2 over the
China mainland on September 8. Addressing Carter, who defended the
overflight proposal, Rusk asked: "Pat, don't you ever let up? How do
you expect me to negotiate on Berlin with all these [U-2] incidents?"
(Khrushchev's diversionary tactic, shifting Washington's attention
from Cuba to Berlin, seemed to be working with Rusk.)

The attorney general, however, didn't buy Rusk's prioritization and
extreme cautiousness. "What's the matter, Dean, no guts?" he snapped.

"Let's sustain the overflights, and the hell with the international
issues," Robert Kennedy added. In the end, Rusk prevailed with

McGeorge Bundy's vigorous support and the attorney general's acquiescence. Peripheral flights over international waters were authorized but on a limited basis, and land overflights in areas known to have Soviet SAMs were blocked. The president ratified that decision the following day.[17]

This unconscionable surveillance downgrade, combined with a few days of inclement weather, left US intelligence agencies without photographic evidence of the strategic buildup for about one month. The Soviets thus were able to unload, unobstructed, medium-range missiles at the port of Mariel on September 15–17 and transport eight of them to the site near San Cristobal in the western part of the island. When Kennedy finally authorized in October the resumption of land overflights, this San Cristobal base—the first one to be photographed—was almost operational.

The Council and the Congressional Joint Resolution (September 20)

The Cuban Revolutionary Council was not privy to the twists and turns of US-Cuba policy, but it seemed to us that Washington was intent on avoiding or deferring the inevitable showdown with Moscow. Major sabotage plans and other paramilitary operations were either placed on hold or pared down, and the anti-Castro guerrillas in the Escambray Mountains, facing a huge Castro scorched-earth offensive, were virtually left to their own fate.

Incensed by Washington's procrastination, the Student Revolutionary Directorate—an anti-Castro organization based in Miami and not directly attached to the Council—decided to take direct action on their own to highlight the Soviet military occupation and dramatize Cuban resistance. On August 24, at 11:30 p.m., a group of exiled students, nineteen to twenty-three years in age, penetrated Castro's coastal defenses in two motorboats and fired their .20-caliber guns on a Havana hotel that housed Soviet bloc military officers. The daring raid produced heavy damages but no casualties and triggered a violent Castro protest.

The incident reached the highest levels of the Kennedy administration, involving the president, the attorney general, and the undersecretary of state, among others. A debate ensued over whether to arrest and prosecute the intrepid students. The president finally decided to issue a statement deploring the raid and warning against any such "spur of the moment" and "counterproductive" actions.[18]

Given these developments, along with alarming refugee reports clearly indicating an acceleration of the Soviet military buildup in Cuba, Tony Varona (then in charge of the Council's external relations) and I met with Miró-Cardona to assess the situation and agree on next steps. Tony and I argued that in view of the reluctance of the White House and the State Department to meet the Soviet–Castro challenge, our only recourse was to alert and enlist the support of Congress. After all, the looming crisis transcended Cuba and endangered the national security of the United States. Miró-Cardona was concerned that our plan might jeopardize his relationship with President Kennedy, but he did not stand in the way. "Just be careful and discreet," he counseled.

Believing that sooner or later some type of military action with overt US involvement would be required to address the threat, Varona and I decided to build a case for the recognition of a Cuban belligerent government-in-exile—not to vegetate in Miami with meaningless titles, but to formalize the alliance and rally our forces for liberation.

We sold the idea to Florida's Democrat senator George Smathers, a staunch anti-Castro advocate and a personal friend of President Kennedy. Working closely with the senator's staff, we found several precedents of US recognition of governments-in-exile during World War I and World War II. These included the Czechoslovak National Council—representing a dismemberment of the Austro-Hungarian Empire not yet constituting an independent state in 1918—and the Free French led by de Gaulle from London in 1940.

Although the historical condition of a formal state of war was missing in Cuba, there were other factors that strengthened our case. The OAS had outlawed Cuba's Marxist-Leninist regime and urged member states to exercise their right of individual or collective self-defense against Soviet intervention in this hemisphere. Moreover, the White House had already given tacit recognition to the Cuban Revolutionary Council as evidenced by President Kennedy's ongoing relationship with Miró-Cardona. All that was needed was to formalize that relationship so that a Cuban belligerent government-in-exile could spearhead collective military action to free their country.

That was precisely the main point that Smathers made in the Senate when he presented his government-in-exile resolution. Such a government, he indicated, could help line up or neutralize some of the wavering Latin American republics before the United States put troops on the ground. And then he added: "If we get a government-in-exile; they [the Democratic Cubans] can be the first wave; they are the people who are trying to free their own country, and we avoid the stigma to a great extent of having to say that we have unilaterally attacked [Cuba]."[19]

Secretary of State Dean Rusk objected in the Senate to the Smathers resolution, saying that he "didn't believe the United States has ever recognized a government-in-exile which did not originate in its home country, and which had [not] been driven out by enemy action, as in the case of World War II." (That, as noted earlier, was not true.) He also pointed out that there was "not a degree of cohesion among the various refugee groups outside of Cuba to support ... a single institutional alternative arrangement for Cuba, given a change in the situation."[20] (True, but a duly recognized government-in-exile under Miró-Cardona, with adequate resources and primed for action, could have rallied the support of most of the Cuban exiles and resistance groups on the island.)

These counterarguments did not mollify Rusk's adamant position. Despite Smathers's gallant efforts, our government-in-exile initiative was dead on arrival.

Somewhat frustrated by this setback, I approached my grandfather Cortina, exiled in Miami, for encouragement and guidance. The former

Cuban foreign minister and statesman was frail but remained lucid and well-informed. He told me that under the circumstances, the most effective way to press the White House to address the clear and present danger of Soviet military intervention in Cuba was through a joint resolution of Congress. When signed by the president, he reminded me, it would have the force of law.

Cortina gave me two good pieces of advice: (1) When drafting a proposed joint resolution, don't rely solely on the Monroe Doctrine, which Latin American countries view with suspicion. Invoke the Inter-American Treaty of Reciprocal Assistance (the Rio Treaty), which authorizes the use of armed forces to safeguard the peace and security of the hemisphere. (2) Be sure to assert the right of the Cuban people to self-determination. "We don't want to give up our sovereignty," he emphasized, while recalling the 1898 congressional joint resolution declaring that "Cuba is, and of right ought to be, free and independent."

I incorporated those pointers into my draft and called for the adoption of all the individual or collective measures deemed necessary to protect the security of the United States and other countries in this hemisphere and to repel Soviet intervention in Cuba. Tony Varona and I shared the draft, on a bipartisan basis, with Senators George Smathers (Democrat of Florida), Strom Thurmond (Democrat of South Carolina), and Bourke B. Hickenlooper (Republican of Iowa), and with Congressman William E. Miller (Republican of New York and national chairman of the Republican Party). They agreed in principle with the proposed joint resolution and promised to seek the backing of their colleagues, particularly those in the Foreign Relations and Armed Services Committees.

The idea of a joint resolution gained momentum, and several senators developed their own drafts, which were discussed on September 17, 1962, at a joint meeting of the Committees of Foreign Relations and Armed Services of the US Senate. Senator Kenneth Keating's proposed resolution declared that the domination of Cuba by international communism jeopardized the peace and security of the hemisphere, and reaffirmed "the right and obligation of the US to take all necessary actions, in cooperation with other Western Hemisphere nations if possible, and unilaterally if necessary, to end such domination."[21]

All the senators in attendance viewed with great concern the Soviet military buildup in Cuba, except for Senator Wayne Morse, Democrat of Oregon, who implied that those colleagues who called for prompt and effective action to address the threat were alarmists and warmongers. Senator Keating defended the use of force by the United States to meet the emergency, unilaterally if necessary, citing President Kennedy's statement of April 20, 1961: "If the nations of this hemisphere should fail to meet their commitments against Communist penetration, then I want it clearly understood that this Government will not hesitate in meeting its primary obligations which are the security of our own nation."[22]

Senator Winston L. Prouty, Republican of Vermont, joined the fray and said, "I think the greatest threat to peace today is a belief on the part of the Russian leaders that the United States and perhaps the Free World will not fight or resist in the event of a real showdown."[23]

The intervention of the chairman of the Armed Services Committee, the Democrat senator of Georgia Richard B. Russell, was the one that carried more weight and proved to be decisive. He first posed some pointed questions to Secretary of State Dean Rusk: "On what do you base your conclusion that there are more agricultural specialists than missile specialists from Russia in Cuba?" Not satisfied with the answer, Russell retorted with manifest edginess: "How can we tell whether he [the specialist] is teaching them to build a power line or whether he is teaching them to engage a radar set so as to fire missiles against the United States?"

Then the chairman addressed the core issue: whether to pass a "concurrent resolution" as recommended by Secretary Rusk and several senators, which would only express the sense of the Congress without committing the president, or whether to adopt a "joint resolution," which would be signed by the president and become the law of the land. Russell's position in favor of a joint resolution was unequivocal. This would require, he explained, striking out. "It is the sense of the Congress." He also said that "the United States is determined." And to emphasize the need to incorporate the president, he asked: "Why ... eliminate the only man in the American government who can really speak for the United States in international relations? He ought to be in there." And he was.[24]

We at the Council were very pleased with the resolution that was passed by the Senate on September 20, by a vote of 86–1, and over-whelmingly by the House a few days later. It was a joint resolution signed into law by the president on October 3. It invoked both the Monroe Doctrine and the Rio Treaty, expressly recognized and sup-ported the Cuban people's right to self-determination, and committed the United States to averting or countering the Soviet military inter-vention in the Caribbean in even stronger terms than we had proposed in our draft.

This is how the joint resolution (Public Law 87-733) reads in part:

> The United States is determined:
>
> A. To prevent by whatever means may be necessary, in-cluding the use of arms, the Marxist-Leninist regime in Cuba from extending by force or threat of force its aggressive or subversive activities to any part of this Hemisphere;
> B. To prevent in Cuba the creation or use of any exter-nally supported military capability endangering the security of the United States; and
> C. To work with the Organization of American States and with freedom-loving Cubans to support the as-pirations of the Cuban people for self-determination.

The Berlin Diversion (September 29)

Meanwhile in Moscow, Khrushchev was concerned that President Kennedy, under mounting pressure, might attack Cuba before the Soviet medium- and intermediate-range missiles were operational. (They were scheduled to become operational between mid-October and late November 1962.) But instead of backing down, he decided to accelerate the shipment in crates of one squadron of IL-28 light bombers with six eight- to twelve-kiloton nuclear bombs, as well as Luna short-range missiles with their nuclear warheads. The Soviet premier wanted to make sure that there was enough retaliatory capability on the island to ward off any US invasion ahead of the strategic emplacements.

To shift US focus away from Cuba and gain time, Khrushchev raised again the specter of Berlin. He told Kennedy's interior secretary, Stewart Udall, who had visited the Soviet Union in early September, that he intended to put Kennedy in a position in which he would have to settle the Berlin problem. "We will give him a choice—go to war or sign a [German] peace treaty" (which, among other things, would enable East Germany to control traffic to and from Berlin).

The Soviet premier then cunningly tempered his threat, saying that "out of respect for your president, we won't do anything until November." En passant, almost as an afterthought, he touched on Cuba—"an area that could really lead to some unexpected consequences." He contended that he was simply redressing in Cuba an intolerable double standard. After all, he added, "You [the United States / NATO] have surrounded us with military bases." His implication was clear: Why can't the Soviet Union do the same in Cuba?[25]

Khrushchev followed up with a letter to the president dated September 28. In it he wrote, "The abnormal situation in Berlin should be done away with. ... And under present circumstances we do not see any other way out but to sign a German peace treaty." Khrushchev then warned that any rash US action against Cuba, as the congressional joint resolution allegedly called for, could unleash nuclear war. Finally, the Soviet premier astutely played the political card, this time more explicitly, asserting that he would not force the Berlin issue until after the US November congressional elections.[26]

To better understand the implications of Khrushchev's letter, Kennedy met on September 29 with two distinguished Soviet experts who had been US ambassadors to Moscow, Charles Bohlen and Llewellyn Thompson. Their discussion centered primarily on Berlin—whether to respond to Khrushchev's Berlin challenge set out in his letter or to ignore it and "just let this thing drop until he comes over in November." Kennedy chose to wait and see what the Soviet premier had up his sleeve after the elections. Khrushchev got what he wanted from the president: a focus on Berlin and allowing the military buildup to continue in Cuba.[27]

The Countdown—While the White House Wavered (October 1–15)

October 1, Cuba

By October 1, the Soviets had covertly unloaded forty-two medium-range ballistic missiles (MRBM), including six fakes, and ancillary equipment at three Cuban ports: Bahía Honda and Mariel on the northern coast, and Casilda in the south. Those missiles, about seventy-four feet long, had a range of approximately eleven hundred nautical miles and could reach any point from Dallas, Texas, to Washington, DC. Each one carried a one-megaton warhead, and all were moved at night to their respective launch sites by sixty-seven-foot Russian trailers.[28]

Within the US intelligence community, reports of suspicious installations steadily increased, but in early October the official line in Washington still was that the buildup was defensive and the emplacement of offensive missiles unlikely.

As disclosed by Sean D. Naylor (national security correspondent, Yahoo News, January 23, 2019), a network of Cuban CIA agents on the island, led by Esteban Márquez-Novo, reported in mid-September 1962 that they had seen a convoy carrying long canvas-covered objects resembling MRBMs. The convoy was headed toward a Soviet-guarded trapezoid perimeter in the far-western province of Pinar del Río bounded by four towns where they believed that a strategic missile base was being built. Márquez-Novo and his radio operator had been trained in the United States by CIA officer Thomas Hewitt and infiltrated into Cuba as part of Operation Cobra. The information they gave, including the grid locations for the four small towns that enclosed the suspected strategic missile base, turned out to be precise and accurate but was not initially taken seriously by the White House.

October 1–2, Washington, DC

When Secretary of Defense McNamara was apprised of intelligence reports that seemed to validate the suspicion that the Soviets were emplacing MRBMs in the far-western province of Pinar del Río, his response was to outline six circumstances in which military operations against Cuba may be necessary. He also ordered that existing plans be updated to cover those contingencies. Again, more planning but no action.[29]

October 4, Cuba

According to Soviet records, the first shipment of nuclear warheads, on the freighter *Indigirka*, reached the port of Mariel on October 4. On board were forty-five one-megaton warheads for the MRBMs plus other warheads for the tactical missiles and the bombers. In total, the ship reportedly carried "over 20 times the explosive power that was dropped by Allied bombers on Germany in all of the Second World War."[30] (The US intelligence community eventually learned that reinforced bunkers in the mountains had been set up as nuclear depots, but they had no positive evidence that the warheads had actually arrived in Cuba.)

October 4, Washington, DC

At a meeting of the Special (Cuba) Group Augmented (Operation Mongoose), Robert Kennedy stated that the president was very dissatisfied with the lack of action in the sabotage field. Visibly annoyed, the attorney general went on a tirade, stressing that nothing was moving forward in that area. CIA director John McCone took sharp exception, saying that "a lack of forward motion [was] due principally to hesitancy in government circles to engage in any activities which would involve attribution to the United States."

Following a heated discussion, it was agreed to develop more-aggressive plans, including the possible mining of harbors, but the White House did not give the green light to proceed. To sharpen intelligence, McCone again requested authorization to conduct U-2 reconnaissance flights targeting suspect areas. This was placed on hold pending further consideration.[31]

October 5, Washington DC

McCone met with National Security director McGeorge Bundy and explained why no major covert actions had taken place in Cuba. He also pointed out that the decisions to restrict U-2 flights had placed the US intelligence community in a position where it could not provide unimpeachable evidence of the suspected development of Soviet offensive capabilities in Cuba. "Bundy took issue[,] stating that he felt the Soviets would not go that far, that he was satisfied that no offensive capability would be installed in Cuba."

In general, Bundy's views on Cuba, as expressed at the meeting with McCone, were that "we should either make a judgment that we would have to go in militarily (which seemed to him intolerable) or, alternatively, we would have to learn to live with Castro and his Cuba and adjust our policies accordingly."[32]

October 8, United Nations and Havana

At the end of his UN address denouncing Washington's aggressive plans, Osvaldo Dorticós, Castro's titular president, stated, "If ... we are attacked, we will defend ourselves. I repeat, we have sufficient means with which to defend ourselves. ... We have the weapons which we would have preferred not to acquire and which we do not wish to employ." Fidel Castro himself made the same claims in Havana: He vowed that Cuba was no longer vulnerable to the whims of Washington. "They will not be able to do that [invade] with impunity," he boasted. Hinting at a newly acquired retaliatory power, Castro added, "They could begin it [an invasion], but they would not be able to end it."[33]

October 9, Washington, DC

At a meeting with the Special (Cuba) Group Augmented, the president finally approved the urgent reiterated request for a U-2 flight covering suspected medium-range missile sites protected by SA-2 emplacements. For nearly a month, John McCone had pressed for such a flight, but Secretary of State Dean Rusk and others had resisted, with Kennedy's concurrence, fearing international repercussions if the U-2 were detected or shot down.

The president at long last ruled in McCone's favor, but he specified that it had to be an in-and-out mission expected to take only twelve minutes.[34] The flight, however, was delayed until October 14 owing to unfavorable weather.

October 10, Washington, DC

At the White House, CIA director McCone showed the president photographs of the crates in Havana believed to contain IL-28's, Soviet bombers capable of carrying nuclear payloads. The crates were transported to air bases in the early days of October. "Kennedy requested that such information be withheld at least until after the [November] elections [because] if the information got into the press, a new and more violent Cuban issue would be injected into the campaign[,] and this would seriously affect his independence of action. ... The president further requested that all future information be suppressed. [McCone] stated that this was extremely dangerous."[35]

October 13, Washington, DC

Soviet ambassador Anatoly Dobrynin assured State Department ambassador-at-large Chester Bowles that Moscow was not shipping offensive weapons to Cuba. "Why, he asked repeatedly, do we get so excited about so small a nation? Although the USSR could not let Cuba down, they had no desire to complicate the situation further. Was it not possible for us to negotiate a modus vivendi with Castro directly?"[36] (Dobrynin later claimed that Moscow had kept him in the dark about the shipment of offensive missiles to Cuba.)

October 14, Miami

Miró-Cardona was asked to meet at the Carillon Hotel in Miami with Adam Yarmolinsky, special assistant to Secretary of Defense McNamara; Robert Hurwitch, in charge of Cuban affairs at the State Department; and several Pentagon officers. Accompanying Miró-Cardona were Tony Varona, the Cuban Revolutionary Council's second-in-command covering external affairs, and Captain Ernesto Despaign, a military adviser. The US government delegation stressed the need to accelerate the enlistment of Cuban refugees into the US Army and to prepare a list of exiled pilots, medical doctors, and professionals who might be available should military action against the Castro regime be required. The leaders of the resistance movement inside Cuba were to be alerted. It all seemed that an invasion was imminent, when in fact it was only contingency planning.

Washington, DC

That same day, October 14, National Security Adviser McGeorge Bundy made the following astonishing remarks on Cuba on ABC's televised program *Issues and Answers*:

> Well, ... I know there is no present evidence and I think there is no present likelihood that the Cubans and the Cuban government and the Soviet government would in combination attempt to install a major offensive capability. ... So far, everything that has been delivered in Cuba falls within the categories of aid which the Soviet Union has provided, for example, to neutral states like Egypt or Indonesia, and I should not be surprised to see additional military assistance of that sort. That is not going to turn an island of six million people with 5,000 or 6,000 Soviet technicians and specialists into a major threat to the United States.

U-2 Flight over Cuba

While Bundy emphatically assured the nation that the Soviet military buildup in Cuba posed no significant threat and said that he expected the buildup to continue, air force major Richard D. Heyser flew a U-2 reconnaissance mission over the western part of Cuba. The target perimeter was based on the one drawn by Esteban Márquez-Novo and his team. It encompassed the San Cristobal area, near San Diego de los

Baños, and was centered in the heavily guarded "Finca of Dr. Cortina at La Güira, where very secret and important work [was] in progress, believed to be concerned with missiles."[37] The "Dr. Cortina" mentioned in the declassified CIA document is my maternal grandfather, and the La Güira farm, confiscated by the Castro regime and controlled by Soviet troops, belonged to him. In one of its lovely valleys surrounded by caves where my family and I used to picnic, the U-2 pilot photographed on October 14 the first of the Soviet MRBM sites in Cuba that startled Washington and led to the Missile Crisis.

October 15, White House

While the photographs of the MRBM base and nearby encampments were being examined by the National Photographic Interpretation Center and scanned by analysts, the president, unaware of what was going on, had a relaxed and cordial meeting at the White House with Algeria's leader Ahmed Ben Bella. A strong Castro supporter, he probed Kennedy about his intentions toward Cuba. The president denied any invasion plans, but this would change, he said, if the Soviets turned Cuba into an offensive base or if Castro attempted to use it as a springboard for expanding communism.

As Ben Bella later recounted to Castro, the president spoke of the possibility of reconciliation with Fidel if Cuba maintained a "National Communist" regime. "Do you mean a Yugoslavia or Poland?" Ben Bella asked. "Yes," the president said, nodding.[38] This dream or delusion of a peaceful, unattached Communist Cuba was shattered the following day.

1. Dr. José Manuel Cortina, author's grandfather, pictured here addressing Cuba's 1940 Constitutional Convention. He subsequently served as Secretary of State.

2. Dr. José Manuel Carbonell, author's grandfather; diplomat and former president of the Cuban Academy of Arts and Letters (1930).

3. Dr. Raúl de Cárdenas, author's wife's grandfather, former Vice-President of Cuba (1944-1948).

4. Dr. Néstor Carbonell-Andricaín, author's father, was Speaker of the House of Representatives (1940-1942). This portrait was displayed in the National Capitol.

5. El Capitolio- Cuba's National Capitol, a grandiose neo classical gem inspired by the Capitol in Washington DC and the Pantheon in Paris, was opened in 1929 and became the seat of Congress.

6. The author and his family invited by Pope John Paul II to a private audience at his summer residence in Castel Gandolfo, September 7, 1998.

7. *The author and President Ronald Reagan at the Oval Office, 1980s.*

To Nestor Carbonell
With best wishes,

Ronald Reagan

8. *The author and former British Prime Minister, Margaret Thatcher, at a private PepsiCo event in Venice, 1990s.*

9. Manuel ("Ñongo") Puig and his wife, Ofelia Arango Puig, author's cousin, in Havana 1950s. Active in the underground, they were both arrested by Castro's security forces in 1961. Ñongo was executed; Ofelia survived and remained committed to the cause in exile.

10. Ramón ("Rino") Puig, and his wife, Ileana Arango Puig, author's cousin, in Miami 1990s. Involved in the resistance movement, Rino was imprisoned for 15 years by the Castro regime. He later resumed the struggle in exile with Ileana.

11. Eddy Arango, author's cousin, in Miami 1970s. He was involved in the first major anti-Castro conspiracy, and was arrested by Castro's police in 1959. He served five years in prison and later went into exile with his wife Madie in the US.

12. Humberto Cortina, author's cousin, at Fort Benning, GA 1963. He landed in Cuba with the Bay of Pigs Brigade in April 1961, and was seriously wounded. After his recovery, he enlisted in the US Army.

13. The author, who attended the OAS conference in Punta del Este, Uruguay, in late January 1962, is pictured here with Dr. Miró-Cardona, President of the Cuban Revolutionary Council (left), and Cuban exile activist Eddy Leal (right), thanking Colombia's Foreign Minister, Dr. Caicedo Castilla, for supporting the Castro regime's expulsion from the OAS.

14. *Vice President Richard Nixon privately met with Fidel Castro in Washington, D.C. in April 1959, during Fidel's visit to the US. As noted by Nixon, "Castro was either incredibly naïve about communism or under Communist discipline."*

15. *Raúl Castro and Ernesto "Che" Guevara shortly after the triumph of the revolution in 1959. Their initial mission was mass executions of alleged Batista supporters (Raúl Castro in Santiago de Cuba, and Guevara at La Cabaña fortress in Havana).*

16. Dr. José Miró Cardona (center), Dr. Manuel Antonio "Tony" de Varona (left) and Manuel Ray (right), leaders of the Cuban Revolutionary Council, declaring war on Castro (April 1961).

17. Carrier USS Essex, part of the naval task force near the Bay of Pigs, was base for jets that could have turned the battle's tide.

18. Admiral Arleigh Burke pressed Kennedy to provide air support to the besieged brigade. Responding to the President, who did not want the US involved in the operation, he said: "Mr. President, we are involved."

19. *President Kennedy and former President Eisenhower posed for pictures on April 22, 1961 at Camp David, where they sharply disagreed on the causes of the Bay of Pigs debacle and the likely Soviet reaction.*

20. *Members of the Bay of Pigs brigade, pictured here, were captured by Castro forces after they ran out of ammunition.*

21. *Thanks to the foresight and persistence of CIA Director John McCone, pictured here coming out of the White House in mid1962, President Kennedy finally authorized the resumption of U-2 reconnaissance flights over suspected areas in Cuba.*

LAUNCH POSITION

MISSILE-READY TENTS

MISSILE ERECTORS

22. *This is the October 1962 aerial photograph of the Soviet medium-range ballistic missile base in Cuba that triggered the Missile Crisis. As disclosed by the CIA the base was located near the town of San Cristobal, Pinar del Río province, at the hacienda La Guira that had been confiscated from Dr. Cortina, the author's grandfather.*

23. In March 1963, the Cuban exile group, Commandos L, headed by Tony Cuesta (left) launched a spectacular raid on the Russian freighter Baku anchored close to the Cuban port of Caibarién. This led to the US crackdown on all future raids against the Castro regime.

24. During his April-May 1963 state visit to Russia, Castro was enthusiastically greeted and feted by the Politburo. Seen here clasping hands with Soviet Premier Khrushchev on May Day in Moscow's Red Square, Castro received the title of Hero of the Soviet Union, the Order of Lenin and the Gold Star.

25. *Fidel Castro warmly bids farewell to Chinese President Jiang Zemin, who visited Cuba in April 2001. Commercial, political and intelligence relations were strengthened between both countries.*

26. *Venezuelan President Hugo Chávez hugs Fidel Castro in Havana in February 2006. The deal they had struck a few years earlier of Venezuela's oil and service fees in exchange for Cuban doctors and spies, seemed to be working well for both.*

27. Raúl Castro congratulated President Obama for ushering in a US-Cuba thaw at a joint press conference in Havana in March 2016. But Castro's actions, in Cuba and abroad, soon thwarted the détente.

28. Raúl Castro hailed Venezuelan President Nicolas Maduro at a conference in Havana in April 2017, and reiterated Cuba's commitment to defend his regime.

29. *Russian President Vladimir Putin embraces Raúl Castro in the Kremlin prior to a Red Square Parade on May 7, 2015. This trip followed Cuba's agreement to increase intelligence cooperation with Russia (March 2014), and Russia's write-off of $32 billion of bad Cuban debt to the Soviet Union (July 2014)*

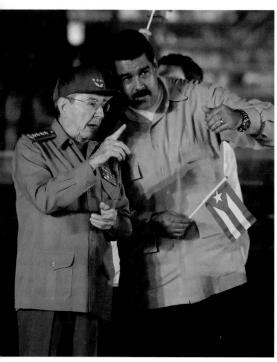

30. *Raúl Castro and Nicolas Maduro, pictured here, attended Fidel Castro's funeral in Santiago de Cuba in December 2016, and reaffirmed their alliance.*

31. Damas de Blanco (Ladies in White) is a peaceful dissident movement founded in 2003 by spouses and relatives of political prisoners in Cuba. They call for the release of all such prisoners and respect for human rigths. After Mass every Sunday, they silently walk throughout the streets, dressed in white, carrying a Gladiolus.

32. Shown here is the harassment often suffered by Damas de Blanco, pounded but not cowed by trained agents of the Castro regime.

33. Cuban dissident leader Oswaldo Payá holds up the European Parliament's Sakharov prize for freedom of expression awarded him on December 17, 2002. After achieving international prominence for his Varela Project (a pro-democracy national referendum) he died in 2012 in a suspicious car crash. His family and a passenger who survived claim that they were rammed by another car. The Castro regime has blocked an independent investigation.

34. Shown here with his wife Elsa, is a prestigious dissident leader, Oscar Elias Biscet, a 59-year old physician. He was imprisoned by Castro in 2003 for eight years in a tiny cell, often tortured. President George W. Bush awarded him the Presidential Medal of Freedom.

35. Pictured here is José Daniel Ferrer, the 50-year-old head of the Patriotic Union of Cuba (UNPACU), the largest human rights coalition in the interior of the island. After eight years in prison from 2003 to 2011, he was again arrested in October 2019 and held incommunicado for more than one month. Reports of torture, while imprisoned, have increased concern for his health.

CHAPTER 9

Eyeball-to-Eyeball: Who Blinked? (October–December 1962)

▌Shock and Disarray (October 16—the White House)

When the president woke up on October 16, McGeorge Bundy jolted him with the news that the U-2 pilot had photographed two nuclear MRBMs and six missile transports in the western part of Cuba. Very disturbed, Kennedy asked Bundy to assemble his foreign policy team from the State Department, the Pentagon, and the CIA, as discreetly as possible, for an urgent meeting that morning at the Cabinet Room. This team was called the Executive Committee of the National Security Council, or Ex Comm. Unbeknown to all its members, save the attorney general, who was in on the secret, the president taped the discussions at the White House during the electrifying "thirteen days" of the Missile Crisis and beyond.

Kennedy had two meetings with the Ex Comm on the sixteenth. The first started at 11:45 a.m. and the second at 6:00 p.m. The tapes of the discussions that day reveal how surprised the president and his team were when they were shown the photographic evidence of the San Diego de los Baños / San Cristobal MRBM complex. It actually encompassed, on second reading, three missile sites with four launchers each.

The president acknowledged how misguided they had been about Khrushchev's intentions. "We certainly have been wrong about what he's trying to do in Cuba," Kennedy said. "There isn't any doubt about that. Not many of us thought that he was going to put MRBMs on Cuba."

"No, except [CIA director] John McCone," interjected McGeorge Bundy.

"Yeah," the president replied, nodding.[1]

Senator Kenneth Keating also got a passing recognition. When the president asked how long they could keep the information about the missiles secret, he was reminded that the senator had already, in effect, announced it on the floor of the Senate. As McGeorge Bundy pointed out, "Senator Keating said this on the floor of the Senate on the tenth of October: 'Construction has begun on at least a half dozen launching sites for intermediate-range tactical missiles.'"[2] The team considered interviewing Keating to identify his source, but the president vetoed the idea.

Perhaps most startling was how befuddled and seemingly unprepared the Ex Comm was to deal with the clear and present crisis on the sixteenth, despite the myriad contingency plans that had been developed and frequently revised for more than a year.

Throughout the discussions that day, most of those in attendance meandered and flip-flopped, drifting with the current or coming up with unrealistic, if not bizarre, proposals. Secretary of State Dean Rusk, the first one to speak at length, stated that "we have to set in motion a chain of events that will eliminate this [missile] base." But then, in the next breath, he added, "I think also that we ought to consider getting some word to Castro, perhaps through the Canadian ambassador in Havana or through his representative at the UN ... that Cuba is being victimized here, and that the Soviets are preparing Cuba for destruction, or betrayal."[3]

Secretary of Defense McNamara sketched out in the morning several military options, including air strikes to destroy the missiles before they became operational. But then in the afternoon he made a surprising turnaround. With an authoritative tone, he averred: "I don't think there is a military problem there [in Cuba]. ... This *is* a [US] domestic problem." By that, he probably meant an electoral backlash if they did nothing, particularly since the president had warned that the emplacement of offensive missiles in Cuba would have most serious consequences. Parsing words, McNamara argued, "We didn't say we'd go in ... [if the missiles were there]. ... We said we'd act ... to prevent their use." As a solution, the defense secretary proposed "open surveillance" (to avert any attempt to fire the missiles) and the "search of suspicious ships coming to Cuba."[4]

In the course of the discussions, the president probed, challenged, and asked many questions as expected under the circumstances. But he also indulged in candid retrospection. Realizing how complex and dangerous the Cuba situation had become with Soviet direct involvement, Kennedy lamented, "That's why it shows the Bay of Pigs was really right. If we had done it right."[5]

The president also regretted having drawn a redline at the emplacement of strategic missiles in Cuba. "Last month I should have said that we don't care," he mused. Now, however, he was forced to do something.

His first inclination was to authorize a limited air strike to knock out the missile sites. But when McGeorge Bundy and McNamara contended that the offensive missiles in Cuba didn't really alter the strategic balance of power and posed no significant threat to the United States, the president started to backtrack. "You may say it doesn't make any difference if you are blown up by an ICBM flown from the Soviet Union or one from ninety miles away," he posited. "Geography doesn't mean that much."[6]

General Maxwell Taylor diplomatically demurred: "I think from a cold-blooded point of view, Mr. President, you're quite right in saying that these are just a few more missiles targeted on the United States. However, they can become a very, rather important, adjunct and reinforcement to the strike capability of the Soviet Union."[7] (According to intelligence experts, had the installation of the twenty-four MRBM launchers and sixteen IRBM launchers in Cuba been completed, they would have increased Moscow's first-strike land-based salvo by 80 percent, from its then very low operational base.)

Other advisers, especially Assistant Secretary of State Edwin Martin, underscored the adverse psychological impact of "sitting back" and letting the Russians "do it to us" (in Cuba). "It makes them look like they're coequal with us," conceded the president. And that "we're scared of the Cubans," added the secretary of the Treasury Douglas Dillon.[8]

Throughout the discussions, the subject of Berlin frequently came up. Would the Soviets "bargain Berlin and Cuba against each other," pondered Secretary Rusk, "or ... provoke us into a kind of action in Cuba which would give an umbrella for them to take action, with respect to Berlin? In other words, like the Suez–Hungary combination [in 1956]."[9]

After several hours of rambling and inconclusive exchanges, Secretary of Defense McNamara suggested outlining in writing the possible courses of action discussed to be evaluated by the Ex Comm with a sense of urgency since they were informed that the MRBMs would be operational in about two weeks. The options included the following:

A. **Overtures to Khrushchev and Castro** to see if the crisis could be peacefully resolved prior to any military action (proposed by Rusk and strongly supported by Undersecretary of State George Ball and UN ambassador Adlai Stevenson).

B. **Limited blockade** to prevent offensive weapons from entering Cuba (suggested by McNamara).

C. **Surgical air strike** to take down MRBMs and IRBMs (favored by the president in the early stages of the discussion).

D. **Extensive air attacks** against not only the strategic missiles but also the SAMs, the bombers, MiGs, airfields, potential nuclear storage sites, and radar installations (recommended by the Pentagon and the CIA).

E. **Invasion** (mainly raised by Robert Kennedy, who said, "If you're going to get into it at all [why not?], get it over with [launching an invasion] and take our losses." To strengthen the case for an invasion, he wondered "whether there is some other way we can get involved in this, through a [provoked or fabricated] incident in Guantánamo Bay … or whether there's some ship that … you know, sink the *Maine* again or something."[10] (The attorney general was, of course, alluding to the mysterious explosion of the US battleship *Maine* visiting Havana, which triggered the Spanish-American War in 1898.)

The meeting ended with no consensus as to what course of action to take.

The Kennedy and Gromyko Face-Off (October 18)

While the Ex Comm was debating what to do about the missiles in Cuba, the president agreed to meet at the Oval Office on October 18 with the dour Soviet foreign minister Andrei Gromyko. Khrushchev had asked him to request the meeting to gauge the mood in Washington and, specifically, to determine whether Kennedy knew about the missiles and was gearing up for military action in Cuba.

After a discussion on Germany and Berlin, Gromyko zeroed in on Cuba. He reiterated that the Soviet Union's assistance to Cuba was pursued solely for the purpose of developing its agriculture and training Cuban nationals in the handling of defensive armaments. Gromyko further asserted that Moscow stood for peaceful coexistence and hoped that the United States would resolve by negotiation its problems with Castro. But he warned that the USSR "could not stand by as a mere observer when aggression was planned and when a threat of war was looming." From his perspective, the recent call-up of one hundred fifty thousand reservists in the United States only served to stoke existing tensions, which could lead to a state of war.

In view of the fact that the president had not yet decided what course of action to take on Cuba, he opted not to disclose to Gromyko that he had irrefutable evidence of Soviet offensive missiles emplaced on the island. But he told the foreign minister that he did not know why Moscow had embarked on a major military buildup in Cuba, since he would have given Khrushchev "assurances that there would be no further invasion, either by refugees or by US forces."

Before the meeting ended, Kennedy read to Gromyko a portion of his September 4 statement on Cuba, which basically said that if the Soviet Union were to install offensive missiles on the island or build an offensive military capability, grave consequences would ensue.[11]

After his parley with the president, Gromyko reported to the Kremlin that he did not sense that Operation Anadyr had been uncovered, and although Kennedy was disturbed by the Soviet arms shipments to Cuba, he did not seem inclined to launch an invasion or retaliate militarily. Two other factors also contributed to Moscow's complacency: attention in Washington had shifted again to Berlin as the principal superpower flash point, and US Congress—perceived by the Kremlin as a hotbed of extremism—had just recessed until after the November elections.[12]

The Ex Comm's Agonizing Reappraisal (October 18–22)

On the eighteenth, the CIA released a thorough "Joint Evaluation of the Soviet Mission Threat in Cuba," prepared by the Guided Missile and Astronautics Committee, the Joint Atomic Energy Intelligence Committee, and the National Photographic Interpretation Center. They drew on the valuable intelligence provided by Soviet colonel Oleg Pendovsky, a spy for the United Kingdom and the United States, who had provided detailed information on Soviet military capabilities, including the size, configuration, and effectiveness of Moscow's offensive missiles.

The evaluation, based on U-2 photography made on the October

14 and October 15 missions, stated that there were at least 8 launchers and 16 medium-range ballistic missiles deployed in western Cuba at two launch sites. These missiles, with a range of 1,020 nautical miles, could be launched about 18 hours after the decision to launch. (Two additional MRBM sites were reported on October 19 east of Havana.) In addition, the report asserted that fixed soft sites had been spotted, probably intended for intermediate-range ballistic missiles. These missiles had a range of 2,200 nautical miles and could be operational by December 1962. Although there was still no positive evidence of nuclear warheads in Cuba, the evaluation assumed that they were available on the island to support the offensive missile capability.

Given these developments, the report concluded that the Soviet Union "intends to develop Cuba into a prime strategic base, rather than as a token show of force. The mixed force of 1,020- and 2,200-nautical-mile missiles posed a common threat to the United States and a large portion of Latin America."[13]

Despite this alarming evaluation and subsequent reports of the Soviet weapons in Cuba, which included twenty-two IL-28 bombers, Secretary of State Dean Rusk raised serious doubts. He "wondered whether these planes were decoys ... [and] whether the Russians were trying to entice us into a trap." CIA director McCone took issue with that supposition, saying that "the Russians would not have sent a hundred shiploads of [military] equipment to Cuba solely to play a trick."[14]

UN ambassador Adlai Stevenson opposed any military action that could lead to an invasion and "urged that we offer the Russians a settlement involving the withdrawal of our missiles from Turkey and our evacuation of Guantanamo base."[15]

After mulling over the tough issues and wavering for several days, the members of the Ex Comm, by and large, fell into two separate camps. On one side were those who propounded decisive action involving air strikes of substantial proportion to destroy the strategic missiles, the MiGs, and the bombers as a prelude to a possible invasion. On the other side were those who favored a gradual approach, starting with a limited blockade and pausing for negotiation before considering other actions.

The most prominent advocate of the first group was General Maxwell Taylor, backed by the Joint Chiefs of Staff and by former president Eisenhower and former secretary of state Dean Acheson, who had been consulted on this matter. Taylor asserted, "If we don't act [decisively] now, the missiles would be camouflaged in a way as to make it impossible for us to find them." He then added, "If we do not destroy the missiles and the bombers, we will have to change our entire military way of dealing with external threats."[16]

The only one of the hard-liners who warned that the missile problem was totally eclipsing the underlying Castro-Communist problem was CIA director McCone. He stated that "the main objective of taking Cuba away from Castro had been lost, and we have been overly consumed with the missile problem."[17]

Defense Secretary McNamara, who initially contended that the offensive missiles in Cuba were a political problem, not a military threat, eventually realized that they could potentially pose a serious national security issue. To address this matter, he joined the blockade camp but indicated that "the US would have to pay a price to get the Soviet missiles out of Cuba. He thought we would at least have to give up our missile bases in Italy and Turkey and would probably have to pay more besides."[18]

The attorney general, who initially favored going in all the way to deal with the threat, started to waver. On the nineteenth, he seemed defiant and unflinching. "In looking forward into the future," he said, "it would be better for our children and grandchildren if we decided to face the Soviet threat, stand up to it, and eliminate it now. The circumstances for doing so at some future time were bound to be more unfavorable, the risks would be greater, the chances of success less good."[19]

But on the twenty-first he changed his mind. He opposed an initial air strike because "it would be a Pearl Harbor–[type] attack, [and] it would lead to unpredictable military responses by the Soviet Union[,] which could ... lead to general nuclear war." Instead, he believed the United States "should start with the initiation of the blockade and thereafter play for the breaks."[20]

The president's varying positions covered the gamut. He initially seemed inclined to act promptly without warning, targeting the MRBMs and possibly the airfields. Later he favored an air strike to destroy only the missiles, pointing out that "we would have to live with the threat arising out of the stationing in Cuba of Soviet bombers." But the president realized that even a pared-down air strike "would lead to a major Soviet response, such as blockading Berlin." Doing nothing, however, or delaying a decision was out of the question since the missile threat got worse each day. As Kennedy considered a less risky alternative, he wistfully remarked, "We might wish, looking back, that we had done earlier what we are now preparing to do."[21]

After a lot of hemming and hawing, the president finally agreed to proceed with a limited blockade, called "quarantine" to avoid comparison with the Berlin blockade. While Kennedy did not preclude a possible air strike and invasion at a later stage, he clearly was tilting toward a political settlement, saying that if a UN resolution calling for "the withdrawal of missiles from Cuba, Turkey, and Italy was proposed, we would consider supporting such a resolution."[22] (As disclosed years later by Dean Rusk, the president had actually developed a secret plan to instigate the UN resolution through Andrew Cordier, the former deputy UN secretary-general then at Columbia University.)

Those who had favored air strikes and a possible invasion, including the Joint Chiefs of Staff, fell in line with the president and backed his quarantine decision.

Moscow: Troubling News (October 21)

While Kennedy was preparing to announce the quarantine, the Kremlin received disturbing reports suggesting some form of US military action in the Caribbean. Soviet intelligence reported that a convoy of military planes had left for Puerto Rico; bombers on duty in the Strategic Air Command had significantly increased; and the US Navy was in full display in the Caribbean, participating in an exercise code-named ORTSAC (Castro spelled backwards).

Khrushchev also received word that Kennedy was about to make a major public statement regarding the Soviet threat in Cuba. Even before he got a copy of the president's declaration and geared up for what he felt "may end in a big war," the Soviet premier lamented in front of his colleagues that he had not signed a Soviet-Cuban defense agreement in late August as Castro had requested. "We didn't deploy everything that we wanted to," he asserted, "and we didn't publish the treaty." What he meant was that had he moved forward at full speed pursuant to a formal treaty and completed the buildup without a cloak of secrecy and deception, it would have been very difficult, if not impossible, for Washington to turn it into a casus belli.[23]

Washington: The Die Is Cast (October 22)

Before the address to the nation and the world on the nuclear crisis, the Armed Forces of the United States started to forge a ring of steel around Cuba. Around three hundred fifty thousand men were mobilized, including the paratroopers of the 82nd and 101st Airborne Divisions and the Atlantic Amphibious Force. One hundred eighty-three ships of the US Navy, encompassing fast destroyers, guided-missile cruisers, eight aircraft carriers, and detachments of submarines, were dispatched to the Caribbean to control the vital sea-lanes surrounding the island. At more than eighty air bases in the United States and overseas, twenty-five hundred aircraft were fueled, loaded with weapons, and readied to fly. And the ICBM launching crews, spread in complexes throughout the United States, were brought to full alert.[24]

No leader had ever spoken from a position of such overwhelming strength as did President Kennedy on October 22, 1962. He also had the full support of French president Charles de Gaulle, British prime minister Harold Macmillan, German chancellor Konrad Adenauer, and other NATO allies, and received the unanimous backing of the OAS (except for one abstention). All he needed before publicly announcing the blockade (quarantine) was the endorsement of key congressional leaders. But what he got from them was skepticism, if not outright opposition.

The most vocal was the chairman of the Senate Armed Services Committee Richard Russell, who demanded stronger steps than a quarantine, meaning military action, and emphasized that no further warning to Khrushchev was necessary or advisable. "If we delay," he said, "if we give notification, if we telegraph our punches, the result will be a more difficult military action[,] and more American lives will be sacrificed."

The more surprising opposition to the blockade came from the chairman of the Senate Foreign Relations Committee William Fulbright. He, who a year earlier had proclaimed that "Cuba is a thorn in the flesh, but not a dagger in the heart," now called for the invasion of the island to resolve the crisis. He argued that the blockade was the worst of the alternatives open to the United States. "An [attack] on a Russian ship, he contended, is an act of war against Russia, [whereas] an attack or an invasion of Cuba [is] an act against Cuba."[25]

The president took issue with that sophistic distinction and pointed out that more drastic action at that time would increase the risk of Soviet retaliation, particularly on Berlin. He did not preclude, however, air strikes and even an invasion if Khrushchev did not remove the missiles.

A few minutes later, Kennedy delivered his stirring televised address. He declared that the Soviet Union had deployed to Cuba, under a cloak of secrecy and deception, offensive missiles and bombers capable of carrying nuclear warheads. To deal with the threat, he announced the establishment of a strict quarantine, to be supplemented by such other actions as may be necessary under the circumstances.

The president called on Khrushchev to dismantle and withdraw those weapons from Cuba and warned him that the United States would "regard any nuclear missile launched from Cuba against any nation in the Western Hemisphere as an attack by the Soviet Union on the United States, requiring a full retaliatory response upon the Soviet Union."

The president recognized that "the cost of freedom is always high, but Americans have always paid it. And [there is] one path we shall never choose, and that is the path of surrender or submission."

Moscow Undeterred (October 23–26)

Kennedy's address and Ambassador Stevenson's bravura performance at the UN displaying photographic evidence of the offensive buildup did not deter Khrushchev from moving forward with the completion of the missile sites. He denounced the blockade as an act of aggression and warned that Soviet ships might not respect the quarantine line. Since Washington had established a twenty-four-hour grace period, the Soviets took full advantage of the brief hiatus.

The ship *Aleksandrovsk*, with an additional cargo of nuclear warheads, beat the clock and arrived safely at the port of Isabela de Sagua on the northern coast of central Cuba. Not so the four ships carrying the intermediate-range ballistic missiles, which were ordered by the Kremlin to turn back, along with other incoming ships loaded with armaments.

Khrushchev raised the alert level of the Soviet Armed Forces and of those of the Warsaw Pact and ordered the commander in chief of the Soviet forces in Cuba (Pliyev) to be at full readiness. He also assured Castro, who had announced a general mobilization of three hundred fifty thousand soldiers and militias, that Moscow would not back down.

On October 24, President Kennedy was having second thoughts about the naval quarantine and its possible consequences. According to James M. Lindsay of the Council on Foreign Relations, Kennedy lamented to his brother Attorney General Robert Kennedy that he had been forced to impose the quarantine. "I just don't think there was any choice," Robert Kennedy assured him. "And not only that, if you hadn't acted, you would have been impeached." The president's response was: "That's what I think—I would have been impeached." (Not a wild speculation given the joint resolution on Cuba that Kennedy had signed into law.)

Despite his initial unwavering stance, Khrushchev realized that the Soviet Union could not keep the offensive missiles in Cuba without going to war and that he would have to find another way to protect the Castro regime.

By October 25, he discussed with his colleagues of the Presidium a possible diplomatic settlement consisting of a US pledge not to invade Cuba in exchange for the removal of the missiles. But, as a good poker player, he was not about to rush with an offer. He first wanted Kennedy to show his hand.[26]

Washington: Back-Channeling and Backpedaling (October 23–26)

The day following the announcement of the quarantine, Robert Kennedy visited the Soviet ambassador Anatoly Dobrynin. According to the ambassador, the attorney general "was in a state of agitation, and what he said was markedly repetitious." Displaying anger and frustration, he said that "the president had virtually staked his political career on the Soviet assurances about Cuba by publicly declaring that the arms were purely defensive—although some Republicans had warned otherwise." That turned out to be, he stressed, "a deliberate deceit." The attorney general did not hold Dobrynin responsible for that, acknowledging that the ambassador had also been misled.[27]

Robert Kennedy kept his lines of communication with Dobrynin open but also used back channels, directly or through reliable journalists, to float ideas to the Kremlin for a possible settlement. One of those intermediaries was Frank Holeman, a *New York Daily News* correspondent. He reportedly conveyed to Soviet intelligence officer Georgi Bolshakov a possible trade suggested by the attorney general's office: The United States would dismantle its missile bases in Turkey, and the USSR would do the same in Cuba. This missile swap was even suggested in his column by Walter Lippman, an influential US foreign policy pundit close to the White House.

The president was indeed prepared to agree to the swap, in addition to a no-invasion-of-Cuba pledge, if the commitment could remain confidential (given the expected opposition of Turkey and other NATO allies). Kennedy thought that the missile swap was an essential condition demanded by the Kremlin to strike a deal and had even developed, as a fallback, a secret plan to have the secretary-general of the United Nations formally propose such a swap. Turkey, however, had not been a critical issue raised in the Presidium discussions during the crisis. In fact, according to Deputy Premier Mikoyan, "we were not thinking about bases in Turkey at all." That is why Khrushchev only asked for a noninvasion pledge in his first proposal to Kennedy. But as the feelers from the Kennedy camp on the missile swap reached him, he decided to include in his second letter to the president a US-Soviet pledge to the UN that they would trade the alleged offensive weapons in Cuba for the Jupiter missiles in Turkey. With this added condition, Khrushchev felt that he could snatch a victory from the jaws of defeat.[28]

The Darkest Day of the Crisis (October 27)

The White House

The US intelligence findings, based on detailed analysis of low-altitude photography taken on October 26 and 27, were indeed alarming. All twenty-four MRBM launchers were fully operational with a capability to salvo within six to eight hours of a decision to launch. Construction of IRBM sites in Cuba continued at a rapid pace. Trenches were being built at the missile sites, and camouflage against aerial photography was being extended. In addition, the Guanajay bunker for nuclear warheads in western Cuba was essentially complete, and other facilities for probable nuclear storage were being set up.[29]

That was the state of affairs when the Ex Comm met with the president on October 27. No sooner had the meeting started at 10:00 a.m. than Kennedy was handed a second letter from Khrushchev, adding the Turkey-Cuba missile swap as a condition to settle the crisis. The president commented that "the Russians had made the Turkish missile withdrawal proposal in the most difficult way. Now that their proposal is public, we have no chance to talk privately to the Turks about the missiles, which, for a long time, we have considered obsolete." Nevertheless, he was inclined to accept the Soviet premier's condition, arguing that "we are in a bad position if we appear to be attacking Cuba for the purpose of keeping useless missiles in Turkey."[30]

While the Ex Comm members debated this delicate issue—most of them objecting to the public acceptance of the missile swap because it would undermine the NATO alliance—distressing news reached the White House. An American U-2 reconnaissance plane had been shot down over Cuba, and its pilot, Major Rudolf Anderson, had been killed. Mounting edginess on the island, amid reports of an imminent US invasion, accounted for this deliberate attack that escalated the crisis. Here's the backdrop of this episode:

Cuba

On October 26, Fidel Castro reportedly got word that the Kennedy administration had prepared an ultimatum to the UN secretary-general U Thant calling for the immediate removal of the offensive weapons. Convinced that this was the prelude to a US attack, Castro ordered the general staff of the Cuban Revolutionary Army to prepare for hostilities. Raúl Castro and Che Guevara took over the Cuban command posts in the far-eastern and western provinces of the island, respectively, and Fidel remained at the national headquarters bunker in Havana.

In the early morning hours of October 27, a deeply disturbed Fidel Castro visited Soviet ambassador Alekseev and delivered a letter to Khrushchev calling for a preemptive (first) nuclear strike: "If they [the Americans] manage to carry out an invasion of Cuba—a brutal act in violation of universal and moral law—that would be the moment," Castro wrote, "to eliminate this danger forever through an act of the most legitimate self-defense. ... However harsh and terrible the solution, there would be no other." The Soviet premier, who was rash but not suicidal, reminded Castro a few days later that "we struggle against [Yankee] imperialism, not in order to die, but to draw on all of our potential, to lose as little as possible, and later to win more" (Cuba Missile Crisis, Khrushchev-Castro letters—Cubanet).

Castro had another macabre plan up his sleeve, one that he was prepared to execute in the event of a US invasion. In the huge penitentiary at the Isle of Pines, which housed close to three thousand political prisoners, the Cuban ruler had ordered that holes be drilled in the tunnels beneath the ground floor of the four circular units and that they be filled with dynamite. The explosives were intended to prevent the "counterrevolutionaries" from staging a prison revolt to join an "imperialist" aggression, should such an attempt be made. Fortunately the explosives were not detonated. (The *Miami Herald* revealed on October 26, 2014, how that dark secret was uncovered.)

The morning of October 27, an American U-2 was sighted in the far-eastern province of Oriente near the town of Banes. Anticipating US air strikes only hours away, the Soviet commanders in Cuba, without consulting Moscow, decided to bring down the plane as an "operational-strategic necessity." An SA-2 rocket exploded near the U-2, causing it to plunge to the ground. Major Anderson died in the crash.[31]

The White House: Afternoon

To the dismay of the Pentagon, the president decided not to retaliate and suspended reconnaissance flights until the following day. Despite the rapidly deteriorating situation, his preference was still "to trade, not invade." Hence his willingness to accept the Turkey-Cuba missile swap proposed by Khrushchev. Bowing, however, to strong pressure from the Ex Comm, he agreed not to do it publicly.

The president thus ignored Khrushchev's second letter, which called for trading away the missiles in Turkey for those in Cuba, and basically accepted the terms of the first letter: Moscow would remove offensive weapons from Cuba under UN supervision and undertake not to reintroduce them, and the United States would lift the blockade and give assurances against the invasion of Cuba.

To clinch the deal, the president also decided to convey confidentially to Khrushchev his willingness to dismantle the Jupiter missiles in Turkey a few months after the settlement of the Cuban Missile Crisis, but not as an explicit quid pro quo. Robert Kennedy was asked to relay this message through Ambassador Dobrynin.

Washington: The Robert Kennedy–Dobrynin Meeting (7:45 p.m.)

The meeting took place at the Justice Department. According to Dobrynin's version, the attorney general stressed the urgency to reach a settlement, particularly after the downing of the US reconnaissance plane. "Delay in finding a way out," he underscored, "could spin out of control." While recognizing that a military action in Cuba could have ominous consequences, Robert Kennedy said or implied that the United States was resolved to get rid of the missile bases and was prepared to bomb them as a serious threat to US security if it came to the worst.

When the attorney general conveyed to the ambassador the president's response to Khrushchev's first letter, Dobrynin asked, "What about the missile bases in Turkey?" Robert Kennedy replied in essence that those missiles would not stand in the way of a settlement. They could be dismantled in four or five months, but given the NATO connection, the president could not announce it as part of the deal. It would have to remain as a confidential understanding.

Dobrynin keenly observed Robert Kennedy's demeanor throughout the meeting. "He was very nervous," noted the ambassador. "Indeed, it was the first time I saw him in such a state. ... He just kept repeating that time was pressing." And indeed it was. Dobrynin got the message with its implicit threat and immediately relayed it to Moscow.[32]

Miami: Early Evening

While this was going on in Washington, Miró-Cardona, the head of the Cuban Revolutionary Council, was summoned to an urgent meeting in Miami with several of his State Department and Pentagon contacts. A US invasion of Cuba to overthrow the Castro regime seemed imminent. According to classified files released by the National Archives in October 2017, US military planners estimated they would need 261,000 troops to seize strategic areas in Cuba within 10 to 15 days. Given this emergency, President Kennedy wanted to make sure that the plans were in place to establish a Free Cuba government on the island.

Miró-Cardona was prepared for that contingency, having lined up a broad representation of both the exile groups and resistance movements on the island for a government of national unity. In the course of the discussion, he made it clear to his interlocutors that he expected to land with the US expeditionary force, along with the other members of the prospective Free Cuba government, and to broadcast to the Cuban people a liberation manifesto that he would draft.

Upon returning to his home in Miami Beach that evening, which was packed with the Council's board members, advisers, and staff, Miró-Cardona took me aside and said in a low, tense voice, "It seems that the invasion could happen any moment. I want you to draft a proclamation in Spanish addressed to the people of Cuba, which I will broadcast upon landing. It should have the vibrancy to lift the spirits and rally for victory, as well as the magnanimity to stimulate defections and unite for peace." He then added, "Lock yourself in a secluded room of the house so that you can write without interruptions. I need the manifesto soon!"

It was not easy for me to concentrate. As I pictured the landing and the new dawn of freedom we had yearned for, I had to temper my emotions. It took awhile for the thoughts to flow. Here is an English version of the proclamation I wrote in Spanish:

My Fellow Countrymen,

We have returned to our homeland after several years of painful expatriation. Marching with us, in close alliance, are the invincible forces of democracy. We do not come with impulses of vengeance but with a spirit of justice. We do not defend the interest of any sector, nor do we intend to impose the will of any ruler. We come to restore the right of the Cuban people to establish their own laws and to elect their own government.

We are not invaders, inasmuch as Cubans cannot invade their own land. We aspire to the glory of liberating our country, which fell under the Soviet yoke through the perfidy and betrayal of some of its sons.

We come to oust forever from our soil the hatred that divides the Cubans, the firing wall that bloodies the families, the misery that ravages the cities and towns, and the foreign domination that subjugates and disgraces our country.

The hour of rebellion—so eagerly sought—has finally struck. Members of the heroic underground: rise and help us rescue the unyielding political prisoners so that all of you can occupy a place of honor among the forces of liberation.

Members of the rebel army and the militias: break your ties with the Communist tyranny and join the legions of freedom. All those who abandon the enemy ranks to embrace the cause of democracy shall be our allies in war and our brothers in peace.

Our fatherland demands of us supreme sacrifices. Let every man be a muscle of rebellion. Let every woman be a torch of patriotism. Let every home be a trench line of dignity.

Cubans: Throw off the hammer and sickle of Communist oppression. Join the new battle for independence. Take up arms to redeem the nation, and march resolutely on to victory. Our sovereign flag proudly waves its splendid colors, and the island rises with the stirring cry of liberty!

As soon as I had finished drafting the proclamation, I handed it to Miró-Cardona. He read it carefully and, to my surprise and satisfaction, didn't make any changes. Deeply moved, he gave me a warm Cuban *abrazo* and asked me to stay at home that evening in case he needed to reach me urgently.[33]

▌The Shaky Settlement (October 28–November 20)

On October 28 in the morning, the world breathed a sigh of great relief. The superpowers had headed off, it seemed, the mortal danger of a direct nuclear confrontation. Khrushchev accepted Kennedy's proposal to settle the Missile Crisis and ordered his generals to dismantle, crate, and return the so-called offensive weapons under United Nations supervision, in exchange for a US no-invasion-of-Cuba guarantee. The Soviet premier also acceded to the president's demand not to disclose the Turkey-for-Cuba missiles side deal, but he spelled it out in a confidential letter that Ambassador Dobrynin handed to Robert Kennedy on October 29.

According to the ambassador, the attorney general confirmed to him the following day that the president would honor the understanding. To underscore the need for confidentiality, Robert Kennedy added that "someday—who knows?—he might run for president, and his prospects could be damaged if the secret deal about the missiles in Turkey were to come out."[34]

Most of the Ex Comm members, particularly those who had opposed the air strikes and the invasion and had insisted that Khrushchev be given a decorous way out, exulted with a sense of triumph. They felt vindicated. This prompted Bundy's remark that, throughout the crisis, "everyone knew who were hawks and who were doves; today was the day of the doves."

Not surprisingly, the hawks were not pleased with the outcome. CIA director John McCone, for one, had earlier warned that if the United States focused only on the removal of the missiles, the Soviets would keep Cuba and Castro would remain in power. His clear-sighted warning continued to be his leitmotif.

The Joint Chiefs of Staff, fearing a Soviet deceptive retreat, voiced their distress and anger. When summoned to the White House, Admiral Anderson cried, "We have been had!" The air force chief of staff, General Curtis LeMay, pounded the table. "It's the greatest defeat in our history, Mr. President. ... We should invade today!" Secretary of Defense McNamara, who was present, said he looked at Kennedy and noted that "he was absolutely shocked. He was stuttering in reply."[35]

Cubans on both sides of the Gulf were also incensed. Most exiles viewed the settlement as US capitulation and a missed opportunity to liberate Cuba. Some harshly called it a second Bay of Pigs betrayal. Others, when they later heard the president proclaim that, under the settlement, there would be "peace in the Caribbean," fired back, saying that those words evoked Neville Chamberlain's "peace for our time" following the infamous Munich pact with Hitler.

In Cuba, an irate Castro, who apparently had heard about the settlement on the radio, accused Khrushchev of ignominiously giving in to Kennedy and called him a leader without cojones (balls), among other flowery epithets. The Soviet premier responded that the conflict was coming to an end with a favorable conclusion for Castro since it would prohibit any invasion of Cuba. Aware of Fidel's explosive personality and hurt feelings, Khrushchev urged him not to give "the mad militarists of the Pentagon any excuse to abort the agreement and take military action against Cuba."[36]

President Kennedy, who emerged from the confrontation with an aura of Churchillian statesmanship, felt that there was no need to seek further safeguards and clarifications before confirming the deal. So as soon as he received Khrushchev's message on October 28, he responded: "I consider my letter to you of October 27 and your reply of today as firm undertakings on the part of both governments which should be promptly carried out." He soon realized, however, that his rush to seal the agreement had perilous consequences.

The Crisis Continues

An essential condition of the Kennedy–Khrushchev understanding was that the Soviet missile bases in Cuba would be dismantled and the missiles removed from the island under United Nations supervision. Yet Castro objected to on-site inspection, and UN secretary-general U Thant and Soviet deputy premier Mikoyan failed to dissuade him from blocking the deal.

To keep the agreement alive, Washington caved in and acquiesced to inspection on the sea. Russian crewmen pulled back the canvas tarpaulins over what appeared to be missiles. This "striptease," as billed by humorists, enabled hovering US helicopters to peak and photograph, but the metal casings that presumably protected the missiles were not removed, and no boarding parties searched for nuclear arms. Nevertheless, Washington was satisfied that the forty-two MRBMs reported by the Soviets had been withdrawn, along with the nuclear warheads that were never photographed or spotted.

Absent on-site inspection, the United States was also unable to ascertain what was stored in cave complexes that had been cordoned off, reinforced, and conditioned with dehumidifying and air-conditioning equipment. Most troubling were the reports that burrowing and tunneling continued at a feverish pace after October 28, under the supervision and control of Soviet military personnel.

A major flaw of the agreement conceived and sanctioned by President Kennedy was that it did not define and specify the so-called offensive weapons that the Soviets were supposed to dismantle, crate, and remove. While it was understood, or at least implied, that they included medium- and intermediate-range ballistic missiles, the list was only submitted by Kennedy to Khrushchev on November 2.

Even then, there was no mention of the dual-use short-range launchers known as Luna (FROG) and some one hundred tactical nuclear warheads on the island. It seems that the Pentagon and US intelligence agencies were unaware that they had been deployed. Fortunately, Mikoyan felt uneasy leaving the tactical nuclear warheads in Cuba, even under Soviet supervision, so they were quietly withdrawn on December 1 on the ship *Arkhangelsk*.[37]

What became a very serious bone of contention, which almost reignited the crisis, was the removal of the IL-28 bombers and their nuclear payloads. President Kennedy did not mention the bombers in the October 28 agreement and voiced not to get "hung up" over them. Pressed by the Pentagon and other members of the Ex Comm, however, he subsequently decided to raise it as a make-or-break issue.

Khrushchev strongly objected, arguing that the bombers had been deployed to Cuba for defensive purposes and their removal had not been part of the agreement. Given the impasse, Kennedy softened the demand, indicating that if the Soviet premier promised to remove the bombers in one month, he would take his word and lift the blockade. This message was relayed by the attorney general through his back channel (Bolshakov) and via Ambassador Dobrynin.

Khrushchev offered two counterproposals. The first of these was a commitment that the bombers would be flown by Soviet pilots only. (This idea was originally suggested by the Kennedy brothers, who subsequently withdrew it.) The other alternative was a private gentlemen's agreement á la the Turkey deal with a promise to withdraw the IL-28's when, in Moscow's judgment, "the time was ripe to remove them." The president rejected both options and reiterated that he would accept Khrushchev's promise with a thirty-day timetable.

To press the Soviet premier for a quick, positive answer to his proposal, the president set a deadline—November 20, the date scheduled for a White House press conference on Cuba. If this veiled ultimatum did not produce the desired result, the Ex Comm recommended the tightening of the blockade in the first instance and the bombing of the IL-28's and other targets as a last resort. Although the president was determined to avoid military action in Cuba, he authorized, as a rehearsal for a possible invasion, a two-day amphibious exercise—the largest since World War II—at Onslow Beach, North Carolina.

The pressure worked. At Mikoyan's insistence, Castro reluctantly accepted the removal of the IL-28 bombers, and Khrushchev promised to ship them back to the Soviet Union within one month. Relying on that assurance, which was honored, the president announced during his November 20 press conference that he was ordering the lifting of the blockade. This formally ended the Cuban Missile Crisis with the United States seemingly in the driver's seat.[38]

▌The Unsettling Aftermath

According to most historians and analysts of the Cuban Missile Crisis, Khrushchev blinked during the eyeball-to-eyeball confrontation with Kennedy and withdrew the Soviet strategic missiles and bombers from Cuba in exchange for a US pledge not to invade the island and withdraw US missiles from Turkey (and apparently also from Italy). The president's performance was viewed by many as "his finest hour," and he was praised for his firmness and prudence in the face of grave danger and for his mastery of Cold War statecraft.

Although the unvarnished historical record does not fully support the glorification accorded the president, the hype caught on. Thanks mainly to the public relations skills of the administration's spinmeisters, and to the sanitized account of the Missile Crisis published by the attorney general and by other cabinet members and White House advisers, Kennedy largely escaped censure for his belated response to the Soviet military buildup in Cuba and for allowing Moscow to keep the strategic base in the Caribbean—a base that became the springboard for Communist subversion in several parts of the globe.

Still, the president was concerned about press reports and leaks, which could tarnish his image. At the meeting of the Executive Committee of the National Security Council on November 20, he asked, "How [can we] control such reports[,] and how [can we] deal with them publicly?" He was referring to various articles on the Missile Crisis, particularly the one written by James Daniels in *Reader's Digest*, which alleged that the administration refused to accept reliable information on offensive missiles in Cuba prior to October 22.

Considering the potential political risks posed by snooping journalists, the president decided that "all press contact with feature writers should be confined to Mr. Bundy and the Attorney General, and that our respective organizations should be advised not to discuss any details of Administration activity in August, September, and October [1962] with such feature writers."[39]

Apart from these steps to control or vet the narrative, the Kennedy administration benefited from the fact that the minutes and tape transcripts of the White House discussions during the Missile Crisis, including those documents that cast a shadow on the president's performance, remained classified for many years. As a result, the administration's version of events was by and large accepted at face value with few refutations.

It was only in 1996, when the State Department declassified the minutes of the 1961–63 meetings of the National Security Council, that we got a clearer picture of what went on behind closed doors. We learned, among other things, that the Joint Chiefs of Staff had urged Kennedy not to lift the blockade before the Soviets withdrew from

Cuba all of their troops and lethal armaments (not just the offensive missiles and bombers).

Displaying considerable foresight, they had warned the president on November 16, 1962, "When the extent of this [military] presence [in Cuba] is known and the weapons systems remaining in Soviet hands are thoroughly appreciated, it will be clear to the Western Hemisphere that it has indeed been invaded and remains invaded by the Soviet Union."[40] Sadly, their warning was not heeded.

The continued Soviet military intervention in Cuba, however, did not mar the president's standing in the United States. As reflected in his approval rating post–Missile Crisis, US public opinion gave Kennedy a thumbs-up. Not so our NATO allies. During the meeting of the National Security Council held on November 19, Undersecretary of State George Ball reported that "he was surprised at the unanimous [NATO] reaction that we had let the Russians off too easily and had not demanded the elimination of the Soviet base in Cuba."[41]

West Germany was mystified by Washington's delayed and half-way response to the Soviet threat in the Caribbean, even though the German intelligence service, relying on their agents on the island, had alerted the CIA to the shipment of Russian strategic missiles to Cuba as early as September.

But the NATO ally who seemed more upset and alarmed by the implications of the superpower settlement was General Charles de Gaulle, who had given Kennedy his total support to confront the Russians in Cuba. He decried the leaked Turkey-for-Cuba missile swap struck behind NATO's back and reproached Kennedy's tacit acceptance of the Soviet Union's continued military involvement in Cuba post–Missile Crisis.

In April 1963, the *Revue Militaire d'Information*, regarded as the most authoritative publication issued under the aegis of the French Defense Ministry, denounced that "there was ... indeed an agreement between the great powers on the 'demissilization' of Western Europe, an operation evidently demanded by the Soviets in return for their own nuclear disengagement in Cuba.

"Western public opinion was tricked," the publication declared. "Under the pretext of modernizing the armaments of Turkey and Italy [with seagoing Polaris missiles], the United States has cleverly disengaged itself [from mainland Europe]."

Kennedy's pledge to remove the Jupiter missiles from Turkey and not to invade Cuba certainly had a profound effect on General de Gaulle. According to journalist C. L. Sulzberger, the French leader years before had told then vice president Richard Nixon, "As the Soviet Union develops the capability to strike the cities of North America, one of your successors will be unwilling to go to nuclear war for anything short of a nuclear strike against North America.

"For the general," noted Sulzberger, "this analysis was confirmed by the 1962 Cuba confrontation. Once the Russians had nuclear-tipped rockets emplaced in the Caribbean, they agreed to remove them only when US missiles were withdrawn from Turkey and if Washington promised to leave Castro alone. De Gaulle reasoned: 'If the Americans will not fight for Cuba, 90 miles away, I must draw conclusions from this.'" And as Sulzberger pointed out, "These conclusions included a weakened NATO—of which France is now a 'yes, but' partner" (a partner which, under de Gaulle, opted to develop its own nuclear force de frappe).[42]

Within our continent, numerous Latin American presidents, particularly those under Castro-Communist fire in Central America, were deeply disturbed by Kennedy's unconditional no-invasion-of-Cuba pledge, coupled with the assurance he gave Khrushchev that he was "confident that other nations of the Western Hemisphere would be prepared to do likewise." The leaders south of our border feared that the pledge would effectively bind them without their consent and would force Washington to accept and even safeguard the permanence of a Soviet-backed totalitarian regime in Cuba.

President Villeda Morales of Honduras, expressing his views and those of his neighbors, publicly reminded the White House that "it is absolutely essential to win the battle of Cuba ...; that battle cannot be considered ended with the mere withdrawal of Russian missiles ...; it must end by returning millions of Cubans to liberty."[43]

To counter the criticism that Kennedy should have obtained a settlement more advantageous to the United States and the free world, McGeorge Bundy asserted that the president had imposed the quarantine simply to get the offensive weapons out of Cuba. Had he broadened that objective to extract a more comprehensive commitment from Khrushchev and Castro, Bundy argued, "we would have soon faced a rapid erosion of support at home and abroad."

Based on that questionable premise, the Kennedy administration claimed to have achieved its central purpose without firing a single shot: the restoration of the situation that existed in Cuba prior to the Missile Crisis—in other words, the status quo ante.[44]

Unfortunately, that was not the case. The Soviets and Castro emerged from the Missile Crisis with much more than what they'd had in Cuba *before* the offensive weapons were shipped to the island. For starters, they got a US pledge not to invade Cuba, or to allow others to attack the island, without a reciprocal Castro guarantee not to engage in subversive activities.

The president tried to back out of the unconditional no-invasion pledge, insisting that it was subject to Castro's good behavior and to the Rio Treaty. Since Khrushchev and Castro would not buy that conditionality, Kennedy refused to formalize the exchange of letters with the Soviet premier that sealed the deal. But, as Michael Beschloss pointed out, "Although the Kennedy–Khrushchev agreement on Cuba was never formalized in a treaty, later presidents and Soviet leaders treated it with almost the same reverence."[45]

According to Soviet deputy premier Anastas Mikoyan, President Lyndon Johnson told him shortly after Kennedy's funeral that he would remain faithful to the US pledge not to invade Cuba.[46] And in 1970, after the United States discovered the construction of a Soviet submarine base in Cuba, the Nixon administration invoked the Kennedy–Khrushchev agreement to include submarine bases as a prohibited offensive installation, thereby recognizing the full force and effect of the accord.[47]

Apart from the no-invasion pledge, which eventually hamstrung Cuban freedom fighters in the United States and abroad, Washington allowed the Soviets and Castro to keep on the island the twenty-four battalions of surface-to-air missiles introduced during the Russian military buildup, along with the short-range, nuclear-capable FROG rockets, Komar ships, and the MiG-21's.[48] These fighter-bombers were upgraded years later with MiG-23's and MiG-27's, which could be quickly conditioned to carry nuclear payloads.

Yet another indication of Moscow's continued military intervention in Cuba post–Missile Crisis was the permanence of part of the Russian forces that were deployed to the island in June–October 1962—a total of 41,902 soldiers, military experts, trainers, and support personnel.[49] According to the summary record of the Meeting of the National Security Council on November 29, the president himself decided not to insist on the withdrawal of all the Soviet forces from Cuba. He commented that "the Russians won't take out their forces until we give a no-invasion assurance. It is better for us to have Soviet units in Cuba than to give a formal [UN] no-invasion assurance."

The attorney general was not particularly concerned about Russian troops on the island. In fact, they apparently gave him a sense of comfort. He wrote in his memoirs, "I didn't see what the problem was—the Russians in Cuba. I mean, I'd rather have the Russians running the SAMs [surface-to-air missiles] than the Cubans running them."[50]

Despite the tacit acceptance of the Soviet Union's military presence in Cuba, Washington seemed surprised and alarmed when the CIA spotlighted in 1979 a Russian combat brigade on the island armed with forty tanks and backed by several thousand military experts and support personnel. The alarm, however, soon subsided, and the brigade and entourage remained in Cuba until the early 1990s.

Unchallenged, the Soviets sent to the island in the 1970s, for resupply and a show of strength, numerous naval task forces that included guided missile carriers and destroyers and nuclear attack submarines. They also conducted reconnaissance missions along the East Coast of the United States with Tu-95 Bear turboprop aircraft.

Moscow had another weighty motive for maintaining a military presence in Cuba: the operation of a major electronic intelligence station whose large antennas eavesdropped on US civilian, military, and space satellite messages and picture relays. This advanced monitoring complex, atop a limestone hill of Lourdes, east of Havana, was deemed at the time the most powerful and sophisticated Russian intelligence-collection facility in the world outside the Soviet Union itself.

But from the standpoint of the Cold War, the most important geopolitical and military advantage that the Kremlin gained from the Missile Crisis was the tolerated use of Cuba as a formidable base to spur Communist expansion through armed attacks, espionage, and subversive activities throughout the Americas, Africa, and other regions. This Soviet sanctuary enabled the Castro regime to ignite and support "wars of liberation or popular insurrections against Yankee imperialism" and to spread the myth that communism was the wave of the future.

Moscow's free rein in Cuba, following the Kennedy–Khrushchev accord, has generally been justified as the necessary price that had to be paid for settling the Missile Crisis without unleashing a nuclear war. Is that a valid explanation? If the United States had tightened the blockade or taken military action to disarm and liberate Cuba, or at least to sever the Soviet military connection, would that have triggered a nuclear war?

When the former policy makers from the Kennedy administration and scholars of the Missile Crisis met in Hawks Cay, Florida, in March 1987, most of them felt, in retrospect, that more could have been accomplished if the White House had taken a tougher stance. The United States had such strategic and conventional superiority in the region that the chances that a war over Cuba could have escalated into a nuclear exchange were viewed by some of the pundits at the meeting as "one in fifty." Others considered that "even one chance in a thousand of nuclear war would be too high."[51]

Still, despite the very low odds, one could not have totally ruled out the possibility of "blundering into disaster," as McNamara put it, or of stumbling into a nuclear war. So, it would seem unfair for us now, with the benefit of hindsight, to blame Kennedy and the "doves" of the Ex Comm for lack of sufficient fortitude when faced with Soviet offensive missiles in Cuba, nearly operational, pointing at the United States.

Yet the teetering on the brink need not have occurred. In fact, it could have been averted if Washington had taken appropriate action *before* the crisis escalated.

True, US intelligence estimates, colored by philosophical misconceptions, political biases, and plain wishful thinking, maintained that the establishment on Cuban soil of Soviet nuclear capability was incompatible with Kremlin policy. Yet CIA director McCone, well-informed senators, NATO intelligence officers on the island, and Cuban exile leaders repeatedly warned the president and his advisers about the serious implications, both conventional and nuclear, of the Soviet military buildup in Cuba.

After considerable prodding, Kennedy did serve notice on the Soviet Union in early September that the emplacement of offensive missiles and combat forces in Cuba would have grave consequences, but he failed to follow through. To avoid incidents with Moscow, he even suspended for almost one month U-2 reconnaissance flights over the suspicious areas of Cuba protected by Soviet surface-to-air missiles and troops.

Moreover, when McCone showed the president on October 10 photographs of crates in Havana believed to contain Soviet IL-28 bombers capable of carrying nuclear payloads, Kennedy told the CIA director to "withhold that information at least until after the [November] elections." National security was apparently deferred for political considerations.

And so the Soviet invasion of Cuba with nuclear striking forces proceeded apace and was nearly completed without US opposition or interference, an invasion over four months involving more than a hundred shipments laden with Soviet lethal weapons and forty-two thousand soldiers and military personnel, an invasion that left in its wake a formidable base that wreaked havoc in several regions of the world, taking the toll of hundreds of thousands of lives.

Yes, Kennedy got the missiles out, but he allowed the Soviets in. And in they stayed for three decades, arming, financing, and protecting the most subversive and long-lasting totalitarian tyranny of modern times.

CHAPTER 10

Did Castro Get to Kennedy before Kennedy Got to Him? (1963)

The Release of the Bay of Pigs Prisoners

After settling the Missile Crisis, albeit without the total withdrawal of Soviet troops from Cuba, the president focused on another priority: the release of 1,113 Bay of Pigs freedom fighters imprisoned by Castro.

The negotiation with Fidel was entrusted by the Kennedy brothers to a shrewd New York attorney, James B. Donovan, who had served as assistant counsel in the Nuremberg trials and had arranged with the Kremlin and East Germany the exchange of Soviet spy Rudolf Abel for the downed U-2 pilot Francis Gary Powers and the Yale student Frederic L. Pryor. This was the subject of the Steven Spielberg 2015 blockbuster film *Bridge of Spies*.

As directed by the White House, Donovan acted in Cuba not as a representative of the US government but as a private US citizen and counsel for the Cuban Families Committee in their efforts to free the Bay of Pigs prisoners.

On December 22, 1962, after several months of intense and often vexing negotiations, Castro agreed to release the prisoners upon receipt, as a down payment, of 20 percent of the stipulated ransom: $53 million worth of pharmaceuticals, medical supplies, foodstuffs, and other products.[1] The following day, the brigade prisoners were flown to Miami. Not all were included in the exchange. Five were executed (allegedly because of crimes committed under Batista), two died in prison, and seven had to serve up to twenty-five years behind bars.[2]

Just before Christmas, on December 23, 1962, the freed Bay of Pigs prisoners arrived en masse at the Dinner Key Auditorium in Miami, which was packed with families and friends. When the veterans entered the hall, the crowd broke and rushed forward. Their tears and screams were seen and heard by millions of Americans watching on television. It was a moving and spontaneous outpouring of relief and jubilation.

Four days later, the president invited the brigade leaders to his villa in Palm Beach, where he was vacationing. Flanked by the first lady and her sister Princess Lee Radziwill, he warmly greeted them. No presidential assistant attended the gathering, save the press secretary Pierre Salinger. After a cordial exchange of pleasantries, Kennedy, turning serious, raised the subject of the Bay of Pigs and expressed his sorrow for what had happened.

As reported by José "Pepe" San Román, the brigade's military chief, the president told them that he did not provide further support to the brigade because the Soviet government had threatened to attack West Berlin if the United States launched more air raids on Cuba. He described his agonizing dilemma: support the Bay of Pigs invasion and face a Soviet military confrontation in Berlin, which could touch off a large-scale war, or maintain world peace and risk the defeat of fourteen hundred Cuban freedom fighters. It was a most difficult and painful decision, the president emphasized, but the priority was clearly world peace. (This was basically the same explanation Kennedy gave Eisenhower when they met on April 22, 1961.)

The brigade chiefs chose not to challenge the president's explanation for having "dumped" them in Cuba without air cover. They withheld their grudges, thinking that Kennedy had not given up on Cuba and would back a new attempt to liberate the island. With that expectation, they agreed with the White House to invite the president to inspect the brigade at the Orange Bowl in Miami and present him with their most treasured possession: the banner that had flown over the command post at the Bay of Pigs for three days and had been preserved by a soldier who was able to obtain diplomatic asylum.

I vividly recall, as a participant, the well-choreographed ceremony at the Orange Bowl, which stirred the spirits of thousands in the stadium. The members of the brigade, clad in khaki uniforms, and their families and friends, waving flags, poured their hearts out when the white convertible carrying the president and the first lady glided over the field. After the bands had played the national anthems of the United States and Cuba, Pepe San Román read his opening remarks and then turned toward the president and said, "Mr. President, the men of the 2506 Brigade give you their banner—we temporarily deposit it with you for safekeeping."

The president unfurled the flag, stepped to the microphone, and replied, "I want to express my great appreciation to the brigade for making the United States the custodian of this flag." He paused, and then his voice soared with emotion: "I can assure you that this flag will be returned to this brigade in a free Havana."

The multitude who attended the ceremony rose and clapped wildly. Shouts of "Guerra! Guerra!" (War! War!) and "Libertad! Libertad!" (Liberty! Liberty!) rocked the stadium for several minutes. I looked around and saw that few eyes were dry. The members of the brigade and the Cuban exiles at large put behind them the Bay of Pigs debacle and, roused by the president's assurance, renewed their vows to continue the struggle. They soon realized, however, to their dismay, that Kennedy was not inclined to wage war but seemed to be tilting toward an accommodation with Castro.[3]

Kennedy's Two-Track Cuba Strategy

Although the president's declared goal was to foster the end of Communist domination in Cuba, he was not about to risk another confrontation with the Soviet Union, which in January 1963 still had some seventeen thousand troops and military personnel on the island.

Moreover, Kennedy had to contend with the global challenge of the Cold War. In that context, he viewed Cuba as a possible negotiating chip.

At a meeting with the National Security Council on January 22, 1963, he mused: "The time will probably come when we will have to act again on Cuba. Cuba might be our response in some future situation—the same way the Russians have used Berlin. ... We can use Cuba to limit their actions just as they have had Berlin to limit our actions."[4]

A Cuba–Berlin give-and-take with the Russians was clearly in the president's mind, but this notion was too defensive and uncertain; it was more a contingency plan than a policy. So Kennedy decided to try a more realistic and proactive Cuba strategy, one involving carrots and sticks, pressures and incentives. Hence the dual strategy, which crystallized following the president's meeting in Palm Beach with CIA director John McCone on April 15, 1963.

At that meeting, McCone "explained to the president that the Cuban problem must be solved in one of two ways ...: by bringing consistent pressure of every possible nature on Khrushchev to force his withdrawal from Cuba, [and] then to bring about the downfall of Castro" or, alternatively, "by working on Castro with the objective of disenchanting him with his Soviet relations, causing him to break ... with Khrushchev, ... reorient his policies with respect to Latin America, and establish in Cuba [a] government satisfactory to the rest of the Hemisphere.

"The president thought both approaches should be carefully examined and suggested the possibility of pursuing both courses of action at the same time."[5] The dual strategy was set in motion without foreseeing Castro's response.

The pressure component called for isolating Cuba as much as possible with the support of the Organization of American States and NATO allies. The objective was to increase the Soviet's carrying cost of the Castro regime. Minor acts of sabotage under strict CIA control were authorized.

Although the secret Mongoose office in Miami was nominally disbanded—its functions were actually transferred to the Special Affairs Staff (Task Force W)—covert action plans continued to be devised to supplement the pressure side of the dual strategy. Indeed, by the fall of 1963, after several bizarre schemes had been discarded, a new CIA plot to assassinate Fidel Castro, without the involvement or knowledge of the Cuban exile leaders, gained momentum.

The attorney general, Robert Kennedy, remained the overall point man on Cuba, but he focused primarily on the cloak-and-dagger operations. The president, for his part, took on with maximum discretion the soft incentive side of the strategy. He earnestly pursued a rapprochement with Castro, hoping that Fidel could be lured to at least relax his ties to Moscow and stop exporting the revolution. Encouraged by Donovan's seemingly constructive dialogue with the Cuban dictator during the negotiations to free the Bay of Pigs prisoners, the president even considered sending his brother to Cuba.

As documented in the declassified December 14, 1962, Memorandum of Telephone Conversation between McCone and Undersecretary of State George Ball, the CIA director said that "the president wants the attorney general to go down [to Havana] because he now has commitments to cover the Castro list." McCone added that the "woman who has been described in various reports as being his adviser, his secretary, or his mistress [Celia Sánchez] can arrange for him to come down. ... They would allow him in[,] and then we would have him charter a Pan American plane to fly down there."[6]

This plan was dropped, apparently because it was deemed too risky politically, so Donovan was asked to advance the accommodation talks himself. When he met Castro in Havana on January 25, 1963, to follow up on the release of twenty-four US citizens imprisoned in Cuba, he proposed to Fidel, as a possible prelude to the normalization of relations, the resumption of Pan American Airways flights to Havana. Donovan also suggested that, "in view of Cuban-Chinese friendship, Castro might be helpful in obtaining the release of Americans imprisoned in China. Donovan told Castro that his difficulties [with Washington] lay in his dependence upon the Soviets. Castro only grunted in reply."[7]

As evidenced by his long, glorious trip to the Soviet Union in April–June 1963 (described later on), Fidel had no intention of breaking with Moscow, despite his passing bitterness at the Russians for having withdrawn the missiles. He feigned interest in exploring a rapprochement with the United States to induce Washington to lower its guard and grant unilateral concessions, while he braced himself to subvert Latin America and beyond with Soviet support.

With that ruse in mind, "Castro warmly re-issued the invitation that Donovan return to Cuba with his wife for a week or so (possibly the first week in March). Castro indicated he wished to talk at length with Donovan about the future of Cuba and international relations in general."[8]

So eager was the president to strike a deal with Castro that he overruled in early March 1963 a State Department official who suggested that Donovan be instructed to tell Castro that breaking Cuban relations with the Sino-Soviet bloc was a nonnegotiable US condition for improved relations. As stated in a top secret / eyes only memorandum recording Kennedy's instructions to National Security Adviser McGeorge Bundy, "The President does not agree that we should make the breaking of Sino-Soviet ties a non-negotiable point. We don't want to present Castro with a condition that he obviously cannot fulfill. We should start thinking along more flexible lines." Kennedy's surprising position shift, which suggested a willingness to accept a Tito-type regime, "must be kept close to the vest," the memo advised. "The President, himself, is very interested in this one."[9]

Donovan returned to Cuba in April, not with his wife but accompanied by his eighteen-year-old son John and two of Robert Kennedy's aides. The discussions of a possible US-Cuba rapprochement did not progress during their five-day enjoyable visit, which included snorkeling with Fidel Castro in the Bay of Pigs.

According to Donovan's son's remembrances of the trip, carried by the *Daily Mail* on October 18, 2015, his father foiled a CIA potential hit on Castro involving a poisoned wet suit he was asked to present as a gift to the Cuban ruler. Donovan gave him instead one he had personally bought in New York without any toxin. (The Senate Select Committee, chaired by Senator Frank Church, which in 1975 gathered evidence on the CIA's failed attempts to kill Castro, reportedly included this episode.)

Cuban Exiles and the Kennedy Administration Clash (March–April 1963)

While Washington was cozying up to Castro, Moscow allowed him to keep thousands of Soviet soldiers and military and intelligence personnel on the island, not only for training and security purposes but also to clamp down on internal resistance. Indeed, they participated in several military and counterinsurgency operations.

To boost internal resistance, put pressure on the Russians to leave the island, and demonstrate that the Kennedy–Khrushchev pact would not block the exiles' efforts to liberate Cuba, anti-Castro commando groups in Miami prepared to strike. On March 18, representatives of the exile organization Alpha 66 attacked the Soviet ship *Lgov* at the Cuban port of Isabela de Sagua, firing several bursts from a heavy machine gun.

Then, on March 28, members of the Commandos L exile group launched a spectacular raid on the Russian freighter *Baku*. This proved to be one of the most daring undertakings because the Cubans and the Soviets had tightened security measures, and the US authorities were no longer winking at the raiders. They were dead set against these provocative attacks carried out by Cuban exiles.

The Commandos L (for liberty) were led by Tony Cuesta, a very tall, audacious, onetime Havana businessman who had become a seasoned seafaring captain infiltrating anti-Castro cadres into Cuba and carrying out coastal forays. After eluding US surveillance, Tony and his crew left Florida aboard a mothership and sailed to an inlet along Anguilla Isles. There they cast off the *Phoenix*, a converted twenty-two-foot speedboat, from the mother vessel and prepared for the bold mission. Just before midnight on March 28, the commandos spotted their imposing target—the bulky, round-bottomed Soviet freighter *Baku*, anchored close to the Cuban port of Caibarién.

Suddenly, a Soviet patrol vessel making the rounds appeared on the scene. The raiders watched breathlessly, holding fast to their guns. Fortunately the launch saw nothing suspicious and disappeared into the darkness. A few minutes later, ten loud explosives shattered the silence. It was Ramón, one of the raiders, firing his cannon at the command bridge of the freighter. At less than ten yards, every rifle aboard the *Phoenix* shot at the deck of the *Baku*. Then Tony impassively said, "Ahora la bomba"—"Now the bomb."

Andrew St. George, the *Life* magazine photographer and chronicler of the venture, described this critical moment:

> Ramón leans out ready to drop the bomb, its fuse lit, overboard. But the bomb won't budge. The line attached to its float is tangled on the deck rail. Ramón tugs and yanks. The burning fuse has three or four minutes to go. ... Ramón crashes his body against the railing. The railing gives, the line swings free. Someone leaps to help and the bomb is overboard. ... Tranquilino [the navigator] swings the *Phoenix* away from the freighter. ... Our boat shudders for a moment. From behind I hear the crash of glass. The rifles on the *Phoenix* keep firing. Then all is silence as we speed away into the night.[10]

The blasting of a thirteen-foot hole in the *Baku* touched off the wildest international dustup on Cuba since the October Missile Crisis. Moscow accused the United States of "dangerous provocation" and threatened to retaliate. Castro ordered two of his MiGs to harass the US transport *Floridian* in the high seas. The Cuban commandos expected howling and pounding from their enemies, but they had not anticipated condemnation and persecution from their friends.

The US authorities lambasted the forays as counterproductive and dangerous, and asserted that such activities would not be tolerated. Washington ordered a crackdown against all future raids on Cuba. Action groups were restricted to the land limits of Dade County, a twenty-five-hundred-square-mile area that includes Miami. Speedboats owned by Cuban exiles were impounded. The coast guard in the area increased its force by 20 percent to thirty-six hundred. To complete the quarantine of the Cuban exiles, Washington enlisted the support of the British authorities in the Bahamas to patrol adjoining seas.

Watching this impressive display of US-British might, columnist Henry J. Taylor sharply commented, "In tragic truth, Castro's Russian masters have outthought us, outmaneuvered us, and cast us out of control of the situation. ... How else could we now find ourselves forced to order a wrong-way blockade against fighters for freedom instead of against Castro?"[11]

At the Miami headquarters of the Cuban Revolutionary Council, its president, José Miró-Cardona, was under tremendous pressure to either obtain the lifting of the quarantine imposed on the commandos or resign.

Sensing that the US policy on Cuba was drifting toward accommodation with Castro, the exile leader sought clarification from John H. Crimmins, who had been charged by the State Department to assume in Miami the interagency coordination of Cuban affairs. Apart from calling for an end to the crackdown in Miami, Miró-Cardona outlined in a memorandum three possible options to liberate Cuba: "Joint Cuban-American military action against the Castro regime; failing that, Cuban military action with the same type of [US] military and financial assistance for the Cuban exiles that the Soviet Union provides for the Castro regime; and failing that, Cuban military action with no US involvement other than a loan to the Cuban Revolutionary Council to prosecute the war."[12]

Not having received a satisfactory response to his query, the exile leader and his executive assistant and interpreter, Ernesto Aragón, followed up in Washington and requested a meeting with the attorney general, Robert Kennedy. The meeting was held on Saturday, April 6, at his office. While Miró-Cardona and Ernesto Aragón were waiting in the anteroom, two of Robert Kennedy's young sons passed by with their huge Newfoundland dog, Brumus. A few minutes later, the Cubans were escorted to the attorney general's office.

Robert Kennedy had removed his jacket, loosened his tie, rolled up his sleeves, and left his shoes under the table. Despite his seeming informality, he was sullen and tense. He meant business. Since the attorney general was alone, Aragón served as interpreter and took notes, which he shared with me.

Not wasting any time with perfunctory remarks, Robert Kennedy bluntly told Miró-Cardona: "You seem to be misinformed. We have not changed our policy toward Cuba. The US government never represented to you that it had committed itself to taking military action against Castro." Miró-Cardona responded: "Since the beginning I was told, I think in your presence, that the Cuban problem was essentially military, requiring at least six divisions, with as many Cubans involved as possible." Visibly irked, the attorney general shot back: "I was not present when you allegedly were told that Cuba was a military problem. That is not true, and besides, there are no military plans against Cuba."

The exile leader was flustered by Robert Kennedy's flat denial, knowing full well that the attorney general had been present when the president affirmed that Cuba was a military problem and asked Richard Goodwin to step up the training of Cuban units at several US camps. His integrity called into question—which Latinos generally take as a personal offense—the usually amiable and diplomatic Miró-Cardona responded with anger. Stabbing the air with his index finger, he told the attorney general, "You are a kid" [*chiquillo* was the term he used], speaking to a university professor ... one of three generations [of Mirós] who have fought for freedom … and I will not allow you to cast a shadow of doubt on my word of honor!"

The acrimonious exchange did not abate. Robert Kennedy blasted the Cuban commando groups for their irresponsible and ineffectual operations. "I will not tolerate any actions from US territory that are contrary to the laws of this country," the attorney general emphatically asserted. Miró-Cardona replied, "How can you say that you support freedom-loving Cubans when you persecute them and bar them from fighting for the liberation of their homeland?"

When Miró-Cardona reiterated his intention to resign, Robert Kennedy clenched his jaw and muttered, "Tell me, Dr. Cardona, what it is, specifically, that you want?" The exile chief outlined the three options he had earlier conveyed to State Department and Pentagon officials, including a US loan to the council to prosecute the war, if Washington preferred not to involve US troops or resources. "What is the order of magnitude?" Robert Kennedy asked.

"I am not prepared to give you an estimate without consulting with military specialists," Miró-Cardona replied. The attorney general pressed him to give him a rough number. "I really don't know," Miró-Cardona said, "but if you insist, fifty … one hundred million?"

Robert Kennedy then changed the subject and seemed to soften his tone. He told Miró-Cardona that he did not understand his desire to resign, and without offering to consider the exile leader's request or suggesting any other alternative to support the liberation effort, the attorney general urged him to think it over for thirty days and then meet with him again. "But if you decide to resign and to issue a public statement," Robert Kennedy warned, "you must clear the text with us first. Sensitive disclosures might be harmful to the security of the United States and could be used against us by enemies of this administration."

According to Aragón's notes, Miró-Cardona stood up and somberly replied, "I came here to seek clarification regarding the Cuban situation. After a careful assessment of the facts and responses received, I have concluded that you have changed your policy toward Cuba and that you have no plans or intentions to put an end to the Castro regime. I outlined possible courses of action, and they have been tacitly rejected. I am, therefore, impelled to resign. I cannot wait thirty days, and I do not intend to consult with anyone on the text of my resignation. I assume full responsibility for my actions. Good afternoon and goodbye."

Before Miró-Cardona tendered his resignation, Robert Hurwitch, the State Department official in charge of Cuban and Caribbean affairs, told Aragón that the exile leader's attitude would lead to a severance of US relations with Cuban exiles. "No single Cuban will ever be received in any government office in the future," Hurwitch reportedly asserted. He also reminded Aragón that there were a number of legal reasons for canceling a US residence permit known as the green card.

These veiled threats did not deter Miró-Cardona. On April 18, he tendered his resignation to the Cuban Revolutionary Council and released for publication a twenty-four-page appendix explaining the motives. It had the effect of a political and diplomatic bombshell. The administration's spokespersons vigorously counterattacked, denying the allegations of the exile leader and implying that the crisis had occurred because Washington had refused to yield to his ultimatum of a $50 million loan and a pledge to invade Cuba.[13]

I saw Miró-Cardona in Puerto Rico a few days after he had resigned. He was well aware that some of the Cubans in Miami who had criticized him for being subservient to Washington's dictates were now reproaching him for his drastic step. Despite the flurry of attacks, the now-retired exile leader seemed at peace with his conscience.

In a brief aside, he told me, "You know, throughout the process, I have been able to withstand the impatience, even the diatribes, of my compatriots because I had confidence in our friends in Washington, who promised me to support the liberation of Cuba. Now, however, with the Kennedy–Khrushchev pact and the resulting change of policy, my faith has been dashed." Frowning more than ever, he added, "Washington is seeking, I am convinced, an accommodation with

Castro ... but I will not be party to that disgrace. The son of General Miró-Argenter will never play the shameful role of Marshal Pétain!"

Miró-Cardona's resignation and the subsequent dissolution of the Cuban Revolutionary Council created a leadership void within the Cuban exile community, but not for long. The head of Bacardi, José (Pepín) Bosch, who supported Castro during the insurgency against Batista and turned against Fidel after he embraced Marxism-Leninism, was exiled in the Bahamas when Miró-Cardona stepped down and the Council broke up.

As vividly described by Tom Gjelten in his book *Bacardi and the Long Fight for Cuba*, Bosch effectively led and funded efforts to keep the anti-Castro resistance fire burning from 1963 to 1965. With the backing of renowned personalities, including Claire Boothe Luce and Admiral Arleigh Burke, he created a Citizens' Committee for a Free Cuba in Washington, DC, and organized a referendum within the exile community to select and empower a five-man directorate to assume the Representación Cubana del Exilio (RECE). Lacking US and Latin American government support, RECE closed up shop in the mid-1960s, but a young, magnetic member of the quintet (Jorge Mas Canosa) later became an inspiring leader.

Bosch was not the only Bacardi CEO who played an important role in the anti-Castro movement. Shortly after retiring as the chairman of Bacardi in exile, Manuel Jorge Cutillas wholeheartedly led the Center for a Free Cuba based in Washington, DC, and supported numerous initiatives to galvanize the prodemocracy resistance in Cuba and abroad.

Washington's New Overture to Castro (April–November 1963)

Having hamstrung the commando groups and subsequently ended the support of the Cuban Revolutionary Council, which led to its disbandment, Washington thought that this would facilitate a rapprochement with Castro. Vain illusion or, to be precise, delusion. Ten days after

Miró-Cardona had tendered his resignation, the international news services reported that the "Cuban premier Fidel Castro, wearing a fur hat and a trench coat with sleeves far too long, flew into Moscow ... and received the warmest, most tumultuous welcome ever accorded a foreign dignitary in the Soviet Union."[14]

During his forty days in Russia—perhaps a record in the annals of state visits—Castro journeyed to fourteen cities; inspected the Northern Fleet and strategic forces rocket base; delivered innumerable speeches at stadiums, factories, and town squares; and reviewed the May Day Parade from the top of the Kremlin Wall. He also received the title of Hero of the Soviet Union, the Order of Lenin, and the Gold Star, and spent scores of hours conversing and chuckling with Nikita Khrushchev and his successor-to-be, Leonid Brezhnev.[15]

Still, the White House renewed its attempt to seek an accommodation with Castro. The back-channel intermediary used this time was Lisa Howard, a reporter for ABC News. A onetime actress and soap opera star who covered the United Nations as a correspondent for Mutual Radio Network in 1960, she became the first US journalist to interview the Soviet premier Nikita Khrushchev. Three years later, the attractive and persistent Howard scored another journalistic coup: an exclusive televised interview with Fidel Castro, which was aired on May 10, 1963. Again the Cuban ruler floated the idea of exploring better US-Cuba relations.

It should be noted that Lisa Howard, the go-between for Castro and the White House, had developed an intimate liaison with "her dearest Fidel." As disclosed in her diary, Castro kissed and caressed her in their first meeting in Havana, "expertly with restrained passion," but would not go all the way. According to Howard, he explained why: "You have done much for us; you have written a lot, spoken a lot about us. But if we go to bed, then it will be complicated and our relationship will be destroyed." (Peter Kornbluh, who had access to Lisa's diary, told the story in *Politico*, May–June 2018.)

It is hard to believe that Castro was sincere in striking a deal with

Washington after basking in adoration in Moscow and reaffirming his commitment to defend and expand International communism. Yet the White House authorized William Attwood, an adviser to the US mission to the United Nations, to establish private contacts with Carlos Lechuga, the Cuban ambassador to the United Nations. The first bilateral talks—an informal exchange of views—took place on September 23 during a social reception at Lisa Howard's spacious Park Avenue apartment. As reported by Attwood, Lechuga "hinted that Castro was indeed in a mood to talk and thought there was a good chance that I might be invited to Cuba."

After a series of phone conversations with Havana in October, Castro proposed to send a plane to Mexico to pick up Attwood and fly him to a private airport near Varadero Beach, where Fidel would talk to him alone. The plane would fly him back immediately after the talk.

As disclosed by Peter Kornbluh, drawing from declassified documents, Castro's invitation set off a flurry of discussions inside the Kennedy administration. "Would such a trip be secure? Should the United States find out first what Castro was willing to talk about? Was Castro sincere, or was he trying to manipulate a reduction of US pressure? What were the political dangers of an accommodation with Cuba? Should a dialogue even be attempted?"[16]

After pondering the pros and cons, it was decided to pursue the talks, preceded by a preliminary meeting in New York between Attwood and Ambassador Lechuga to review Castro's agenda. As Attwood testified behind closed doors to a special Senate committee, he was told that after he received the agenda, the president wanted to see him to determine what to say and whether Attwood should go to Cuba, or what to do next. This message was relayed to Attwood on November 19, three days before the president's assassination.

In those last three days, Kennedy himself sent two indirect messages to Castro. The first one was conveyed in a speech before the Inter-American Press in Miami. Referring to Cuba's effort, backed by external powers, to subvert the other American republics, the president

stated that "this and this alone divides us. As long as this is true, nothing is possible. Without it, everything is possible." What Kennedy said,
in essence, was that a Communist Cuba would be negotiable if Castro
ceased to export his revolution.

Kennedy's second message, more explicit than the first one, was
delivered to Castro on November 22 by French journalist Jean Daniel.
As requested by the president, Daniel told Fidel that the US trade embargo against Cuba could be lifted if Castro stopped his support for
leftist movements in the hemisphere. When an aide interrupted their
conversation to report that Kennedy had been shot, Castro turned to
Daniel and said, "This is an end to your mission of peace. Everything
is changed."[17]

Against this backdrop, can we conclude that, had it not been for the
president's assassination, we would have achieved a historic turning
point in US-Cuba relations, leading to a stable rapprochement? Not really. As the record shows, Castro was not truly interested in giving up
his Communist ideology, expansionist grand design, and Soviet support
for the sake of a peaceful entente with the detested Yankee imperialism
he had vowed to defeat. And the Kennedy brothers, who were wary of
Castro's machinations, did not rely solely on diplomatic overtures to
settle the Cuban crisis. They actually played a perilous, indeed fateful,
double game.

JFK's Assassination and the Suspected Cuban Connection (November 1963)

On the very same day that President Kennedy was assassinated,
November 22, 1963, CIA case officer Néstor Sánchez in Paris handed
to one of the intrepid frontliners of the Cuban Revolution who held
high military rank an ingeniously crafted poison-tipped ballpoint pen
to kill Fidel Castro. The Cuban plotter, code-named AM/LASH, was
Rolando Cubela, a young, engaging "comandante" with a thick beard

and a mercurial personality. (In his prerevolutionary days, he was nick-named Torpedo.)

The AM/LASH conspiracy began in 1961, when a CIA official approached Cubela in Havana to determine if he would be willing to cooperate in efforts to bring down the Castro regime. The comandante, who seemed disturbed by Fidel's totalitarian direction, manifested more interest in defecting than in conspiring. However, as his relationship with the agency drew closer, he warmed up to the idea of remaining on the island, "if he could do something really significant for the creation of a new Cuba." To achieve that, he was willing to plan the "execution" or "elimination" of Fidel Castro. (He objected to the term *assassination*, not to the act.)[18]

As documented by Brian Latell, a former US National Intelligence officer for Latin America and author of *Castro's Secrets: Cuban Intelligence, the CIA, and the Assassination of John F. Kennedy*, Cubela's professed desire to eliminate Castro was music to the ears of the top CIA leaders. The agency was frequently prodded, particularly by the attorney general, to produce tangible results. That meant to "come up with some ideas to kill Castro," as one CIA official would later testify in a congressional hearing.[19]

The agency had earlier discarded as cockeyed or impractical two plots to assassinate Castro. The AM/LASH conspiracy, however, seemed more promising since it would be led by an insider—a senior government official who was close to Fidel—who had cold-blooded killer instincts. Before Castro seized power in 1959, Cubela murdered Batista's chief of military intelligence, Antonio Blanco Rico, while the feared officer was watching a show at the Montmartre nightclub in Havana.

Carried away by Cubela's gung-ho demeanor and background, and under mounting pressure to act, the CIA dismissed troubling signs that cast a shadow on the comandante's bona fides. According to Brian Latell, Cubela had refused to take a lie detector test—a standard procedure for new recruits—and he apparently had unlimited time and money to travel and meet with CIA officials in distant locations. He also failed to provide any significant inside information on the Castro regime. Still, the agency decided to go ahead with AM/LASH—a grave mistake. As Cuban defectors from Castro's intelligence services (DGI) would later testify, Cubela was a double agent, feeding every detail of the US plot back to Havana.[20]

The CIA plan was discussed with Cubela in Brazil on September 7, 1963. It called for covert action by him and his military coconspirators to "neutralize" (kill) Castro, overthrow the regime, and form a new pro-US government that would, if necessary, request US military assistance to quash any resistance.[21] Cubela was on board with the plan but requested military supplies, including a weapon to carry out his mission and protect himself, as well as a meeting with Robert Kennedy. He wanted proof that the Kennedy brothers were involved in, and supportive of, the plot.

At the CIA headquarters, Cubela's request for a parley with the attorney general was turned down, but to assure him that the plan presented to him had presidential blessing, Desmond Fitzgerald met with him on October 29 at a safe house in Paris. Fitzgerald was an East Coast socialite, friend of the attorney general, who was chief of Task Force W charged with covert operations against the Castro regime. Although Fitzgerald did not reveal at the meeting his real name and title, he identified himself as Robert Kennedy's personal representative and gave additional evidence of the Kennedy involvement, which seemed to satisfy Cubela. The only thing missing was the assassination weapon.

The comandante had requested an FAL rifle with a silencer, but instead he got an intricate device delivered to him in Paris, on November 22, by CIA case officer Sánchez. It consisted of a pen fitted with a syringe that could be filled with poison to be injected into Castro. The needle was so fine that Fidel would not feel its insertion. While Sánchez was showing Cubela how to operate the device, an urgent call came from Fitzgerald in Washington: President Kennedy had just been shot in Dallas.[22]

The question arises: Is there any connection between the CIA–Cubela plot to kill Castro and the assassination of President Kennedy by Lee Harvey Oswald, a lifelong Marxist and ardent supporter of Castro and the Cuban Revolution? Or was it just coincidence? Circumstantial evidence suggests a possible linkage.

On September 7, 1963, a few hours after the CIA discussed with Cubela the plan to kill Castro, Fidel gave an interview to an Associated Press reporter in which he put the United States on notice that "aiding terrorist plans to eliminate Cuban leaders" would mean that "they themselves will not be safe."[23]

Whether in connivance with Havana or simply aroused by the Cuban Revolution and eager to defend it against US "aggression," Oswald apparently backed up Fidel's threat. As early as 1959, Oswald, then stationed at the Marine Corps Air Station El Toro in Southern California, was mesmerized by the bearded leader's saga and made contact with the Cuban Consulate in Los Angeles. According to Latell, this prompted the Castro regime to open a dossier on Oswald.

Just a few months before Kennedy's death, Oswald staged in New Orleans, where he was living, several one-man demonstrations representing the pro-Castro Fair Play for Cuba Committee. He scuffled with anti-Castro activists and was briefly arrested. Then in late September 1963, he went to Mexico City to get a visa at the Cuban Consulate to travel to the island, but the visa was not forthcoming.

During his five-night stay in Mexico, reports Latell, Oswald also visited the Soviet Embassy, where he met with "an officer of the notorious Department 13, responsible for assassination and sabotage operations" and for training Cuban intelligence agents.[24]

The CIA, which closely monitored the Cuban and Soviet embassies and consulates in Mexico City, as well as the hotel where most of their visiting agents stayed, was suspicious of Oswald and kept him under surveillance. However, the investigation was abruptly ended. As highlighted by the *Wall Street Journal* editor Mary O'Grady in her November 17, 2013, column, when the US ambassador to Mexico Thomas Mann pushed hard for more information about Oswald's sojourn in the country, his request was surprisingly denied. In his memoir, Mann wrote: "The Embassy received instructions to cease our investigation of Oswald's visit to Mexico and to request that the Mexican government do the same." Mann asked for reconsideration and was turned down.[25]

What accounted for the virtual blackout, which resulted in withholding from the Warren Commission investigating the Kennedy assassination critical information about Oswald's Cuban-Soviet contacts in Mexico and about the CIA–Cubela plot to kill Castro? Was the hush decision made for security reasons, to avoid compromising the CIA and triggering a Cuba casus belli? Was it prompted or influenced by political considerations, to shield the president's legacy and not ruin his brother's political aspirations? Or was it a combination of these and other concerns?

There are still many questions not satisfactorily answered regarding the Cuban connection and whether there was a second gunman involved in the assassination. But pending the release of thousands of JFK assassination records not yet declassified, what appears so far to ring true is Brian Latell's assertion that Fidel Castro was at least aware that Oswald was going to shoot the president.

This was brought to light by Florentino Aspillaga, considered the most valuable defector ever to flee Cuba's DGI intelligence service. He told his CIA debriefer when he escaped in 1987, and recently he told Latell, that the DGI had instructed him shortly before the assassination to drop his routine radio surveillance of the CIA and Cuban exiles and focus on signals from Texas—"any little detail, small detail from Texas," his boss said. And about three hours later, just after midday on November 22, 1963, Aspillaga had something to report that was much more than a small detail: the assassination in Dallas of the president of the United States.[26]

While Aspillaga's testimony and other pieces of information seem to link Castro, at least indirectly, to the crime, no hard evidence has yet surfaced implicating him in the organization of the plot. And yet

President Lyndon Johnson, who was privy to state secrets surrounding Kennedy's tragic death, confided to his friend, journalist Howard Smith, in October 1968, shortly before leaving office: "I'll tell you something that will rock you," he said. "Kennedy was trying to get to Castro, but Castro got to him first." Smith begged for detail, but Johnson refused to provide any, saying only, "It will all come out one day."[27]

Then in September 1969, when Johnson was interviewed for a CBS series about his presidency, Walter Cronkite asked him in connection with Kennedy's assassination if he was satisfied that there was no foreign conspiracy. "I can't honestly say that I've ever been completely relieved of the fact that there might have been international connections," Johnson replied. Cronkite, intrigued by the answer, pointedly asked him if his suspicions involved Cuba. In response, Johnson cautiously said, "Oh, I don't think we ought to discuss the suspicions, because there's not any hard evidence that would lead me to the conclusion that Oswald was directed by a foreign government."

Three weeks before the segment aired, Johnson insisted that the exchange be deleted on grounds of "national security." CBS reluctantly obliged, but in April of 1970 the story that Johnson "expressed fundamental doubts of the Warren Commission's conclusion" during the Cronkite interview leaked out anyway.[28]

In July of 1973, six months after Johnson's death, *The Atlantic* carried an article by Leo Janos, a journalist and former Johnson speechwriter, which refers to Johnson's belief that Kennedy's assassination was the result of a conspiracy organized from Cuba. "I have never believed that Oswald acted alone, although I can accept that he pulled the trigger," he reportedly explained to Janos. Johnson thought such a conspiracy was hatched in retaliation for US plots to assassinate Fidel Castro. Johnson stated that after taking office he had found that the government "had been operating a damned Murder Inc. in the Caribbean."[29]

Joseph Califano, a former high-level government official in the Kennedy and Johnson administrations, who was coordinator of Cuban affairs at the Pentagon, concurred with Johnson's opinion about Castro's complicity in the Kennedy assassination. He wrote in his memoir, "I have come to share LBJ's view [that Castro] 'got him first.' ... Over the years I have come to believe that the paroxysms of grief that tormented Robert Kennedy for years after his brother's death arose, at least in part, from a sense that his efforts to eliminate Castro led to his brother's assassination."[30]

CHAPTER 11

Castro's Détente Game: From Johnson to George H. W. Bush

After John F. Kennedy's assassination, Washington ceased to pursue plans to take out or overthrow Castro and started to wind down covert operations such as commando raids and sabotage to undermine his regime. Without the Soviet strategic missiles, Cuba did not seem to pose any serious threat, so numerous US attempts were made to reach a rapprochement with the Cuban ruler that could lead to normalization of relations or peaceful coexistence. This chapter tells the story of Castro's deceptions and Washington's delusions.

Cuban Americans, myself included, warned Washington that at least as long as Castro's Cuba was subsidized, armed, and protected by Moscow, and as long as it remained a sanctuary for subversion, it would fuel the so-called wars of national liberation against Yankee imperialism in the Americas and beyond.

Faced with the emergence or threats of potential Cubas, US presidents post-Kennedy intervened militarily in several countries but left untouched the principal source of the insurgencies: the Castro-Soviet safe haven in the Caribbean. That's mainly why the Cuban ruler emerged as a dauntless David defying the Goliath of the North, and why his Marxist revolutionary movement, perceived at the time as the wave of the future, spread like a contagious disease to several regions of the world.

Lyndon Johnson (1963–1969)

After John Kennedy's tragic death, the Attwood-Lechuga talks in New York, exploring a possible US-Cuba détente, were put on hold by the National Security Council. President Johnson was concerned about appearing soft on Castro-Communism during the 1964 election.

However, according to Peter Kornbluh, the tenacious Lisa Howard, Fidel's emissary and lover, did not give up. She brought back from Havana in February 1964 a memorandum containing a "verbal message" from Fidel to Johnson. The key points he reportedly conveyed were startling: "Please tell President Johnson that I earnestly desire his election to the presidency in November." He then added: "If the president feels it necessary during the campaign to make bellicose statements about Cuba or even to take some hostile action—if he will inform me, unofficially, that a specific action is required because of domestic political considerations—I shall understand and not take any serious retaliatory action."

Castro also stressed, "I seriously hope that Cuba and the United States can eventually sit down in an atmosphere of goodwill and of mutual respect and negotiate our differences. I believe that there are no areas of contention between us that cannot be discussed and settled in a climate of mutual understanding."[1]

Some historians blame the Johnson administration for having shied away from the seemingly propitious opportunity to break down the barriers to normalizing relations with Communist Cuba. But was Castro really straightforward in his friendly gesture, or was he playing anew a duplicitous game? The facts point to a smoke screen.

While Castro was intoning the alluring song of peaceful coexistence and reconciliation with Yankee imperialism, he was stepping up his campaign to propagate communism through all of Latin America. As disclosed by CIA director McCone before the House Foreign Affairs Subcommittee on March 1, 1963, between one thousand and fifteen hundred Latin Americans had received guerrilla and sabotage training in Cuba in 1962. McCone warned, "Today, the Cuban effort is far more sophisticated, more covert, and more deadly. In its professional trade-craft, it shows guidance and training by experienced Communist advisers from the Soviet bloc, including veteran Spanish Communists."[2]

But the CIA was not the sole source of alarm. The Special Consultative Committee on Security of the Organization of American States (OAS) also had concluded, in its February 8, 1963, report, that the Castro offensive was linked to Moscow's design to further Communist expansion by exploiting the desire of the West to avoid war and by using hidden aggression or subversion—the most effective and "least costly way of acquiring peoples and territories without exaggerated risks."

The OAS report described in detail the techniques used to spur subversion and pinpointed nine training centers in Cuba used to form cadres of men and women "who will dedicate not only their free afternoons to the revolution, but their entire lives."

Although the OAS report raised the level of awareness of the growing threat, the real wake-up call came in November 1963, when a fisherman discovered three tons of war equipment hidden in a place called Macana on the seacoast of Falcón state in Venezuela. The arsenal, which included automatic rifles, bayonets, submachine guns, mortars, and rocket launchers, came from Havana and was to be used for raids by Venezuela's Armed Forces of National Liberation, whose leaders had been trained in Cuba.

Having verified the origin of the arms, the OAS condemned the Castro regime and imposed sanctions in July 1964. Most member states severed diplomatic and economic relations with Cuba. The near-isolation of the island was acclaimed as a breakthrough. Many in Washington thought that the ostracized Castro would wither on the vine or mellow with time. They did not realize that the Soviet Union was not about to abandon its strategic stronghold in the very heart of the Americas.

US Intervention in the Dominican Republic

The next international incident exploited by Castro occurred in the Dominican Republic in April 1965. A breakdown of law and order in the country was rapidly degenerating into a civil war. As described by the respected Brazilian ambassador Ilmar Penna Marinho, "It was a no-man's-land. There had been a complete collapse of public authority. … Arms had been given to a disorganized nation of fanatics and adolescents who were in a frenzied state, egged on by subversive broadcasts. … Anarchy reigned, and any organized group that made a landing in the Dominican Republic could have dominated the situation."[3]

The struggle erupted when soldiers sympathetic to the leftist president Juan Bosch, who had been ousted and was living in exile in Puerto Rico, attempted to overthrow the feckless triumvirate then ruling the country. This resulted in a bloody clash between the right-wing "loyalist" generals and the pro-Bosch "rebels," who were largely inspired by the Cuban Revolution.

The US Embassy in the Dominican Republic feared that Castro, who had in Santo Domingo some forty-five Cuban-trained and well-armed Marxist operatives fanning the flames of rebellion, would try to fill the ensuing power vacuum with support from Havana. Most of Johnson's inner circle didn't buy this alarming report, but the president was determined not to run the risk of having a second Cuba in the Caribbean. Yet he proceeded cautiously, ordering a first wave of only four hundred marines ashore, ostensibly to protect the embassy and facilitate the evacuation of foreign nationals. He soon realized, however, that a tentative, piecemeal approach would not end the bloodshed and stabilize the country.

As noted by Peter Felten, "At a meeting on the morning of April 30, the president complained of being in a bind. He feared a Communist takeover in Santo Domingo if he failed to act decisively, but he worried the United States would be isolated in the hemisphere if he ordered an assault on the rebels."[4]

Following a brief period of zigzagging decisions and confusing public statements, the president dispatched some seventeen thousand troops from the Eighty-Second Airborne Division to Santo Domingo and placed them under the symbolic umbrella of the OAS's Inter-American Peace Force. The OAS cloak served to blunt the charges of US unilateral intervention and gunboat diplomacy.

Concurrently, Johnson stepped up the efforts to find a political solution to the violent crisis with broad support. He ceded the mediation role to an OAS three-member team headed by the US ambassador to the OAS Ellsworth Bunker. The president established general guidelines but did not attempt to micromanage the negotiation.

The settlement orchestrated by the OAS committee was both blessed by Dominican factions and endorsed by the White House. Following a cease-fire, a nonpolitical provisional government took over the country and paved the way for free elections supervised by OAS observers. The clear, indisputable winner over Juan Bosch was Joaquín Balaguer, a mild-mannered, pro-US politician who ushered in a relatively democratic and stable era.

Winding Down Anti-Castro Operations

Having averted a possible Castro-Communist takeover in the Dominican Republic, Johnson proceeded to deemphasize Cuba. After all, he had other, higher priorities to address—his Great Society agenda and Vietnam—and Castro did not seem to pose any further threat. So the president continued winding down all paramilitary operations, including limited sabotage, against the Castro regime.

The Student Revolutionary Directorate, which had played an important role in the Cuban underground movement and in the exile fronts, was one of the first organizations under Johnson that was ordered by the CIA to cease its anti-Castro belligerent activities. José María de Lasa, a twenty-two-year-old Cuban student who later earned a law degree at Yale University and became general counsel of a major multinational corporation, shared with me the inside story of this bitter and unexpected development:

In early 1964, José María was summoned to CIA headquarters in Washington. He was received by then CIA deputy director Richard Helms, whom he had previously met through family connections. After a cordial greeting, Helms told him in no uncertain terms to refrain from launching any further forays; otherwise the students involved would be expelled from the United States.

Back in Miami, José María relayed the stern warning to his colleagues of the Student Revolutionary Directorate. Trying to avoid a head-on confrontation with the agency, they decided to conduct their operation from an offshore base, beyond the jurisdictional bounds of the United States. They were, however, in for a big surprise.

After raising funds at a concert held in Miami, the students obtained authorization from the government of the Dominican Republic to use a small military camp on the island of Catalina, off La Romana. Following several months of drills and preparation, just when the students were about to launch their first assault, the Dominican authorities informed them that because of "pressure from the Americans," they had to abort the operation and dismantle the base.

For José María and his colleagues, this was a stunning blow. It proved to them, without any doubt, that the Kennedy no-invasion pledge, apparently ratified by Johnson, protected Castro from any attacks, even if planned and executed outside the United States. In the words of José María, "Washington had sadly become the custodian of the Soviet satellite in Cuba."

Even the CIA-financed training camps in Central America operated by Manuel Artime, the civilian leader of the Bay of Pigs invasion, and his MRR group would suffer the same fate. They had been allowed by the agency to launch a few raids in 1963–64, but after those forays, their US lifeline was cut and they had to dismantle their camps.

Having determined that it was unnecessary or impracticable to attempt to overthrow or destabilize the Castro regime, Washington's attention shifted to its victims. Back in October 1965, President Johnson had declared "to the people of Cuba that those who seek refuge here in America will find it. The dedication of America to our tradition as an asylum for the oppressed is going to be upheld."

In that spirit, Congress passed in November 1966 the Cuban Adjustment Act, which gave Cuban refugees permission to apply for permanent residence in the United States. That Act, and subsequent legislation, virtually guaranteed an open door to Cubans fleeing the Castro regime. With the extraordinary assistance of humanitarian organizations—mainly the International Rescue Committee—the refugees were provided a most generous safety net, which enabled them to rebuild their lives in a free and prosperous society.

Castro's Global Offensive and Che Guevara's Demise

Meanwhile, the Cuban ruler did not remain idle. In the steadfast pursuit of his hegemonic dream, Fidel founded in Havana on January 3, 1966, the Organization of Solidarity with the Peoples of Asia, Africa, and Latin America (OSPAAL). The avowed purpose was to defend those who were being crushed by the onslaught of globalization, imperialism, and neoliberalism.

According to the Staff Study submitted in 1966 to the Subcommittee on Internal Security of the Senate Judiciary Committee, the five hundred delegates assembled by Castro in Havana from thirty-five countries was "the most powerful gathering of pro-Communist, anti-American forces in the history of the Western Hemisphere."

Castro carried the day with his revolutionary credentials, incendiary rhetoric, and theatrical demeanor. The declarations and resolutions of the conference bore his imprint: "The struggle is to the death. ... The peoples of three continents must reply to imperialist violence with revolutionary violence to safeguard hard-won national independence, as well as to achieve the liberation of the peoples who are fighting to shake off the colonial noose."

In his closing remarks, Castro defiantly proclaimed with a melo-dramatic tone, "The world is big, and the imperialists are everywhere, and for the Cuban revolutionaries the field of battle against imperialism takes in the whole world. ... Hence we declare that Cuban fighters can be counted on by the revolutionary movement in any corner of the earth."[5]

Che Guevara—an unwavering practitioner of the all-out confronta-tional strategy espoused by the conference in Havana—was determined to "create two, three ... many Vietnams." Having resigned his posts in Cuba, he tried in 1965–66 to ignite or buttress radical insurrections in Africa, particularly in the Congo, but was unable to make any signifi-cant headway.

He then turned his sights to a more familiar region, Latin America, and chose Bolivia as his next target. On November 3, 1966, Guevara secretly arrived in La Paz, Bolivia, with a wig and under a false name. He soon started training at a camp in a remote region of the country. His guerrilla force initially numbered fifty and operated as the National Liberation Army of Bolivia. The well-equipped units started to grow and scored a number of early successes against Bolivian Army regulars. But by August 1967 the tide turned against the rebels.

Guevara realized, albeit belatedly, that his Bolivian assumptions, fueled by his feverish imagination, were not well-grounded. The social and agrarian reforms implemented by the national government had brought some relief to the inhabitants of rural areas and mitigated their desire to launch a revolution, or at least to support one spearheaded by a foreigner. As Guevara wrote in his diary, "Peasants do not give us any help, and they are turning into informers."

Not even the leaders of Bolivia's Communist Party and leftist move-ment, which followed Soviet guidelines, stood by Guevara during the struggle. Moscow held that his "adventurism" was counterproductive and was miffed that, amid the Sino-Soviet rift, he had sided with Beijing and openly criticized the Kremlin for advocating a policy of peaceful coexistence with the United States.

But Guevara's belief that the Bolivian Army, ill-prepared to snuff out a guerrilla insurgency on its own, would not be bolstered by the United States was perhaps his most glaring misjudgment. The CIA's Special Activities Division sent to Bolivia a team of commandos and other operatives, including two experienced Cuban exiles, Felix Rodríguez and Gustavo Villoldo, to aid in the hunt for the guerrillas. And the US Army dispatched an elite unit of Green Berets, steeped in jungle warfare, to supply and train the 640-man Second Ranger Battalion of the Bolivian Army.

On October 7, 1967, an informant apprised the Bolivian rangers of the location of the rebels' encampment. Encircled the following day, Guevara and his scant guerrilla force surrendered. "Don't shoot! I am Che Guevara, and I am worth more to you alive than dead," he reportedly shouted as he lay wounded, beset by a severe asthmatic condition, his clothes shredded and his hair matted with dirt.[6]

The US government wanted to take Guevara to Panama for interrogation before being tried, but the Bolivian president at the time, René Barrientos, would have none of that. He feared that the guerrilla warrior would turn a public trial into a Communist propaganda spectacle. On Barrientos's order, Guevara was summarily executed on October 9 and secretly buried in Bolivia.

Fidel Castro, who had had tactical differences with Guevara, possibly combined with a tinge of jealousy, did not evince much interest in supporting or rescuing his embattled comrade in Bolivia. But now, upon learning of his death, he was quick to magnify his epic and glorify him. Better to praise the potential rival dead than alive, the calculating Fidel probably thought.

In his impassioned eulogy on October 18, before a huge crowd in Havana of inflamed mourners, Castro reminisced and rhapsodized: "If we wish to express what we want the men of future generations to be, we must say: Let them be like Che. ... If we want the model of a man who does not belong to our times but to the future, I say from the depths of my heart that such a model, without a single stain on his conduct, is Che."

The legend of a romantic Guevara driven by noble ideals, who sacrificed his life to set free the exploited and the oppressed, was spread by Castro and by the international Communist propaganda network. Those who have fallen for that myth revere the icon, whereas those who witnessed or learned of his heinous crimes, including the execution in La Cabaña fortress of hundreds of Cubans without fair trial, revile the man.

Whether revered or reviled, Guevara stands as an example of cold-hearted consistency, of acting out what he preached. Without remorse or regret, he did what he said a true revolutionary must do: "hate the enemy" without relent, and become "an effective, violent, selective, and cold killing machine."[7]

Richard Nixon (1969–1974)

Cuba was not a major concern when Nixon took office, nor was it viewed as a priority by his administration. The president had other fish to fry: disentangle Vietnam, a war he had inherited that had polarized the nation; reduce tensions with the Soviet Union, initiating a period of détente that led to the signing of an Anti-Ballistic Missile Treaty; and open diplomatic relations with Communist China.

The prevailing view in Washington, following Guevara's demise in Bolivia, was that Moscow, in the spirit of détente, would keep Fidel in check and not provoke any new incident with the United States over Cuba.

The Castro-Communist regime was, therefore, downgraded in the corridors of power from a looming menace to a vexing but manageable nuisance, and all attempts to subvert or overthrow the regime were ended. Whatever was left, if anything, of a regime-change strategy was scrapped, and containment became the paramount objective to avert other Cubas.

Within the exile community, some of us could understand why Cuba did not figure among Nixon's top priorities when he was elected president, but we were surprised and disappointed that he had apparently downplayed or disregarded the danger he himself had flagged after the Cuban Missile Crisis: that the island near our coast could become a Soviet launchpad for espionage, military assaults, and subversion.

After Nixon had lost the race for governor of California and moved to New York, the former prime minister of Cuba, Tony Varona, and I were invited to brief Nixon on lessons learned from the Bay of Pigs and the Missile Crisis. We were told that he was planning to write a paper on the subject and wanted to get our perspective. The meeting took place at the residence in Key Biscayne, Florida, of Nixon's close friend, the banker Charles "Bebe" Rebozo.

I well remember that our interlocutor probed us with incisive questions, took copious notes on his yellow pad, and displayed an impressive command of foreign affairs. Much of what we discussed that day was later sharpened and expanded by Nixon in very clear terms. In April 1964, he told the American Society of Newspaper Editors, "We have goofed an invasion [the Bay of Pigs], paid tribute to Castro for the prisoners [the brigade], then given the Soviets squatters' rights in our backyard."

And in his lucid piece "Cuba, Castro, and John F. Kennedy" carried by *Reader's Digest* on November 5, 1964, Nixon wrote, referring to the Missile Crisis, "The United States pulled defeat out of the jaws of victory." He went on to say, "Weak-kneed foreign policy encouraged the enemy to bolder and bolder action. Shiploads of Soviet arms have continued to pour into Cuba—until today, except for the United States and Canada, the island is the strongest military power in the Western Hemisphere." He also wrote, "For world Communist leaders the battle for Cuba is not about Cuba. It is about Latin America. And the eventual target is the United States."

Did Nixon at the White House dismiss the Cuban threat and pursue the same weak-kneed foreign policy he had keenly criticized? Not for long.

Renewed Military Buildup in Cuba

Moscow took advantage of Washington's Cuba policy shift post–Missile Crisis to resume its military escalation in Cuba. As noted in a well-researched study by Christopher Whalen, an analyst at the Heritage Foundation, the buildup this time was carried out in a tentative and gradual way. Each incremental move was a test; each minor achievement was a precedent to build on.[8]

The arrival in Cuba, in July 1969, of a seven-ship Soviet naval squadron, which included a guided missile carrier, two guided missile destroyers, and a November-class nuclear attack submarine, marked this new chapter of Russian expansionism. For the first time since the Spanish-American War in 1898, the naval force of a rival extracontinental power entered "mare nostrum"—the Caribbean Sea. The submarine did not put into any Cuban ports, but several surface vessels visited the port of Cienfuegos. There was no Washington reaction.

The Soviets then decided to include Cuba in their global naval exercises, Okean-70, and to start flights from Murmansk to Havana of Tu-95 Bear turboprop reconnaissance aircraft. Unchallenged, the aircraft soon conducted from Cuba reconnaissance missions along the East Coast of the United States.

A second naval squadron visited Cuba in May 1970, including an Echo II–class nuclear-powered cruise-missile submarine equipped to carry nuclear warheads. According to the Center for Strategic and International Studies of Georgetown University, "the visit of the nuclear Echo II to Havana is believed to be the first time that a Soviet nuclear attack submarine has entered a non-Russian port."[9] On this visit, the Russian ships openly used Cuban ports for resupply, thus moving another notch in their escalation. Still no Washington reaction.

Then in September 1970, a third Soviet squadron was sighted en route to Cuba. This force, including submarine tenders and a barge to handle nuclear waste, rendezvoused outside Cienfuegos harbor. It was there that the Soviets had been secretly building a submarine base to extend the range of their nuclear-powered fleet. The specter of a US-Soviet confrontation loomed anew.

Although the 1962 Kennedy–Khrushchev agreement on Cuba was "never formally buttoned down" and did not explicitly prohibit a Soviet submarine base in Cuba, Henry Kissinger, Nixon's national security adviser at the time, took the position that such a base violated the 1962 accord. During his tense meeting with Soviet ambassador Anatoly Dobrynin on September 25, 1970, Kissinger's message to Moscow was direct and unambiguous: "We would view it with utmost gravity if construction [of the submarine base] continued," he pointedly warned. Having underscored the seriousness of the crisis, he then told Dobrynin that "it is now up to the Soviets whether to go ... the route of conciliation or the route of confrontation."[10]

The Soviets elected to back down, but not totally. They did not go ahead with the construction of the submarine base and thus avoided a direct clash with the United States. Yet less than three months after the 1970 understanding, another nuclear-powered November-class submarine, accompanied by a Kresta-I guided missile cruiser and a submarine tender, put into Cienfuegos and was serviced. Since then, numerous submarines from the USSR called in Cuban ports and patrolled the southern and eastern coasts of the United States.

While the Nixon administration was wrestling with the Soviet submarine base issue in Cuba, news from Chile jolted the White House. On September 4, 1970, Salvador Allende had won the presidential election in a close three-way race with a plurality of 36.3 percent of the votes cast. He was about to become the first Marxist president, with KGB-Castro ties, to be elected in a Latin American country.

Surprise in Chile

Allende, a Chilean physician born into an upper-middle-class family, had run unsuccessfully for the presidency as a member of the Socialist Party in 1952, 1958, and 1964. As revealed by Vasili Mitrokhin, a Soviet defector who had access to the KGB's foreign intelligence files, the KGB first contacted Allende in 1953. That relationship grew much closer when the Soviet-Chilean diplomatic relations were established in 1964.

The Chilean Communist Party initially viewed Allende as a "weak and inconsistent politician" with Maoist sympathies and a hefty dose of arrogance and desire for glorification. He also had a reputation as a licentious bon vivant. During his visits to Havana in the 1960s, some of Castro's entourage privately mocked him for his bourgeois tastes, fine wines, tailored suits, and elegantly dressed paramours.[11]

Despite those troubling traits, Moscow had confidence in Allende (codenamed LEADER by the KGB) and decided to support him as their best bet to seize power in Chile. The chances for success significantly improved when he ran again for president in 1970. His candidacy was backed by an enlarged left-wing coalition, and the anti-Marxist vote was split between two other contenders.

What perhaps tilted the balance in Allende's favor was the half a million dollars he got through KGB channels. The CIA spent a comparable amount on the campaign but was barred by those in charge of covert action (40 Committee) from supporting any of the candidates opposing Allende. The agency could only alert Chileans to the danger of a Communist takeover.[12]

Allende's narrow victory by only thirty-nine thousand votes out of a total of the three million cast was hailed by a Moscow commentator as "second only to the victory of the Cuban Revolution in the magnitude of its significance as a revolutionary blow to the imperialist system in Latin America."[13]

At the White House, according to Henry Kissinger, "Nixon was beside himself" when he heard the news. Having excoriated the

Democrats for over a decade for allowing Cuba to go Communist, he himself now faced the same prospect in Chile.[14] Richard Helms, CIA director, blamed Nixon and Kissinger for failing to heed his calls for covert action: "It was their own damn fault for letting things go until it was too late."[15] Nixon, writes Kissinger, now insisted on "doing something, anything, that would reverse the previous neglect."[16]

Agustin Edwards, owner of the leading newspaper in Chile (*El Mercurio*), played an important role in alerting Nixon to the ominous consequences of an Allende takeover. I knew the amiable and talented Agustin well, since at the invitation of PepsiCo's CEO Donald Kendall, he joined the company where I was working. He and I spoke at length about the Castro-Communist penetration in Latin America.

As disclosed by Kissinger in his memoirs, after Edwards met with Nixon at the White House on September 14, the president told Helms that he wanted a major effort to see what could be done to prevent Allende's accession to power.

Under great pressure from the president, the CIA developed two covert courses of action. The first one (denoted as Track I) involved the Chilean congress. Since no presidential candidate had won an overall majority, Chile's constitution mandated that a joint session of its congress choose between the two candidates who had garnered most votes. The task was to persuade enough members of congress to vote into office not the front runner (Allende) but the candidate who had come in second (Jorge Alessandri). The other course of action (Track II) called for engineering a military coup.

According to Helms, Nixon ordered both tracks to be followed simultaneously, despite the reservations of the CIA's station chief in Santiago, who warned, "Parameter of action is exceedingly narrow[,] and available options are quite limited." In a follow-up message to Washington, he added, "Urge you do not convey impression that station has sure-fire method for halting, let alone triggering, coup attempts."[17]

Nixon and Kissinger offered their respective versions of this episode. The president stated in his memoirs that having been "informed that our efforts were probably not going to be successful ... I instructed the CIA to abandon the operation."[18] He seemed to be referring to the coup attempt. Kissinger, for his part, asserted in his memoirs that Track II was "terminated by me" on October 15.[19]

The fact is that both tracks either were aborted or failed to materialize, and Allende was confirmed as president by the national congress on October 24, 1970. As a result, Chile became an important theater of the Cold War. Moscow and Havana would try hard to consolidate their momentous gain, and Washington would seize every opportunity to thwart it.

During the first year of Allende's term in office, things seemed to be going his way. With his class warfare rhetoric, combined with agrarian reform, the nationalization of industries, and heavy spending, he was able to boost GDP growth by nearly 8 percent and fire up large swaths of the population. The Kremlin was pleased with the initial implementation of Allende's socialist agenda and continued to provide guidance and substantial funding to his government.

Castro also lent Allende his full support and carefully planned a grandiose trip to Chile to bolster him. Like a Roman proconsul, Fidel arrived in Santiago in November 1971 with a large retinue of bodyguards, intelligence officers, and government aides and turned his state visit into a three-week nonstop roving spectacle.

He visited nine provinces and rallied the workers, incited the farmers, and aroused the students. But not all was show and harangue. Under the radar screen, Fidel strengthened Allende's Praetorian Guard—the black beret Grupo de Amigos Personales—mainly comprising an elite Cuban paramilitary force of proven loyalty to the Communist cause.[20]

By early 1971, the economy began to turn against Allende, and the situation got worse the following year. Productivity had fallen, growth had virtually vanished, and the world market price of copper—Chile's main source of income—had collapsed. Since Allende's election in 1970, Chile's currency had been devalued on the open market by a stunning 10,000 percent.

The CIA could not take credit for "making the [Chilean] economy scream" as instructed by Nixon; the crisis was mainly triggered or aggravated by Allende's dismal policies. But the agency did take advantage of the ensuing malaise, fomenting angry protests that destabilized the government and paved the way for the military coup.[21]

The KGB started to downgrade Allende's prospects of survival. They pointed to his "distractions"—frequent carousing as an inveterate womanizer. Although married, he had a collection of mistresses, but his favorite seemed to be his personal secretary, code-named MARTA by the KGB. There were reports of orgies held in a hideaway outside Santiago where Allende and other lecherous bigwigs and their courtesans watched sex films and cavorted.[22]

But what worried the KGB the most was not Allende's dissipated life; it was his inability to purge the armed forces and security system and to bring them under his control. He was also criticized for his reluctance to crush the opponents who were stirring unrest. These deficiencies, the KGB highlighted, increased his vulnerability to a military coup.

Sure enough, irate protests escalated in 1973, along with several waves of strikes by truckers, among others. To complicate matters for the president, the opposition won the parliamentary elections held in March, and soon thereafter the congress declared that Allende's flagrant violations of the charter had given rise to a "constitutional breakdown," which called for appropriate action to restore law and order.

The stage had been set for the overthrow of the regime. Allende had declared that "if the hour comes, the people will have arms." By that he meant that he would mobilize militias and left-wing paramilitary groups if faced with an army revolt. The hour came, however, and he failed to live up to his promise.

The CIA certainly had sown the seeds of regime change, but the agency apparently learned of the coup only two days before it was launched and was not directly involved in the planning or execution of the overthrow.[23]

When General Pinochet and his military junta rolled the tanks on September 11, 1973, Allende entrenched himself in his presidential offices, defended by only fifty to sixty of his mostly Cuban Praetorian Guard and half a dozen officers from the Servicio de Investigaciones. Faced with inevitable defeat, Allende reportedly sat on a sofa of his office, placed the muzzle of an automatic rifle (a gift from Castro) beneath his chin, and blew his brains out.[24] (There is, however, a different account of Allende's death. According to several Cuban exiles with intelligence background and links, the Chilean president was shot by one of Castro's guards when he was about to surrender to the military.)

In the context of the Cold War, the overthrow of Allende's regime by the anti-Communist military junta was viewed as a victory by those who did not camp with the Soviets and with Castro. A second Cuba, with Chilean characteristics, had been averted. But the victory was not damage-free. It left in its wake a political casualty: the temporary eclipse of democracy.

This was the same fate of Argentina, Brazil, Uruguay, and other Latin American countries: when assailed by the Castro-Communist onslaught, they could not find a better option than military dictatorships. Democracy was not strong enough to fend off the threat and survive.

▌ Gerald Ford (1974–1977)

The spirit of détente, which led to the opening of China and the lessening of tensions with the Soviet Union, lived on after Nixon's resignation. It prompted his successor, Gerald Ford, to make a serious attempt to put behind the "perpetual antagonism" between the United States and Cuba. The goal was to remove the obstacles that had impeded the normalization of relations. Past failures did not deter a further try.

This new rapprochement was actually initiated by Secretary of State Henry Kissinger late in the Nixon administration. Congressional pressure to turn over a new leaf on Cuba was mounting. Senators

William Fulbright, Frank Church, and Edward Kennedy, among others, had introduced legislation to lift unilaterally the US embargo on Cuba.

In addition, several Latin American governments wanted to rescind the multilateral diplomatic and economic sanctions imposed by the OAS on Cuba. They believed that Castro-Communist subversion was a thing of the past. In any case, they argued, it was better to bring the chief instigator (Castro) back to the fold than to keep him out.

Still, Cuba remained a controversial political issue in the United States, so Kissinger guardedly looked for an intermediary to make initial contacts with the Castro regime (as President Kennedy had done with journalist Lisa Howard following the Missile Crisis). The choice this time was Frank Mankiewicz, a freelance journalist and former spokesman for Robert Kennedy who had recently shot a documentary on Cuba for CBS and was returning to Havana to interview Castro and write a book for Playboy Press.[25]

According to Kissinger, Nixon was not enthusiastic about the emissary, but he went along with a message to Castro along these lines: "America in principle was prepared to improve relations [with Cuba] on the basis of reciprocal measures agreed in confidential discussions ... and was willing to show our goodwill by making symbolic first moves." The message stressed that "any substantial progress would depend on the strictest reciprocity on the part of Cuba."[26]

Castro, who enjoyed playing the diplomatic game when it suited him, promptly responded with finesse. He asked Mankiewicz to bring back to Kissinger a box of Cuban cigars, courtesy of Fidel, along with a message expressing interest in a "relaxing of tensions."[27]

A preliminary meeting was held on January 11, 1975, at a cafeteria in New York, by Deputy Undersecretary of State Lawrence Eagleburger with two Castro representatives: Ramón Sánchez Parodi, a senior official of the Cuban Communist Party, and Néstor García, first secretary of Cuba's UN mission.[28] This was followed by a substantive discussion on July 9 at the Pierre Hotel in Manhattan, led by Assistant Secretary of State for Inter-American Affairs William Rogers, who covered some of the steps approved by Secretary of State Henry Kissinger to relax tensions, phase out the embargo, and normalize relations.[29]

After touching on several not-too-controversial issues like the release of eight Americans held in Cuban prison and giving the green light for family visits in both directions, the US delegation raised sensitive matters but toned them down to avoid early clashes. These included a reasonable limit to the continued Soviet military buildup in Cuba; restraint in the Castro regime's campaign calling for Puerto Rico's independence; containment of subversive activities in other countries; and compensation for US properties confiscated by the regime. (Discussion of potential break points, such as respect for human rights, transition to democracy, and nonalignment with the Soviet bloc, was left for subsequent meetings.)

As expected, the Castro delegates raised their own issues and demands, such as the lifting of the US embargo; payment of damages to Cuba; the end of CIA conspiracies, and the return of the US base of Guantánamo.[30] But they did not engage in diatribes or walk out of the meeting. The members of the US delegation were quite satisfied with the results of the discussion and felt there was room for negotiation and ultimate compromise.

Eager to clinch a deal with Castro, the Ford administration offered several inducements to the Cuban ruler without any quid pro quo. First, the United States voted in favor of the July 29, 1975, OAS resolution, effectively ending the multilateral diplomatic and economic sanctions against the Castro regime. Then on August 19, President Ford eased the US embargo, allowing foreign subsidiaries of US companies to trade with Cuba, dropping foreign aid penalties on countries trading with the island, and permitting ships en route to Cuba to refuel in the United States.

▌ Castro's Military Airlift to Angola

Clearly, Washington went out on a limb with these unilateral concessions, but the ultimate goal of engaging Castro in constructive negotiations seemed well worth the wooing. So what was the Cuban dictator's response? Not quite what the White House was expecting. He brazenly airlifted to Angola, with Soviet assistance, thousands of Cuban combat troops to support the Marxist-dominated Popular Movement for the Liberation of Angola (MPLA), which seized control of most of the country following independence.

This was not an isolated foray into Africa since Castro had previously shipped arms, troops, and guerrilla instructors to bolster Communist movements in Algeria, Guinea, Somalia, Congo, Mozambique, and Malawi. But the involvement in Angola was not just a token or small-scale military intervention. It was an outright invasion.

According to Cuba's Communist newspaper *Granma*, at the crest of the 1975–76 war in Angola, Cuba had thirty-six thousand troops in that country, commanded by Division General Abelardo Colomé.[31] "In relation to Cuba's population of 9.4 million" (at the time), noted professor Jorge I. Domínguez, "these troops were the equivalent of a US deployment of over eight hundred thousand troops, more than the United States had in Vietnam at the peak of that war."[32]

What accounted for Castro's startling provocation while Washington was earnestly trying to reach an accommodation with him? Some scholars and historians, particularly those who tend to give Fidel a pass, argue that the United States did not go far enough with its concessions. Others contend that it was unrealistic, if not delusional, to think that Castro would trade his leading role as an intractable Marxist-Leninist revolutionary, propped up with massive Soviet aid, for a rapprochement with "Yankee imperialism."

But what is indisputable is that Secretary of State Henry Kissinger tried in good faith to break the impasse with Communist Cuba as he had done with Red China and the Soviet Union, but instead of reciprocating, Havana's master of deceit rebuffed Washington's honest offer of détente.

President Ford ended this ill-starred overture, declaring to the press on December 20, 1975, that "the action of the Cuban government in sending combat troops to Angola destroys any opportunity for improvement in relations with the United States. They have made a choice. It, in effect, and I mean very literally, has precluded any improvement in relations with Cuba."[33]

Yet the president's emphatic statement did not really end this episode. After a new attempt to reopen negotiations with Cuba fizzled out without producing any positive results, Kissinger pondered his next move. He felt that the United States had to respond to Castro's brazen and humiliating challenge in Angola.

There were also internal political considerations in play. The Ford administration's conciliatory Cuba policy had become a hot issue during the 1976 presidential campaign and had placed Ford on the defensive. Conservatives led by Ronald Reagan characterized the policy as an iteration of failed détente.

Kissinger's main concern, however, transcended politics. He posited, "If there is a perception overseas that we are so weakened by our internal debate so that it looks like we can't do anything about a country of eight million people, then in three or four years we are going to have a real crisis." Kissinger argued that Castro's Cuba needed to be stopped in Africa. Otherwise, he asserted, Rhodesia and Namibia would be next, and possibly later South Africa.[34]

As revealed by William M. LeoGrande and Peter Kornbluh, drawing on recently declassified documents, Kissinger concluded that contingency plans to "clobber" Castro's Cuba had to be prepared. With President Ford's approval, he convened on March 24, 1976, a small team of national security officials, including Secretary of Defense Donald Rumsfeld, the CIA's deputy director Vernon Walter, and National Security Adviser Brent Scowcroft.

The team, known as the "special action group," was tasked with developing political, economic, and military plans "to move against Cuba" in response to any further intervention in Africa or Latin America. The basic objective was to "prevent the creation of a pattern of international conduct in which Cuba and the USSR arrogate to themselves the right to intervene with combat troops in local or regional conflict."[35]

By mid-April, the Cuban contingency plans had been drafted. They outlined possible options, such as deterrence (involving punitive, economic, and political measures), cease and desist, interdiction, and military retaliation. These last two included blockade, air strikes to destroy selected Cuban military targets, and invasion.

The possible consequences of US military intervention in Cuba were discussed at length by the team. Kissinger's aides pointed out, "A Cuba/Soviet response could escalate in areas that would maximize US casualties and thus provoke [a] stronger response. The circumstances that could lead the United States to select a military option against Cuba should be serious enough to warrant further action in preparation for general war."[36]

Given the ominous warning of a potential superpower confrontation if US force were used in Cuba, the contingency plan, including the nonmilitary options, was tabled. Absent any meaningful deterrent, Castro and the Kremlin geared up for yet another African foray. Since Ford was not reelected in November, that became one of Jimmy Carter's predicaments.

Jimmy Carter (1977–1981)

Carter was not discouraged by the Ford administration's failure to achieve a rapprochement with Castro. He felt confident that with a more open, congenial, and flexible approach, he could pierce the veil of distrust and induce the Cuban dictator to accept a harmonious modus vivendi.

Toward Normalization of Relations

On March 15, 1977, shortly after he took office, Carter signed a classified presidential directive that stated unambiguously, "I have concluded that we should attempt to achieve normalization of our relations with Cuba."[37]

With that goal in mind, the president took three major steps in just six months, from March to September 1977. He lifted the sixteen-year ban on travel to Cuba, basically accepted the fishing and maritime boundaries proposed by the Castro regime, and agreed to the opening of Interest Section offices—quasi embassies—in Havana and Washington.

This new Cuba policy seemed inconsistent with Carter's overarching commitment to human rights. He had upbraided the military dictatorships of Argentina and Chile for violations of civil liberties, and now he was accommodating the most egregious violator: the Castro regime.

Even famous international writers who had fervently supported Castro, like Jean-Paul Sartre, Susan Sontag, Mario Vargas Llosa, Octavio Paz, and Jorge Edwards, had broken with him when he arrested the Cuban poet Heberto Padilla in 1971 for having mildly criticized literary intransigence within the government bureaucracy. Castro detained Padilla and forced him to repent publicly and denounce some of his confreres.

This "Padilla Affair" marked a redoubling of repression, not only against political dissidents but also against intellectuals deemed ideological deviationists. Castro had earlier warned Cuban journalists, writers, and thinkers of his dogmatic rule: "Everything within the revolution; nothing outside the revolution." And the prohibited "outside the revolution" sternly applied to both politics and culture.

Cuban exiles were furious with Carter's perceived appeasement of Castro. A few of the extreme militants resorted to violence, setting off bombs near the Soviet Embassy in Washington and on the premises of an airline scheduling flights to Cuba. But most of the exiles, while fuming, were respectful of US laws and vented their anguish and anger in peaceful demonstrations, statements to the press, and letters to the president.

Perhaps the letter that got the most attention came from Juanita Castro, Fidel's undaunted sister who was living in exile in Miami. In her missive to the president, she warned him not to cozy up to her cruel and deceitful brother, and poignantly added: "At the beginning of your War of Independence in 1775, Benjamin Franklin wrote to his old friend in England, William Straham: 'Look upon your hands! They are stained with the blood of your relations!' Mr. President, I submit that your decision in this matter [normalizing relations with Castro] might well determine if you will ever again be able to look at yours."[38]

Carter felt that Juanita's letter warranted a reply. At the president's request, National Security Adviser Zbigniew Brzezinski assured her that the administration was just "seeking to determine whether relations with Cuba can be improved on a measured and reciprocal basis."[39]

Within the Carter administration, some believed that the subsequent release by Castro of some three thousand political prisoners, negotiated by a committee led by Cuban American banker Bernardo Benes, with Washington's discreet support, was a clear sign that Fidel was reciprocating Carter's overture.

Exiles in Miami were divided on this issue, but most of them strongly rejected the notion of a breakthrough in US-Cuba relations. Although happy that prisoners unjustly incarcerated had been released, they warned that Castro's seemingly humanitarian gesture was a ploy to gain legitimacy and numb the United States into inertia or complacency. Nothing has fundamentally changed in Cuba, the unflinching exiles cried out. The Castro regime's totalitarian apparatus designed to crush dissent remains intact, they asserted, and its dreadful prisons are still geared up for new tenants.

▌*Ethiopia Foray*

There was indeed some complacency toward Castro in the State Department. Our diplomats did not seem particularly alarmed by Cuba's 1977 foray, jointly with the Soviet Union, into yet another African country, Ethiopia. As a result of this impassive attitude, a clash ensued between Secretary of State Cyrus Vance and National Security Adviser Zbigniew Brzezinski. Vance held that the so-called Ethiopian crisis was a local incident triggered by a territorial dispute between two African nations, whereas Brzezinski maintained that the issue could mushroom into an international conflict with geopolitical implications.

Anticipating the influx of Cuban soldiers and Soviet war matériel to Ethiopia, Brzezinski warned that if Ethiopia and South Yemen were to link up with Moscow, access to the Suez Canal could be threatened. Given this potential risk, Brzezinski recommended the deployment of an aircraft carrier to the area as a show of US force.[40]

Brzezinski was very much alone in his advocacy of a strong stance in Ethiopia. Wayne S. Smith, who oversaw Cuban affairs at State at the time, displaying what Jeane Kirkpatrick called a "Blame America First" proclivity, sharply criticized Brzezinski for his alleged "irresponsible rhetoric and his loose cannon approach to foreign policy."[41] And Secretary Vance, evincing uncharacteristic bursts of temper, flatly rejected any show of force in the Horn of Africa that could put US prestige on the line.[42]

In the course of heated discussions, Brzezinski cautioned that lack of a meaningful US response to deter or restrain the Soviets and their Cuban proxies in Africa and elsewhere could jeopardize not only the desired détente but also a high foreign policy priority of the Carter administration: the ratification by the Senate of SALT II—the Limitation of Strategic Offensive Missiles Treaty to be signed by Carter and General Secretary of the Central Committee of the Communist Party Leonid Brezhnev.

Brzezinski lost this battle, but the ensuing developments gave credence to his concerns. By February 1978, Cuban troops in Ethiopia had increased to ten thousand or eleven thousand; Moscow had sent there four hundred tanks and some fifty MiG jet fighters; and the first deputy commander in chief of Soviet ground forces, Petrov, was the one providing direction for the Ethiopian military operations.[43]

On May 25, 1978, Carter felt compelled to declare, "There is no possibility that we would see any substantial improvement in our relationship with Cuba as long as [its government] is committed to this military intrusion into the [internal] affairs of the African people."[44]

▌ *The Soviet Combat Brigade in Cuba*

There were other nails in the coffins of Cuban détente and of SALT II. One of these was the disturbing news, leaked in November 1978, that the Soviets had shipped to Cuba MiG-23 fighter-bombers, which could potentially be reconfigured for a nuclear role. Much more serious, however, was the subsequent report of a Soviet combat brigade in Cuba. US intelligence agencies knew that Moscow had stationed on the island several thousand military personnel to advise and train Castro's army. But the encampment in Cuba of an actual three-thousand-strong motorized Soviet brigade with headquarters and readiness to strike, if necessary, seemed to have caught Washington by surprise and created quite a stir in the Senate.

Thinking that the United States had no real leverage to induce Moscow to back down short of threatening military action, the president in his televised address on October 1, 1979, tried to deemphasize the implications of the brigade, indicating that such a small force, with no airborne or seaborne capability, posed no threat to the United States.

Then, in an effort to salvage the SALT II treaty signed in June 1979, the president stated that "the brigade issue is ... no reason for a return to the Cold War. ... The greatest danger to American security is the breakdown of a common effort to preserve the peace, and the ultimate threat of a nuclear war." Carter ended his remarks by making an impassioned plea to the Senate to ratify SALT II, but to no avail. The treaty was doomed.[45]

The Mariel Exodus

The Mariel exodus, masterminded by Castro, was another incident that jolted the Carter administration. It was set off in April 1980 when a handful of desperate Cubans trying to flee the country crashed into the former residence of my wife's great-uncle in Havana, occupied by the Peruvian Embassy. When the ambassador refused to surrender those who had sought asylum to the Cuban authorities, Fidel exploded and said something like, "If you people want to leave, go ahead and leave! Everyone who wants to leave, go to the Peruvian Embassy."

Within hours, some ten thousand men, women, and children thronged the courtyard and spacious garden of the embassy. The police had to cordon off the area because there were thousands more trying to get in.[46]

Had Castro lost his mind in a rage? Not so. His emotional outburst seemed irrational, but the actions he took were coldly devised and meticulously carried through. Aware of the restlessness in the country, beset by stagnancy, repression, and despair, Fidel needed a safety valve to release tensions. The embassy incident (contrived or not) served him well to stage a mass exodus. After encouraging the Cubans to break into the Peruvian Embassy, he himself publicly announced, "All those who want to leave [the island], go to the docks at Mariel" (a port west of Havana).

About one hundred twenty-five thousand people flooded the Mariel area before it was shut off. A "freedom flotilla," composed mainly of small, leaky boats manned by Cuban exiles from Miami, came to the rescue of relatives and friends. Most of the refugees belonged to the working class—poor fishermen, state tillers, laborers: the very Cubans Castro had promised to save from "capitalist exploiters" and "Yankee imperialism."

Among the refugees who were sealifted, Fidel infiltrated several thousand ex-convicts, misfits, and spies—a malicious surprise that angered and embarrassed the Carter administration. But more serious than that was the implied warning embedded in the exodus itself—an unspoken Castro warning that overhanged the United States like a sword of Damocles: "If you continue to blockade our country with economic sanctions, we'll unleash an even bigger mass exodus that will overwhelm Florida."

Amid the Mariel exodus that rattled Carter's administration and may have contributed to his reelection defeat, the president did not confront Castro but rather offered him a deal if he would close Mariel and end the migration crisis with US cooperation. Carter would then be prepared to hold bilateral negotiations in the first quarter of 1981 to address all major issues with the ultimate goal of lifting the US embargo and normalizing relations between the two countries.

According to William M. LeoGrande and Peter Kornbluh, the offer was first conveyed to Castro in Havana by Paul Austin, CEO of the Coca-Cola Company, who apparently exceeded the terms of the White House offer, and subsequently by Peter Tarnoff, executive assistant to the secretary of state, who set the record straight. Both returned to Washington buoyed by Castro's seemingly positive frame of mind, which was not put to the test because of the president's electoral defeat. Yet to this day Carter regrets not having been more flexible with Castro and established full diplomatic relations with Cuba.

Who Lost Nicaragua?

Carter ended his presidency facing major crises not only in Iran and Afghanistan but also in Central America with the emergence in Nicaragua of a Marxist–Sandinista government linked to the Castro regime and intent on subverting neighboring countries.

There are those who lay the blame for "losing" Nicaragua squarely on Carter's dithering. This skewed accusation is unfair as there is

enough blame to go around. No one is more culpable than the dictator Anastasio Somoza, who obstructed a democratic transition.
The non-Sandinista opposition and the governments of several Latin
American countries, particularly Costa Rica, Venezuela, and Panama,
also share responsibility for eventually joining or supporting the insurrection led by the radicals. And the Carter administration bears blame
for belatedly and half-heartedly attempting to avert the Sandinista
takeover without any show of force or credible clout.

The inside story of this unfortunate development was shared with
me by Washington's man in Managua during the critical 1977–79 period, Ambassador Mauricio Solaún. A short, dark-haired, unassuming
scholar who peppers his intellectual acuity with dashes of wit and
banter, Solaún was born and raised in Cuba. He studied law in Havana,
earned an MA degree in economics at Yale University and a PhD in
sociology at the University of Chicago, and for ten years was professor
of sociology at the University of Illinois.

Given my long-standing friendship with Mauricio, which goes back
to our college years at the University of Villanueva in Havana, I asked
him point-blank: Considering his Cuban experience, was he truly unable to detect the Marxist ideology or tendency of the Sandinista leaders
and their road map to seize power? Mauricio told me that he was well
aware of the danger, but his hands were tied.

This is how he described his predicament. "I was to be a catalyst
for change [pressing human rights] amid increasing turmoil, but I was
forbidden to mediate the crisis, steer the process, and help to avert a
political vacuum that could be filled by the radicals."[47]

Robert A. Pastor, director of Latin American and Caribbean affairs
on the National Security Council from 1977 to 1981, seemed to concur
with Solaún's portrayal of his quandary in Managua. Pastor wrote,
"There was a special poignancy in Solaún's service in Nicaragua. As
a Cuban American, he, more than anyone, knew the cycle of events
that had led to Castro's triumph and wanted to avoid a repetition. Yet

Solaún could do little as he watched the worst-case scenario unfold before his eyes."[48]

The ambassador's primary goal in Nicaragua, as outlined by the State Department, was to "promote democratization and improvement in the human rights situation while maintaining neutrality." The initial impact of his human rights thrust was encouraging. Somoza lifted the state of siege imposed at the end of 1974 and allowed the civic opposition to be more vocal in criticizing the dictator and calling for reforms.

However, a tragic event occurred that inflamed the nation. On January 10, 1978, Pedro Joaquín Chamorro, the director of the newspaper *La Prensa* and one of the most prestigious anti-Somoza civic leaders, was shot dead as he drove to his office. Most of the enraged population held the dictator responsible for the assassination without hard evidence. Mass demonstrations, strikes, and violent clashes with the police rocked the major cities, and the Committee of National Dialogue canceled the meeting with Somoza.

Under those unsettling circumstances, the moderate opposition leaders hoped that the United States would weigh in to help arbitrate the power struggle and prevent chaos. But Ambassador Solaún was again instructed by the State Department not to meddle in the internal affairs of Nicaragua.

Since the ambassador was barred by Washington from taking an overt stance or even playing a mediation role, he privately approached Somoza's respected uncle Luis Manuel Debayle in the hope that he might persuade his nephew to foster an orderly path to the rule of law and elections before it was too late. Given the growing opposition to the dictatorship from all quarters, Solaún stressed that, in his view, not as ambassador but as a friend of Nicaragua, the status quo would not likely hold through 1981.

Somoza was fuming when he summoned Solaún to his office. "What is this message that you have sent me through my uncle," he sputtered, "that the Nicaraguans accuse me of being a dictator and have turned against me … and that the Somoza dynasty has to end before 1981?"

The ambassador let Somoza blow off steam and calmly explained why it behooved him to seek a political solution to the acute crisis that was convulsing the nation. He then touched on the delicate subject of the dictatorship. With disarming frankness (which Somoza occasionally accepted and even enjoyed), Solaún quipped with a roguish smile: "I know you don't like to hear about the dictatorship. But after all, Mr. President, with all due respect, you *are* a dictator." More surprised than annoyed by the blunt remark, Somoza dropped his pretense and chuckled.[49]

Solaún's unconventional approach produced some positive results. In June 1978, Somoza announced a series of liberalization measures that included the amnesty of some political prisoners, an invitation to the OAS Human Rights Commission to conduct a survey in Nicaragua, and guarantees for the safe return of an elite exiled group of nonradical Nicaraguans known as the Twelve who were backing the Sandinistas.

Then, instead of keeping the pressure on Somoza to make sure he honored his promises and shortened his term, the White House made an incredible about-face and decided to send a letter of appreciation to the dictator over Carter's signature. Solaún objected to the letter on the grounds that it would send the wrong signals to Somoza, but he was overruled.

The letter was leaked to the *Washington Post*, which published on August 1 a front-page article headlined "Carter Letter to Somoza Stirs Human Rights Row." The lead paragraph read: "President Carter, overriding State Department objections, has sent a personal letter congratulating Nicaraguan president Anastasio Somoza for promises to improve the human rights situation in his country." The article concluded that the human rights policy "seemed to veer back and forth, drawing charges that its policy toward Somoza is confusing, inconsistent, and ineffective."[50]

In Nicaragua, the word spread that Carter had sold out to Somoza.

Three weeks later, on August 22, the Sandinistas raided the national palace and captured the fifteen hundred people in it. Somoza, who was away, decided not to storm the palace and gave in to most of the Sandinistas' demands, including the release of fifty-nine political prisoners, the payment of $500,000 in cash, and the publication in the newspapers of the rebels' call to arms to overthrow the Somoza dictatorship.

As a result of the successful commando-type assault on the palace and Somoza's seeming capitulation, the insurrection led by the Sandinistas gained momentum. They soon were able to propel guerrilla attacks and popular uprisings in four major cities of the country.

In December 1978, following the failure of a mediation initiative sponsored by the United States, Castro started to play a more visible role in the struggle. He unified the three factions of the Sandinista Front meeting in Havana and persuaded them to accept a Marxist hard-liner, Tomás Borge, as the coordinator of the amalgamated Sandinista forces. Between late May and July 19, 1979, Castro shipped to the guerrillas in Nicaragua, via Costa Rica, a large amount of arms in twenty-one flights.[51]

In June, after the Sandinista offensive had peaked, Carter finally decided to end his "noninterventionist policy" toward Nicaragua. Hoping to secure broad support for collective action, the United States advocated the creation of an OAS peacekeeping force that would ease out or remove Somoza, ensure the cessation of hostilities, and help to establish a provisional government of national reconciliation that would hold free elections.

The precedent was the 1965 OAS peacekeeping force that stabilized the Dominican Republic during Lyndon Johnson's presidency. But there was one salient difference: Johnson obtained the reluctant support of the OAS only after he had deployed US troops to Santo Domingo, whereas Carter ruled out any US unilateral armed intervention. Not surprisingly, Carter's feckless proposal was resoundingly rejected by the OAS.

Absent a strong US stance backed by boots on the ground, most of the moderate opposition sectors in Nicaragua, as well as the leaders of Venezuela, Costa Rica, and Panama, cast their lot with the Sandinistas. And when both the OAS and the United States finally called for the immediate and definitive end of the Somoza dynasty—an ultimatum no longer couched in diplomatic language—the dictator resigned and left the country on July 17, 1979.

However, the caretaker government that replaced the Somoza regime with some moderates on board was short-lived, and the demoralized national guard collapsed after most of its chiefs left the country and went into exile. The political and military vacuum that ensued enabled the Sandinista junta to seize effective control of the country without much difficulty.

While the Sandanista takeover in Nicaragua was not precisely a carbon copy of the Castro ascent in Cuba ten years earlier, ominous signs were similar. The Sandinistas began to build a powerful army and repressive system, and some of the hard-liners holding key positions in the junta did not conceal their Marxist-Leninist tendency and hatred of Yankee imperialism. Their hearts were clearly with Fidel, who covertly shipped Soviet arms to Managua, along with military advisers to train the soldiers and schoolteachers to indoctrinate the students.

Still, the Carter administration decided to give the Sandinistas the benefit of the doubt. This seemed to be the White House's rationale, or mirage, to engage them: "Whether the Sandinistas were Communists or not, perhaps it would be better to treat them like Democrats, and maybe the Sandinistas—or rather some of the key leaders—might even begin to behave like Democrats. As they dealt with the hard realities of governing ... the new Nicaraguan leadership might come to realize that the United States and the Nicaraguan private sector had more to offer than Cuba or [Marxist] ideology."[52]

Imbued with wishful thinking, Carter invited Daniel Ortega, the Sandinista leader, and other members of the governing coalition to the White House in September 1979. In the course of the cordial conversation, Ortega told the president that they would welcome "frank and unconditional support from the United States." He also stressed that their principal task was reconstruction and that they "were not a factor in the radicalization of El Salvador ... or of Guatemala."[53]

Confident that US relations with the Sandinistas could improve by offering them more incentives, Carter increased the economic aid to Nicaragua up to $100 million in humanitarian assistance, loans, and grants. But in January 1981, shortly before the inaugural of President-Elect Ronald Reagan, Carter's rapprochement fell through.

US intelligence reports, backed by aerial photography, revealed that the Sandinista government was providing significant amounts of arms and military equipment to the radical insurgents in El Salvador. The shipments, which originated in Havana, were made from Managua by boat, by land (through Honduras), and by air.

This conclusive and alarming evidence forced the president to suspend aid to Nicaragua—a recognition that his attempt to normalize relations with the Sandinistas had failed, and a further embarrassment to his beleaguered administration, struggling in the final hours of his presidency to obtain the release of the American hostages in Iran.

Ronald Reagan (1981–1989)

When Reagan took office, he quickly became aware that a major immediate threat to US security lay in Soviet-Cuban expansionism in our backyard: Central America.

A few days prior to his first press conference, Reagan had received reliable intelligence confirming that the Soviet Union was providing the arms that were being shipped through Cuba and then distributed by Nicaragua's Sandinista National Liberation Front to radical guerrillas in El Salvador.

▌ *The Rising Threat*

The president clearly understood the grave geopolitical implications. "Although El Salvador was the immediate objective, the evidence showed that the Soviets and Fidel Castro were targeting all of Central America for a Communist takeover. El Salvador and Nicaragua were only a down payment. Honduras, Guatemala, and Costa Rica were next and then would come Mexico."[54]

To sound the alarm, Reagan authorized in February 1981 the release of evidence of Soviet-Cuban involvement in a white paper. This indictment, along with a credible show of will and power to thwart the Communist attempt to subvert the region from Nicaragua, marked a sharp departure from Carter's accommodation policy. As noted by Robert Pastor, "The Carter administration had tried to paste the mask of democracy on the Sandinistas' face, [whereas] the Reagan administration tried to remove the mask and show the world they were really Communists."[55]

Early in March, CIA director William J. Casey presented to Reagan and his national security team a covert plan to counter the Soviet advance in the Third World. It included a $19 million US-funded operation to defend El Salvador against a Communist takeover by halting the flow of arms from Nicaragua to the insurgents. "If we can't stop Soviet expansionism in a place like Nicaragua," argued Casey, "where the hell can we?"[56] This plan was approved by the president on March 9, 1981.

Reagan's secretary of state, Alexander Haig, who had crowned his distinguished thirty-one-year army career serving as the supreme allied commander of NATO forces in Europe, was not happy with the incremental and narrow approach to the challenge in Central America. Haig felt strongly that it was not enough to provide the Salvadorian government with the limited military and economic aid approved by the president.

In Haig's view, it was also necessary to bring the overwhelming economic, political, and military power of the United States to bear on the source of the problem: Cuba. For it was Castro's Cuba, the secretary contended, that was supplying Soviet arms and training Communist guerrillas for the Salvadorian insurgency. In 1980 alone, the Castro regime had trained up to twelve hundred guerrillas.[57]

Haig's proposal to stop Cuba's forays, displaying "the reality of US military power," including a possible blockade of the island, was rejected by the president and his inner circle. Some feared that the Soviet Union might retaliate against the United States and its allies in other parts of the world. Others doubted that Congress or the public would support such action without direct provocation by Cuba. Still others felt that Reagan should not get entangled in the Central American sideshow and should focus on domestic priorities, such as the tax cut.

Haig, by his own admission, was left "virtually alone" with his proposal, but the president did authorize in November 1981 a contingency plan to respond to "unacceptable military actions by Cuba." He also ordered naval maneuvers off Puerto Rico as part of a NATO exercise and authorized the funding for a five-hundred-man Nicaraguan force aimed primarily at the "Cuban infrastructure in Nicaragua that was training and supplying arms to the Salvadorian guerrillas."[58] That force, known as the "Contras," was later increased not only to interdict the shipment of arms from Nicaragua but also to foster regime change.

Attempts at Détente

Those who claim that Reagan exacerbated the crisis in Central America by eschewing diplomacy and obsessively pursuing or provoking confrontation seem to overlook three major overtures attempted by his administration during the period 1981–82, not devoid of wishful thinking.

First, Assistant Secretary of State Thomas Enders held six meetings with the Nicaraguan leaders in August–September 1981 to defuse the crisis and seek a peaceful solution. He told the Sandinista hierarchs that if Nicaragua would end its support for foreign insurgencies and cease its military buildup, the United States would pledge not to intervene in Nicaragua's internal affairs and would renew economic aid to the country.

Daniel Ortega tacitly rejected the proposal, complaining about Washington's military exercises in the area and its failure to constrain the Nicaraguan exile groups. But Daniel's brother and minister of defense, Humberto Ortega, was more candid and direct in explaining where they stood. In a September speech, he declared, "We are anti-Yankee, we are against the bourgeoisie. ... Sandinism without Marxism-Leninism cannot be revolutionary."[59]

Still, Reagan persisted in his efforts to pursue a rapprochement, not only with Nicaragua but also with the key instigator of the Central American crisis, or in the words of Alexander Haig, "the source": Castro's Cuba.

At the president's request, Haig held in Mexico City, on November 23, 1981, a secret meeting arranged by Mexican foreign minister Jorge Castañeda with Cuba's deputy chairman of the State Council, Carlos Rafael Rodríguez. This very senior government official was one of the most sophisticated and articulate leaders of the historic Communist Party of Cuba, an early supporter of the Castro revolution, and, most important, a trusted standard-bearer of the Kremlin.

Sporting a white goatee, a well-cut suit, and polished shoes, he had, according to Secretary Haig, "the easy manner, the self-assured speech, the surface good humor of a man who is at ease with great affairs and famous people" (including, of course, Haig himself).[60]

Following are the highlights of their engrossing and, at times, testy parley extracted from the declassified stenographic record received by the Soviet ambassador to Cuba from Carlos Rafael Rodríguez:[61]

In his opening remarks, Haig pointed out that the United States had mostly recovered from the traumatic experiences of Vietnam and Watergate and was in a stronger position to address international conflicts threatening peace. In that context, the secretary clearly indicated that the Reagan administration viewed Cuba's series of armed interventions in Africa and the Middle East, in concert with the Soviet

Union, "as a challenge to [US] national interests. Haig then alluded to the Castro regime's subversive actions in this hemisphere, recently targeting Central America.

The secretary clarified that Washington's clash with Cuba had nothing to do with the latter's government system. The existing tensions were geopolitical, not ideological. "Our capability for coexistence," Haig emphasized, "is manifested most graphically in [our] relations with other Communist regimes: China, Yugoslavia, and the growing number of countries in Eastern Europe." Haig then held out the olive branch of normalizing relations with Communist Cuba if the Castro regime ceased to intervene in the internal affairs of other countries in collusion with the Soviet Union.

In response to Haig, Rodríguez first zeroed in on geopolitics, refuting the secretary's allegation that the major impediment to normal US-Cuba relations and peace was the Castro government's alleged subservience to the Soviet Union's hegemonic grand design. Referring to Angola, he said: "I can assure [you] unequivocally, inasmuch as I played a direct role in this matter, that when the decision to dispatch Cuban forces in Angola was made, we communicated nothing about it to the Soviet Union. ... We had absolutely no concept of the geopolitical ... importance of Angola in light of the interests of the Soviet Union. We saw in Angola a friendly country ... struggling against colonialism, against South Africa, and [we] embarked on all of this."

Rodríguez then turned to Nicaragua. He acknowledged that Cuba "helped the Sandinista front in every way that we could." He also told Haig, "You know that there were several governments in Latin America who helped them substantially more than we did."

Rodríguez denied that Cuba had any forces in Nicaragua. "We have there 2,759 people, of which 2,045 are teachers ... and 159 are doctors. ... We [also] have several dozen military advisers ... rendering assistance in the organization ... and training of the Nicaraguan army."

Regarding El Salvador, Rodríguez also rejected the claim that Cuba had any troops or military advisers there supporting "the revolutionaries who are struggling ... against the right-wing junta." With a hint of sarcasm, he challenged Haig to produce any evidence of "these fabled Cuban troops" in El Salvador or of any shipments being funneled by Cuba through Nicaragua.

Rodríguez summarized his opening remarks defending Cuba's sovereignty, its right to support the countries of the Third World, particularly in Latin America, and its friendship with the Soviet Union, grounded on "a common ideology" and on the "significant assistance" received from Moscow. He did point out, however, that such assistance was not "incompatible with ... normalized relations between the United States and Cuba."

When Haig took exception to the "benign picture" that Rodríguez had painted of the Castro regime's subversive activities, the exchange became quite contentious:

> RODRÍGUEZ. The information that you are spreading about Nicaragua is a complete falsification.

> HAIG. Cuba's activities in Nicaragua and El Salvador constitute a threat to the continent. ... We are in possession of comprehensive proof of such involvement. ... We have photographs, documents, minutes of interrogation. ... You have seen the "White Paper," but we have another fifty of them.

> RODRÍGUEZ. You have a good factory of White Papers ...

> HAIG. Nobody gave Cuba the divine right to interfere in the internal affairs of the countries in this hemisphere, regardless of what arguments may be advanced to justify it. ... I believe that you would render [the Sandinistas] the

greatest form of solidarity, if you would bring
the Cubans home. ...

RODRÍGUEZ. Return doctors? Teachers?

Haig concluded his remarks with this stark warning: "If the Cuban
Revolution has matured to this point, then that is fine. If that is not the
case, then we are on a path toward confrontation, and soon." To avoid
this, "we must find a solution to these problems. ... We believe that
time is slipping away."

Rodríguez did not back off in his rebuttal. Challenging the accuracy
of some of Haig's allegations, he said, "I remember that the 'Bay of Pigs'
was brought about by information from people located in Cuba that
led the CIA to a mistaken conclusion." Regarding Haig's allusion to a
possible military clash, Rodríguez claimed that Cuba was not afraid.
He did recognize the risk of miscalculation and called for more direct
contacts, but he did not soften his intractable positions or retract any of
his questionable explanations and outright mendacities.

Given the discouraging outcome of the Haig-Rodríguez meeting,
the prospects for a détente with the Castro regime seemed rather dim,
but Reagan decided to try anew. For the next attempt, the president
asked General Vernon Walters to explore a rapprochement directly
with Fidel Castro in Havana. The general was an ideal envoy to carry
out the mission. Formerly deputy director of the CIA, he had a distinguished diplomatic and military career that enabled him to work closely
with many of the world's leading statesmen.

Other advantages for the task were Walters's linguistic skills (fluent
in Spanish and five other languages), engaging personality, and the fact
that he had gotten along well with Castro as his interpreter during the
Maximum Leader's visit to the United States in 1959.[62]

As recounted by Walters in his book *The Mighty and the Meek*,[63] a
few days prior to his trip to Havana in March 1981, Reagan summoned
him to the Oval Office to gauge the chances of accomplishing the two

main objectives of his mission: wean Castro from Moscow's camp and stop the military aid he was sending to Nicaragua and leftist guerrillas in other Latin American countries.

The general candidly replied that he did not think his chances of success exceeded 5 percent. He "thought that Castro was a true believer in all of the Marxist claptrap," and he doubted that Fidel would want to give up "the aura of being Moscow's man in the Caribbean ... the Communist David standing up to the capitalist Goliath," in exchange for US diplomatic relations and financial assistance. Fidel would view that "as apostasy from what he regarded as his lay religion." Reagan reportedly nodded, smiled, and said, "Do your best." Walters assured him that he would.

On March 4, Walters and his executive assistant, Commander Lee Martiny, flew from Fort Lauderdale, Florida, to a military base near Havana in an unmarked Learjet provided by Washington. Shortly after arrival, they were taken to Cuba's pre-Castro presidential palace, where they were warmly greeted by Fidel and Deputy Chairman of the State Council Carlos Rafael Rodríguez (Haig's interlocutor).

At the outset, Castro expressed his earnest hope that "we can reach some sort of agreement that will benefit both our countries." After a brief pause, he said, "But if you have come here to threaten me, you should know that I have been threatened by every [US] president since Kennedy ... and I know that your Congress will not let your presidents do to me what they would like to do." (It's ironic that the indomitable Cuban leader, paladin of Marxism-Leninism, relied for protection on the checks and balances of the very democracy he denigrated.)

Before addressing the threat issue, Walters decided to set the record straight. He recalled that when Castro met in 1960 with Vice President Nixon and Secretary Herter, the glorified revolutionary leader repeatedly denied he was a Communist. "What threw you into the arms of the Soviets?" Walters pointedly asked Fidel. "Was it Washington's insensibility to your needs, as alleged by Herbert Matthews of the *New York Times* and other pundits?"

Castro flatly rejected that theory. "No one threw me into the arms of the Soviets," he affirmed. "I became a Communist at the age of seventeen. I am still one and will be one until the day I die."

Walters told Castro that he had come to Havana at President Reagan's behest, "not to threaten you" but to explore any possible arrangement to put an end the quarter of a century confrontation. He then shared with Fidel what he described as "a truth as old as history." He said, "When a great country like mine feels threatened in what it regards as its vital interests, as for example in Central America, then we are prepared to consider all options, without exceptions."

Castro's immediate response was, "Well then, everything is negotiable." But instead of offering suggestions to allay the existing US-Cuba animosity and reach a settlement, he let loose a tirade against the United States and doubled down on his allegiance to Marxism-Leninism as the wave of the future. Castro spoke for nearly three hours, his words flowing like a torrent. Walters opted to let him talk and only corrected his most glaring falsehoods. The Cuban ruler "made it abundantly clear that he was not only a believing Communist but [also] a practicing one who felt that it was his revolutionary duty to help liberation movements like his own to overthrow the tyrants put in power by the Wall Street imperialists."

When Walters told Castro that in the light of what he had said, there did not seem to be much that could be negotiated, Fidel raised both hands in a gesture of rebuff and repeated, "Oh, no! Everything is negotiable." This was, of course, his typical double game, which had duped so many government officials and pundits, but not Vernon Walters.

The general recognized, however, that Fidel, who was unfailingly courteous throughout the discussion, "had a charismatic and somewhat attractive personality and gave a childlike impression of sincerity when he spoke of communism." Walters noted, "At times, it was difficult to remember when speaking to him how many people he had shot, imprisoned, and driven to desperate flight from their native land."

Toward the end of the meeting, followed by a courtesy dinner at a sumptuous guesthouse confiscated by the regime, Castro said to Walters, "Well, despite our differences, we have at least one thing in common."

"And what is that?" asked Walters.

"We are both pupils of Jesuit schools," replied Fidel.

"But, Mr. President," interjected the general, "there is one fundamental difference: I remained *fidele* [faithful]"—a play on Castro's name.

The Cuban ruler shook his head and said, "What a pity that you are on the other slope." They both let it go at that.

The general left the island convinced that it would be futile to make further attempts to engage Castro at that time. When Walters debriefed Reagan, the president asked him if he thought Castro really believed in communism. "Yes," replied Walters, "and the ideology seems to drive his conduct and decisions." The president then asked him if there was any indication that Castro was willing to halt his support for revolutionary and anti-American movements. "I heard nothing that could lead me to this conclusion," said Walters. The president thanked him for having taken on the delicate mission and seemed pleased that it was handled very discreetly.

Based on Walters's report, Reagan turned the page and concentrated on beefing up the Contra forces to counter the Communist onslaught in Central America. With Cuban and Soviet help, the Sandinistas had built the most powerful military force in that region in a relatively short time. They augmented their armed forces from about five thousand in 1979 to eighty-eight thousand in 1983. During that same period, they increased their tanks from three to fifty, their antiaircraft guns from two to one hundred fifty, and their missile launchers from none to thirty.[64]

US Invasion of Grenada

While Reagan was grappling with Congress over the funding and expanded role of the Contra forces, another burgeoning regional crisis, with humanitarian, security, and geopolitical implications, was brought to his attention in October 1983. A bloody military coup, staged by the staunch Communist deputy prime minister of the small Caribbean island of Grenada, had ousted the socialist government led by Maurice Bishop and destabilized the former British Commonwealth.

Reagan was wary of the safety of the eight hundred US medical students enrolled at St. George's University School of Medicine on the island. The nightmare experienced by the US hostages in Iran was still fresh in his memory.

But there was something else that concerned the president: the presence in Grenada of some seven hundred Cuban construction workers, combat engineers, and military personnel who were building a nine-thousand-foot airplane runway. According to US intelligence sources, the large runway and the numerous fuel storage tanks being installed were primarily intended not for commercial use but to accommodate Soviet-Cuban aircraft to transport weapons to radical insurgents in El Salvador and neighboring countries.

In March 1983, seven months prior to the US invasion of Grenada, Reagan had denounced in a televised address the progressive Soviet-Cuban militarization of the island. To back his assertion, he displayed an aerial photograph of the construction by Cubans of the oversized airfield.

By October, it became evident to the US intelligence community that the purpose of the airstrip was to provide a base for arms shipments from Cuba to Central American guerrillas. In light of the findings presented to him, the president decided not to risk having another Communist-controlled beachhead in the Caribbean, and he preemptively launched the invasion of Grenada on October 25.

British prime minister Margaret Thatcher felt that the invasion, named Operation Urgent Fury, was unwarranted and opposed it. However, the seven member islands of the Organization of Eastern Caribbean States, which viewed the Castro regime's progressive military control of Grenada as an imminent threat to their security, supported the operation and contributed troops to the seven-thousand-strong expeditionary force. That gave Reagan some cover to exercise the right of self-defense against clear and present danger without prior OAS clearance.

Meanwhile in Havana, when it became obvious that the United States was preparing to invade Grenada, Castro summoned Colonel Pedro Tortoló, a hefty black Cuban officer who had led the Cuban military mission in Grenada from 1981 until mid-1983, and sent him back to the island to command the Cuban troops there.

Tortoló arrived less than twenty-four hours before the landing of the US-Caribbean security forces, along with one hundred fifty to two hundred additional Cuban soldiers. Although the colonel lacked combat experience, Castro relied on his unquestioned fealty and courage to fight to the death in what was to be the first (and only) really head-on confrontation with the "Americanos" in the Caribbean.

Castro himself trumpeted at a press conference Tortoló's historic mission and compared him to the great military hero of Cuban independence Antonio Maceo. To Castro's dismay and embarrassment, Tortoló fell short of the mark, to put it mildly.

As one of the Cuban worker-combatants in Grenada later declared, "I was standing next to Comandante Tortoló. When I looked around, he had run away." The Cubans, who never lose their pungent sense of humor, promptly spun the joke around Havana that "if you want to get [anywhere] first, you must have Tortoló's shoes."[65]

In the end, twenty-four Cubans were killed and fifty-nine wounded during the lightning Operation Urgent Fury. Some six hundred taken prisoners by the US-Caribbean security forces were allowed to return to Havana, where they were greeted by a sullen and uncharacteristically silent Fidel Castro. Although he pretended that everything was all right and dutifully visited the wounded soldiers in the hospitals, his seething anger for the humiliating surrender of his men in Grenada did not subside. He demoted all of them to low-level positions. As for the commander, the ineffable Tortoló, who had become a figure of scorn and ridicule, he was court-martialed, degraded, and banished to Angola.[66]

The United States also sustained some casualties during the victorious invasion: 19 dead and 116 wounded. Although the discovery of thousands of infantry weapons hidden on the island and of several secret military assistance agreements between Grenada, Cuba, and the Soviet bloc seemed to validate Washington's geopolitical and security concerns, the UN censured the United States for violating international law.

Still, for Reagan, Grenada was an unmitigated success. The invasion thwarted the establishment of another Soviet-Cuban forward military base in the Caribbean, served as a warning to the Sandinistas in Nicaragua, and enjoyed broad popular support in the United States. As for the people of Grenada, grateful for the freedom and stability brought about by the US-led Operation Urgent Fury, they celebrate the date of the invasion as their Thanksgiving Day.

The Iran–Contra Scandal

After Grenada, the president was riding high in the polls, but not in Congress, over the US secret war in Central America. Despite the report of the 1983 National Bipartisan Commission on Central America (Kissinger Commission), which underscored the strategic importance of the Caribbean–Central American Zone, the bipartisanship achieved was short-lived.

Congressional support for the Contra insurgency was progressively restricted. Under the so-called Boland Amendment, the Contras were authorized to interdict arms but not to overthrow the Sandinista government in Nicaragua. Then, in the spring of 1984, after a series of disclosures of CIA covert involvement in the mining of three Nicaraguan harbors, the Senate passed a more drastic Boland Amendment. This one explicitly prohibited military or paramilitary support for the Contras by the CIA, Defense, "or any other agency or entity involved in intelligence activities" during the period from October 1984 to December 1985.[67]

While the United States was barred from providing military aid to the Contras, Nicaragua received in 1985 eighteen thousand tons of Soviet arms, including advanced attack helicopters. Along with shipments came military advisers from the Soviet Union and East Germany, who joined some eight hundred from Cuba already in Managua.[68]

In light of the Soviet-Cuban offensive, Reagan was determined to find covert means to keep the Contras together "body and soul." To circumvent the congressional ban, the responsibility for supporting the Contras passed from the CIA to the National Security Council at the White House, and a convoluted scheme was concocted to obtain external funding.

The scheme merged two secret transactions: the sale via Israel to Iran of US TOW antitank missiles in exchange for the release of several US hostages held by Hezbollah, and the diversion of the profits from the arms sale to Iran to fund the Contras. This scheme led to the Iran–Contra imbroglio that rocked the Reagan administration and the president himself.[69]

A few months before the scandal exploded, Reagan explained why he felt so strongly about continuing to support the Contras. In a speech to the nation on June 24, 1984, he confided that he was ashamed when he read the remarks of a Nicaraguan Contra: "You Americans have the strength, the opportunity, but not the will. We want to struggle, but it is dangerous to have friends like you—to be left stranded on the landing beaches of the Bay of Pigs. Either help us or leave us alone."[70]

The specter of the Bay of Pigs did haunt the president, but that was no legal justification for the cover-up that was devised to funnel the Iran funds through fourteen corporations and thirteen bank accounts.[71]

On November 25, 1986, just before the details of the Machiavellian story were fully known, Reagan held a press conference. It was probably the most humiliating moment of his presidency. In a brief statement, he disclosed that an inquiry by the attorney general had revealed that on one of the activities undertaken by his National Security Council staff in connection with an Iranian initiative, "serious questions of propriety" had been raised.

Reagan did not provide information of the questionable activity but indicated that the inquiry had concluded that he had not been "fully informed." He then added: "While I cannot reverse what has happened, I'm initiating steps ... to [en]sure that the implementation of all future foreign and national security policy initiatives will proceed only in accordance with my authorization."

The seriousness of the situation became apparent when the president announced that National Security Adviser John Poindexter had resigned and Colonel Oliver North had been relieved of his duties. Unable to cope with the barrage of questions that followed his cryptic statement, the president handed over the press conference to Attorney General Edwin Meese and departed.[72]

Although Reagan was not impeached, the congressional hearings on the Iran–Contra cover-up and the judicial investigation conducted by Lawrence E. Walsh incriminated him and shed opprobrium on his standing. And yet a string of positive developments in the last three years of his presidency, largely attributed to his stewardship, enabled him to burnish his image and gain recognition as a farsighted and courageous leader of the free world.

Recovery and Vindication

In Nicaragua, the US-backed Contras were unable to overthrow the Marxist regime, but the casualties and high costs of the struggle sustained by Managua, compounded by the downswing of its economy, forced the Sandinista leaders to accept in 1987 the pacification and democratization plan proposed by the president of Costa Rica of the time, Óscar Arias.

The Arias ten-point plan, backed by the other Central American governments, led to the phaseout of Soviet-Cuban military assistance to insurrectionists in the region and to free elections in Nicaragua. To the dismay of the Sandinistas, the opposition leader, Violeta de Chamorro, won the elections and ushered in a democratic transition. The much-reviled Contra war promoted by Reagan, and the pressure it exerted on the Sandinistas and its allies, had, after all, produced some positive results.

In Afghanistan, Reagan's crucial decision to supply the mujahideen with handheld Stinger heat-seeking missiles contributed to the withdrawal of Soviet forces from Afghanistan in 1988.[73] But where Reagan's statesmanship reached its climax was in the broader theater of the Cold War within the Soviet bloc. For it was he who, in conjunction with Pope John Paul II and British prime minister Margaret Thatcher, devised and steadily pursued the comprehensive strategy not just to contain but to roll back and bring down the "Evil Empire."

With the support of his inner circle, Reagan's strategy further crippled the sagging Russian economy and undermined the Kremlin's grip on its satellites. Fired up by Radio Free Europe[74] and not choked off by the Soviet military, the dissident movements in Central and Eastern Europe gained momentum and won over their freedom.[75]

Castro's Reaction

Castro took note of Reagan's decisive leadership in the final stages of the Cold War and opted to temper not his anti-Yankee rhetoric but some of his provocative actions. He blasted the president when, at the behest of the young, charismatic Cuban American exile leader Jorge Mas-Canosa, he authorized the funding and launch of Radio Martí to break the Castro regime's stranglehold on the free flow of information.

He also chastised Reagan for having appointed the heroic Armando Valladares, imprisoned and tortured by Castro for twenty-two years, US ambassador to the United Nations Commission on Human Rights.

Yet the Cuban dictator refrained from broad-scale retaliation, as he had vowed to do, and actually retreated in a number of areas.

Castro ended Cuba's military intervention in Central America following the signing of the Arias peace plan and reached a settlement with Angola and South Africa, which resulted in the withdrawal of some fifty thousand Cuban troops from that region. Castro also accepted the return to Havana of the twenty-six hundred delinquents, misfits, and spies he had dumped on Florida during the Mariel exodus, and he formalized an immigration agreement with the United States.[76]

Reagan clearly fared better with his muscular stand against Castro's expansionism than with his and his predecessors' earlier attempts at détente without much leverage. Wily and ruthless dictators like the Cuban ruler soar aggressively when they sense weakness and recoil cautiously when confronted with strength.

◼ George H. W. Bush (1989–1993)

During his presidency, the elder Bush had to devote much of his time to foreign affairs. This was not a problem. Given his distinguished public service credentials as ambassador to the United Nations, US envoy to China, director of the CIA, and vice president of the United States, he had an ample reservoir of talent and experience to draw from when dealing with complex international issues. And he certainly had no shortage of those.

Bush put together an impressive and well-integrated team of advisers, including Brent Scowcroft, national security adviser; James Baker, secretary of state; Dick Cheney, secretary of defense; and Colin Powell, chairman of the Joint Chiefs of Staff. Another prominent counselor was Robert Gates, who served the president as deputy national security adviser and later as director of the CIA.

The US Invasion of Panama and the
Noriega-Castro Drug Connection

During the first two years of Bush's presidency, while he ably addressed the breakdown of the Soviet Union and Hussein's invasion of Kuwait, Panama became a serious national security and political issue. Its military ruler, Manuel Noriega, who had been a valued CIA "asset" during the Contra war against the Sandinista regime in Nicaragua, had turned against the United States and was indicted by a federal grand jury in 1988 on drug trafficking charges.

The well-documented indictment accused Noriega of virtually selling his government to drug traffickers for millions of dollars in bribes and turning Panama into a center of money laundering and cocaine smuggling, the cocaine mostly bound for the United States. According to the indictment, Noriega provided secure airstrips and haven for some of the world's most violent dealers, including the infamous Medellín cartel.[77]

The president was pressed by congressional leaders to bring Noriega to justice in the United States, but since Panama was under his ironfisted rule, the general would block any attempt to extradite him. Bush began to focus on removing Noriega from power but opted not to support a covert internal coup attempt, which was haphazardly planned and easily quashed on October 3, 1989.

The president decided instead to plan an overt military operation to oust Noriega and bring him to trial on drug charges in the United States. On December 20, 1989, a few days after Bush was notified that Noriega's military forces had killed a US serviceman and attacked another one and his wife, Bush launched Operation Just Cause with about ten thousand forces landing in Panama and joining some thirteen thousand already there.

When they overtook the Panamanian military without much resistance, Noriega sought refuge at the Vatican's embassy in Panama City. He surrendered to US forces in early January and was flown to Miami,

Florida, where he was tried and convicted in September 1992 on eight counts of drug trafficking, racketeering, and money laundering, and sentenced to forty years in prison.[78]

The United States was chastised by the UN and the OAS for the unilateral armed intervention in Panama, bypassing these organizations and violating international covenants and procedures. Most Americans, however, hailed the military operation that ended Noriega's despotic rule and brought him to justice, and the Panamanians by and large were happy to have regained their freedom.

A direct outgrowth of the Noriega US trial in 1992 was the case against the Castro regime. Testimonies implicating Raúl Castro in Noriega's drug trafficking were provided by Cuban defectors and Medellín cocaine cartel chieftain Carlos Lehder Rivas, who was serving life plus 135 years in the United States after being convicted on drug trafficking charges in Florida in 1988.

Lehder testified that in 1982 he met with Raúl Castro, defense minister and second-in-command of the Cuban regime, to strike a deal. In exchange for millions of dollars, Raúl agreed to facilitate the Medellín cartel's cocaine shipments through Cuba. Using special radio frequencies provided by the regime, the drug traffickers were able to exit Cuban airspace without interference. They also were allowed to land on Cuban soil with their loads of cocaine.[79]

Since 1982, US officials had been aware that the Castro regime was using drug trafficking as a means of both raising hard currency for Cuba and undermining the hated "empire." Four Cuban officials, including a vice admiral in the Cuban navy, were charged with importing marijuana into Florida. But they were never arrested or brought to trial. Then in 1984, a Drug Enforcement Administration informant, Barry Seal, penetrated a cartel plot hatched by the Castro and Sandinista governments to send 1,462 pounds of cocaine to Miami. The drugs were seized by the US authorities, but no Cuban or Nicaraguan officials were charged.[80]

By 1989, Fidel Castro realized that evidence linking senior officials of his regime to the Medellín drug cartel and to Noriega was extensive and incriminating. To preempt or blunt a possible indictment, he decided to assemble a kangaroo court to convict some of those Cuban government officials who were involved in drug trafficking. The irony is that the leader who conceived and negotiated the smuggling deal with the Medellín cartel, Raúl Castro, was the one who pressed charges against his partners in crime.

Ten officers of the army and the Interior Ministry were sentenced to prison terms ranging from ten to twenty years. Among the four who were convicted of treason against the Cuban Revolution on charges of corruption and drug dealing, and executed on July 13, 1989, was the decorated general and former commander of the Cuban forces in Angola, Arnaldo Ochoa. Well-informed sources on the island believe that Fidel Castro may have had ulterior motives to execute the popular general and shining star of the regime: He knew too much and had risen too high.

During his videotaped mea culpa, redolent of the Stalin era's forced confessions, Ochoa dutifully swore that all his actions were "the artifice of my [own] mind," and neither Fidel Castro nor his brother Raúl, nor anyone else in the Communist Party or government, "ever had anything to do with it [the drug trafficking]" (English translation).

Ochoa also said, "I want to tell my comrades-at-arms that I believe I betrayed my country, and I say in all honesty, one pays for treason with one's life." To complete the government-concocted confession, the general unctuously declared that if he faced execution, "my last thought will be of Fidel and the great revolution that he has given our people."[81]

Castro's show trial and partial purge did not deter the prosecutors at the US Attorney's Office in Miami from drafting a proposed indictment against the Cuban government. It charged the regime as a racketeering enterprise and Defense Minister Raúl Castro as the chief of a ten-year conspiracy to send tons of Colombian cartel cocaine through Cuba to the United States.[82]

Prosecutor Bob Martínez, who spearheaded the thorough

investigation implicating the Cuban government and Raúl Castro in drug trafficking, was ready to make a final presentation to a federal grand jury in Miami and file formal charges. But Washington blocked that move. As reported by ABC News, the Justice Department—by then under the Clinton administration—overruled the US Attorney's Office in Miami and quashed the indictment in 1993, alleging national security and intelligence issues.[83] As a result, the Castro regime walked away from incrimination unscathed.

Castro Dug in His Heels

In April 1989, while trying to invigorate the decaying Soviet Union with an infusion of liberalization and drastic government spending cuts, Mikhail Gorbachev flew to Havana to have a candid conversation with comrade Fidel Castro. He was greeted with a great deal of pomp and bear hugs. But the warm reception quickly turned cold when the Soviet leader advised Castro that Moscow could not continue providing massive aid to Cuba and urged him to launch his own glasnost and perestroika.[84]

The Cuban dictator, however, was not willing to temper his radicalism or institute even modest economic reforms. Not quite yet. He would have to bear a little later the full brunt of the Soviet collapse to allow a limited and temporary opening of the state-controlled economy.

Gorbachev was not the only personality who beseeched Castro to change course. Adolfo Suárez, who in 1976 led Spain's peaceful transition from Francisco Franco's autocracy to a democratic parliamentary monarchy, also tried to persuade Fidel to foster a more pluralistic and efficient system of government, reuniting the fractured Cuban population and attracting foreign capital and technology.

At the request of Carlos Alberto Montaner, distinguished Cuban exile, syndicated journalist, and active member of the International Liberal Movement, as well as other compatriots interested in exploring a constructive engagement with the Castro regime, Suárez met with

Fidel in Havana in mid-1990 to test the waters. The meeting was cordial but fruitless. The Cuban ruler showed no interest in softening his intractable position. His most memorable statement during the colloquy was that "Cuba would sink in the ocean before abandoning Marxism-Leninism." Confident that he was on the right track, Castro boasted that the Cuban example would be followed by many other countries "when humanity recovers its senses."[85]

Castro was emboldened by the Foro de São Paulo, a conference of leftist/Marxist political parties and organizations from Latin America. It was launched by Brazil's Workers Party, headed by Luiz Inacio Lula da Silva, in São Paulo, in 1990. Lula, a strong Castro supporter, was later elected president of Brazil, and the Foro remained a vital platform for both Lula and Castro.

Bush Pressed to Harden Cuba Policy

Sensing US complacency, Castro not only intensified repression against peaceful dissidents but also scrambled the transmissions of TV Martí, which began broadcasting to Cuba in March 1990, and jammed Radio Martí. The objective was clear: total blackout of non-government-filtered news on the island.

Under those circumstances, with no likelihood of a rapprochement with the Castro regime, Cuban exile leaders submitted to President Bush in 1992 a three-hundred-thousand-signature petition to rescind the 1962 Kennedy-Khrushchev no-invasion-of-Cuba pledge so that the exiles could pursue their struggle for Cuba's freedom without US interference. The president declined to abrogate the accord and refused to condone violations of US neutrality law.[86]

Since the White House refused to allow any military action against the Castro regime, Cuban exile leaders then proposed the strengthening of the US commercial embargo. They argued that the combined impact of the cancellation of Soviet aid and the reinforcement of US sanctions would compel Castro to start liberalizing the island, at least with economic reforms.

Bush was reluctant at first to support a bill in Congress (the Cuban Democracy Act) that significantly tightened the US embargo, but when presidential candidate Bill Clinton opportunistically endorsed it during the 1992 campaign, the president promptly followed suit.

The Cuban Democracy Act, presented by US congressman Robert Torricelli, was passed by Congress and signed into law by President Bush on October 23, 1992. It prohibited foreign-based subsidiaries of US companies from trading with Cuba; barred travel to the island by US citizens; and established strict limits on family remittances to the island.

Donations of food to nongovernment organizations in Cuba, however, were not restricted, nor were medical supplies and medicines sent to the Cuban people. The tightened embargo would be lifted and financial support provided when Cuba held free elections under international supervision.

For the first time the US embargo, absent Soviet aid to compensate for it, truly had "bite." Its impact, however, was lessened a few years later when the Castro regime got a new life preserver, this one courtesy of the Venezuelan president Hugo Chávez.

CHAPTER 12

Clinton, Castro, and the Pope (1993–2001)

No More Soviet Windfall

Following the implosion of the Soviet Union and the shutdown of Cuba's vital lifeline in 1991, the island lost more than 35 percent of its GDP in one fell swoop. While Cuba was receiving Moscow's massive aid, estimated to have totaled $65 billion over thirty years, Castro could dismiss and even deride the US "blockade" (economic embargo). This he did at a public rally in January 1969, asserting, "The blockade is now a matter of scorn and laughter." That was then, however, but such was not the case in the 1990s.

The dire situation that ensued forced Fidel Castro to introduce for the first time some market-oriented reforms (his miniperestroika) in the summer of 1993, which he labeled "the Special Period in Time of Peace."

Although most of the economy remained under government control, Castro allowed state farms to form cooperatives and licensed self-managed microbusinesses (no employees permitted), like home-based restaurants, bed-and-breakfasts, small artisan shops, and a slew of menial services. Fearing creeping capitalism, which could undermine the regime's totalitarian control, these reforms were later curbed and partly reversed.

Given the island's urgent need of capital, Castro amended the Communist Constitution to allow foreign companies to invest in Cuba in certain areas, but only in partnership, on a minority basis, with the government. Among the corporations that flocked to Cuba and invested there were Meliá from Spain (tourism), Sherritt from Canada (mining/oil), Pernod Ricard from France (rum), Imperial Tobacco from the UK (cigars), Nestlé from Switzerland (ice cream and soft drinks), Domos from Mexico, and Telecom Italy (telecommunications).

Most of these corporations experienced obstacles and frustrations, but nothing comparable to FirstKey's nightmare. As reported in a lengthy *Wall Street Journal* article dated June 28, 1999, FirstKey signed a joint venture agreement with the Cuban government in 1997 to increase the generation of power, which had dropped to a very low level, causing frequent outages across the island. The company's CEO at the time, Clarence Boudreau, a lanky thirty-four-year veteran of major engineering projects spanning the globe from Canada to China, thought he had hit the jackpot with the deal. "Everybody was pushing Cuba. It was the place to invest," he said.

His ecstasy, however, was short-lived. The Castro regime reneged on the contract, and FirstKey lost about $9 million spent on developing the project. To add insult to injury, the regime used FirstKey's plans to lure European firms to the very same project. "First there is [the] love affair," Boudreau bitterly complained, "and then they dispose of you like a wet rug."

The Clinton administration applauded Castro's miniperestroika and, to encourage deeper reforms, decided as a first step to ease US restrictions on US travel to the island. Visits were authorized under a "people to people" program fostering cultural and religious activities. The president and his inner circle were deluded by Castro's limited economic reforms, thinking they would lead to the liberalization of the regime. The Cuban ruler, however, had other plans to address the simmering unrest on the island.

■ The Tugboat Massacre and the "Maleconazo"

A Castro heinous crime in 1994 was the sinking of the tugboat *13 de Marzo*. This was not an isolated or uniquely atrocious episode. It was preceded by the July 6, 1980, Canimar River massacre, when a large excursion boat attempting to flee the island was attacked by a Cuban air force plane and sunk by a freighter that rammed into it. According to the Cuban Archive (in exile), several dozen passengers, including children, were killed.

Regarding the *13 de Marzo* tugboat mass murder, the Inter-American Commission on Human Rights reported that in the early morning hours of July 13, 1994, four boats belonging to the Castro regime sank the old tugboat seven miles off the Cuban coast. It was fleeing the island with seventy-two people on board.

The regime's boats attacked the runaway tug with their prows while at the same time spraying everyone on the deck, including women and children, with pressurized water. The pleas of the women and children to stop the attack were in vain, and the *13 de Marzo* sank, killing forty-one people, including ten minors. Thirty-one passengers survived and bore witness to this abhorrent crime, which the Castro regime called "an accident."[1]

Even inside Cuba, under tight government censorship, the news of the massacre at sea spread like wildfire and added fuel to the restlessness spiked by the grave economic crisis. These two factors, along with false rumors that ferries in Havana had been seized and were available to flee the island, contributed to a major antigovernment protest, or short-lived uprising, known as the Maleconazo, which preluded the Rafter Crisis.

The Malecón is the wide waterfront avenue that gracefully circles the bay of Havana like a dazzling necklace. It had generally been a peaceful area to relax, stroll, and enjoy the sea breeze, particularly when power outages, such as those endured by the population in the 1990s, made it unbearable to remain inside the crowded, dilapidated houses nearby.

However, on the morning of August 5, 1994, the Malecón turned into a battlefield. What sparked the spontaneous popular revolt is still open to debate, but the underlying causes are well-known: hunger, scarcities, despair, and oppression. Hundreds, perhaps thousands, of enraged Cubans began pouring into the streets shouting, "Libertad," "Viva Cuba Libre," and "Cuba, sí. Castro, no."

The regime promptly unleashed its plainclothes shock troops (the Rapid Response Brigades), who lashed out against the unarmed crowd with sticks and iron bars. Despite the unremitting violence of the repression, it took the government thugs several hours to quash the rebellion, which had started to spread to surrounding streets. Only then did Castro show up in the Malecón to proclaim their great victory before the TV cameras.

The Rafter Crisis

Castro was well aware of the existing restlessness across the island and realized that he needed a safety valve to release tension. Since the 1980 Mariel exodus worked well for him without any US reprisal, he decided immediately after the Maleconazo to launch another such exodus. Blaming the US immigration policies for encouraging Cubans to leave the island illegally, he announced that his government would not stand in the way of those who wanted to flee. That led to what is known as the Rafter Crisis.

During the months of August and September 1994, some thirty-five thousand Cubans of all ages took to the sea, mostly on flimsy inner-tube rafts. The objective of the rafters, known as *balseros*, was basically the same as that of the Mariel escapees: to reach the safe haven of Florida. But this time those fleeing Cuba were interdicted at sea by the US Coast Guard and diverted to the US naval base at Guantánamo, Cuba.

Many of the intercepted rafters were suffering from heat injuries and had no food or fresh water left. The few rafts with engines were mostly out of fuel and were drifting in the current. Several young boys and girls under the age of ten were found floating alone on inner tubes. They talked of how their mothers or fathers had been taken by sharks during the voyage.

A large number of rafts were found completely empty or broken into several pieces. It is estimated on the low side that 25 percent of the rafters were lost at sea—a heartbreaking tragedy.

Those who were picked up and sent to Guantánamo were housed in large tent cities rapidly constructed by military personnel at several sites of the US naval base. Camp conditions were challenging due to high heat, water shortages, and the large amount of trash. Thanks to the commendable efforts of the US Joint Task Force 160 in charge of Operation Sea Signal, and the assistance of the Cuban American (Miami) medical doctors who volunteered to treat the ailing rafters, the overall situation gradually improved.[2]

Yet not all was orderly and peaceful. Owing to lingering uncertainties about their future—without a country and enduring indefinite detention—some of the Cuban balseros at the camp grew restless and staged riots. President Clinton realized that he could not keep thousands of Cuban refugees indefinitely fenced in Guantánamo. Mounting pressure to find a humanitarian solution forced the president's hand. After several months in limbo, most of the rafters were paroled into the United States.

Castro's Maneuver

While the migration turmoil Castro had set off was still rattling the Clinton administration, the Cuban ruler sent an unusual emissary to meet with the president and advocate on his behalf the normalization of US relations with Communist Cuba: the renowned Colombian novelist and Castro devotee Gabriel García Márquez.

The meeting between the novelist and the president took place in September 1994 at the Martha's Vineyard summer house of the distinguished writer William Styron. When the cordial conversation over lunch turned to Cuba, Clinton explained why under the 1962 Cuban Democracy Act it would be very difficult, if not impossible, for him to lift the embargo absent a fundamental change in Cuba.[3] However,

bowing to pressure from Havana, the president made some concessions. He agreed to take in at least twenty thousand legal immigrants
from Cuba annually, and in return he relied on Castro's word to use
"mainly persuasive methods" to stop the rafter exodus.[4]

The White House also announced in May 1995 that, under the new
immigration policy, Cuban refugees intercepted by the US Coast Guard
at sea ("wet foot") would be sent back to Cuba, while those who made it
to US soil ("dry foot") would be allowed to remain and apply for expedited US residence. The weird logic or inconsistency to appease Castro
was evident. Those caught before touching US soil would be treated
as illegal immigrants and turned over to the Cuban dictator, whereas
those who were able to sneak in were accorded the privilege of staying
and applying for the coveted green card. With the "wet foot" provision,
Castro got part of what he wanted.[5]

The Shoot-Down

Emboldened by the Clinton administration's conciliatory response to
the rafter exodus, Fidel Castro, along with his brother Raúl and the
upper echelons of the regime, masterminded the 1996 shoot-down by
Cuba's air force MiGs of two small unarmed Brothers to the Rescue aircraft. This vile aggression killed three US citizens and one US resident
flying on a humanitarian mission over international waters.

Brothers to the Rescue was a nonprofit organization founded in May
1991 (four years before the wet foot, dry foot policy was announced)
for the purpose of assisting and rescuing raft refugees fleeing Cuba
and supporting nonviolent efforts of the Cuban people to regain their
freedom. Under the leadership of José Basulto, a Bay of Pigs veteran,
the Brothers included some thirty young pilots of various nationalities
who volunteered to fly in rickety Cessnas over the Florida Straits to
carry out search and rescue missions.

When a rafter was spotted and needed urgent assistance, the
Brothers promptly alerted the US Coast Guard and circled the rafter

until help arrived. They would also toss down plastic water bottles, food, T-shirts, life jackets, and even radios bundled up in a bubble wrap. In their first eight months of operation, they reportedly flew 202 missions and saved 143 rafters. By 1996, lives saved by the Brothers at sea exceeded four thousand.[6]

Apart from their humanitarian mission, Brothers to the Rescue relayed to the world films of desperate men, women, and children fleeing Communist Cuba on anything that floated. Castro, of course, was not happy with the negative publicity, but what really infuriated him was Basulto's daring incursion in January 1996, when he and three other pilots flying on two separate planes reached Cuban territorial airspace and dropped half a million flyers, which fell like confetti over Havana. The flyers listed articles of the UN Declaration of Human Rights and urged the Cubans to exercise those rights.

Castro, having viewed that foray as an intolerable provocation, vowed revenge. He instructed his "Wasp Network" of spies in Miami, engaged in infiltrating the US Southern Command and several Cuban American militant groups, to target Brothers to the Rescue. One of the spies who infiltrated the organization was Juan Pablo Roque, a dashing former Cuban air force pilot who feigned defection to the United States in 1992.

Roque joined the Brothers as a pilot and alerted the Castro regime to the fateful flight on February 24, 1996, of the three unarmed planes of Brothers to the Rescue, two of which were shot down by Cuban fighter aircraft over the Florida Straits. The day before the downing, Roque slipped out of Miami and returned to Cuba, where he later denounced Brothers to the Rescue as a terrorist organization.[7]

The Brothers were unaware of the deadly plot hatched by the Castro regime when three of their Cessna planes took off from Opa-locka airport on February 24 at 1:11 p.m. on a humanitarian mission to search for rafters. It was a beautiful, cloudless afternoon with ceiling and visibility unlimited, or CAVU in military jargon.

While the Brothers' aircraft were flying north of Cuba's twelve-mile airspace, the Cuban air force ordered the scrambling of two fighter planes, a MiG-29 and a MiG-23, carrying short-range missiles, bombs, and rockets. Following instructions imparted by both Fidel and Raúl Castro, the Cuban military aircraft shot down, without warning, over international waters, two of the Brothers' Cessnas, piloted by three young US-born citizens and one Cuban-born US resident.[8]

The third Cessna, piloted by their leader, José Basulto, and by Arnaldo Iglesias, and carrying the president of Mothers Against Repression (MAR por Cuba), Sylvia Iriondo, and her husband Andrés, managed to evade the hot pursuit of the Cuban MiGs and return to the Opa-locka airport.

After the downing of each plane, the Cuban pilots could be heard vaunting their heinous feat, and the ground control in Havana could be heard congratulating them. The MiG pilots' radio transmissions, taped by the United States, included the following brag (English version) when the first plane was shot down: *"We hit them! We hit them—cojones! This one won't fuck around anymore."* Then, when the second plane was downed, the crow was: *"Destroyed! We destroyed the other one! Fatherland or death, cojones!"*

A day after these exclamations of glee and profanity were aired at a special meeting of the United Nations Security Council, US ambassador to the UN Madeleine Albright famously declared, "Frankly, this is not cojones. This is cowardice."[9]

In its report on the downing, the Inter-American Commission on Human Rights concluded: "The fact that weapons of war and combat-trained pilots were used against unarmed civilians shows not only how disproportionate the use of force was, but also the intent to end the lives of those individuals. ... The extracts from the radio communications between the MiG-29 pilots and the military control tower indicate that they acted from a superior position and showed malice and scorn toward the human dignity of the victims."[10]

From the time the Cuban MiGs were spotted by the United States, F-15's at Homestead Air Force Base in Florida had been waiting for instructions with their engines running. They could have been off the ground in two minutes and in the area within ten. Why then was no attempt made to prevent the aggression by deploying intercept jets? The North American Aerospace Defense Command stated in its October 13, 1996, report that the failure to intercept or scramble was the result of "miscommunication" but claimed that, given the speed of events, it was unlikely that the F-15's could have deterred the shoot-down.

Brothers to the Rescue, however, did not buy the "miscommunication" explanation. Having conducted their own investigation, they found out that the F-15's were grounded because the pilots received a clear order: "Stand down battle stations."[11]

Fidel Castro admitted to *Time* magazine and to Dan Rather on a special edition of *CBS Evening News* that he gave the order for the shoot-down. "You can only take so much provocation," he averred. But he did not concede that the alleged "pirate aircraft" of the "terrorist organization Brothers to the Rescue, which may have been carrying arms," were shot down in international waters as the evidence showed.[12]

Judicial Watch and human rights organizations called for indictment. The editorial board of the *Miami Herald* urged Clinton to charge the Castro military clique with murder. The president, however, decided not to press legal charges. The responsibility fell to the Bush administration, which indicted the Cuban air force general who relayed the immediate order to shoot down the planes, as well as the pilots (the Pérez-Pérez brothers) who executed the order. Fidel Castro, however, was excluded from the indictment on the grounds of immunity as head of state, and so was his brother Raúl, who could not claim such protection. Regardless of immunity, the Castro brothers continued to enjoy impunity.

The Libertad Act

The downing of the planes did have legislative consequences that Castro did not foresee and Clinton could not forestall. The president was not keen about maintaining the US embargo on Cuba, much less strengthening it. But given the uproar caused by the shoot-down of the Brothers to the Rescue planes without any US attempt to avert it, Clinton could not overcome the pressure to strengthen sanctions against Cuba.

The calculating Castro, for once, miscalculated. To perpetrate his aggression against the Brothers to the Rescue, he relied on Clinton's antiembargo stance to evade retaliation. He certainly did not expect that Congress would not only reinforce but also codify the embargo, meaning that no president could abrogate or nullify its essential provisions without congressional approval. The congressman who pushed hardest to achieve that goal was none other than Castro's former nephew, Lincoln Díaz-Balart.

On March 12, 1996, Clinton reluctantly signed into law the Cuban Liberty and Democratic Solidarity (LIBERTAD) Act (also known as the Helms–Burton Act), which several Democratic filibusterers in the Senate had managed to table in 1995. The Act strengthened the trade and financial sanctions against the Castro regime and subsequently was broadened to include a ban on US tourist travel to the island.

Under the Act, foreigners who trafficked in confiscated properties in Cuba were exposed to lawsuits in the United States and denial of US visas. The application of this "extraterritorial" provision, which had been suspended by all presidents prior to Trump, was reinstated by Trump in April 2019. The Act also barred any US economic assistance to Cuba while the island remained subjugated by the Castro brothers.[13]

Faced with the restrictions imposed by the Act, which tied the hands of the president and made a US-Cuba détente very difficult, Castro realized he had to stage a dramatic tactical shift to improve his image and relieve both internal and external tensions. With this in mind, he decided to make peace with the Catholic Church and to welcome the visit of its preeminent spiritual leader, who he believed would join him in denouncing the US embargo: Pope John Paul II.

The Historic Pilgrimage

Hoping that the pope would accept the invitation, Castro moderated his antichurch stance and reestablished Christmas as a public holiday. Was this a sincere U-turn or a tactical move? Was the Jesuit-educated "lost son" signaling a desire to rejoin the flock, or was he playing one of his deceitful games to burnish his image without changing his stripes? The Vatican seemed to harbor some doubts about Castro's intentions but was not about to turn down the opportunity to thaw relations with the Communist regime. If Paris was well worth a Mass for the Huguenot King Henry IV, how could the bishop of Rome spurn a pilgrimage to Havana?

The pope decided to go, and the Clinton administration, eager to encourage constructive engagement with Castro, relaxed the ban on travel to Cuba and allowed the church to charter flights and a cruise ship to carry all those interested in joining John Paul's journey.

Among Cuban Americans, the announcement of the papal visit spawned heated debate. Most favored the visit but feared that Castro would attempt to manipulate it to buttress his regime. I shared that concern and wrote an article in Spanish titled "Reconciliación o Resistencia—el Dilema de la Iglesia en Cuba" (Reconciliation or Resistance—the Dilemma of the Church in Cuba). The article was published in the Miami newspaper *Diario Las Américas*—owned and directed by Horacio Aguirre, a stalwart supporter of the Free Cuba cause—several weeks prior to the pope's trip.[14]

What prompted me to write the article was a reliable report that the church hierarchy in Cuba (with a few notable exceptions) wanted the pope to be very accommodating toward the regime during his visit and to call for reconciliation while skirting or downplaying sensitive "political" issues, such as human rights and freedom. Seeking more space to carry out their evangelical mission, the Cuban cardinal and some of the bishops advised the Vatican not to rock the boat, in other words, refrain from encouraging dissent lest Castro stymie further reforms and retaliate against the church.

To me, that overly cautious, if not submissive, approach would serve only to legitimize the Communist regime, discourage freedom-loving Cubans yearning for recognition and support, and tarnish the waning prestige of the church on the island.

I realized that Cuba was not Poland, that the frail pope in 1998 was not the vigorous crusader who galvanized his homeland a decade earlier, and that the dissident movement on the island was not as widespread, cohesive, or vibrant as the one led by Solidarity. Yet I implored the pope to light a candle to liberty in Cuba by infusing the despondent population with a heavy dose of courage and hope. *Nolite timere* (Be not afraid)—the watchword of John Paul's papacy—should be the rallying cry of his visit to Cuba, I wrote.

To my great surprise, the article reached the desk of John Cardinal O'Connor, archbishop of New York, who invited me to discuss with him the pope's forthcoming trip to Cuba. I had not met the cardinal and was, of course, delighted and honored to see him. The meeting, coordinated by Mario J. Paredes, executive director of the church's Hispanic Center of New York, was held at the center's office on December 18, 1997. At my request, two distinguished members of the Cuban American community joined me: Otto Reich, former US ambassador to Venezuela, and Frank Calzón, executive director of the Center for a Free Cuba.

The tall, imposing cardinal, dressed all in black with a resplendent gold cross hanging over his chest, arrived alone at the meeting. He walked down the hall with a long martial stride, a hallmark of his twenty-seven years at the US Navy, where he rose to rear admiral and chief of chaplains. But what struck me the most was his warm, congenial smile, which tempered his austere bearing.

At the outset, the cardinal told us that, at the Vatican's behest, he was involved in the planning of the Holy Father's trip to Cuba and would appreciate our views and suggestions to ensure the success of his pilgrimage.

I reiterated our main concern: Castro's likely attempt to portray the visit as the Vatican's endorsement or validation of his Communist regime. To forestall Fidel's machination, my colleagues and I stressed, the pope should stand up for human rights on the island and provide faith and encouragement to the oppressed Cubans in their pursuit of justice, dignity, and freedom. We also urged the Vatican to insist that the pope's Masses and homilies be broadcast live to the Cuban people. Otherwise, we added, the trip should be canceled.

The cardinal understood our concern since he himself could attest to Castro's stratagem. We then pointed out that Fidel in all likelihood would avail himself of the pope's visit to raise the red herring of the US embargo, knowing full well that the church, and the pope himself, had repeatedly condemned it. "What to do?" the cardinal asked us as he took out from his pocket a white piece of paper to jot down some notes.

Measuring my words, I said, "With all due respect, Your Eminence, I believe it has been ill-advised for the church to condemn Washington's *external* embargo on Cuba without also denouncing Castro's *internal* embargo on the Cuban people. The only way out of this predicament, in my opinion, is for the pope to call for the end of the two embargos, thereby ensuring that the much-needed opening of Cuba run in both directions—inward and outward."

After discussing other steps to maximize the positive impact of the pope's visit, O'Connor summarized the salient points we made and told us he would share them with the Holy Father during his upcoming trip to the Vatican. To temper unrealistic expectations, he said that he did not know what the outcome of his intervention would be since the pope's trip agenda, including his homilies and public statements, had already been mostly finalized. But he assured us that our suggestions would reach the highest level (meaning the pope), adding with a light-hearted smile, "And I don't need intermediaries [to get to him]."

My colleagues and I left the meeting grateful for the opportunity to convey our views to the Vatican through our illustrious interlocutor. Given O'Connor's positive response to our proposals and his close relationship with John Paul II as one of his most trusted and influential counselors, we were confident that the cardinal would deliver on his promise.[15]

When the pope and his entourage arrived at the airport in Havana, Castro, wearing a dark suit, warmly greeted him. Those who believed that Fidel was genuinely moved and contrite were taken aback when he veered from his welcoming remarks and accused Spain and the Catholic Church of exterminating seventy million Natives and twelve million Africans during the colonization of North America.[16] Was this blast a Fidel gaffe or a mere lapse of protocol? Not really. It was a premeditated, true-to-type show of power and defiance.

Seemingly unperturbed, the pope did not deviate from his prepared remarks and spelled out in his reply the main themes of his pilgrimage: "love, truth, and hope." Well aware, based on his own experience in Poland, that totalitarianism bred godlessness and conformity, he told the Cuban people, "Be not afraid to open your hearts to Christ." This, his signature leitmotif, he reiterated throughout the trip.

The pope then touched on the controversial issue of the US embargo without naming it. He implied that the opening of Cuba required more than the lifting of US sanctions. It called for the removal of both internal and external barriers. This is how he diplomatically phrased his dual appeal, which was widely circulated by the international press: "May Cuba open itself to the world, and may the world open itself to Cuba."

When I heard from afar the pope interconnecting for the first time, at least indirectly, both sides of the embargo, I could not help but surmise that Cardinal O'Connor had had a hand in crafting the felicitous phrase. (I was able to confirm my hunch a few weeks later.)

The pope ended his arrival remarks "with the prayer that this land [Cuba] may offer to everyone a climate of freedom, mutual trust, social justice, and lasting peace."[17] *Not a bad start,* I said to myself.

Despite his frail health, undermined by the onset of Parkinson's disease, Hurricane Wojtyla, as he was called in Cuba, crisscrossed the island, celebrating multitudinous, open-air Masses in four large cities. In his homilies, which were broadcast live in Cuba following tense negotiations with the Castro regime, the pope covered a wide range of topics from education and marriage to moral values and reconciliation. But the two themes that drew most frequent and enthusiastic applause were human rights and freedom. The young people in the central city of Camagüey were particularly roused when the Holy Father urged them, as protagonists of Cuba's future, "to be bold in [the search of] truth, courageous in [the pursuit of] freedom, constant in responsibility, generous in love, invincible in hope!"

In the far-eastern city of Santiago de Cuba, many were uplifted by the valorous words of the elderly archbishop of Santiago, Pedro Meurice, who introduced the pope. Not mincing words like most of the fainthearted bishops on the island, he reproached those Cubans who had confused "patriotism with [political] party ... and culture with an ideology." He stressed the need to debunk "false messianism" and denounced how the church, and the nation, had been "impoverished by a state-provoked ideological confrontation with Marxism-Leninism." He also called for the unification of the divided Cuban family, but not one resulting from government-imposed uniformity.[18]

The pope followed suit with a vigorous homily, advocating "true freedom, which includes recognition of human rights and social justice." He said that the church "does not seek any type of political power in order to carry out her mission" and added that the freedom the church claims for itself it also claims for all individuals and families who have "a right to their own sphere of autonomy and sovereignty."

Putting to rest any impression of Vatican timidity or capitulation, he asserted that "the church is called to bear witness to Christ by taking courageous and prophetic stands in the face of the corruption of political or economic power." He closed his eloquent remarks by evoking Cuba's Christian traditions, exemplified by the devotion of the Cuban people to the Virgin of Charity (Virgen de la Caridad del Cobre).

John Paul II crowned his Cuban pilgrimage with an open-air Mass at the Plaza de la Revolución in Havana attended by close to one million people, including Fidel Castro and members of his cabinet. His message was deep, but his language was clear. It resonated with the huge crowd, which interrupted him with applause more than twenty times. Even though the pope followed the ill advice of Cuba's cardinal Jaime Ortega not to meet privately with leaders of the dissident movement lest it enrage Castro, John Paul II made up for that blunder, or missed opportunity, by choosing freedom as the central theme for his final Mass in Havana.

Having earlier called for the liberation of all political prisoners on the island, the pope invoked the Gospel according to Saint Luke and declared that "the Spirit of the Lord has sent me to proclaim release to the captives ... to set at liberty those who are oppressed." Some in the crowd responded with this refrain: "El Papa, libre, nos quiere a *todos* libres" (The pope, free, wants us *all* free).

The Holy Father's good humor won the hearts of those attending the Havana Mass. Following one of many bursts of applause that interrupted the flow of his homily, he quipped, "I am not against the applause, because when you applaud, the pope rests." Even the stern-looking Fidel could not help but smile.

The Cubans, for their part, also displayed their pungent wit as evidenced in one of the refrains that emanated from the crowd: "El Papa, amigo, llévatelo contigo" (The pope, friend, take him [Castro] with you).[19]

John Paul II left the island tired but in high spirits. Although Castro gave no indication that he would liberalize his Communist regime—in fact he scoffed at any comparison between Cuba and Poland—the pope was pleased with the response of the Cuban people to his pilgrimage and his messages. He felt that an epiphany of faith had occurred, which, if further stimulated by the church on the island, could eventually (most likely in a post-Castro era) create an environment conducive to a peaceful transition to freedom and justice under the rule of law.

Cardinal O'Connor, who helped sharpen some of the key messages of the pope, was most appreciative of the suggestions I gave him, and surprised me with a very special invitation. Through his kind intercession, the Vatican accorded me and my family the rare privilege of attending on September 7, 1998, the pope's early morning mass at the tiny chapel of his Castel Gandolfo summer residence, followed by a brief private audience with him. The cardinal also honored me and three other Hispanic community leaders with a papal award at the Solemn Pontifical Mass held at Saint Patrick's Cathedral on October 16 to celebrate the twentieth anniversary of the pontificate of John Paul II.

I was, of course, deeply touched by O'Connor's deference, but what heightened my esteem and admiration for him was his keen interest, indeed his zeal, to follow up on the pope's visit to Cuba. He told me and other colleagues that the seeds planted by the Holy Father had to be nurtured if they were to fructify, then he started to discuss with us possible next steps. Sadly, on May 3, 2000, a very aggressive cancer extinguished the life of this spiritual leader. Freedom-loving Cubans lost his invaluable support but gained the inspiration of his exemplary legacy.

The Elián González Affair

The impact of the Cuban saga was felt, yet again, in the United States following a wrenching episode with political ramifications that became a cause célèbre: the Elián González affair.

On November 21, 1999, five-year-old Elián, his mother, and twelve friends fled Cuba on a small aluminum boat with a faulty engine. Elián's mother and ten others died when the boat capsized under stormy weather in the crossing. However, the young boy and two other survivors were found floating on inner tubes by several fishermen, who turned them over to the US Coast Guard.

The Immigration and Naturalization Service released Elián to his paternal great-uncle Lázaro, living in Miami, who contended that the boy should remain in the United States as his mother, divorced from her Castroite husband, fervently wished. Indeed, she had sacrificed her life so that her son could be raised in freedom.

But Elián's estranged father, Juan Miguel, induced or encouraged by the Castro regime, laid claim to the boy and insisted that he be returned to his care in Cuba. The custody battle that ensued became an inflammatory political issue, particularly when Fidel Castro took center stage and confidently anticipated that Elián would be sent back to the island. "It's inevitable," he emphatically declared. Cuban American leaders warned that if that were to happen, Elián would be brainwashed and turned into a poster boy for the Communist regime.

During the widely publicized legal battle, it became evident that the Clinton administration favored reuniting Elián with his father, despite his mother's wishes and the likelihood of Communist indoctrination. Supporters of that position held that it was based solely on legal grounds—in the absence of the mother, the father's will prevails. Critics argued that it was driven or influenced by political considerations—Clinton's desire to ingratiate himself with Castro to seek a rapprochement.

As soon as a Florida family court judge revoked the great-uncle's temporary custody of Elián, Attorney General Janet Reno ordered heavily armed federal agents to seize Elián in Miami and bring him to Washington. In the predawn hours of April 22, 2000, an elite Border Patrol force, brandishing machine guns and employing pepper spray and mace against on-site protesters, barged into the house where Elián was staying with his relatives, grabbed the boy, and flew him to Andrews Air Force Base in Washington to meet with his father.[20]

The White House arranged for their stay at the Aspen Institute Wye River Conference Center in Maryland (formerly known as Wye River Plantation) while they awaited a final court decision on the asylum plea filed by the great-uncle on behalf of Elián. During their sojourn at the plantation, the *Miami Herald* reported that at least two dozen Castro diplomats, their spouses, their kids, and aides visited them. In addition, US visas were issued to Elián's classmates and teachers from his hometown in Cuba so that they could join him at the plantation. They flew to Washington along with a Cuban doctor carrying antidepressants, which were seized by US Customs agents at Dulles International Airport. Elián's relatives in Miami, barred from visiting him, denounced that the feared reprogramming of the boy had already started, sadly in the United States.[21]

On June 28, 2000, the US Supreme Court declined to review the 11th US Circuit Court of Appeals ruling that Elián's great-uncle and other Miami relatives lacked legal standing to file for the boy's asylum. Later the same day, Elián, his father, and their entourage flew to Havana and were accorded a rapturous welcome by Fidel Castro.

The outcome was not surprising. Fidel took Elián under his wing, attended his birthday parties, and hoisted him as a symbol of the revolution in its struggle against Yankee imperialism. Shortly after the boy's return to Cuba, he donned the Communist Young Pioneer uniform. On September 28, 2005, Elián, then eleven, stated in an interview with CBS's *60 Minutes* that he considered Fidel "not only as a friend, but also as a father."[22] In 2008, he dutifully joined the Young Communist Union of Cuba.

The Elián González affair had political repercussions in the United States. The seizure of the boy in Miami by armed federal agents and his subsequent return to Communist Cuba produced a significant swing to Republicans from irate Cuban American Florida voters in the 2000 presidential election. Pundits believe that this swing may have influenced the close outcome of the election, clinched by George W. Bush by winning the critical state of Florida by a margin of only 537 votes.

CHAPTER 13

Divergent Paths: George W. Bush and David Rockefeller (2001–2009)

Shortly after taking office, George W. Bush declared that US sanctions on Communist Cuba were not just a policy tool but also were a "moral statement." Aware that the Castro regime continued systematically to violate civil and political rights, the president stipulated no weakening of the embargo until the regime released political prisoners, allowed free speech, and held democratic elections. However, the Bush administration did not oppose or hinder the unofficial rapprochement made by the Council on Foreign Relations to Fidel Castro.

The council, a highly regarded and powerful nongovernment organization that often shapes or influences US foreign policy, felt that a new attempt should be made to seek, or at least explore, an accommodation with Communist Cuba. With that mission in mind, it decided to send to Havana in February 2001 a most impressive delegation of nineteen renowned foreign affairs experts, business leaders, former senior government officials, academics, and council executive staff. The delegation was to be led by David Rockefeller, former chairman of Chase Manhattan Bank, who helped to found and support numerous internationally oriented think tanks and nonprofit organizations.

The Castro-Rockefeller Encounter in New York

David Rockefeller's long-standing interest in engaging Castro spiked in October 1995 when the Cuban ruler attended the celebration in New York of the fiftieth anniversary of the United Nations. As Rockefeller recounted: "El Presidente wanted especially to meet me. ... At the formal reception hosted by Secretary-General Boutros-Ghali at the UN, Castro spotted me, charged across the delegates lounge, and grabbed my hand, shaking it warmly." Rockefeller attributed Fidel's effusiveness, in part, to his daughter Peggy Dulany, who "had visited Cuba a number of times since 1985 and developed a good rapport with President Castro."[1]

Prior to Castro's arrival in New York, the media reported that David Rockefeller and his daughter Peggy were planning to host a reception in Fidel's honor at the Rockefeller country estate in Pocantico Hills, New York. The news infuriated the highly sensitive Cuban American community. The psychological and political implications of the announced reception, likely viewed as paying homage to the Cuban dictator, also concerned me. So, given my personal relationship with David, stemming from our involvement in the Council of the Americas, I decided to drop him the following note:[2]

October 17, 1995

Dear David:

I am deeply disappointed and saddened to learn that you and your daughter are planning to host a private reception in honor of Fidel Castro.

Given your high profile and prestige, the reception is bound to have negative repercussions. Castro, desperately searching for supporters, would be emboldened by your gracious hospitality, while freedom-loving Cubans would feel rebuffed by the perceived insensitivity.

David, you don't need this controversy. As a friend, please reconsider your decision.

Sincerely,

Néstor Carbonell

True to form, David promptly replied on October 19, explaining in a long, cordial letter why he believed that engaging Castro was advisable and could be fruitful. He clarified, however, that he and his daughter Peggy had not planned a private reception honoring Fidel, but he said that a meeting with him at some neutral location in New York was possible.

While David shared many of my concerns, he still felt that dialogues even with dictators could be useful. He referred in general terms to a number of instances where autocratic leaders have come to realize that their policies had failed and were hurting their own people. Rockefeller was hopeful that a private conversation with the Cuban ruler could lead to fruitful negotiations at the government level.

He ended his missive invoking our friendship and conveying his warm regards.

I greatly appreciated that David had taken the time to explain his position, but I begged to differ. The candid, soft-power approach he advocated to engage Castro may have worked with other dictators, but with the cunning and intractable Fidel, such attempts had only served to boost his ego and steel his stand. In my respectful rejoinder, I warned David that "with Castro, there is more monologue than dialogue," and I added, "Castro is no Franco, and he certainly is no Gorbachev. He is not even Pinochet. He repudiates the slightest political opening." As for the limited economic reforms he had initiated, I pointed out that they stemmed "not from diplomatic parleys, but from sustained and painful pressure."

David Rockefeller met privately with Castro on October 23 at the

Council on Foreign Relations building on Park Avenue, but we do not know what was discussed. What we *do* know is that at the United Nations, where Castro drew more applause than President Clinton, he blasted the US embargo on Cuba. With his finger jabbing the air for emphasis, he declared: "We lay claim to a world without ruthless blockades [a term he used for the Cuba embargo] that cause the death of men, women, and children, youth and elders, like noiseless atom bombs."

And to his enthusiastic supporters in Harlem, who might have thought that he had changed his revolutionary stripes by wearing a tailored suit at the United Nations and socializing with fawning celebrities in Manhattan, he said, "Others might change because they are not in the right. We won't because we *are* right."[3]

The Summit in Havana

Although Castro had shown no indication of tempering his uncompromising stand, the Council on Foreign Relations went ahead with the planned trip to Havana on February 14, 2001. Among the members of the high-powered delegation headed by David Rockefeller were Peter Peterson, former secretary of commerce in the Nixon administration and chairman of the council; William Rogers, former undersecretary of state; Carla Hills, former US trade representative; Jim Jones, former US ambassador to Mexico; Mario Baeza, a Cuban American attorney and investment banker in New York; and Mark Falcoff, a resident scholar at the American Enterprise Institute for Public Policy Research, former senior staff member on the Senate Committee on Foreign Relations, and author of well-documented books on Latin America and Cuba.

The main purpose of the trip was to discuss with senior government officials in Cuba, including Fidel Castro, the proposals made by a council task force to normalize US-Cuban relations and "contribute to a rapid, peaceful, democratic transition in Cuba."

The 2001 task force report titled "The US-Cuban Relations in the 21st Century" outlined four areas of recommendations submitted to the Castro regime: "family reunification and migration; the free flow of ideas to speed the dynamic currently under way; security proposal to develop relationships and deepen counternarcotics cooperation and military-to-military exchanges; and trade, investment, property, and labor rights."

The four-day visit to Cuba was chronicled by Mark Falcoff, who gave me a copy of his notes, punctuated with insightful observations and colorful anecdotes.

Although the VIP tour that was arranged by the Castro regime was "guided" and not too extensive, the council members were able nevertheless to get a pretty good grasp of the current situation on the island. Those who had not previously visited Cuba were impressed by the splendor of Old Havana, enhanced by the restored colonial architectural gems, but most were depressed by the bleak surroundings, which were saddled with dilapidated buildings crowded with sorely wanting dwellers.

The very full and intense program of meetings started with a visit to the thirty-four-year-old foreign minister Felipe Pérez Roque. Following the cordial greetings, "his message was simple: lift the embargo [unilaterally] and everything will be okay." He reluctantly conceded that some of the council's proposals were "constructive" (lifting the ceiling on remittances, allowing more-frequent family visits, antinarcotics cooperation), but echoing the party line, he insisted on nothing less than "a complete turnaround on US policy."

The delegation then met with the ministers of basic industry and tourism, who proudly recited facts and figures about new joint ventures with foreign investors. When Falcoff later asked Pete Peterson what he thought of the numbers, the former US secretary of commerce and council chairman reportedly replied, "It was a drop in the bucket, nothing at all even for a fairly small country."

In their conversation with both ministers, the council members broached an issue that they felt might be of concern to prospective foreign investors. It had to do with the "curious labor law," which required investors to hire employees selected by a government agency and to pay their salaries in hard currency to the same agency that pocketed 90 percent (sometimes 95 percent) of the remunerations and doled out the balance to the employees in local currency. The ministers dismissed the issue, saying that the system in place did not bother or hold back foreign investors.

The council group met with several other high-level government officials, as well as with ambassadors, artists, and intellectuals. They also had the opportunity to converse with a few prominent dissidents and human rights activists at the former residence of the US ambassador, then occupied by the head of the US Interests Section in Havana. All of these individuals were very critical of the oppressive Castro regime, but they expressed divergent views of US foreign policy—some in favor of the embargo, other against it.

The time finally came for the meeting with Fidel Castro. It started at about 10:30 p.m. and ended at 4:00 a.m. Following are the highlights gleaned from Falcoff's detailed notes:

"David Rockefeller started out the conversation by complimenting Castro and his educational achievements. This was the cue for Castro to talk for probably an hour and a half, wandering all over the terrain. A follow-up question produced more floods of oratory"—from the Bay of Pigs to a school of social work he had just opened. "At about 2:45 a.m.," wrote Falcoff, "Bill Rogers managed to get to the [main] point of the meeting, which was to pin down Castro on our report. What did he think of the [council's] specific proposals?"

Castro didn't see why the council persisted in "half measures," when in his view the real problem was the embargo, which had to be lifted. "He thought that this report was more 'rightist' than the last one … and he spoke [disparagingly] of the language of the report—particularly the constant reference to the 'post-Castro' era, spitting out the words with venom and sarcasm."

According to Falcoff's notes, Walter Mead and Julia Sweig of the council intervened to explain to Castro that the "Left" in the United

States, which has always been "in solidarity" with the revolution and favored a change in US policy, had to gain support of the "Right"—thus the language used by the council's task force in its report. This did not appease the irate ruler, who "interrupted to say that it was terrible that an injustice like the embargo had to be corrected through immoral means."

Trying again to focus the discussion on the central theme, Bill Rogers asked Castro what he thought of the council's specific proposals, for example, US food and medical sales to Cuba. Fidel flatly responded that even if they were offered, "we can't buy anything from you because you don't buy anything from us." (Despite Castro's brusque turndown, the United States soon became one of Cuba's major suppliers of food and medicine. Fidel's obstinacy was overridden by necessity.)

At a certain point, the irrepressible Bill Rogers jumped in again and asked Castro what his brother Raúl meant when he declared on Cuban television that the United States would be well-advised to make its peace with his brother now, rather than wait till later, when "things would be more difficult." Deflecting the question, Castro asked Rogers what *he* thought Raúl meant. Bill said: "I don't know." Fidel replied: "I don't either." Everyone in the room burst out laughing. "This was the only light moment in the whole meeting," wrote Falcoff.

At about 3:15 a.m., Castro invited the council delegation for a dinner served in a separate room. At the end of the copious meal—five courses and two wines—it was time for toasts. David Rockefeller raised his glass and thanked Castro and the Cubans for their warm hospitality—a courteous one-minute tribute. The group remained standing when Castro took the floor to toast his guests. He said, "Don't worry, I'm not going to make a long speech," and then proceeded to do just that.

About five minutes into Castro's meandering remarks, Bill Rogers collapsed into his chair. Mark Falcoff, who recounted this episode, turned to him and asked if he was all right. "Yes, fine, just a little weak," he said. Castro droned on. Bill looked worse and worse, noted Falcoff, slumping down over the table. The entire room became alarmed, except Castro, who continued to talk, oblivious to it all.

After Fidel concluded his seemingly endless toast, one of his aides apparently whispered in his ear what was going on. In a flash, an emergency team, including Fidel's personal doctor, appeared on the scene and carried Rogers to an upper floor, along with his wife, Julia Sweig, and Peggy Dulany.

Meanwhile, Castro bid farewell to the rest of the council delegates as they filed out of the room toward the elevators. It was 4:00 a.m.

Thus ended the touted visit to Cuba of the council's heavyweights. The good news was that Bill Rogers got excellent medical care—the type reserved for the ruling elite and foreign dignitaries—and in an hour returned to the hotel feeling better. The bad news was that the council's mission to engage Castro failed. He rejected the "half measure" proposed by the task force and demanded the total and unconditional lifting of the US embargo with no indication that he would liberalize the regime.

David Rockefeller wrote in his memoirs, "Castro harangued us continuously throughout the night. When I intervened to ask him if there were areas where he had not achieved his goals, he paused briefly but had trouble thinking of one." Rockefeller concluded: "I think there is little possibility for change while Castro remains in power, although he does seem willing to negotiate on many important issues." (David did not mention what those issues were.)[4]

Castro's Superspy

On September 21, 2001, ten days after the horrific terrorist attacks against the World Trade Center and the Pentagon, the FBI arrested Ana Belen Montes, a forty-four-year-old highly decorated US intelligence official charged with conspiracy to commit espionage for the Castro regime.

Born in 1957 to Puerto Rican parents, and armed with impressive academic credentials from Johns Hopkins and the University of Virginia, Montes rose through the ranks of the Defense Intelligence Agency (DIA) while spying for Castro. For seventeen years, reported the *Washington Post*, "she blindsided the intelligence community with brazen acts of treason." Intelligence experts consider her among the most harmful spies in recent memory.

Hired by the Pentagon's major producer of foreign military intelligence as an entry-level research specialist, Montes was frequently promoted and became the DIA's top political and military analyst for Cuba, or as she was known in those circles, "the Queen of Cuba."

Ana Belen Montes not only passed on to Castro military secrets of the United States but also "proved adept at shaping [and often softening] US policy toward the island nation."⁵ She persuaded many in the Defense Department and the intelligence community that the Castro regime no longer posed a threat to the United States or the region and subtly suggested that it should be engaged and brought into the fold.

It is truly astonishing that Montes was able to get away with such treacherous acts for so long. As disclosed by the *Post*, by day she was a buttoned-down GS-14 in a Defense Intelligence Agency cubicle, and by night she was on the clock for Fidel Castro, listening to coded messages over shortwave radio, passing encrypted files to handlers in crowded restaurants, and slipping undetected into Cuba wearing a wig and clutching a phony passport.

The FBI would have preferred to monitor Montes a bit longer, hoping that she could lead the agency to others in Cuba's vast spy network. However, given Montes's possible access to classified information about the impending US and NATO military intervention in Afghanistan, and given Castro's long history of selling secrets to US enemies, the FBI decided not to take any chances. After her arrest, Montes pleaded guilty and was sentenced to a twenty-five-year prison term. Her plea bargaining possibly saved her from the death penalty.

Montes was not the only spy working for Castro in Washington. Two others were convicted in 2010: State Department officer and part-time faculty member at the Johns Hopkins School of Advanced International Studies Walter Kendall Myers and his wife Gwendolyn. Walter was sentenced to life imprisonment, and Gwendolyn was given seven years. They reportedly had spied for thirty years and managed to influence numerous intelligence estimates and policy recommendations on Cuba, downplaying the continued risk or potential threat posed by the Castro regime.

The Varela Project and the Black Spring

Trying to divert attention from the highly publicized arrests, Castro extended an informal invitation to Jimmy Carter to visit Havana in early 2002. The former president accepted the invitation, thinking that his visit would help to improve US-Cuba relations, and agreed to deliver a televised speech at the University of Havana with no strings attached. In his address, Carter called on US Congress to lift the embargo on Cuba. That was music to the ears of Fidel and the members of his politburo. But the following part of the address was not to their liking. Indeed, it riled them deep inside. Carter endorsed the Varela Project, which petitioned the Castro regime for a referendum on civil liberties.

The project, named after Father Félix Varela, revered by many as a precursor of Cuba's independence, was launched by a coalition of dissident groups led by the fifty-year-old devout Catholic engineer Oswaldo Payá. Backed by more than double the ten thousand minimum required signatures for citizens' petitions to be considered by the National Assembly (putative parliament), the project called for a national referendum on draft legislation guaranteeing freedom of expression, association, religion, and private enterprise.

The day after his speech, Carter met with Castro and suggested several economic and political reforms consistent with the Varela Project, which would not only benefit the Cuban people but also help neutralize US congressional opposition to the lifting of the embargo. Carter emerged from the meeting very disappointed. According to his adviser

Robert Pastor, "he just shook his head." Castro had turned down all his proposals. The former president reportedly imagined that "Fidel might play a role like Deng Xiaoping in China, catalyzing reform. Their conversations convinced him otherwise."[6]

The Black Spring

To allay any illusion that he might become a true reformer, Fidel Castro tabled the Varela Project shortly after Carter left the island. He also mobilized the masses to denounce US stratagems to undermine his regime and secured enough signatures (almost unanimity, he claimed) to approve a constitutional amendment declaring socialism "irrevocable."

Yet Fidel was not satisfied with a mere legal formality. After all, he owed his permanence in power not to the rule of law but to the use of force. Realizing that the dissident movement, spurred by the Varela Project and other initiatives, was gaining strength, he decided to crush it. During a three-day span in mid-March 2003, as the world watched, with shock and awe, the US-led invasion of Iraq, Castro ordered a sweeping crackdown. The regime's security forces arrested some seventy-five peaceful dissidents—independent journalists, librarians, democracy advocates, and human rights activists, many of whom were involved in the Varela Project.

Adolfo Fernández-Saínz, one of the journalists arrested, was accused of "subverting the internal order of the nation" with a small home-based news agency alleged to be spreading lies planted by the US media. This is how his wife, Julia, described the raid: "Over the course of eight long hours, plainclothes state security agents, pistols on hip, ransacked the apartment, confiscating items considered proof of Fernández-Saínz's crimes: a typewriter, stacks of the Communist Party daily (*Granma*) with Fidel Castro's remarks underlined, and outlawed books such as George Orwell's *Animal Farm* and *1984*."[7]

Convicted in one-day show trials, the seventy-five dissidents were sentenced to prison terms ranging from twelve to twenty-eight years.

The "decent, quiet, no fighting, no yelling" Fernández-Saínz, as described by one of the agents involved in the raids, was sentenced to fifteen years behind bars.

The unsparing crackdown, known as Cuba's Black Spring, was strongly condemned as a "flagrant breach of human rights" even by the generally ambivalent or accommodating European Union. This time the EU stiffened its resolve and imposed sanctions on the Castro regime. Amnesty International, among other human rights organizations that took a stand against the brutal repression, adopted the seventy-five arrested dissidents as "prisoners of conscience."

Bush's Free Cuba Program

In light of these despicable developments, Bush blocked a congressional drive to seek a rapprochement with Castro. Instead of making unilateral concessions to the Cuban ruler—like offering tourist dollars, which would only serve to subsidize his tyranny—the president approved between October 2003 and May 2004 a number of measures to tighten the embargo and hasten "democratic change" on the island. The multiagency program included steps to reduce the flow of hard currency and visitors from the United States to Cuba.

The program also allocated up to $59 million over two years to intensify public diplomacy, broadcasting, and support for democracy-building trailblazers on the island. These included human rights activists and relatives of dissident leaders imprisoned by the Castro regime.

To coordinate the program, Bush created the Commission for Assistance to a Free Cuba, designed to hasten a transition to democracy and establish the "core institutions of a free economy, modernize infrastructure, and meet basic need in the areas of health, education, housing, and human services."[8] Referring to the strategy underpinning the commission's work, the president declared, "It is a strategy that says we're not waiting for the day of Cuban freedom, we are working for the day of freedom in Cuba."[9]

The commission's undertaking, coordinated with five US government agencies, was perhaps the most comprehensive effort to advance the cause of democracy in Cuba through peaceful means. However, it was not able to overcome the jamming by the Castro regime of the transmissions of Radio Martí and TV Martí and could not rally many of the Latin American and European countries (or the Vatican) to support the Free Cuba program. Although inspired by Reagan's playbook to roll back communism in Poland (and other Eastern European countries), the program lacked the technical and financial resources, backing, and persistent follow-up that had enabled Solidarity to turn the tide.

Still, the commission made significant headway in reenergizing the dissident movement in Cuba, which had been implacably battered and demoralized by the crackdown.

Corporal Cason

In that endeavor, the point man in Havana was James Cason, a fifty-seven-year-old US Foreign Service officer with an MA from the School of Advanced International Studies (SAIS), Johns Hopkins University, and extensive diplomatic experience in Latin America. Cason served from 2002 to 2005 as principal officer at the US Interests Section in Havana (the de facto US ambassador) and later as US ambassador to Paraguay.

The Castro regime regarded Cason as a subversive agent of Yankee imperialism and made it very difficult for him to carry out his task. He could not have more than fifty-one Americans working at the Interests Section in Havana and was not allowed to hire local employees directly. He had to accept those selected by the regime (most of whom were spies). His ability to travel across the island was sharply restricted, and he was effectively barred from interacting with government officials, professionals, and academics and from airing his views in the national press.

Despite the hurdles he faced, Cason managed to meet with

dissident leaders in the Interests Section in Havana and give them books, shortwave radios, and humanitarian aid. In solidarity with the seventy-five human rights and prodemocracy activists who were imprisoned during the crackdown, Cason placed in front of the Interests Section building the number 75, in neon light, atop a thirty-foot replica of the Statue of Liberty smuggled in for the Fourth of July celebration. At Christmastime, he also prominently displayed the symbolic 75 between a giant Santa and a Rudolph the Red-Nosed Reindeer gracing the facade of the building.

Castro and his minions were not amused. Realizing that Cason's campaign was not only propping up the buffeted dissident movement but also creating considerable buzz in Havana and beyond, they promptly launched their counteroffensive. They put up a hundred-foot-high banner on an apartment house adjacent to the Interests Section building that depicted Cason as a Santa on a sleigh pulled by twelve marines dropping bombs on Iraqi kids. Castro's propagandists also ran attack cartoons on TV against "Cabo Cason" (Corporal Cason) as part of a series designed to ridicule and discredit the Yankee corporal.

Cason was happy with the free publicity he got, which bolstered his standing and put the regime on the defensive. So he kept it going by placing corporal stripes on the guayabera shirt he wore for National Day parties and by affixing his cartoon persona to a flag he flew on the front of his car. Needless to say, Castro was relieved when the intrepid Cason was replaced in 2005 as the principal officer of the US Interests Section in Havana.[10]

Cason's successor, Michael E. Parmly, who initially seemed intent on lowering the section's profile, eventually continued the psychological campaign to awaken civil society and incite peaceful dissent. In January 2006, he erected a three-foot-high scrolling electronic news billboard across the length of the fifth floor of the Interests Section building. The screen displayed excerpts from the Universal Declaration of Human Rights, the works of Martin Luther King, and other inspiring messages.

In response, Castro denounced the "insolence" of the Bush administration at a public rally next to the Interests Section and ordered the erection of 138 black flags outside the US mission to obscure the billboard.[11] With those flags flapping in the wind like gigantic bat wings, the regime effectively smothered the billboard's prodemocracy messages but was unable to quell what it feared most—the unabated yearning for freedom of the Cuban people.

Raúl Castro at the Helm

In July 2006, Fidel Castro shocked the nation, announcing that his illness (complications from an acute intestinal infection that forced him to undergo several operations) made it necessary for him to cede power temporarily to his brother Raúl and a leadership team of six high-level government officials. The dynastic succession was consummated in 2008 when a frail Fidel resigned and anointed Raúl head of state.

Many in Washington were heartened by the succession, thinking that Raúl Castro—the chief operating officer of the regime who had revamped and led Cuba's armed forces and installed its totalitarian system with Soviet assistance—was more pragmatic and open to change than his obdurate brother.

Even President Bush, who was not as sanguine with the succession as most of the foreign experts, welcomed the news while traveling in Rwanda and expressed his earnest hope that Raúl's accession to the highest level of government would mark the beginning of a democratic transition in Cuba. He also pledged that "the United States will help the people of Cuba realize the blessings of liberty."[12]

Seeking to create a climate conducive to constructive engagement, Bush extended an olive branch to Raúl in 2008, following the three hurricanes that devastated the island. The president offered Cuba $6.3 million in humanitarian assistance, $5 million of which would be provided directly to the Castro regime. Bush no longer insisted that the entire donation be channeled through nongovernmental organizations on the island.

Despite this concession, the cagey Raúl threw a monkey wrench into the negotiations by demanding, as a condition, that the US embargo be lifted, at least for six months, so that Cuba could buy construction materials to rebuild damaged homes.[13] This condition killed the offer and forestalled yet another attempt to thaw US-Cuba relations.

CHAPTER 14

Raúl Castro's Rule and Bogus Opening

In 2008, Raúl Castro took over the Communist regime by virtue of the dynastic succession decreed by his ailing brother. He faced a most serious challenge. It was not an external military threat but an internal economic and financial crisis with far-reaching consequences.

It Doesn't Even Work for Us Anymore

In August 2010, the frail Fidel Castro, still evincing flashes of lucidity, confessed to Jeffrey Goldberg of *The Atlantic* magazine: "The Cuban model doesn't even work for us anymore." (He later recanted his Freudian slip, alleging that he had been misunderstood.)

In December 2010, the curt, no-nonsense Raúl Castro, at the helm of the regime, addressed the rubber-stamp parliament and, in his deep guttural voice, somberly warned the delegates: "We can either rectify the situation, or we will run out of time walking on the edge of the abyss, and we will sink."[1] Cubans sardonically dubbed these apocalyptic remarks the "Titanic speech."

Cuba was facing a severe economic and financial crisis, aggravated by a series of calamities: three hurricanes in 2008, estimated at $10 billion in damage; a 25 percent drop in the price of nickel (a major source of foreign exchange); and the decline of revenues from tourism caused by the global recession.

Marc Frank, Reuters' correspondent in Havana, sounded the alarm on April 23, 2009. "A cash crunch that began last year for Cuba," he wrote, "appears to be getting worse as state-run banks insist they have little foreign currency." A subsequent Agence France-Presse dispatch from Havana carried this unnerving headline: "Power Cuts and Fewer Beans for Crisis-Hit Cubans."[2]

An angry Raúl Castro blamed the populace for much of the island's decay and depravation without acknowledging the root cause: the oppressive, inefficient, and corrupt totalitarian system he continued to uphold.

■ "Resolving" on the Island

Coping with the crisis, which has not significantly abated, remains a daily ordeal. Every morning most Cubans wake up wondering how they will meet their basic needs. Their conundrum: how to supplement a thirty-day government food ration that lasts at best a couple of weeks with a monthly state salary of slightly over $40 on average (following a minimum salary raise in June 2019). Each day becomes a survivalist zigzag around the impediments of a miserable, regimented life. Islanders have a name for this artful dodging. They call it "resolving."

Resolving describes the scramble for essentials in a nation that lacks "everything except police and disillusion"—the words of a European visitor. The shortages are less felt by the fortunate Cubans who receive remittances from family abroad. They are able to exchange the hard currency they get for CUCs, the local convertible currency at parity with the dollar, which gives them access to the better-supplied hard currency stores.

The large swaths of nonprivileged Cubans who depend solely on the government's meager stipend or pension must be more creative. They barter, moonlight, or perform any service—legalities notwithstanding—as long as a fee is involved. And when there is no fee, they take what they need. Pilfering is so prevalent that job seekers are less interested in the pittance they'll be paid than in the swag they can pocket.

One could say, without overstretching this point, that the Castro regime has democratized stealing.

Shortages have tested the Cubans' creativity, particularly during the "Special Period" in the 1990s, following the end of the Soviet subsidies. Some Cubans have punched holes in the bottom of a water bottle to make a showerhead. Women have used colored classroom chalk for makeup, shoeshine paste for their eyelashes, and ground-up battery charcoal to darken their hair.[3]

Cubans have made deodorants with bicarbonate of soda, and shampoos with vinegar and soap (if available) or with rainwater and detergents. Absent toilet paper, government newspapers (not widely read) have become very handy. In the culinary department, the Cubans' resourcefulness is also manifest. People have made coffee from peas and cooked picadillo, a hash-like staple, with soy and banana peels in lieu of meat.

Belt Tightening ... and a Few Surprises

To avert the meltdown of the heavily indebted and stagnating economy, Raúl Castro initially took some drastic steps. He slashed imports, except food products, by about one-third, closed or consolidated a number of inefficient ministries and government-controlled businesses, and capped energy use across the board.

Belt tightening was certainly needed. But Raúl crossed the line by taking several arbitrary and alarming steps in 2009. He froze local bank deposits of foreign investors and suppliers up to $1 billion[4] and temporarily suspended international transfers. He also unilaterally converted some major overdue accounts payable by the Castro regime into medium-term loans bearing very low interest with no collateral.

Even one of the leading nongovernment foreign investors in Cuba, the Canadian Sherritt Corporation, reportedly had to accept a five-year deferred payment of its $162 million past due accounts. Only a police state holding investors, suppliers, and speculators as virtual hostages can pull that off without a grumble or whimper.

The Purge

While tackling the crisis, the sly Raúl Castro set the stage for a purge. Seeming to recognize that the state-controlled economy was broken, he urged Cubans to express their views and suggestions, even at the regime's expense. He said: "The best solutions can come from a profound exchange of differing opinions"—startling words from a career Marxist-Leninist. But they proved to be nothing more than a ruse to spotlight deviationists lurking in the shadows and punish overly ambitious functionaries. It seemed to echo Mao's deceitful campaign "Let 100 Flowers Bloom."

Despite his purported respect for dissenting views, Raúl proceeded to purge several high-level government officials he did not trust. These people included Carlos Lage, fifty-seven, senior vice president of the regime and czar of the economy, and Felipe Pérez Roque, forty-four, who rose from the ranks of the Young Communist League and became foreign minister under Fidel. They were accused of maligning the revolutionary leaders (allegedly dubbed "dinosaurs" or "living fossils") and harboring sordid political ambitions.

After vilifying Lage and Pérez Roque for three hours in the presence of Communist Party honchos, Raúl forced the two to bow their heads and repent for their imputed transgressions. Following their Stalinesque self-flagellation and a period of house arrest (dubbed by dissidents "Operation Pajama"), Lage was relegated to the post of administrator of a modest hospital, and Pérez Roque was ordered to serve as an engineer in an industrial park on the outskirts of Havana. A woeful outcome for the two renegades, but at least they saved their skin.

After tackling the purge, Raúl Castro had to face the severe impact of the economic crisis on the regime's education and health-care systems.

Education

The free education system launched by the Castro regime has gone from hyped star to crashing meteorite. Early on, after closing down all private schools and universities, the regime embarked on an intense drive to raise literacy across the island. Reaching deep into Cuba's most remote villages, teams of teachers and assistants made significant progress.

According to most published statistics, literacy on the island rose from a respectable 77 percent in 1958 (the fourth-highest in Latin America) to over 90 percent today—the regime claims 99 percent.

But Cuba's high literacy rate came at a steep price. The curriculum aggressively promoted communism, distorted history, and glorified Fidel Castro, Che Guevara, and other revolutionary leaders. Young students were separated from their parents for extended periods and sent to ad hoc education-cum-work camps in the countryside, where supervision was lax and promiscuity rampant. Opportunity to pursue higher education and university degrees largely depended on loyalty to the Cuban Revolution and compliance with the official diktats.

In recent years, however, Cuba's education system has sharply declined. A shortage of funds for school maintenance is matched by a dearth of teachers, many of whom have been sent to more than thirty countries as part of Cuba's Yes I Can literacy program to generate hard currency for the Castro regime while spreading the Communist gospel.

To address the island's educational deficit, the government relies on unlicensed or "emerging" teachers and exhorts retired professors to return to the classroom. The Cuban Education Ministry acknowledged a shortfall of about ten thousand teachers in the 2018–2019 school year.[5]

A Cuban American writer, José Manuel Prieto, had something to say in 2011 when he visited the school he'd attended in the 1970s—the Escuela Vocacional Lenin, still deemed Cuba's best. "It's a pale copy today of what it was when Leonid Brezhnev inaugurated it in 1975," wrote Prieto in the *New York Review of Books*. "Back then it offered an impressive education." Now, given the shortage of professors, "more than half of the classes are televised … and many parents pay private tutors for classes in mathematics and science."[6]

During his visit, a former classmate of Prieto, whose daughter was in her senior year, told him about "constant pilfering—even mattresses are stolen from the school dormitories," further evidence of widespread poverty and moral degradation in Cuba today.[7]

Health Care

Like education, health care used to be a much-lauded crown jewel of the regime's social support system, boasting one of the highest per capita ratios of physicians in the world.

The real star in the medical firmament was the municipal program of family doctors: teams of physicians and nurses dispatched to serve community clinics, schools, urban workplaces, and agricultural villages free of charge.

Among the benefits of dispatching a medical team to every 130 families—to live and work in the communities they serve—is a low mortality rate for live births. And that's what Cuba purportedly achieved. According to Index Mundi, Cuba's 2018 rate was 4.4 deaths per 1,000 live births—among the lowest in the world.

This lauded statistic reflects, in part, the island's staggering abortion rate. It is also worth noting that Cuba's pre-Castro infant mortality rate—32 per 1,000 live births in 1957—was already the lowest in Latin America and the thirteenth-lowest in the world, ahead of France, Belgium, West Germany, Japan, Austria, Italy, and Spain.[8]

Today, however, the overall situation is markedly different. More than fifty thousand of the island's licensed physicians and medical personnel have been stationed abroad (along with teachers) to generate hard currency and support the Castro-Communist goals. The cash-strapped regime pockets the huge fees and related expenses charged to foreign governments and pays only a paltry salary to the Cuban professionals.[9]

To help cover the deficit of doctors and other health-care personnel on the island, diagnosis and treatment have often become the bailiwick of nurses and medical students. As reported by reputable independent economists, most of the rural hospitals were closed in 2011, and 9 percent of the polyclinics were shut down. Those that remain open are typically in disrepair.

The Tale of Two Cubas

Given the continuing deterioration of the Cuban health-care system, why is it still praised by professed experts on Cuba, and why do foreign visitors, government officials, and celebrities continue to flock to the island for medical and cosmetic treatment?

The answer is simple. There are two Cubas today: the resplendent island that coddles affluent foreign visitors and dignitaries (along with Raúl Castro and other high-level government officials), and the grim redoubt of totalitarian rule that is driving the locals deeper into despair. Cuba is indeed a model of deception, a Potemkin village set in the tropics—bright for foreigners with hard currency but dim for locals who have none.

An example of the special care and attention lavished on well-heeled visitors and celebrities is the case of Diego Maradona, an Argentine regarded as one of the best soccer players of all time. Having suffered a heart attack in 2000 caused by an overdose of cocaine, Maradona was invited by Fidel Castro to detox at the exclusive La Pradera health farm and resort outside Havana—off-limits to the local population.[10]

The extended treatment seemed to work, but a few years later Maradona suffered another severe heart attack, again triggered by cocaine. Shipped back to Cuba by his family and placed under Fidel's guardianship, Maradona underwent a more rigorous treatment at one of the island's exclusive upscale facilities specializing in mental health.

Although stricter this time, "Papa" Fidel maintained his soft spot for the athlete's celebrity (not to mention his hard currency). Maradona's treatment included a daily round of golf and the uplifting company of a gorgeous nineteen-year-old Cuban girlfriend.

In August 2011, Venezuelan president Hugo Chávez underwent emergency surgery to remove a baseball-size cancerous tumor in the pelvic area that had metastasized. He subsequently returned several times to Havana for chemotherapy and further surgery before his passing. Needless to say, the top-notch hospital facilities and special medical treatment accorded Chávez are not available to regular Cubans.

You don't have to be a dignitary or a celebrity to be pampered by the Castro regime so long as you are a friend of the revolution and carry hard currency. Foreign visitors and tourists can have access to various first-rate hospitals and health facilities, like Cira García. As reported by Laurie Garrett, a senior fellow for global health at the Council on Foreign Relations, "Aside from posters of Che Guevara and Fidel Castro, Cira García feels like a top European or North American clinic, as the thousands of patients who arrive every year from more than seventy nations could attest."

Package deals, reports Ms. Garrett, cover a wide range of services at very competitive prices—from a new knee ($6,850) to a titanium implant to correct a herniated vertebral disk ($4,863); from thigh liposuction ($1,090) to a face-lift ($2,540).

The key, according to Ms. Garrett, is that "all of the clinic's equipment appears to work, the pharmaceutical supplies are plentiful, the daily patient loads are small, and the doctors [sixty full-time physicians and forty specialist adjuncts] feel as though they have the tools and the time to do what they have long been trained to do."[11]

What a stark contrast between the showcase hospitals that provide world-class care for Cuban government officials and well-heeled foreign visitors and dignitaries, and the public polyclinics that have become shells of their former selves. Since the free fall of the economy, many of Cuba's celebrated polyclinics lack stethoscopes and sterile gloves.

Syringes are recycled, and disinfectants are in short supply. Patients must bring their own gowns and bedding and then clean them when they return home.

Here is the testimony of an American, Christopher P. Baker, who in 2012 escorted a *National Geographic* expedition to Cuba. During that trip, he accompanied one of the female participants who fell ill with a serious dental problem to the Clínica Internacional—a well-equipped, foreigners-only hospital in the large southern city of Cienfuegos. Having detected an abscess, the doctors referred her to the dental ward at Cienfuegos Hospital, open to the general public.

This is how Baker describes what he saw: "The hospital's broken windows and screens were an ill omen of worse to come. … Dental instruments were sitting in a tray that hadn't been cleaned—not even wiped—in ages. A microscopic study might well have revealed every known bacteri[um] under the sun. … Fortunately, the dentist didn't need to place any instrument in her mouth." An antibiotic was prescribed, which the international clinic had in stock.

Baker continues: "The next day, while walking along Cienfuegos's main shopping street, the group paused to peruse the local pharmacy that serves local Cubans. I counted barely a handful of drugs (all locally produced) for sale in the sparsely stocked shelves. What a study in contrasts! The bare[-]bones Cubans-only pharmacies and the foreigners-only pharmacies fully stocked with imported drugs."[12]

This is not an unusual or isolated occurrence. In November 2015, a couple from Canada, Barbara and John Johnston, were enjoying a most pleasant stay at a Cuban resort hotel in Cayo Santa María, reserved for foreigners, when Barbara became seriously ill. Following incessant vomiting and septic shock, she was transferred to a mainland hospital in the city of Santa Clara that serves the community.

This is how her husband describes the contrast: "When you're on the island and the resorts are beautiful and what you see is all really nice, but you get into Santa Clara and it was really a shock." According to John, there was no running water at the hospital, no antiseptic, and no blankets. The beds were stained, and the staff wore their street clothes in the intensive care unit.

The Johnstons' story did not have a happy ending. After enduring a thirty-six-day nightmare at the local deteriorated hospital where Barbara was poorly treated without any clear diagnosis, her family was able to airlift her to the United States, but alas it was too late to save her. Given her critical condition, she was flown to her hometown in Canada, where she passed away surrounded by her heartbroken husband, sons, and relatives.[13]

Myths and Realities of Raúl's Reforms

Despite the shocking realities faced by the islanders, many foreigners were duped by Raúl Castro's seeming pragmatism when he declared that Cuba must loosen central control of the economy, slash state subsidies and payrolls, increase private enterprises, and attract more foreign investments.

He later postulated, however, that he was just "updating Cuba's socialism," veering toward a model where central planning remains the leading force and capitalism is rejected, "but the market will not be ignored." Let's see what he meant:

The Agro Uphill Battle

Before the Castro-Communist takeover, Cuba was blessed with exceptional agricultural resources. Today it is in dire straits.[14] Once known as the "sugar bowl" of the world, Cuba with its 163 mills produced over 20 percent of the global output of cane sugar.

Under Fidel Castro, brigades of soldiers, students, homemakers, and state employees from the cities were sent to the countryside to produce ten million tons of cane. The government even invited foreign sympathizers to cut cane in solidarity with the socialist revolution.

Following the artificial peak of close to eight million tons in 1989, sugar output plummeted. Cuban authorities then shuttered more than one hundred of its refineries and converted some three million acres of cane field to other crops or left them untilled. In 2017–18, sugar production fell to 1.1 million tons, a 105-year low.

Even Cuba's richly flavored, slow-burning tobacco, the envy of the world, has not fared any better. According to official data from the National Statistics Office, accessed by the *Wall Street Journal*, Cuba produced ninety-one million cigars in 2014, down 58 percent from 2006. A number of the island's finest tobacco plantations are now mostly fallow farmland covered with thorny bushes.

Why? Tobacco farmers face two major problems: lack of resources and getting paid too little by the government, which is the sole buyer of 90 percent of what they produce. Efforts have been made to boost production, with some progress, but the industry fears that it may not be ready for any significant demand boom.[15]

Once an exporter of other product categories such as coffee, fruit, seafood, and even meat, the island now cannot even cover local demand. Having to import nearly 80 percent of what Cuba consumes at a cost of about $2 billion per year—a burden the island can no longer carry—the Castro regime decided to boost agricultural productivity by doling out several million acres of fallow state land to over two hundred thousand small farmers.[16]

This was a step in the right direction, but major drawbacks have lessened the impact of the reform. The state retained title to the land, granting only ten-year renewable leases (now renewable for twenty years) without providing the essential financing, input, and tools.

Despite efforts to raise agricultural productivity, Cuba is producing less food than it did in 1989. Farmers have to sell most of their production to a state agency (Acopio) at prices that are below what they could get in a free market.

The dismal distribution system in the countryside, crippled by a shortage of trucks in good working condition, remains controlled by the state. As a result, fruit spoils before it reaches the final market.

Layoffs and Self-Employment

Raúl Castro realized that the state could no longer afford to keep the bloated bureaucracy and plethora of hangers-on, so he signaled the need to lay off over one million government employees (about 20 percent of the workforce).

To assuage the impact of the phased layoffs, the regime rekindled and expanded the licensing of self-employed service providers called *cuentapropistas*. The cash-starved state fostered the conversion of home-based shops and services that had been covertly operating in the black market into taxable businesses, as was done in the 1990s before the Castro brothers curtailed them for fear of capitalist contamination. This time, however, the regime authorized the hiring of nonfamily employees.

Since in Cuba what is not expressly permitted is generally forbidden, the list of services that may be licensed is very long. However, following the recent consolidation of licenses, these services have now been reduced from 201 to 123.[17]

Some of the allowed occupations cover such menial, if not odd, activities as pruning palm trees, sewing buttons, peeling natural fruit, refilling disposable cigarette lighters, and performing as clowns. One may repair box springs, mattresses, and umbrellas for a fee but may not sell them. Fortune-telling with tarot cards is also authorized.

Castro's purported liberalization wave has not yet reached Cuban professionals. Architects, engineers, doctors, and attorneys have been excluded from government licenses and barred from forming private firms.[18]

The most substantial and potentially profitable of the authorized self-employed occupations are those that cater to tourists with hard currency, particularly in-home restaurants (*paladares*) and bed-and-breakfasts (*casas particulares*). Propelled by a rise in tourism, the licensed minienterprises now account for close to six hundred thousand self-employed Cubans, or 13 percent of the workforce.[19]

But are these operations true privately owned and legally recognized businesses? Not really. They cannot be incorporated as private enterprises and are subject to licenses that the government issues, suspends, curtails, or revokes at its discretion without effective recourse. And these licenses are not transferable.

These micro-operations are subject to stifling taxes to rein in "excessive" wealth and don't have access to wholesale markets to buy the necessary input at reasonable prices. As a result, many resort to the black market for supplies. Since the self-employed are barred from importing goods for use or resale, some employ couriers known as mules. This practice, which used to be tolerated (often with bribes), is now harshly penalized with confiscations and severe fines.[20]

Cars and Homes for Sale

One of the recent reforms, billed as a major step in the Communist island's economic transformation, is the right to purchase new and used automobiles from the state, without special permission, for the first time in half a century.

In Cuba, where nine out of ten households do not own a car or other vehicles, the news was heartily praised, but not for long. Markups of 400 percent on the cars sold by state-run retailers—the only ones authorized to operate—dashed the expectations of most Cubans, who, as previously mentioned, only earn on average slightly over $40 a month.

At a Peugeot dealership in Havana, prices that ranged from $91,000 for a 2013 Model 206 to $262,000 for a 508 led prospective buyers to walk away, shaking their heads in anger and frustration. Elsewhere, used cars in poor condition went on sale for prices generally starting at $25,000. Said artist Cesar Perez, looking at a 2005 Renault: "These prices show a lack of respect for all Cubans. What [I find] here are wrecks. I now have no hope of getting a car for my family."[21]

A more meaningful reform, enacted in November 2011, allows the purchase and sale of homes. For decades, Cubans could only swap equal-value properties—a complicated barter arrangement that often took years to carry out. Although no cash was allowed to pass from buyer to seller, payments were frequently made under the table.

The regime, eager to grab a piece of the action, has now legalized the black market transactions and imposed an 8 percent tax on the assessed value of the homes, equally split by the buyer and seller. Were it not for the financial constraints attached to this reform, it could bring significant relief to thousands of Cubans who live in crumbling, overcrowded homes with many families and even divorced couples living together for lack of a better option.

The critical housing problem was underscored by Miguel Coyula, a prominent government architect who specializes in urban planning. He said that "an average of three buildings collapse in Havana each day, victims of neglect, overcrowding, and improvised construction." According to official sources, it would cost about $3.6 billion to build the six hundred thousand houses Cuba needs.[22] The deficit is now estimated at close to one million units.

Stepping Up Construction

The Castro regime, which for decades remained the sole authorized housebuilder, has at last legalized private construction and repairs. Black marketers don't have to deliver cinder blocks at night, as in the past, and purchasing a bag of sand is no longer a concealed and convoluted process.

Still, it is generally small-scale stuff with many drawbacks. No private mortgage lenders or real estate brokerage firms are permitted. House-hunters mostly rely on word of mouth or leaflets, and prices are based on guesstimates rather than appraised values. It is a crude market where financing must go through government banks offering few loans, credits, or subsidies.

The new law allows only citizens and permanent residents to buy and sell real estate, and limits ownership to two homes (a residence and a vacation property). Then there is the unresolved issue of the titles to old properties, which could expose current buyers to future claims by the legitimate owners of confiscated homes. And there is the fear of revealing to the government the true value of the transactions and the source of funds.

When Raúl Castro launched the above-mentioned reforms, most independent economists pointed out that they did not constitute systemic changes and would neither generate the needed growth nor improve living conditions in a meaningful way. To the chagrin of the Cuban people, that somber prediction turned out to be true. According to Joaquin P. Pujol, former assistant director of exchange and trade relations at the International Monetary Fund, "While there has been some liberalization in agriculture and the labor market [with self-employment] … the Cuban model is still very close to the one used in the former Soviet Union," with its inherent inefficiency, corruption, and sluggishness.[23]

A Thriving Business: Sex Tourism

There is, however, a business that is sadly growing in Cuba today: sex tourism. The prevailing poverty and corruption are gnawing at the social and moral fabric of the nation and fueling a new type of prostitution that is tolerated, if not encouraged, by the regime.

This is not the traditional and contained prostitution transacted by seasoned professionals, mainly in established brothels (such as those that operated in pre-Castro Cuba). The current prostitution is more diffuse and unconventional, carried on independently by young women, mostly amateurs in their teens, who offer their charms to tourists for hard cash to survive or for a marriage license to escape.

They are called *jineteras* (horsewomen), who saddle visitors for a while and then return to their poorly paid jobs, if they have jobs. Young men are also available for a fee. This widespread depravation has turned Cuba into a preferred destination for sex tourism, competing with Bangkok. Not an achievement to be proud of.

Investors at the Gate?

Despite dim hope for a true opening in Cuba under Raúl Castro, some international investors, including US corporate executives, are still interested in exploring business opportunities on the island. Most, however, do not seem too keen on risking significant capital there, even if the US embargo were lifted. Current conditions in Cuba are very troubling—a stagnant economy nearing recession, low purchasing power (about half of what it was in 1989), appalling infrastructure, and lack of minimum legal safeguards.

Those who have done their homework do not blithely dismiss or downplay the Castro regime's egregious confiscation of US properties and businesses in the 1960s—a monumental $8 billion robbery at present value. Nor do they minimize the implications of Raúl Castro's 2008 decision to freeze the dollar accounts of foreign joint venture partners and suppliers.

Prospective foreign investors are particularly concerned about pervasive corruption in Cuba and the risks it poses, both financial and personal. In 2011, as part of an alleged corruption sweep, the Castro regime summarily shut down several Western companies operating on the island, including two Canadian trading companies (Cy Tokmakjian and Tri-Star Caribbean) and a British firm involved in tourism, factories, and docks (Coral Capital). The assets in Cuba of the respective companies were confiscated, and their senior executives landed in prison on trumped-up charges.[24]

Of those arrests, the one that gained more media coverage (outside of Cuba, of course) was the shocking episode involving Coral Capital. The British investment firm, which set up office in Havana in 2000, was a leading promoter of the Cuban tourist industry. In partnership with the Castro regime, Coral turned the dilapidated Saratoga Hotel into a swanky property and designed the €400 million Bellomonte Golf and Country Club project, which reportedly was approved by the regime.

Then in 2011, Coral's chief operating officer Steven Purvis, who had resided with his family in Cuba for ten years, was arrested as he was about to take his children to school. He was first accused of spying (revealing secrets), but the outrageous charge was dropped. He was later accused of "economic crimes" (i.e., conducting foreign currency transactions without specific government permission).

Purvis was incarcerated, along with another Coral executive, initially in a dungeon ironically called a villa (Villa Marista). He was kept there with three other prisoners in a filthy eight-foot-by-eight-foot cell with the lights on round the clock and exercise limited to fifteen minutes a week.

This is how Purvis described his ordeal: "They decide absolutely everything about your life, even personal grooming. The idea is to separate you from your personal identity, so you lose a sense of who you are. Several inmates who passed through my cell during my time went cuckoo, and there was an attempted suicide about once a month. You'd be trying to sleep at night and suddenly there'd be this terrible wail from some other cell."[25]

Purvis was fortunate to have been released in 2013 for time served (two and a half years), thanks presumably to the diplomatic pressure exerted by the British government. He did not break down, but he did lose fifty pounds in weight and all his major investments in Cuba. As to the Bellomonte Golf and Country Club flagship project he had spearheaded, it was handed over to a Chinese firm—courtesy of the Castro regime.[26]

Other Business Disincentives

Some of the other disincentives include a dual foreign exchange system that splits the economy, muddles transactions, and invites corruption, as well as a host of legal restrictions that hamstring foreign investors. For example, investors can only partner, mostly on a minority basis, with state-owned enterprises and are barred from hiring and firing employees of the joint ventures. That is the prerogative of government agencies, which collect the hard currency salaries paid by the foreign investors and pass on to the workers in local currency a small portion of the amounts received.

Not even Raúl Castro's 2014 megaproject—the Mariel Development Zone west of Havana—has attracted major investments. Funded by Brazil's National Bank for Economic and Social Development with a nearly $1 billion loan, the zone surrounds the port of Mariel and is expected to become a regional shipping hub—"the first large terminal port for containers in the Caribbean," it is claimed.[27] The huge contract for the project was awarded to Odebrecht, the Brazilian company whose bribery practices to strike shady deals shook the foundations of many corrupt governments in Latin America.[28]

At the end of March 2018, there were reportedly only thirty-five approved companies of significant scale in the zone, of which ten were in operation and twenty-five were in the process of investment. Fewer than five thousand jobs were created, and only 9.5 percent of the projected investment for the period 2014–18 was received.[29] Not a bright picture, for sure.

Tourism is one of the few industries that continue to attract investors to meet the surge of visitors—somewhat abated following Trump's restrictive measures. But the front-runner is no foreign company; it's Gaviota, part of Cuba's state-owned empire linked to the army, which generates a major portion of the tourism business revenue.

Proudly hailed by the regime as "the fastest-growing hotel holding company in Cuba," Gaviota has reserved the choicest tourism opportunities and sites for itself and generally restricts its foreign partners to management contracts. The island's three most luxurious hotels recently opened by foreign firms in Havana—Grand Hotel Manzana Kempinski, Iberostar Parque Central, and Hotel Paseo del Prado—are owned by Gaviota.

Despite the regime's unwillingness to introduce significant economic and political reforms, Raúl Castro managed to renegotiate the island's $11.1 billion debt to the Paris Club, of which $8.5 billion was pardoned. Moreover, Japan forgave nearly $1 billion of outstanding Cuban debt, and Mexico pardoned 70 percent of Havana's $487 million overdue loan.[30]

But Raúl Castro's singular feat was the one-sided deal (in his favor) that he extracted from the US-Cuba thaw negotiated with President Obama. The next chapter sheds new light on this pivotal episode.

CHAPTER 15

The Delusive Obama-Castro Thaw and the Trump Aftermath

The US-Cuba thaw, pursued by President Obama during his second term in office, was an attempt to achieve—through unilateral incentives and soft diplomacy—the historic rapprochement with the Castro regime that had eluded Obama's ten predecessors.

Following is the story of Obama's expectations and Raúl Castro's machinations with insights into the secret negotiations, the outcome of the deal, and what ensued under the subsequent Trump administration:

Obama's Policy Shift

In May 2008, campaigning for the presidency in Miami, the Democratic candidate Barack Obama asserted, "My policy toward Cuba will be guided by one word: *libertad*. And the road to freedom for all Cubans must begin with justice for Cuba's political prisoners, the rights of free speech, a free press, and freedom of assembly, and it must lead to elections that are free and fair."[1]

This explicit commitment was made to woo Cuban American voters, and it worked. Obama won Florida. He truly believed, however, that Washington's hard-line Cuba policy had not worked and had to be drastically changed.

Soon after assuming the presidency in January 2009, Obama took several steps aimed at clearing the way for a détente with the Castro regime. The fact that all previous US presidents had failed in their efforts to bridge the chasm between the United States and Communist Cuba did not deter the young, self-confident Obama.

Many in Washington felt that since the seemingly pragmatic Raúl Castro had succeeded his ailing, intransigent brother as head of state, the circumstances were more propitious than in the past for constructive engagement.

President Obama did not wait for positive signals from Havana to start revising the Cuba policy. In April 2009, he lifted restrictions on travel of Cuban Americans to the island and on their remittances to family members there. The president declared that the changes were designed to "reach out to the Cuban people in support of their desire to freely determine their country's future."[2]

It should be noted that Cubans on the island who have relatives living in the United States benefit from cash remittances and shipment of much-needed goods. But so does the Castro regime. According to well-informed analysts, cash and goods sent to Cuba by families and friends living abroad represent a combined annual inflow of close to $6 billion. This virtual subsidy helps sustain the failed Communist system by providing financial assistance to many of those who have been laid off by the government or who otherwise struggle to make ends meet.[3]

To advance the desired accommodation with Castro, the Obama administration voted in June 2009 in favor of lifting Cuba's suspension from the Organization of American States despite the 1962 OAS resolution that declared that Marxism-Leninism was incompatible with the Inter-American System.

For those of us who had pressed hard to expel the Castro-Communist regime from the OAS, it was painful to watch this obsequious travesty, which did not mollify the Castro brothers. They flatly rejected the invitation to rejoin the regional organization, reiterating that their country did not want to be part of an imperialist grouping.

The Economist promptly responded with this fine-edged quip: "Like

Marx (Groucho, not Karl), [they] would not join any club that would have [them] as member[s]."

Several Cuban American colleagues and I believed that Obama's first steps on Cuba would lead to something much broader. Our issue was not engagement but unilateral concessions to the Castro regime with no strings attached. That concern prompted me to write two articles in April 2009—one posted in *Forbes* ("Bailing Out the Castro Regime?") and the other in *Foreign Policy* ("Think Again: Engaging Castro").

The president announced in January 2011 a series of measures authorizing "purposeful travel" to Cuba by all Americans, nonfamily remittances to the island, and charter flights to and from Cuba. The purposeful travel, first launched in 1999 by President Clinton as part of a "people to people" program, was intended to "enhance contact with the Cuban people and support civil society" through cultural, religious, and educational activities.

The program seemed fine on paper. Who would quarrel with increased contact with Cubans on the island? The catch, however, was that the visits were generally shepherded by government "tour guides," who would expose the visitors to those settings, activities, and people preselected and monitored by the Castro regime.

The choreographed tours, divorced from the somber realities of Cuba, not only provided a propaganda tool for the regime; they also constituted an important source of income for the military sector, which substantially controls the island's tourist industry.

Obama did not disclose at the time that he was preparing to scrap the two-track policy toward Cuba and call on Congress to lift the embargo without preconditions. Nor did he make it clear that he would soon make a sub-rosa overture to the Castro regime to break the long-standing impasse that had impeded the normalization of US-Cuba relations.

The president's Cuba plan started to gain traction in early 2013. With his final election behind him, Obama privately expressed his intention to make Cuba a priority and to see how far he could push the envelope, preceded by getting a USAID subcontractor out of prison on the island. With that in mind, he asked Ben Rhodes, his thirty-seven-year-old deputy national security adviser for strategic communications, to be "our man in Havana."

In his White House memoir, *The World as It Is*, Rhodes describes his reaction when the designate chief of staff first approached him with the Cuba offer: "I didn't want to betray that I was nervous, that I might not know how to do this; the only thing I knew for sure about Cuba was that every effort to improve relations so far had failed."[4]

Before proceeding with the plan, Obama's senior Latin America adviser at the White House, Ricardo Zúñiga, was asked to check in Miami if indeed the influence of the older, hard-line Cuban Americans had significantly waned. Encouraged by the feedback, Obama felt he could blunt any meaningful opposition, whether from the Cuban American community or Congress, with a well-packaged deal presented as a fait accompli. But, as an extra precaution, he insisted that the negotiations be conducted secretly by his young advisers—Rhodes and Zúñiga—excluding at first the secretary of state and other foreign policy officials. Under those guidelines, the back-channel talks with the Cubans commenced in June 2013.[5]

Raúl Castro's Game Plan

Raúl Castro was agreeable to the talks and ready to pursue them with a game plan he apparently had developed shortly after Obama won reelection in 2012. Without committing to anything other than to talk, Castro made clear at the outset that there could be no normalization of US relations without the total and unconditional lifting of the US embargo.

But before grappling with that "must," Castro raised a thorny issue that almost derailed the negotiations. He demanded the release of three Cuban spies (part of the Wasp Network convicted by a federal jury in

2001). One of them, Gerardo Hernández, was serving a life sentence for conspiring with the Castro regime to shoot down over international waters the civilian planes of the humanitarian organization Brothers to the Rescue.[6]

Castro was confident he had enough leverage to secure the release of the Cuban spies, touted as heroes by his regime. Beyond a president anxious to make a deal, he had an American hostage to swap: Alan Gross, a USAID subcontractor. Gross had been arrested in December 2009 for distributing communications equipment to the Jewish community in Havana to access the internet. After a typical show trial, he was sentenced to fifteen years and kept behind bars, pending what Castro had envisaged all along—an exchange for the Cuban spies.

Obama rejected a straight trade but instructed his negotiators to find a more plausible alternative.[7] In the meantime, Gross was in ill health and rapidly deteriorating, so the president asked Castro to provide better treatment for him—a reasonable request, but not without a price. The Cuban ruler demanded in return that the Cuban spy serving a life sentence be allowed to ship his sperm to Cuba so that he could inseminate his wife living there and become a father while in prison. This bizarre proposition was accepted by the White House. and arrangements were promptly made for a "quiet" shipment of the spy's sperm to Havana.[8]

Reacting to the "in vitro diplomacy," as some in the press facetiously dubbed it, several US lawmakers, led by Ileana Ros-Lehtinen, blasted the Obama administration for having bent over backward to enable the murderer to have a family, the very same murderer who had robbed some of his victims of the possibility of having families of their own.[9]

To make the exchange of prisoners more palatable to the president, Castro agreed to dress it up by releasing several dozen Cuban political prisoners. This is a concession that both Fidel and Raúl have made when convenient and then reneged on it by rearresting most of the freed prisoners.

But this finagling did not lead to a swap of spies since Obama would not accept Castro's contention that Gross was spying for the United States. So, to provide political cover for the president, Gross was released as a humanitarian gesture and the three Cuban spies were exchanged for a mysterious US intelligence agent who had been imprisoned in Cuba since 1995.

Papal Blessing

Obama remained uneasy not only with the prisoner swap, but also with the other, unilateral concessions demanded by Castro to strike a deal with the United States. The president needed the intervention and seal of approval of an unimpeachable world personality. Who better than Pope Francis? Following a briefing at the White House, Cardinal Theodore McCarrick, the former archbishop of Washington (who recently resigned amid a huge sexual abuse scandal), was helpful in getting the pope involved in the final stages of the negotiation.[10]

Castro also was interested in having the Vatican bless a deal—to legitimize and bolster his regime, which was (and still is) facing a serious financial crisis, compounded by the reduction of Venezuela's vital oil supply to the island on credit. He counted on Cuba's Cardinal Ortega to advocate in Rome the normalization of US-Cuba relations, including the unconditional lifting of the US embargo, as beneficial to the church and the Cuban people.

The pope endorsed the deal in letters delivered by Ortega to Castro and Obama, apparently overlooking or dismissing the concerns of his diplomatic envoy to Cuba, the apostolic nuncio Bruno Musaro, who had excoriated the Castro regime. While on vacation in Italy in August 2014, Musaro declared that the Cuban people are "victims of a socialist dictatorship that has kept them subjugated for the past fifty-six years."

The nuncio went on to say that "in Cuba, everything is controlled by the state, even milk and meat. ... People don't have work and don't know what to do to feed their own kids." Without mincing words,

warning perhaps the wishful thinkers who were betting on a rapprochement with Castro to improve the situation on the island, Musaro
categorically affirmed, "Only liberty can bring hope to the Cuban
people."[11]

It seems that Musaro's clear-eyed and courageous assessment was
not well received by the Vatican and the island's submissive Cardinal
Ortega. To the regret of freedom-loving Cubans, the nuncio was replaced shortly after the US-Cuba deal was announced and assigned to
Egypt.

Other Concessions to Castro

Castro surmised that Obama was keen on restoring diplomatic relations
with Cuba as soon as possible. So, taking advantage of the president's
desire to speed up the process, Raúl insisted that before the reopening
of embassies and Obama's visit to Havana, Cuba must be removed from
the list of state sponsors of terrorism.

Obama yielded under pressure. After a brief, superficial review of
the Castro regime's egregious record as an abettor and supporter of
terrorism in collusion with rogue states and subversive organizations,
Cuba was removed from the list. This was done despite the Castro
regime's clear record of smuggling arms to North Korea, establishing
a reign of terror in Venezuela, and harboring dozens of fugitives, drug
traffickers, and terrorists from the United States and other countries.

Castro also reiterated that the reopening of the embassies did not
mean normalization of relations. He insisted that to achieve that, the
embargo would have to be totally lifted and other conditions met.

Those conditions set by Castro included reparations for the alleged
damages caused by the US embargo (over $100 billion), the repeal of
the Cuban Adjustment Act, which grants immigration privileges to
refugees fleeing the island, the closing of Radio and Television Martí,
and the end of all prodemocracy programs on the island financed by

the United States. Last but not least was the return to Cuba of the US naval base of Guantánamo.[12]

Although the president could not deliver all those conditions without congressional approval, he further eased unilaterally—mostly by executive order—travel, export, banking, and investment restrictions. Castro took what he got but gave nothing meaningful in return and continued to press for more.

The Negotiators

Who were the American negotiators involved in the deal, and how did they stack up against the Castro team? As noted earlier, the lead US negotiator was Ben Rhodes, deputy national security adviser for strategic communications. Having graduated from New York University majoring in creative writing, he started working for Obama as a speechwriter in 2007 and remained close to him after he was elected. In May 2016, Rhodes was featured in the *New York Times Magazine* as "the aspiring novelist who became Obama's foreign policy guru."

The *Times* piece suggests that Rhodes successfully leveraged his creativity to manipulate young, inexperienced reporters into "retailing" the administration's sugarcoated narrative of the Iran deal. Rhodes proudly implied that by creating that "echo chamber," he was able to tilt public opinion in favor of the controversial Iran agreement sealed by the Obama administration.[13]

On the Cuba deal, Rhodes's role was more ambitious. It was not just to spin, but to make history. The president assigned him the responsibility of conducting secret negotiations with Castro's envoys, mostly at Canadian government facilities in Ottawa, to break the impasse that for decades had separated the United States and Cuba. Although Rhodes was not lacking in intelligence and audacity, he had no diplomatic experience, in-depth knowledge of Latin American and Cuban affairs, or proven ability to detect and counter the maneuvering of trained Communist deceivers.

During more than seventy hours negotiating with the Cubans, he was assisted by Ricardo Zúñiga, senior director for Western Hemisphere affairs at the National Security Council, who had limited international experience, including stints in Havana.[14] But it was Rhodes who carried the ball with direct and frequent communications with the president.

Once Rhodes and Zúñiga had agreed to the key provisions of the deal, Roberta Jacobson, a seasoned US diplomat who was assistant secretary of state for Western Hemisphere affairs, carried on the balance of the negotiations and kicked off the implementation stage.

The Cuban negotiators were not skilled in conventional diplomacy but excelled in double-dealing. Through most of the negotiation, Castro relied on his alter ego—his son Alejandro Castro Espín, an army colonel and intelligence expert who had studied and honeymooned in Moscow. For more than a decade, Alejandro had worked by his father's side, charged with a portfolio in the Ministry of Interior, including state security, foreign intelligence, and national defense.

Once the key elements of the deal had been scoped out, the officer who took charge of finalizing and executing it from the Cuba side was Josefina Vidal. A versatile and sharp intelligence officer-cum-diplomat of the younger crop, she is fluent in English and experienced in US affairs. The fifty-five-year-old Vidal received KGB training in Moscow's Institute of Foreign Relations and rose through the ranks in Cuba's primary foreign intelligence service (MINREX), heading its North American division.

As first secretary of Cuba's Interests Section (quasi embassy) in Washington during the period 1999–2003, Vidal lectured at Columbia University and Harvard and was viewed in academic and media circles as a thoughtful diplomat well versed in social, economic, and political challenges facing the Americas. Few suspected that her lecturing and socializing was a cover for espionage in the United States.

In 2003, when seven officers at the Cuban Interests Section in Washington, including Vidal's husband, were expelled as spies from the United States, she opted to depart without having to be forced out.

In recognition of her service to the Castro regime, she was invited to join in 2011 the all-powerful Central Committee of the Communist Party of Cuba.

Vidal's deputy in the final negotiations with the United States was Gustavo Machín, whose father, one of Castro's historic "comandantes," was killed with Che Guevara in Bolivia during the failed Communist insurgency. Machín, a senior officer of Cuba's foreign intelligence service, was expelled from the United States for espionage when he served as a member of Cuba's United Nations mission in 2002.[15]

Consistent with their background and training, the three Cuban envoys effectively bluffed, cajoled, and deceived to gain the upper hand in the discussions. They followed the old Soviet ploy: mine is mine; yours is negotiable. No wonder the deal turned out one-sided in Castro's favor.

Supporters and Opponents

Although Obama declared in 2008 that significant steps toward democracy would have to precede the normalization of relations with Cuba, he dropped the precondition in order to strike a deal with Castro.

What prompted this drastic change? Most supporters of Obama's new Cuba policy dismissed any inkling of naivete on the part of the president or of opportunism to shore up his international record. In their view, he rightly concluded that to insist on democratic reforms in Cuba ahead of a détente would only prolong the impasse.

Opponents did not object to engagement but argued that Obama's new Cuba policy went beyond a thaw to offer substantive unilateral concessions to the Castro regime. The president called for the immediate and unconditional removal of all US sanctions that precluded or limited financing and investment in Cuba.

Opponents cautioned that the inflow of US capital and bank credits under current conditions on the island would be tantamount to a bailout of the Castro regime, which would only harden and prolong its grip on power. That's what happened, they adduced, when Hugo Chávez came to Fidel Castro's rescue following the end of Soviet subsidies to Cuba. Venezuela's aid enabled the Cuban leader to roll back or restrict most of the economic reforms he had earlier introduced under dire circumstances.

The advocates of lifting the US embargo on Cuba with no strings attached contended that it would have the salutary effect of denying the Castro dictatorship the scapegoat for their utter failure. They seem to forget—the opponents averred—that the Castro brothers have never been short on pretexts to blame Yankee imperialism for their glaring blunders and self-inflicted calamities.

The antiembargo champions claimed that by ending that "relic of the Cold War" outright, the United States' progressive engine of capitalism would erode and eventually sweep away the decrepit edifice of totalitarianism in Cuba, as it had behind the Iron Curtain. Those who demurred pointed out that tourism, trade, and foreign investment were not the key drivers of change within the Soviet bloc. As Charles Krauthammer wrote, "We contained, constrained, squeezed, and eventually exhausted the Soviets into giving up."[16]

And the debate went on.

The media standard-bearer of the antiembargo thaw, above all, was the *New York Times*. The influential newspaper wrote a series of editorials from October to December 2014, crusading for what essentially was announced on December 17: the president's new Cuba policy.

Among the think tanks that called for and applauded the new Cuba policy, the one that took the lead with two open letters to the president was the Council of the Americas. The letters were signed by several dozen former US government officials and foreign policy experts and by some prominent Cuban American businessmen and former corporate executives led by Carlos Saladrigas, president of the Cuba Study Group.[17]

The US Chamber of Commerce also weighed in, urging the

president to eliminate all legal barriers that impeded or held back US tourism, commerce, and investment in Cuba.

Among the media critics of Obama's new Cuba policy, the *Washington Post* editorial board took center stage as a counterpoise to the *New York Times*. *The Post* underscored the serious implications of rewarding the deceitful Castro regime with major concessions and getting nothing substantive in return. *The Wall Street Journal* and the *Miami Herald* also took issue with the one-sided aspect of the policy.

Echoing and elaborating on those concerns, the Center for a Free Cuba, a nonprofit organization based in Washington, then headed by Ambassador James Cason, published an open letter to Congress in the *Washington Post* titled "The New Cuba Policy: Breakthrough or Bailout?" It was signed by fifty-eight former US diplomats, government officials, and senior executives of multinational corporations (myself included), along with US scholars and several leaders of the dissident movement in Cuba.[18]

At the forefront of the debate were the eight Cuban American senators and members of Congress: Marco Rubio, Robert Menendez, Ted Cruz, Ileana Ros-Lehtinen, Mario Díaz-Balart, Carlos Curbelo, Albio Sires, and Alex Mooney. They could not forestall Obama's unilateral concessions to Castro by executive orders, but they secured enough congressional support to impede the unilateral lifting of the US embargo under totalitarian rule in Cuba. Backing the Cuban American legislators with insights and powerful arguments was Mauricio Claver-Carone, then executive director of Cuba Democracy Advocates.

The Cuban American community appeared somewhat divided in Miami and other cities with the younger generations more amenable than the older ones to the announced détente. Yet despite the gap reflected in some surveys, the hard-line Cuban American lawmakers and the militant exile organizations maintained their principled leadership.

In Cuba, the agreement to restore US-Cuba relations was generally greeted with cautious optimism. Many seemed to believe that it would bring economic relief, most likely without a political opening. However, as time passed, not even the relief was forthcoming.

Within the dissident movement, some human rights activists were hopeful that the new US-Cuba policy would at least help shake the status quo and eventually serve as a catalyst for a democratic transition in Cuba. But most were skeptical. They warned that a one-sided deal, as the one unveiled by the president, would oxygenate the struggling Castro regime and abandon dissidents to their fate.

Summit in Havana

Having announced the US-Cuba détente in December 2014 and having restored diplomatic relations in July 2015, Obama decided to play it up in March 2016 with a summit meeting with Raúl Castro in Havana. He went ahead with his historic trip to the island—the first by a sitting US president in eighty-eight years—even as the Castro regime intensified the beating and arrest of peaceful dissidents and triggered the largest exodus of Cuban migrants to the United States since the rafter crisis of 1994.

Why did Obama visit Cuba after having vowed that he would do so "only if, in fact, I with confidence can say that we're seeing some progress in the liberty and freedom and possibilities of ordinary Cubans"?[19] The White House offered no clear answer to this question except to suggest that the president's trip to Cuba, even with no easing of repression, was the most effective way to foster change on the island.

Convinced that with incentives, diplomatic finesse, and a warm embrace he could induce Castro to turn the page, Obama stated in his televised remarks to the Cuban people that "the United States and Cuba are like two brothers who've been estranged for many years, even as we share the same blood."

Evoking the former clashes of geopolitics and personalities, he stressed, "I know the history, but I refuse to be trapped by it." He then added, "The United States has neither the capacity nor the intention to impose change in Cuba. What changes come will depend upon the Cuban people."[20]

Yet the president, to his credit, also used the visit to meet with some of the dissident leaders and to preach the gospel of democracy during his remarks to the Cuban people. Invoking universal human rights, he said, "I believe citizens should be free to speak their mind without fear, to organize, and to criticize their government, and to protest peacefully, and that the rule of law should not include detentions of people who exercise those rights. I believe that every person should have the freedom to practice their faith peacefully and publicly. And, yes, I believe voters should be able to choose their governments in free and democratic elections."[21]

Obama was confident of making progress with his Cuba agenda, so he decided to forge ahead without securing a congressional green light. Exercising his executive power and perhaps exceeding it, he eased travel restrictions to the island under the so-called people-to-people program, facilitated dollar transactions with the Castro regime, and allowed several US companies to manage hotels owned or controlled by the Cuban military and make other investments on the island.

Disregarding infrastructure and security concerns, Obama also authorized cruises and more than one hundred daily commercial flights to nine cities in Cuba, a country that maintains close relationships with rogue states and is still viewed by the director of national intelligence as one of the top counterintelligence threats to the United States.

The president's expectation was that these and other US "gives" would induce the Seventh Cuban Communist Congress, scheduled for April 16–19, 2016, to liberalize its policies. Obama did not envisage dramatic changes in the short term but was looking for the start of a gradual transition to a brighter, freer, and more inclusive future.

This is how Ben Rhodes summarized their demands or expectations: "We wanted Cuba to expand its nascent private sector. We wanted Cuba to reform its economy, to allow foreign businesses to hire Cubans directly, and to show more restraint in its treatment of protesters."[22]

Surprise and Disappointment

The anxiously awaited Seventh Congress of the Cuban Communist Party, controlled by Raúl Castro and other members of the Old Guard, poured cold water on the feverish illusion of a new direction. *The Economist* soberly commented: "No serious student of Cuba imagined that Mr. Obama's visit and his televised call for free elections would prompt overnight change. But the party congress proved to be a disappointment even by the cautious standards of the reforms that Raúl Castro ... has set in train."[23]

Perhaps the most disturbing outcome of the Seventh Communist Congress was the reaction of the Castro brothers to Obama's goodwill visit and tactful reference to democracy and human rights. In what was clearly interpreted as a pushback against the president, Raúl Castro said in his wide-ranging speech: "We are not naive," adding that "powerful external forces" hoped to "create agents of change to end the revolution."[24]

He accused the US government of trying to "adjust the world to its convenience" and called on the members of the Communist Congress to fight "political subversion" and step up the "ideological work with youths, exposed to expanding actions designed to encourage the values of consumer society, apathy, rootlessness, and despair."[25]

Fidel Castro also lambasted the president with disdain. Frail but undaunted, he delivered what sounded like his valedictory to the Communist Congress. Then, in a scathing article addressed to "Brother Obama," he emphatically stated that "we don't need any gifts from the empire."

Fidel added that Obama's "syrupy" words about brotherhood and shared history, and his call to leave behind the enmity of the past, were enough to give Cubans "a heart attack," particularly after the failed

US-sponsored exile invasion in 1961 and "nearly sixty years of ruthless blockade" and "mercenary attacks." He then condescendingly conveyed a "modest suggestion" that the US president reflect on that history "and not offer elaborate theories about Cuban politics." In plain language, don't meddle in our internal affairs.[26]

Raúl Castro's Ploy

The Obama administration and many pundits who closely followed the decisions (or lack thereof) of the Cuban Communist Congress were taken aback by Raúl Castro's contemptuous attitude toward the United States and his implicit rejection of any meaningful political and economic opening in Cuba.

The surprise can be attributed to a mirage, namely, the belief that Raúl is a pragmatist, not a rigid Communist ideologue like his brother Fidel. The reality, however, is markedly different. Raúl Castro is not a true reformer but a cagey survivor. His seeming flexibility is nothing but a ploy to stay in power. A student of Leninism, he seems to be taking a page from Lenin's New Economic Policy—a tactical liberal move that enabled Moscow to invigorate the sputtering Soviet economy in the early 1920s and reverse its course after tricking the West into providing diplomatic recognition, political legitimacy, and humanitarian aid.

Castro's reforms, instituted before Obama's détente, were not spurred by a sudden conversion to the free market faith. Raúl is no Saul of Tarsus, struck by divine lightning on his way to Damascus. The reforms were driven by the exigencies of a cash-starved, credit-squeezed, fossilized Cuban economy gasping for increased revenues.

Raúl's brand of capitalism is, and always has been, state capitalism steered by the military. Moreover, the licensing of small-scale, heavily taxed, strictly controlled microenterprises (the self-employed *cuentapropistas*) that he has authorized could be halted or reversed at any time by fiat.

Proof of these assertions was borne out by the following developments that took place after the launch of Obama's détente.

In August 2016, the Cuban military took over the business operations assigned by the Castro regime to the historian Eusebio Leal,
the man who led the transformation of Old Havana's crumbling historic center into a World Heritage Site, funded by UNESCO. In what
looked like a military operation, the armed forces assumed control of
the largest business arm of the historian's office comprised of twenty
hotels, thirty stores, and twenty-five restaurants in Old Havana gener-
ating more than $170 million a year. This is how the Associated Press
headlined the takeover: "Cuban Military Expands Its Economic Empire
Under Détente."[27]

One of the key objectives of Obama's new Cuba policy was to encourage the expansion of the so-called private sector represented by
the cuentapropistas. However, the Castro regime thwarted that goal.
In August 2017, it announced the suspension of the licenses for the
most popular self-employed microbusinesses—the in-home restaurants
and the bed-and-breakfasts. The suspension also included construction
services, music and language teachers, party organizers, and other
professions.

What prompted these drastic measures? The regime mentioned it
was putting the brakes on the *cuentapropista* expansion pending new
regulations to curb wrongdoings such as tax evasion and illegal expansion. One of the examples of transgression given was "one same person
[having] two, three, four, and even five restaurants."

The real reason for the suspension, however, seems to be that the
number of self-employed on the island had more than tripled to 567,982
since Raúl Castro, under economic pressure, had decided to expand
the private minienterprises in 2010. They now reportedly account for
13 percent of the total number of employed.[28] The regime apparently
views this escalation as a potential threat to the totalitarian system
because it threatens to generate too much individual economic independence and accumulation of wealth.

When the licensing was reinstated, new restrictions were imposed. For example, those who had legally obtained several licenses could only keep one—the maximum allowed per family. So intense was the protest of the cuentapropistas that the government dropped or softened some of those restrictions, including a cap of fifty guests per restaurant. In most cases, the promised flexibility is on a case-by-case basis, at the discretion of the designated authority.

As for foreign investments, the current ground rules were not changed as the Obama administration had requested. Investors still have to partner with state or military enterprises and cannot hire or fire employees or pay them, except through a government agency that collects the hard currency and pays the workers a fraction in local currency.

What about the Castro regime's human rights record postrapprochement? Sadly, it turned worse, despite the appearance of leniency projected by the regime, which now grants (and revokes), at will, special permits to some dissidents to travel abroad. They can sporadically speak their minds outside Cuba but not on the island.

According to the Havana-based Cuban Commission for Human Rights and National Reconciliation, there were nearly ten thousand documented political detentions in 2016, accompanied in many cases by pounding by the regime's trained thugs, who don't spare women or minors. This count compares to 8,616 in 2015.[29]

Given the foregoing facts, it's fair to say that the US-Cuba thaw was largely one-sided. Even a staunch ally of the United States, former president of the government of Spain, José María Aznar, who favored engagement with the Castro regime, decried the virtually unconditional deal that was struck, which legitimized and beefed up the Cuban dictatorship.[30]

Trump Enters the Fray

During his first year in office, President Trump did not address the Cuba situation right away. Other, more pressing, and more dangerous international issues grabbed his attention.

In November 2017, the Trump administration announced new rules "intended to steer economic activities away from the Cuban military, intelligence, and security services ... and encourage the government to move toward greater economic freedom" for the Cuban people. US commercial relations with one hundred eighty entities owned or controlled by Cuba's security forces (now more than two hundred) are no longer allowed. And US visitors (henceforth required to travel in groups licensed by the Treasury Department) are barred from staying in hotels and eating in restaurants owned or controlled by those entities.

However, the Trump administration maintained diplomatic and commercial relations with the Castro regime, and US companies already authorized to do business in Cuba, such as Starwood (hotels), John Deere, and Caterpillar, were grandfathered. Moreover, US airlines continued to operate across the island under the 2017 regulations,[31] but were later restricted to Havana, and US cruises were suspended.

Given the Castro regime's continued support of the Venezuelan dictatorship, in collusion with Russia and China, the Trump administration has imposed additional sanctions against the regime. These external factors may have a significant impact on the situation in Cuba in the months ahead.

Mysterious Brain Attacks

A most serious crisis arose when it was reported that some twenty-six US diplomats (including intelligence officers) stationed in Cuba had sustained "injury to widespread brain networks" in late 2016 under Obama and through 2017 and early 2018 under Trump. Their neurological symptoms were headaches, dizziness, nausea, and hearing loss, as well as vision, sleep, and mood disorders.

Nearly a year after the reported injuries, at least fourteen of the diplomats were not well enough to go back to work. Most-recent tests indicate significant abnormality in the brains, including reduced volume of white matter (nerve fibers) and impaired connectivity within subnetworks of the brain. These findings dismiss the theory spread by the Castro regime that the symptoms were caused by mass hysteria.

Given these troubling developments, the Trump administration in late 2017 significantly reduced the size of the US Embassy in Havana, warned Americans not to travel to the island for several months, and expelled fifteen Cuban diplomats from Havana's embassy in Washington.

The State Department has not yet given definitive answers on the cause or source of the neural disorders, but several preliminary conclusions apparently have been reached. These were "targeted attacks" (resulting, some experts believe, from high-intensity microwave beams), and they were aimed specifically at American officials who were staying at US diplomatic residences assigned by the Cuban government. A few of the officials, temporarily deployed to the mission, were staying at a couple of hotels near the embassy, but no other guest or hotel employees were reportedly affected. Several Canadian diplomats based in Cuba, however, also suffered similar brain injuries.

Given the Castro regime's police state apparatus with eavesdropping tentacles across the island, it is inconceivable that it would not have been aware of, or involved in, twenty-six targeted attacks occurring over a span of more than one year. The big question is whether a hostile power experienced in this type of aggression was involved. No conclusive answer yet, but the prime suspect among intelligence experts seems to be Russia, not China.[32] As reported by NBC News on September 11, 2018, signal intelligence (meaning intercepted communications) points to Russia.

The investigation was widened in mid-2018, when the State Department had to evacuate several US diplomats from China who experienced illnesses similar to those that had struck US Embassy officials in Havana.[33]

In a detailed article carried by the *New York Times*, experts explain why they believe that the specific features of the diplomats' brain injuries—including signs of concussion without having received any blows to the head—fit the hypothesis of a microwave attack. They also point out that during the Cold War, Moscow was seeking to turn microwave radiation into a covert weapon of mind control, which they called "psychophysical" and "psychotronic." The US Defense Intelligence Agency warned in 1976 that Soviet research on microwaves for "internal sound perception" showed great promise for "disrupting the behavior patterns of military or diplomatic personnel."[34]

Not having yet reached definitive conclusions on the brain attacks and the perpetrators is indeed worrisome. One wonders if the answers to the puzzling questions will ever be found or revealed.

Back to the Future

The other important news from Cuba was the announcement in April 2018 that Raúl Castro had stepped down as president of the Council of State and the Council of Ministers and had designated as his successor a fifty-nine-year-old subservient apparatchik, Miguel Díaz-Canel.

This change did not mark the end of the Castro era, as some assumed, because Raúl retains the reins of power as first secretary of the Communist Party and de facto head of the army until 2021. He also continues to groom his son and former son-in-law, along with a few trusted bureaucrats and military chiefs, as successors apparent to the regime."

Still acting as the supreme leader, Raúl headed the commission in charge of "updating" Cuba's 1976 Stalinist constitution. Among the many amendments that were made, some reporters underscored that, as a sign of advancement, the regime had ditched the constitutional goal of progressing toward a "Communist society." However, the island will continue to be ruled by a single party—the Communist Party—with no real separation of powers or checks and balances. The citizens will not be able to elect their representatives directly, and the exercise of all individual rights must conform to the aims of the socialist state as ultimately determined by the rulers.

Although the president (head of state) will share power with a prime minister (head of government), the regime will remain effectively controlled by the militarized politburo.

Also presented as a breakthrough is the "legalization" of private property, including the minienterprises of the self-employed (*cuentapropistas*). But the so-called legalization is up to now a sham because the enterprises still depend on revocable government licenses and cannot be registered as independent businesses, sold or transferred. Overall, the rules are now stricter, even after having been softened somewhat following strong protests aired through social media.[35]

The new constitution does not introduce any meaningful, systemic change that would uplift the island nation. Sadly, the country remains subjugated and impoverished. Given this predicament, what then is the outlook for the Cuban people? Regardless of the confluence of external factors that may impact the future, does the yearning for freedom beat in the hearts of the Cubans on the island? The answer is found in the next chapter, which highlights sixty years of incessant resistance.

CHAPTER 16

Two Sides of the Cuban Saga: Repression and Resistance

▌Totalitarian Stranglehold

Some of those who have recently flocked to the hitherto verboten island seemed oblivious to the misery of most of the population. They relished Cuba's mojitos, salsa, cigars, and colorful vintage cars and enjoyed their stay in the still alluring country.

But other, more sensitive and inquisitive visitors were able to see through the Castro regime's facade of normalcy and posed some piercing questions when they left the island. Why, they wonder, aren't there mass demonstrations to protest against the alleged iniquities of the regime? Others often ask: If Castro is so bad, why don't Cubans rebel as they did against Batista?

Apart from forgetting or ignoring the underground movement that preceded the Bay of Pigs invasion and the guerrilla warfare that followed it, they don't seem to realize that what has subjugated Cuba under Castro is a totalitarian stranglehold, not a political dictatorship like those experienced in this hemisphere. This ironclad control—political, economic, social, and cultural—has reduced ordinary citizens to mere serfs, dependent on and oppressed by an omnipotent state. Those who have lived under totalitarian rule in Europe are familiar with this type of absolute domination.

The Castro regime's tentacles control every endeavor and facet of human life, including sources of information, channels of communication, education, religion, food supply, health care, commerce, agriculture, industry, science, and arts and letters. Even sports and entertainment are under the mastery of the state.

As Amnesty International denounced on November 16, 2017, "Ordinary Cubans perceived to be even subtly critical of life in the country face a future of harassment at work or unemployment, as authorities use their control over the job market as an additional tool of repression." There are no free labor unions, no collective bargaining, no right to strike, and no independent courts, so workers are at the mercy of the repressors.

The Castro regime, not content with the list of political crimes broadly covered in its penal code, added a new catchall category: the proclivity of an individual to commit a crime or engage in activities that could potentially be deemed "antisocial." This category penalizes "dangerousness," as perceived by the government, before any crime or misdemeanor is committed.

To impose its total control, the regime not only relies on its security forces but also counts on the Committees for the Defense of the Revolution (CDRs), which are civilian militias created by the Castro brothers in 1960 to serve as the eyes and ears of the revolution. The CDRs combine elements of both the gestapo and the Stasi. They operate in virtually every block across the island and monitor the activities of each individual in the neighborhood—whom they meet, what they discuss, and whether they comply with the diktats of the regime.

The surveillance goes beyond the nightmarish eavesdropping so vividly described by George Orwell. In Cuba, "Big Brother" watches you and listens to you. The CDRs are backed by scores of goons (Rapid Response Brigades) spread throughout the island, whose task is to intimidate, pound, and detain human rights activists and other peaceful dissidents. This snooping and repressive apparatus has enabled the Castro regime to preempt uprisings and quash mass demonstrations.

▌The Firing Squad

On April 5, 2001, this is what Fidel Castro declared at the Plenary Session of the 105th Conference of the Inter-Parliamentary Union held in Havana (translated from Spanish): "In our country, there have never been death squads, not a single disappearance, no political assassination, not one person tortured. ... Travel around the country, ask the people, [and] find just one shred of proof, somebody [who can] demonstrate that the revolutionary government has ordered or tolerated any such act, and I will never again assume a public role."

It's easy to demolish this outrageous mendacity, which attempts to whitewash the Castro brothers' heinous crimes. What is difficult is to count and identify all their victims. The Cuba Archive: Truth and Memory, founded in 2001 by the late professor and economist Armando Lago, and currently headed by the government affairs consultant and analyst María Werlau, has taken on this arduous task.

According to the archive's updated December 30, 2017, report, the political executions by firing squad, extrajudicial assassinations, forced disappearances, and other deaths attributed to the Castro regime have exceeded 7,325. The archive only includes in its database reliable confirmations from multiple sources of clearly identified victims. However, the well-documented *Black Book of Communism*, written by Stéphanie Courtois and others, published by Harvard University Press in 1999, estimates that from 1959 through the late 1990s, between fifteen thousand and seventeen thousand people were shot by the Castro regime.

These estimates, however, do not encompass the thousands of Cubans believed to have drowned trying to flee the island in rickety boats or man-made rafts. Nor do they include any of the hundreds of thousands killed by Communist guerrillas in Latin America abetted or inspired by Castro. Just in Colombia, government tallies indicate that the killings exceeded two hundred twenty thousand over five decades. Equally high is the number of casualties estimated in Castro-supported wars in Guatemala and other Central American countries.

According to the Cuba Archive, the mass killings by firing squad on the island started on January 12, 1959, just eleven days after the triumph of the revolution. Seventy-one men in the far-eastern city of Santiago de Cuba—most of them career officers of the island's armed forces and police—were accused of being Batista supporters. They were subjected to a summary trial by an ad hoc "revolutionary tribunal" and found guilty without due process or evidence of the alleged crimes. By order of Raúl Castro, who was stationed in Santiago, they were sentenced to death.

In the early morning hours of the twelfth, they were lined up in pairs and shot by firing squad in front of ditches that had been dug in a shooting practice field in San Juan Hill. The mass graves were then filled by a bulldozer. Witnesses report that several of the men were buried alive.

Since numbers don't show the full human impact of the killings, consider one particularly heart-wrenching narrative. It describes how seven Resistance students and young graduates, accused by the Castro regime of counterrevolutionary crimes, faced the firing squad on April 17, 1961—the day of the Bay of Pigs landings.

The report was chronicled by an eighteen-year-old *bachillerato* (high school) graduate, Tomás (Tommy) Fernández-Travieso, who was in the same holding area in La Cabaña fortress in Havana with his seven young compatriots just before their execution. Tommy was also going to be executed, but considering his age, he was sentenced at the last minute to thirty years in prison. He served nineteen, after which time he came to the United States and wrote several books and other publications, including the following intimate account of his comrades' last goodbyes:

Tommy described the show trial, which lasted only twenty minutes, interrupted by the roar of tanks that were rushing to the Bay of Pigs. Pending execution by firing squad, the prisoners were kept in a holding area at La Cabaña fortress in Havana. The cell, with fluorescent light, had two bunk beds without mattresses and a hole in the floor that served as toilet.

The first to be escorted by two armed guards to the execution area was Carlos. He hugged Tommy through the bars and asked him to look after his daughter. He left her his ring. The second to go was Efrén. He left his cigarette lighter to his wife. The third, Virgilio, lifted the spirits of the remaining prisoners when he told them that he was going to scream in front of the firing squad: "Long live Christ the King, and long live Free Cuba!" And he did. Others defied their executioners by singing the national anthem as they left the cell.

Of the eight young prisoners in La Cabaña holding area awaiting execution on April 17, 1961, only one was left to tell the story: Tommy Fernández-Travieso.

▌Castro's Prisons: A Living Hell

Thousands of anti-Communist Cubans have recounted, privately or publicly, their horrific stories of torture, including putrid food and squalid living conditions, in Castro's prisons. They all suffered immensely behind bars, but no one longer than Mario Chanes de Armas. He fought side by side with Fidel Castro against the Batista dictatorship but turned against Fidel when the latter embraced communism and betrayed his pledge to restore freedom in Cuba.

Chanes de Armas was in prison for one day short of thirty years, longer than Nelson Mandela, and became a leader in prison of the *plantados*—those who rejected "rehabilitation," involving submission to Communist brainwashing and repudiation of democracy. Planted squarely on his principles, and with faith in God, Mario endured countless periods of isolation, as well as brutal physical and mental torture. He remained unbowed during his ordeal, came to Florida after he was finally released, and rested in peace in 2007 without uttering a word of hatred or revenge.[1]

Another giant of the resistance movement, Armando Valladares, became one of the most renowned prisoners of conscience. As an early young supporter of the revolution, he took a job in the Office of the

Ministry of Communications of the Castro regime as a postal clerk. His allegiance ended when he witnessed the totalitarian trend of the regime. Having voiced his philosophical opposition to communism, and refusing to put on his desk the slogan "I'm with Fidel," he faced fabricated charges of terrorism in 1960 and was given a thirty-year sentence. He served twenty-two.

After he was released, thanks to strong pressure from numerous personalities, including French president François Mitterrand and human rights organizations, Valladares wrote a book in the United States titled *Against All Hope* (English version). It was published in 1986 by Alfred A. Knopf and became a best seller. It vividly narrates his harrowing prison experiences.

Armando gives us a picture of the hell he suffered after he refused Communist "rehabilitation" (like Chanes de Armas) and tried to escape. He said: "I spent eight years locked in a blackout cell, without sunlight or even artificial light. ... [The dreaded "drawer cell"] was ten feet long [and] four feet wide, with a hole in the corner to take care of my bodily needs. No running water. Naked. Eight years."

In those punishment cells, guards would dump buckets of urine and feces over the prisoners, who warded off rats and roaches as they tried to sleep. Guards constantly woke them with long poles to ensure they got no rest.

Valladares added: "All of the torture, all of the violations of human rights, had one goal: break the prisoners' resistance and make them accept political [Communist] rehabilitation.

"For many people," Armando noted, "it wasn't practical to resist. Better to sign the paper and leave. But for me ... it would have been spiritual suicide."[2]

The Hidden Gulag

Not content with persecuting dissidents and human rights activists, Castro went after males seventeen years and older who were deemed unfit for the revolution and required rehabilitation. Those males, profiled by the Cuban ruler as "scum of society, deadbeats, and degenerates," were mainly active homosexuals (or effeminates deemed prone to homosexuality) and religious "zealots." Among the latter were Jehovah's Witnesses, Protestants of several denominations, and Catholics, including a priest who later became the cardinal of Cuba, Jaime Ortega.

To corral and subject them to forced labor and corrective measures, Castro created in late 1965 the so-called Military Camps to Aid Production (UMAP was the acronym in Spanish) in the east-central province of Camagüey. One of the first people to reveal the existence of those camps, hidden within the lush vegetation of sugar fields, was a Canadian correspondent (Paul Kidd) who managed to enter one of the two hundred units where some thirty thousand to thirty-five thousand internees were confined at one point. In the 1966 article he wrote for United Press International before being expelled from Cuba, Kidd described the camp he saw—enclosed by ten-foot-high barbed wire with machine guns in each watchtower and ferocious dogs keeping watch below.

Living conditions were horrible, lacking running water and basic hygiene. Most internees slept in bunk beds (or hammocks, if no beds were available) with jute sacks slung between wooden beams for mattresses and were obliged to work at least sixty hours per week planting and harvesting sugar or performing other agricultural tasks. Those who refused or failed to meet the daily production quota were denied food for several days, family visits, and the paltry seven dollars a month (in local currency) that some of the well-behaved received. In his report of the brutality that prevailed in the concentration camp, coupled with Communist indoctrination every night, Kidd wrote: "The Cuban population has now been carried to the brink of Stalin-type era of persecution."[3]

The UMAP's camps have been described in eerie detail by prolific Cuban American author and resistance leader Enrique Ros, who called them Castro's Gulag, and by Néstor Almendros and Orlando Jiménez Leal in their 1984 documentary *Improper Conduct*.[4] According to their reports, Jehovah's Witnesses, along with Gideons International and Pentecostals, were particularly targeted because Castro viewed these secretive "pseudoreligious [fanatics] as agents of the CIA, State Department, and Yankee policy." If they refused to wear the camp uniforms or failed to comply with their guards' orders, they faced harsh punishments including beatings, being buried in the ground up to their necks, or standing in latrines filled with excrement up to their waists.

Homosexuals were also exposed to inhuman treatment. They were housed in segregated camps featuring a sign that read "Work Will Make Men Out of You." Apart from forced labor and frequent torture, the gays were exposed to Pavlovian experiments. According to several internees, if they did not respond like "machos" after watching films of heterosexual sex shown to them, they were not only denied food but also given electric shocks that left them temporarily catatonic. That's how the Castro gurus thought they could "cure" homosexuality.

By mid-1968, under tremendous pressure from international organizations, including the Inter-American Commission on Human Rights, which recorded the atrocities of Castro's concentrations camps, the Cuban ruler ended the UMAP's forced labor camps and turned most of them into military units. Two former Cuban intelligence agents estimated that of the approximately thirty thousand to thirty-five thousand UMAP internees at its peak, about five hundred ended up in psychiatric wards, seventy died from torture, and one hundred eighty committed suicide.[5]

The Exodus

The Castro regime, second to none in this hemisphere as the longest and most vicious violator of human rights, also holds the infamous record of having triggered the largest migration of political refugees, relative to population, who have fled to the United States in the last six decades.

According to Pew Research Center, over two million Cubans from all walks of life, including the refugees' direct descendants, resided in the United States in 2013—the date of the survey. They represent close to 20 percent of the island's current population. The additional Cuban refugees who arrived here during the last six years were not included in the survey.

Many of the refugees and US-born descendants have excelled as doctors and teachers, bankers and entrepreneurs, scientists and artists, entertainers and athletes. Taken as a whole, Hispanics of Cuban origin rank higher in most measures than the rest of the Latino population in the United States (calling all Latin Americans Hispanics, disregarding multiple nationalities, idiosyncrasies, and races, is a misnomer, but that is the census classification).

As reported by Pew, in educational attainment, one-quarter of Cubans ages twenty-five and older—compared with 14 percent of all US Hispanics—have obtained at least a bachelor's degree. In income, the median annual earnings for Cubans ages sixteen and older was $25,000 in 2012—greater than the median earnings for all US Hispanics ($21,000). And in homeownership, the rate of Cubans owning homes (55 percent) exceeded that of all US Hispanics (45 percent).[6]

Despite their encouraging record, Cuban Americans would require further progress to close the achievement gaps versus the total US population. They could possibly do so if they continue to work hard and aim high.

The Cuban exodus sharply increased after the Bay of Pigs debacle and the Missile Crisis settlement, which froze the island in the Cold War, ended anti-Castro military operations from the United States and Latin America, and dashed all hopes to liberate the island anytime soon.

Among the largest waves of Cuban exiles were the Freedom Flights, which from 1965 to 1972 brought about two hundred seventy thousand Cubans to Miami. Also important was the 1980 Mariel boatlift, which in a few weeks flooded Florida with one hundred twenty-five thousand refugees, including several thousand convicts, misfits, and spies seeded by the Castro regime.

But the most daring wave was the one in 1994 by some thirty-eight thousand rafters (*balseros*) who braved the treacherous Florida Straits on anything that floated, including the inner tubes of pneumatic tires. Many never made it.

Another moving chapter of the Cuban exodus story is known as Operation Pedro Pan. It involved the airlift from 1960 to 1962 of more than fourteen thousand unaccompanied children sent by their Cuban parents to the United States, before the latter could also leave or escape from their captive country.

In her *Operation Pedro Pan* book, published in 1999, Yvonne Conde, a distinguished freelance writer and a Pedro Pan refugee herself, explains what prompted the airlift and how it was carried out. She also vividly describes, with dozens of personal stories, the odyssey of the children spirited out of Cuba without their parents.[7]

As noted by Yvonne, Castro's minister of education said in 1960 that "the teacher has an unavoidable obligation to transmit revolutionary thinking to students." That meant Communist indoctrination, military drills, Castro glorification, anti-American slogans, and grueling work in a promiscuous environment at government labor camps in the countryside.

Alarmed parents who could not leave the country immediately desperately sought ways to send their children to the United States and secure temporary care for them. Two key individuals responded to the rapidly spreading panic: James Baker, former headmaster of the private American school in Havana, Ruston Academy, and the priest Bryan O. Walsh, who headed the Catholic Welfare Bureau in Miami, Florida.

They initially worked separately but soon joined efforts to lead what turned out to be a complex, large-scale, and risky humanitarian mission. Baker, in Havana, with the assistance of a group of volunteers (mainly women and a few men), covertly processed the applications involving unaccompanied children between five and eighteen years old and secured airline reservations to Miami. Walsh, in Florida, was able to obtain thousands of visa waivers for the children, exceptionally authorized by the State Department, and handled emergency accommodations, including shelters managed by the Catholic Welfare Bureau, food supply, and where possible, scholarships for schooling.

This passage to liberty, under trying circumstances, was starkly personified by a little Cuban girl who arrived unaccompanied at Miami International Airport. She was spotted by a volunteer with a sign pinned to her dress. It read: "My name is Carmen Gómez. I am five years old. Please be good to me."

Relatives in the United States and foster families who generously opened their homes to the refugees generally did their best to fill temporarily the absence of the children's parents. For some children, the reunification with their mothers and fathers took months; for others it took years; still for others, it never happened.

The children's initial adjustment was hard and, in certain cases, painful with psychological breakdowns along the way. But by and large, the children matured with steel in their spines and gratitude in their hearts, rose to the challenges over time, and seized the opportunities afforded by this generous country, in freedom.

One of them was Carlos Eire, who as a Pedro Pan was airlifted to Miami when he was twelve. Several years ago, he wrote about his personal saga as an unaccompanied refugee in his book *Learning to Die in Miami*.[8] Carlos poignantly describes his lost childhood in a vanished but not forgotten country (Cuba), as well as his onerous but inspiring assimilation into the United States. Here he became a National Book Award–winning author and a highly regarded professor of history and religious studies at Yale University.

Sadly, the Cuban exodus has never stopped, but it has taken different modalities. Here's one of the most remarkable ones: Eager to escape, and depending solely on their ingenuity and audacity, several Cuban self-made mechanics and friends converted a 1951 Chevy pickup truck into a vessel, attaching the driveshaft to a propeller and using fifty-five-gallon drums for flotation.

These refugees, in the dark of night, boarded the craft on July 16, 2003, and cruised to Florida at eight miles per hour. To their surprise and chagrin, the US Coast Guard intercepted them just south of Key West, sank the vessel, and repatriated them back to Cuba. The only satisfaction these hapless refugees got was the title bestowed on them by the press: "truckonauts."

Despite being harassed and closely watched by Castro officials, three of the original truckonauts made a second attempt to reach Florida in February 2004. Their new and improved vessel, with a passenger count of eleven, was crafted from a 1959 Buick. The interior was welded to be watertight, the prow of the boat was attached to the front of the car, and, amazingly, the car remained fully operational with its tires on. The bold objective was to reach landfall near Miami, discard the boat parts, and leisurely drive to a relative's home in Lake Worth, Florida—all as befit truckonauts, in style.

Although the truckonauts could not fully carry out their plan as originally conceived, this ocean crossing had a happier ending than the first attempt. Detained by the US Coast Guard, the group this time was sent to the US base in Guantánamo. After a lengthy stay there, they were granted safe passage to Costa Rica. From there, they covertly crossed three countries and sneaked through the Mexico-US border. Having made it to the US mainland, they qualified under the wet foot, dry foot policy of the 1966 Cuban Adjustment Act to remain in the country and apply for expedited resident status and subsequently US citizenship.[9]

Since the wet foot, dry foot policy is no longer in effect, the difficulties for Cuban refugees to enter the United States are now much greater. Yet the exodus surged in 2015 and 2016, surprising those who felt that the Obama-Castro thaw would minimize or at least contain the urge to leave the island.

Notwithstanding the numerous waves of Cuban refugees seeking asylum abroad, the anti-Castro resistance on the island has remained alive for more than sixty years. Its genesis and evolution over time merits a brief review.

Genesis of the Human Rights / Dissident Movement

Under President Lyndon Johnson, the United States stopped pursuing or supporting regime-change attempts in Cuba. The CIA, for its part, started to dismantle the camps used by Cuban exiles in the United States, Central America, and the Caribbean to launch raids against the Castro regime.

It took awhile for anti-Castro activists on the island in the late 1960s to adjust to this stunning reality. Most, however, did not give up the struggle for freedom and remained in Cuba. But since it was not feasible to obtain military aid from the United States and neighboring countries, they shifted gears and decided to pursue their resistance through peaceful means. One of those activists, Adolfo Rivero-Caro, provided details of the birth of this movement in Cuba in a paper he circulated in Miami on September 28, 2003.

Inspired by the 1975 Helsinki Security and Cooperation in Europe accords, designed to lessen Cold War tensions, and by the human rights organizations that emerged behind the Iron Curtain, two anti-Communist Cuban leaders, Ricardo Bofill and Marta Frayde, founded in Havana, in 1976, the Cuban Committee Pro Human Rights (CCPHR). Their objective was to foster a democratic transition in Cuba, and their strategy was civil disobedience and peaceful resistance.

Frayde, who was a fervent supporter of Castro's revolution until he publicly embraced Marxism-Leninism, became a target of Fidel's rage when she started to oppose him. Convicted on fabricated espionage charges, she was sentenced in 1977 to twenty-nine years in prison. Frayde was eventually released and expelled to Spain, where she continued her human rights crusade until her passing in 2013 at the age of ninety-three.

Bofill was imprisoned in 1980 and remained committed to the cause behind bars with other dissidents who had also been arrested. He later went into exile in the United States, and the brothers Gustavo and Sebastian Arcos-Bergnes then succeeded him at the helm of the CCPHR on the island.

As a result of mounting international pressure, largely spurred by the CCPHR, Castro decided, for the first and only time, to allow the visit in 1988 of a United Nations delegation to assess the human rights situation in Cuba. During that visit, more than one thousand Cubans conveyed to the delegation firsthand accounts of major violations of human rights on the island. Their detailed testimonies were included in a four hundred-page UN report, which made an impact on those who were oblivious to the plight of the Cuban people.

The CCPHR then proposed a National Colloquium in Cuba with representatives of all the sectors of the population, including the Castro regime. The proposal (which did not materialize) infuriated the anti-Communist hard-liners, who accused the proponents of collaborating with the oppressors. The heated debate that ensued turned ad hominem and caused unfortunate clashes. But when passions subsided, the human rights cause regained strength and stimulated the creation of other dissident organizations on the island, including covert in-home librarians with publications outlawed by the regime, and independent journalists, professionals, and artists.

Among the writers on the island who dared to take a stand against the Castro tyranny, Roberto Luque Escalona managed to smuggle out of Cuba the manuscript of a combative book he wrote, which was published in the United States in 1992 under the English title *The Tiger and the Children: Fidel Castro and the Judgment of History*. It lays bare Castro's deceitfulness and brutal repression and explains why history will unequivocally condemn him.

While this was going on in Cuba, most of the exile activists in the United States also shifted to peaceful resistance after the botched Bay of Pigs invasion and the Missile Crisis. They all basically had the same goal—the freedom of Cuba—but their strategies and methods of operation differed.

The distinguished Cuban exile professional Luis V. Manrara was one of the first activists who recognized the urgent need to counter Castro's deceptive propaganda campaign to seduce or neutralize US government officials and opinion leaders. In 1961, he founded the Truth About Cuba Committee, which disseminated solid, unadulterated information on the Communist regime, the suffering it inflicted on the Cuban people, and the threat it posed to the rest of the hemisphere.

With unwavering tenacity and devotion, Luis and his colleagues circulated a large number of publications in English and Spanish that set the record straight on the Castro revolution, and he personally participated in over six hundred interviews, lectures, and debates on Cuba. Luis's goal—to enlighten public opinion on Cuba—did not vanish with him. It was pursued, professionalized, and expanded later, with additional resources, by the Institute for Cuban and Cuban American Studies at the University of Miami under Jaime Suchlicki and by the Cuba program offered by Florida International University.

Another stalwart anti-Castro activist was Elena Mederos—a scholar and staunch defender of human rights and women's rights throughout most of her adult life. Castro appointed her minister of social welfare when he seized power in 1959, but she only remained five months in that post. She fled to the United States in 1961 and a few years later founded Of Human Rights in New York, along with Monsignor Eduardo Boza-Masvidal, Frank Calzón, and other activists.

The main purpose of this nonprofit organization was to denounce human rights violations in Cuba and advocate, through all available means, the release of political prisoners. Cuban American students from Georgetown University were engaged in this initiative. Moreover, several personalities, including Ambassador Jeane Kirkpatrick, supported the effort and gave national and international standing to the organization and its indefatigable torchbearer, Elena Mederos.

It is generally recognized that the most powerful and influential

Cuban American leader in the decades of the 1980s and 1990s was Jorge Mas-Canosa. He came to the United States as a penniless refugee in mid-1960, when he was twenty-one; participated in one of the armed anti-Castro expeditions to Cuba; and like many others, initially held a succession of blue-collar jobs.

However, working nonstop and leveraging his business foresight and the contacts he made, Jorge built a major multinational infrastructure, engineering, and construction company, MasTec, involved in energy, utilities, and communications. He also had the good judgment to gradually turn over the management of the enterprise to his sons so he could pursue his highest personal priority: the liberation of his homeland, Cuba.

More than a priority, the freedom of Cuba was his passion. He realized over time that the military option was not available, so he and several other compatriots founded in 1981 the Cuban American National Foundation, designed to achieve or at least advance the liberation goal mainly through peaceful means.

In that quest, the foundation identified and supported "partners" on the island committed to spurring systemic political, economic, and social change through civic engagement, nonviolent activism, and community building. The foundation gathered inside information on the horrid conditions that prevailed in Cuba and disseminated this information worldwide to increase pressure on the Castro regime to end human rights violations and release political prisoners. As part of the work, the foundation also conducted extensive research and analysis to assess US policy proposals that could foster a democratic transition in Cuba.

But the one who personally sold to the White House and Congress actionable recommendations on US Cuba policy was Mas-Canosa himself. As noted by the *New York Times* on November 24, 1997, "For more than a decade, three American presidents [Ronald Reagan, George H. W. Bush, and Bill Clinton] have sought [Mas-Canosa's] advice on Cuban affairs. ... Every significant piece of legislation on Cuba since 1980 has borne his imprint, from the establishment of Radio and TV Martí to last year's [1996] Helms–Burton Act tightening the economic embargo on Cuba."

In his patriotic mission, the combative Mas-Canosa was not exempt from criticism and, at times, heated controversy. His detractors slammed him with the epithets of intransigent, authoritarian, and power seeker. But that did not deter him from his noble pursuit; it energized him.

What Mas-Canosa did not foresee was that in 1997, when he was fifty-eight, at the apogee of his influence, lung cancer and other ailments would sap his strength and end his life. The Castro regime rejoiced with the news that the man they reviled and called the main leader of "the counterrevolutionary Miami mafia" was gone. But for the foundation and numerous Cuban American militants, his passing was a tragedy and a very big loss.

Nevertheless, the struggle continues, and although other anti-Castro organizations in the United States have also lost distinguished leaders with the passage of time, strong replacements have risen to carry the torch.

Jumping the Censorship Firewall

Many people, including recent visitors to the island, don't quite realize that the Cuban population is still subjected to brainwashing by the state, which controls not only education but also all newspapers and radio and television stations on the island. And to avert the free flow of information through social media that gave impetus to the Arab Spring, the Castro regime's agency ETECSA has kept until recently a very tight rein on telecommunications.

As a result, only a small percentage of Cubans had home access to the internet, and most of those who enjoyed that privilege were subservient to the government. Moreover, not many of Cuba's eleven million people had cell phones.[10]

In early 2015, the Castro regime agreed with a United Nations agency to get the Web into 50 percent of Cuba's households by 2020 and to achieve 60 percent mobile phone access.[11] The announcement was welcomed by many, but the initial steps taken by the regime were ludicrous. To expand access to the Internet, only three dozen Wi-Fi hot spots were introduced in 2015 around the island with restricted connectivity, continued surveillance, and largely unaffordable fees. By 2017, several hundred Wi-Fi connection points had opened in parks and plazas across the country.

Despite the slow Wi-Fi expansion, the Obama administration decided to terminate some of the USAID programs it had launched or supported to circumvent the Castro regime's censorship firewall with technologies and devices, including satellite phones.

The Cuban ruler, not content with jamming the broadcasts of the US-financed Radio and Television Martí, modeled after Radio Free Europe / Radio Liberty during the Cold War, demanded that the Martís be closed altogether as a condition to normalize relations with the United States.[12]

But what threw cold water on Obama's expectation that the US-Cuba thaw would induce Castro to relax censorship was Google's surprising rebuff on the island. Hoping to have better luck in Cuba than Telecom Italia in 1995–2011 and France's Alcatel in 2011–2012, Google made an offer in 2015 that it thought the Castro regime could not refuse: free Wi-Fi access to all of Cuba. The regime's response: Thanks, but no thanks.

After repeated attempts to strike a deal with the Castro regime, Google was allowed in December 2016 to "speed up internet service" on the island. But since the vast majority of Cubans did not have access to the internet, the deal then benefited only a small percentage of the population.

José Ramón Machado Ventura, Cuba's first vice president of the Council of State and of the Council of Ministers, explained why the government turned down Google's offer in an interview with *Juventud Rebelde* newspaper quoted by the *Havana Times* (English version):

"Everyone knows why there isn't more internet access in Cuba: because it is costly. There are some who want to give it to us for free, but they don't do it so that the Cuban people can communicate. Instead their objective is to penetrate us and do ideological work to achieve a new conquest. We must have internet, but in our way, knowing that the imperialists intend to use it ... to destroy the revolution."[13]

Even more telling than Machado Ventura's Communist tirade was the Castro regime's announcement that telecommunications will remain a state monopoly. This means, of course, that private investors and suppliers interested in modernizing and expanding telecommunications in Cuba will have to deal solely with the control-freak government.[14]

Despite the hurdles and risks involved, Cubans continued to search for loopholes to penetrate the thick censorship wall. One of the loopholes they exploited was provided by some of those managers, doctors, and academics loyal to the regime who were allowed to have home internet accounts. A number of them used this perk to supplement their meager salaries by selling their usernames and passwords for around $30 a month, often several times over.[15]

A host of ingenious and daring Cubans managed to set up clandestine Wi-Fi networks in various neighborhoods across the island before the state security started to clamp down. These networks offered their members, for about $10 a month, access to unfiltered news, movies, TV shows, and computer games. The fee often included a weekly *paquete*—a compilation of movies, telenovelas, sports, and news reports put together abroad and passed around using DVDs or USB flash drives.[16]

Among the talented communications risk-takers in Cuba are the independent bloggers who ply their computing skills to find a space, albeit narrow, for free expression. The most prominent is the forty-one-year old Cuban philologist Yoani Sánchez, best known for her blog *Generation Y.* She circumvents government censorship by emailing entries to friends outside Cuba, who in turn post them online.

A self-taught wizard in information technology, Yoani started her blog in 2006—"an exorcism, a virtual catharsis," she calls it. Translated into seventeen languages, this "catharsis" is read worldwide. It vividly describes what life is like in Cuba today, smashing the myths disseminated by the Castro regime and revealing the suffering and yearnings of the Cuban people.

In 2014, Yoani launched Cuba's first independent general-interest website called *14ymedio*, committed to defending truth, liberty, and human rights, but without a militant, ideological agenda. Although it avoided any frontal criticism of the dictatorship, the project was hacked by Castro's propaganda department, directing viewers inside Cuba to a website critical of Ms. Sánchez. The cyberattack did not affect viewers abroad. Given Yoani's celebrity status and deft balancing act, she has so far escaped imprisonment.[17]

Despite the fact that most Cubans had little or no internet access, a significant number of locally generated blogs and portals popped up on the island. Most were tolerated by the regime because they avoided directly challenging the government. However, the government has not hesitated to take action against bloggers and other journalists who report on topics deemed sensitive.

According to Freedom House, an international organization promoting democracy, those actions by the Cuban government included "short-term detentions, beatings, threats against journalists and their family members, internal deportations, house arrest, 'public repudiations,' and demotions."

The Castro regime announced in December 2018 that it would offer the population internet access for mobile phones. The problem is that the price of the 3G service to be provided in stages by the government telecommunication agency (ETECSA) is out of reach for most Cubans. Still unknown is the degree of censorship that the government will apply and the number of sites that it will block.

Despite these drawbacks, Cubans are now increasingly using social media to air their grievances. The Castro regime, however, has not remained idle. On July 4, 2019, it issued a decree prohibiting Cubans from running websites hosted outside the country. The decree dealt a heavy blow to the island's growing independent media sector, where most of the media sites and blogs use foreign hosting services and blogging platforms.

But what generated greater opposition was the July 29, 2019, law stipulating that the state would take control of the largest private network, SNET, which does not rely on the internet but on wireless connections and cables strung between houses and buildings. Observers say it has more than forty thousand users in Havana, who mostly use it to play games or discuss sports. Mounting protests were harshly repressed by the government.[18]

The Defiant Opposition

The most daring militants, who face not only repression but also brutal imprisonment and death, are the nonviolent human rights activists who take a public stand against injustice and oppression, regardless of the risks.

One of the early resistance heroes who died in prison, defiant and undaunted, was Pedro Luis Boitel. A young, charismatic student leader, Pedro fought against Batista and initially embraced the revolution. However, given his Christian belief and anti-Communist stance, he was seen as a threat to the Castro regime and was sentenced in 1961 to ten years in prison. Having rejected Communist "rehabilitation," he was kept behind bars after his sentence had ended. In protest, he went on a hunger strike. After fifty-three days of receiving only liquids and deprived of medical assistance, he died of starvation in 1972. He was forty years old.

His stirring example inspired others to brave the Castro onslaught and not to yield. One of the most recent stalwarts was Orlando Zapata Tamayo, a forty-three-year-old modest but resolute bricklayer who died in prison.

Then in October 2011, Laura Pollán, a former teacher and relentless human rights campaigner, age sixty-three, fell ill following a beating by a vicious government-instigated mob when she was peacefully demonstrating. She was taken to a hospital and died shortly after being admitted. Since the regime hastily cremated her corpse without performing an autopsy, as her family had requested, suspicions abound as to the cause of her death.

Laura's story is engrossing and inspiring. When her husband, Hector Maseda, and seventy-four other stalwart dissidents were arrested in March 2003 in an island-wide crackdown known as Cuba's Black Spring, she and other women whose loved ones also had been jailed organized a simple act of protest. Every Sunday, after attending Mass at Santa Rita Church in the suburbs of Havana, they marched in the street, dressed in white, symbolizing the purity of their cause. The women, known as "Damas de Blanco" (Ladies in White), are disciplined and nonconfrontational, but the regime grew restless and ordered its trained thugs to vilify and attack them. Video entries posted on YouTube and reposted on other websites show how the unflinching Ladies in White were mauled, punched, kicked, and even bitten by the goons.

Under great international pressure, the regime finally agreed to release Laura's husband and the other seventy-four dissidents of the Black Spring. Most of them, however, were deported to Spain. Not satisfied with the outcome, Laura and her Ladies in White decided to continue marching with their single-stem gladioli as long as other freedom-loving Cubans remain behind bars and as long as the regime retains the arbitrary power to fill the prisons again without due process of law.

Another stalwart dissident, Wilmar Villar, died on January 19, 2012, after staging a hunger strike to protest incarceration. He had been convicted of "contempt" for resisting arrest when he participated in a peaceful demonstration in eastern Cuba. Weakened by cruel treatment in prison—he had been placed naked in solitary confinement in a small, cold cell—and by his seven-week hunger strike, Wilmar succumbed to pneumonia at a hospital to which he had been belatedly transferred by the local authorities.

The leading international human rights organizations sounded their outrage, and the White House issued the following statement: "Wilmar's senseless death highlights the ongoing repression of the Cuban people and the plight faced by brave individuals standing up for the universal rights of all Cubans."[19]

A few months later, in July 2012, the internationally renowned Cuban activist and leader of the Christian Liberation Movement, Oswaldo Payá, was killed in a car crash in the far-eastern province of Cuba under suspicious circumstances. A young human rights fellow activist who accompanied him, Harold Cepero, also died in the crash.

The Castro regime claimed that the driver of Payá's car, a member of Spain's Popular Party who supported Payá's movement, imprudently slammed the vehicle into a tree, killing Payá and Cepero and injuring himself and a Swedish passenger, who also backed the prodemocracy cause in Cuba.

Payá's wife and daughter, however, challenged the government's version, saying that they had received reliable information that the car was repeatedly rammed by another vehicle. "So we think it's not an accident," they emphasized. "The government wanted to do harm[,] and they ended up killing him." The family also disclosed that Payá was targeted in a similar incident a few weeks earlier in Havana.

The Spanish survivor, under duress, toed the government's line, and the Swede alleged he was asleep. Only then were they released by the authorities and allowed to leave the island.

After they recovered, back in their respective countries, they recanted their previous testimonies and corroborated the ramming of the vehicle denounced by Payá's family. Despite international pressure to permit a thorough and independent investigation of the suspicious circumstances surrounding Payá's and Cepero's tragic deaths, the Castro regime has adamantly blocked such an investigation.

The mourned dissident leader, a sixty-year-old engineer and devout Catholic, founded in 1987 the Christian Liberation Movement, which called for civil liberties and national reconciliation. Despite the terror prevailing in Castro's police state, Payá managed to launch a campaign known as the Varela Project. Backed by twenty-five thousand courageous militants, he petitioned the Castro regime to guarantee freedom of speech and assembly, and allow the Cuban people to decide in a national referendum, with international supervision, if they wished to install a multiparty democratic system of government under the rule of law.

In recognition of Payá's work and of the harassment he suffered for defending his noble ideals, the European Parliament awarded him its Sakharov Prize for Freedom of Thought in 2002. He was nominated that year for the Nobel Peace Prize with the endorsement of world personalities including Václav Havel, the Czech president. Given the traction that Payá's movement was starting to gain, it seems that Castro decided to nip it in the bud by cutting down its leader.

Orlando Zapata-Tamayo, Laura Pollán, Wilmar Villar, Harold Cepero, and Oswaldo Payá are gone, but their inspiring examples live on. Civil resistance, while not yet a threat to the Castro regime, is picking up, and the calls for freedom are echoing across the island. Despite seemingly insurmountable barriers, the new media is starting to play a role, although limited, in spreading the narrative, firing up dissent, and increasing connectivity.

Even some of the regime's own supporters who enjoy government perks, including artists, economists, and writers, have begun to speak up in favor of more openness and less uniformity dictated from above.

Among the boldest and most highly respected dissident leaders who remain at the forefront of the prodemocracy human rights movement are Berta Soler, the current torchbearer of Damas de Blanco; Guillermo "Coco" Fariñas, who went on a drawn-out hunger strike in defense of political prisoners and was awarded the 2010 Sakharov Prize for

Freedom of Thought; and Jorge Luis García Pérez ("Antúnez"), jailed for seventeen years and known as Cuba's Nelson Mandela.

Oswaldo Payá's daughter, the talented and courageous Rosa María Payá, apart from demanding an independent investigation of her father's suspected assassination, has launched a movement, Cuba Decide, calling for an internationally supervised prodemocracy plebiscite. This initiative has received the backing of many of those in Cuba who had joined her father in his quest, as well as the support of various international personalities.

Among other renowned activists, the one who seems to be leading the largest grassroots organization, mostly in the eastern part of the island, is José Daniel Ferrer. He was one of the seventy-five political prisoners jailed in the 2003 crackdown known as Cuba's Black Spring. After being freed, Ferrer founded the Cuban Patriotic Union (UNPACU), which not only organizes street protests but also lays the groundwork for a political party that aspires to play an important role in a democratic transition. In October 2019, he was again arrested by Castro security forces, held incommunicado for one month, and reportedly tortured. As of this writing, no charges have been filed against him.

Also prominent in the struggle for freedom is the forty-one-year-old Cuban physicist Antonio Rodiles who, after spending twelve years studying in Mexico and the United States, returned to his homeland and founded For Another Cuba. This movement demands that the Castro regime ratify the UN International Covenants on Human Rights, taking inspiration from the 1975 Helsinki Final Act, which gave impetus to the triumphant Velvet Revolution in Czechoslovakia. While participating in a peaceful demonstration in Havana in 2015, Rodiles had his nose fractured by one of Castro's henchmen.

One of the most prestigious and unyielding opponents of the Cuban dictatorship is Oscar Elias Biscet. Biscet is a fifty-year-old physician and the president of the Lawton Foundation for Human Rights. He follows the nonviolent teachings of Mahatma Gandhi and Martin Luther King and calls for intensifying civic resistance to end the Castro regime and uproot its totalitarian apparatus.

After numerous detentions in 1998 and 1999, he was arrested and given a twenty-five-year sentence in 2003 during the summary trials against the seventy-five Black Spring dissidents. While Biscet was in prison, President George W. Bush awarded him the Presidential Medal of Freedom. Released in 2011 after having been held for eight years in a tiny cell, often tortured and kept incommunicado, Biscet has vowed to continue his crusade regardless of the risks.

Although historically divided, the dissident movement in Cuba is trying to build a broad coalition – one that can set aside partisan squabbles and reconcile divergent strategies. To that end, many of the organizations ratified in October 2019 the "Agreement for Democracy." That document, originally signed in 1989, sets forth the overarching principles for the transition to democracy under the rule of law, consistent with Cuba's pre-Castro 1940 constitution.

Since the Castro regime seems unwilling to loosen its grip on power or even to engage in dialogue with the opposition, most of the dissidents believe that a true opening in Cuba will require a multipronged approach: greater civic resistance on the island plus strong external diplomatic and economic pressure. If more than fifty democratic nations stand today with the Venezuelans opposing Maduro, why shouldn't they also support brutally repressed Cubans in their struggle for freedom?

Looking Ahead

Several factors will likely affect prospects for a democratic transition in Cuba. Within the island, after Raúl Castro and other aging die-hards leave, the clamor for change may intensify – as Cuba's economy continues to struggle and the long-shackled population, increasingly connected to the outside world, presses its demands for a better life.

Externally, among the factors that may bear strongly on the

prospects for a democratic transition will be the outcome of the Venezuelan crisis, including the possible end of Cuba's oil lifeline, as well as how the United States and other countries of the region respond to the looming threats posed by Russia, China, and rogue states in the United States' backyard and beyond.

The next chapter addresses these pivotal developments.

SECTION III

The Promising Future

CHAPTER 17

The Dawn of Freedom

In the words of Danish physicist Niels Bohr, "Prediction is very difficult, especially about the future." That's particularly true when it comes to Cuba, where even the present is uncertain.

That said, it seems clear that although the eighty-eight-year-old Raúl Castro stepped down in 2018 as president of the Council of State and of the Council of Ministers, he retains the reins of power as first secretary of the Communist Party and de facto head of the armed forces until 2021.

As noted earlier, Castro designated as his nominal presidential successor the electrical engineer Miguel Díaz-Canel, fifty-nine. Having earned his spurs in Communist youth groups, Díaz-Canel spent fifteen years as provincial party secretary before becoming minister of higher education and, in 2012, vice president of the Council of Ministers.

Díaz-Canel does not have any outstanding revolutionary or military credentials. He is unimpressive in public, short on charisma, and viewed as a subservient apparatchik—praised by Raúl Castro for his "ideological firmness."

This was manifest during his address before the General Assembly of the United Nations in September 2018. Dismissing speculation that he is a reformer in the style of Mikhail Gorbachev, Díaz-Canel stated, "The generational change in our government should not give hope to the adversaries of the revolution. We are continuity, not a rupture." He also declared that the new Cuban constitution being finalized will ratify the "irrevocable character of socialism."[1]

Díaz-Canel recently designated Manuel Marrero as his Prime Minister (approved unanimously by the National Assembly). Marrero, fifty-six, was Minister of Tourism for sixteen years and, like Díaz-Canel, has no strong revolutionary credentials. This civilian facade does not make Cuba's regime a parliamentary government. The real power will continue to rest in the militarized politburo.

Raúl Castro is well aware that his biological clock is ticking, along with those of other hard-line octogenarians of the Old Guard.[2] To make sure that continuity is firmly in place when they are gone, Castro is lining up several loyal generals and admirals, mostly in their seventies, to control the politburo and hold the fort beyond the transition.[3] But his overriding goal, according to informed insiders, is to perpetuate his family's dynasty.

He cannot count, however, on Fidel Castro's sons, who either are not deemed qualified or are just not keen on assuming leadership responsibilities. The exception might have been Fidel's eldest son, Moscow-trained nuclear physicist Fidel Castro Díaz-Balart, sixty-eight, who reportedly committed suicide in February 2018.

The other sons are more interested in enjoying the dolce vita. They inherited Fidel Castro's wealth and debauchery but not his stealth to keep a part-time opulent life under wraps. That life included fleeting paramours, multiple mansions, a hunting preserve, and a luxury yacht—even a paradise islet (Cayo Piedra) with private accommodations, a heliport, and a marina. All this was revealed by his former bodyguard—a witness to Fidel Castro's double life.[4]

Raúl Castro's clan, however, seems eager and ready to take on the dynastic mantle—some of the family members to govern and others to relish the Castro fortune abroad. Raúl's son Alejandro Castro Espín, an adroit six-foot colonel, fifty-four years of age, who has served as chief of the Commission of Defense and National Security with sway in several ministries, lost all or part of the vision in one eye while training in Angola, where the Castro regime sent forces from 1975 to 1991 to defend a Marxist government against South African– and US-supported insurgents.

In 2009, Alejandro wrote a book called *The Empire of Terror*, which must have pleased his father. It portrays the United States as an imperial power bent on subjugating humanity to satisfy its interests and hegemonic goals. Though not yet a general or a member of the rubber-stamp parliament (the National Assembly) or the politburo, Alejandro is one of his father's closest aides. He played a major role in the secret US-Cuba negotiations that led to the thaw during Obama's presidency, as well as in strategic intelligence accords with Russia.[5] However, since then he has remained out of sight.

The most flamboyant and politically outspoken of Raúl's offspring is his daughter Mariela Castro Espín, fifty-seven, married to an Italian businessman. As director of the National Center for Sexual Education, she has crusaded for gay, lesbian, and transgender rights.

But Mariela's real agenda is to keep her family in control of Cuba. During her visit to the United States in May 2012, she wrapped herself in the rainbow colors of the gay rights movement to bestow a patina of progressiveness on her father's grim tyranny. Mariela proclaimed "the power of emancipation through socialism," and echoing the Castro regime's vitriolic propaganda, she lashed out against the Cuban exile community, dubbed the "Miami mafia." Although she is not expected to play a leading role in the post-Castro transition, she was recently elected to the National Assembly.[6]

The one who is likely to be one of the pillars of the dynastic succession is Raúl Castro's former son-in-law Luis Alberto Rodríguez López-Callejas, fifty-nine, who was married to Raúl's daughter Deborah. He was described by The *Economist* as a "shadowy figure who speaks English with an impeccable upper-class British accent, which he says he picked up from his KGB tutor while a student in the Soviet Union."[7] Rodríguez, who has spent his life around the elite of the Castro revolution, was recently invited to join the Central Committee of the Cuban Communist Party and was promoted from colonel to general.

Without much fanfare he has served as the main architect and promoter of "Castro, Inc."—the embodiment of Raúl Castro's vision of state-militarized capitalism. Thanks to his former father-in-law, the business empire under Rodríguez's purview was vastly expanded in the past five years. He is now chairman of a gigantic conglomerate (GAESA) that comprises at least fifty-seven companies owned by the Revolutionary Armed Forces.

GAESA includes almost all the retail chains in Cuba, foreign-run hotels, state restaurants, gasoline stations, rental car fleets, and export–import agencies. Rodríguez is now also in charge of the island's most important base for global trade and foreign investment: the new container ship terminal and 180-square-mile foreign trade zone in Mariel.

Having gauged the power that Rodríguez wields as gatekeeper for most of the Castro regime's state-controlled economy, *Bloomberg Business News* wrote an in-depth piece that carries this message to those planning to invest in Cuba: "Prepare to partner with the general ...; all roads lead to Raúl Castro's [former] son-in-law." This crisp caveat says it all.[8]

For years Rodríguez did not seem to have political aspirations. However, he recently raised his public profile, meeting foreign dignitaries abroad, and was rumored to be designated prime minister (head of government) under Díaz-Canel. He didn't get the post, but remains so far extremely powerful as czar of the economy.

Succession planning is by no means the only daunting challenge facing Raúl and the fading regime. The economy is in a tailspin. On July 8, 2016, Castro's economy minister, Marino Murillo, announced that the country would have to lower its fuel consumption by 28 percent in the second half of the year and cut imports by 15 percent. A week after Murillo sounded the alarm, he was removed from his post.[9]

The alarm, of course, was warranted. The economy ended the year in a recession and, as reported by independent experts but denied by the Castro regime, showed no real growth in 2017. The outlook is further darkened by the mounting crisis in its patron nation Venezuela, which has accounted for 12–20 percent of Cuba's gross domestic product.[10]

According to a recent study by the Inter-American Development Bank, led by the respected economist Pavel Vidal, the island has not yet recovered from the loss of the Soviet subsidies—more catastrophic than originally reported. Still today, the Cuban gross domestic product is 23 percent below the precrisis level of 1989.[11]

Foreign investors and suppliers operating in Cuba's struggling economy have been told by state agencies to wait longer for payment of overdue accounts. Some fear they might face a repeat of Cuba's liquidity crisis in 2008–9, which led the government to freeze (or grab) hard currency bank accounts.

Raúl Castro, for his part, warned Cubans during his April 20, 2019, speech to brace for an economic crisis. Most of the population is already experiencing shortages of food, medicine, and power.

Apart from Venezuela's cutback on shipments of oil on credit to Cuba (down about 40 percent since 2016), the island expects a sharp decline in its principal source of hard currency: selling to foreign governments the services of temporary professionals and workers in various fields—mostly health and education, but with an intelligence sideline.

According to Castro regime officials, the services rendered by over fifty thousand Cubans in numerous countries generated more than $8 billion in 2015. (Other estimates exceed $11 billion.) The bulk of that revenue came from Venezuela and Brazil.[12]

Not many are aware of how the Castro regime exploits the doctors, teachers, and other workers it rents out to foreign governments. In Brazil, for example, the government paid the regime about $4,000 per month for each Cuban doctor performing services in the country under stringent control and harsh living conditions. But the doctors got only 25 percent of their salaries. Moreover, they were barred by the Castro regime from taking their children to Brazil and from getting their college degrees validated in the country. No wonder scores of them filed suits in Brazil to be released from what one judge called a "form of slave labor." Indeed, human rights organizations denounced the hiring out by the Cuban regime of thousands of "indentured" state servants as a new and abhorrent form of human trafficking.[13]

The recently elected president of Brazil, Jair Bolsonaro, declared in November 2018 that if the Castro regime did not recognize the rights of the eight thousand Cuban doctors in Brazil, his government would— allowing them to remain and work in the country as residents—bring their children, receive their full salaries, and validate their medical degrees. Whereupon Castro canceled the agreement with Brazil and ordered the Cuban doctors to return to the island, but many of them, "tired of being treated as slaves," opted to stay.

Cuba's severe trade imbalance and hard currency shortage has forced the regime to start "dollarizing" part of the economy (as it did in the early 1990s when Soviet aid was terminated). From now on, instead of having to buy home appliances and spare parts abroad, or having to import them through third parties (known as mules) with markup, Cubans with dollars or euros from offshore remittances or other means will be able to purchase locally, at competitive prices, some of the needed goods in state-owned hard currency stores. To have access to those stores that are now being opened, the buyer will have to obtain a bank card from a local account with hard currency. So the dollar or euro stays in Cuba. But as those with hard currency deposits have recently experienced, they may not withdraw them at will – not while Cuba remains stifled by a major liquidity crisis.

Beyond this ongoing development, no meaningful liberalization of the economy is foreseen at this time, even within the confines of a political tyranny as in China. The politburo fears that, given the entre- preneurial zeal of the Cubans and the island's proximity to the citadel of pernicious capitalism (the United States), too much economic leeway could undermine its grip on power.

But could the Castro regime cope with worsening economic and fi- nancial conditions without introducing major reforms? It could conceiv- ably muddle through, at least temporarily, if a new US administration, with congressional approval, were to lift or weaken the embargo on Cuba and if Russia and/or China were to increase their economic support.

However, that won't resolve the core problem. The crisis facing Cuba today is not peripheral or transitory, but integral and deep-rooted. Few truly embrace the Marxist-Leninist ideology, and the revolution has lost its relevance and mystique. The rot is so pervasive that the only real cure lies in removing the state's stifling corset to open the economy and unleash the nation's creative energies.

It may take time, however, to achieve that objective. The Castro regime has been able so far to neutralize or contain the anger and frustration of large swaths of the population. But the current unsettling situation is bound to get worse, particularly if the regime loses the Venezuelan subsidy. The gap between the shallow reforms and the bulging needs of ordinary Cubans is widening, and total dependency on the welfare state, which bred conformity and inertia, is no longer sustainable. So as the government safety net contracts, the unrest will grow along with the clamor for liberty.

▌The Price of Freedom

Cubans, on the surface, seem resigned to their current fate as they struggle to overcome their daily ordeal. But history suggests they have not renounced their right to chart their own course and determine their own future. Throughout sixty years of Castro tyranny, thousands of Cubans from all walks of life have paid the ultimate price in their quest for liberty.

Now a new generation of Cubans—led by the surging prodemocracy dissident movement—is trying to reignite the "hope of the hopeless" and the "power of the powerless," in the words of Václav Havel, the late Czech statesman and dissident. Although public protests and peaceful demonstrations have so far been limited, activists and a growing number of Cubans who have been silent or uninvolved are now turning to social media (Twitter, Facebook, and other applications) to express their discontent and demand essential changes.

Despite relentless repression and lack of unified leadership, the dissidents have not been cowed or quelled. They remain adamant in their pursuit, realizing that it will take unflagging perseverance and coordinated efforts to energize civil society. They are convinced that if pressure is increased from inside and outside the island, those in power will have to recognize the legitimacy of the democratic opposition and negotiate a peaceful transition.

This, however, may not happen until Raúl Castro and his Old Guard are gone and their succession scheme is stymied by a galvanized population, including young marginalized officers of the army and disaffected apparatchiks. Not a far-fetched scenario if we recall what occurred in the Soviet bloc following the end of Stalinism under the reformist Gorbachev.

For all their apparent puissance, airtight totalitarian governments, grounded on lies and fear, tend to crack when they are forced to introduce substantial reforms, particularly political reforms. They tend to propel rising expectations and growing demands, and through the crevices that ensue, the winds of freedom start to blow.

But this does not occur by coddling tyrants with unilateral concessions and charm offensives or by enriching their domains with tourism, commerce, and investment. In shackled countries like Castro's Cuba, where the economy is largely controlled by the ruling elite, mainly the military, the inflow of capital and financing bolsters the oppressors and does not effectively empower the oppressed.

To help bring about the largely peaceful transitions from totalitarianism to democracy and free enterprise in the Soviet bloc, the Reagan administration engaged Gorbachev. But it did not rely solely on the soft power of diplomacy. It simultaneously exerted extraordinary economic, political, psychological, and military pressure (including an arms race that almost crippled the Soviet Union). It also supported the dissident movements jointly with Pope John Paul II and British prime minister

Margaret Thatcher. The comprehensive strategy was clearly outlined in three ultrasecret National Security Decisions Directives: No. 32 of May 20, 1982, No. 66 of November 29, 1982, and No. 75 of January 17, 1983.

Most Cuban dissident leaders and human rights activists do not oppose US conditional engagement with the Castro regime (or its successor), but they do warn against the dictator's ploy to promise and not deliver, to take and not give. They harshly criticize the 2014 one-sided Washington-Havana deal that was secretly negotiated without their knowledge or involvement, and they call on the United States and the democratic world to uphold and support their cause.

Cuban American community leaders and activists,[14] often backed by legislators of Cuban descent led on a bipartisan basis by Senators Marco Rubio and Robert Menendez, have submitted to Congress and the White House a number of suggestions to spur democratic change on the island. Among those suggestions are the following:

1. Place Castro's Cuba again where it belongs, among state sponsors of terrorism, and apply the corresponding sanctions. This appears to be under consideration, given the dozens of terrorists and fugitives harbored in Cuba and the close links of the Castro regime to terrorist organizations.

2. Indict Raúl Castro for having ordered, among many other crimes against humanity, the deadly 1996 shoot-down, over international waters, of two unarmed planes of a Cuban American humanitarian organization carrying three US citizens and one US permanent resident. This campaign is spearheaded by Orlando Gutierrez, leader of the Cuban Democratic Directorate, and other prominent activists.

3. Enforce Titles III and IV of the Cuban Liberty and Democratic Solidarity Act, authorizing claims in the United States against those who "traffic" in confiscated property in Cuba, and deny US visas to those who engage in that illicit practice. (The Trump administration ended the periodic suspension of these titles, and the European Union announced that it would challenge the "extraterritorial"

impact of this move and retaliate. The outcome of US court rulings on the outstanding claims is still pending.)

4. Ban US cruises to Cuba, which foster American tourism prohibited by the US embargo and serve mainly to enrich the military in charge of most of the economy. (Suspension of those cruises and restrictions on commercial flights to Cuba have been decreed by the Trump administration.)

5. Apart from penalizing the Castro regime for human trafficking, call on the International Labor Organization to condemn the regime for installing in Cuba a virtual slave labor system that denies all basic rights and that pockets most of the hard currency salaries paid by foreign investors. Warn those investors that they could be held accountable for complicity in the crime.

6. Denounce Castro's new constitutional sham, and support those who are engaged in civil disobedience to press for the release of all political prisoners, for respect for human rights, and for the adoption of a new constitution approved by freely elected representatives of the Cuban people.

7. Fend off, in accordance with the Rio Treaty, the military and subversive intervention of hostile powers in this hemisphere, in collusion with the Castro regime and other Latin American authoritarian governments.

8. Intensify support for the dissident leaders on the island, and encourage them to unify their efforts.

As noted, the United States already has adopted some of the suggested measures. Yet to emerge, however, is a comprehensive, forward-looking strategy. Such a strategy would address the Castro succession scheme as well as the very real threats posed by Russia, China, and rogue states in the Caribbean and throughout Latin America. Importantly, it would also engage and leverage the dissident movement's prodemocracy leaders, whose involvement in any major negotiation affecting the future of their homeland will be essential.

The US Role

Some have asked: Why should the United States get involved in the Cuban plight? One good reason is that we cannot be indifferent or neutral when human rights and individual liberties are systematically trampled on by any government in this hemisphere. This would go against not only our values but also the 2001 Democratic Charter of the Organization of American States, which calls for collective action when democracy is threatened or suppressed in the Americas.

But there is another, even more compelling reason to be involved. The island, dominated by a cruel tyranny supported by anti-American powers and rogue states, is too close to the United States to be abandoned or ignored. As Secretary of State John Quincy Adams presciently pointed out in 1823: "Cuba, almost in sight of our shores, from a multitude of considerations has become an object of transcendent importance to the commercial and political interest of our Union" (and to its national security, I would add).

As noted earlier, the security of the United States and the region is again potentially endangered by and from Castro's Cuba. Both the former head of the US Southern Command, Admiral Kurt Tidd, and his successor, Admiral Craig Faller, have flagged the brewing geopolitical and military threat posed by Cuba in collusion with Russia, China, Venezuela, other rogue states, and terrorist organizations. So hands-off in Cuba is not really an option for the United States, nor is lifting the embargo without quid pro quo. A one-sided engagement is no engagement; it is capitulation, which only emboldens the tyrant and his allies and demoralizes his opponents.

Consistent with US national interests, commitments, and values, Washington should encourage and support the young prodemocracy and human rights activists in Cuba (as it did with the leaders of the Solidarity movement in Poland), for they, and not their aging oppressors, are the island's best hope for a free, peaceful, and prosperous future.

Finally, it's important to bear in mind that a Communist Cuba is an unavoidable reality today, but it is not destiny. It's a tragic aberration that eventually will pass. Freedom still beats in the hearts of the captive population.

As the island's foremost hero, José Martí, who led the final struggle against colonial rule in the Americas, put it so eloquently: "Liberty never dies from the cuts it receives. The dagger that wounds it carries in its veins new blood."

A New Beginning

When change finally comes to Cuba, what will it look like? Will it look like China or Vietnam, open to state and private capitalism but closed to democracy? Or will it look like Poland, where roundtable talks between the government and the dissident movement (Solidarity) gave rise to a gradual democratic opening? Or will it look like Czechoslovakia, where communism's stunning collapse, known as the "Velvet Revolution," brought swift and peaceful transformation? Will it look like Romania's bloody coup or the Soviet Union's unraveling, following Gorbachev's glasnost and perestroika reforms?

It is difficult to predict. But it's reasonable to assume that the Castro regime's likely successors (the military-controlled politburo, including the dictator's protégés and designated family members) will try to retain as much authoritarian power and perks as possible and forestall or delay systemic reforms.

Continuity with minor changes may be achievable, but not for long, given the conditions of the waning regime—its foundations eroded, its resources wasted, and its vitality exhausted. The revolutionary élan spawned by the Castro brothers in their heyday has largely evanesced. What will likely subsist is the raw force and greed of factions at the helm, struggling to remain in power without any inspiring goals to proclaim or cause to defend. Not the best recipe for resurgence.

Absent the ability to cut the Castro Gordian knot, what will it take to liberalize the captive island, subjugated for more than half a century by Communist oppression? Probably a combination of top-down and bottom-up pressure. As fear subsides, frustration grows, and protests escalate, the airtight totalitarian apparatus will likely splinter or crack. The army then will have no choice but to yield to the clamor for fundamental change led by young reformists within the government and by an invigorated dissident movement backed by large swaths of civil society.

The popular outbreak, however, could take time to gain traction since it may lack the strong external boost that spurred post-Communist transitions in Central and Eastern Europe. However, it is encouraging to note the extraordinary backing that the United States, Canada, and numerous Latin American and European countries have given the anti-Maduro democratic forces in Venezuela. This could set a positive precedent for Cuba.

Tyranny will eventually end on the captive island, but liberty under the rule of law will not spring up overnight. The journey from totalitarianism and a command economy to democracy and free enterprise may be staggered, rocky, and contentious.

But those leading the transition will not have to improvise or start from scratch. Drawing on the experiences of Central and Eastern Europe and other regions, jurists, economists, and sociologists from the Cuban American community and the island, as well as US government officials and academics, already have worked on blueprints that could help address the roadblocks that may arise.

Challenges Ahead

One of the biggest initial challenges that post-Communist Cuba will face is the restoration of law and order while fostering national unity and reconciliation. To achieve that, a broad-based provisional government will have to be formed, possibly including noncontroversial representatives of the prior regime, along with leaders of the dissident movement, civil society, and the Cuban diaspora.

Following the release of all political prisoners and the dismantling of the island's repressive apparatus, those accused of major crimes should be brought to justice and tried, with due process of law, by a new, not politicized supreme court. But the purge of those who actively collaborated with the Communist regime (known as "lustration" in Central and Eastern Europe) should not become a witch-hunt driven by personal vendettas. In the interest of healing and reconciliation, lustration, if applied in Cuba, should be limited in scope, duration, and severity.

A constitutional framework, not cast in the Castro-Communist mold, will be needed during the transition before free and multiparty elections are held. Such temporary charter, if based on the applicable provisions of Cuba's last democratic constitution, promulgated in 1940, would carry legitimacy and provide legal guarantees for all. That constitution became the leitmotiv of the struggle against the Batista dictatorship, and its principles embedded in its bill of rights are today espoused by most of the prominent leaders of the dissident movement and the diaspora.[15]

Turning to economic challenges, the transition government will have to renegotiate Cuba's stifling foreign debt and seek urgent relief from the World Bank, the IMF, USAID, and other institutions. It has been estimated that the island will need to stabilize the economy and kick off the recovery anywhere from $500 million to $2.5 billion a year in emergency aid for three to five years.[16]

Well-thought-out measures will be required to unify the exchange rates, deregulate prices, reduce excessive taxes and trade barriers, and gradually phase out unsustainable government subsidies. And to stimulate investments, private property and contractual rights will have to be legally protected against confiscations and arbitrary decrees.

At the same time, the interim government should stave off any extreme nationalistic or protectionist tendency that would shun or discourage reputable foreign investors willing and able to bring to Cuba much-needed capital and technical know-how. Lech Walesa, the first directly elected president of post-Communist Poland, was on the right track when he reportedly declared, "I want the US to send me its best generals: General Motors, General Electric, and General Dynamics."

Privatization will be the linchpin of Cuba's economic recovery, disgorging most of the assets gobbled up and squandered by the Castro regime. The transition government will have to decide which of two basic models to follow: the *big bang* or *shock therapy*, involving an accelerated top-down privatization process (as pursued in Poland) or a phased bottom-up approach, leaving privatization of the largest government enterprises for the final stage. Most independent Cuban economists seem to favor the gradual process, along with a safety net to assuage the impact on the displaced and unemployed.[17]

The transition government should be prepared to counter possible attempts to co-opt the privatization process by corrupt officials of the Castro regime, trying to replicate the plunder of the enriched Russian oligarchs or the pillage of the crooked Nicaraguan Sandinistas.

Another delicate challenge that will arise is how to resolve the outstanding claims of rightful owners of businesses and properties confiscated by the Castro regime. Since the transition government will not have the funds to provide the claimants with monetary compensation, resolution will likely call for restitution of the confiscated property, or of one similar in value where feasible, or payment with government bonds or privatization credits known as "vouchers." Both approaches should entail a commitment to reinvest in Cuba.

The task of verifying titles, estimating the value of the confiscated properties, and determining the rights of competing claimants is fraught with complexity and prone to controversy. It behooves the transition government to study what worked and what didn't in Central and Eastern Europe.[18]

Cuban émigrés and their descendants—viciously dubbed by Castro the "Miami mafia" and accused by him of plotting to oust the islanders from their homes—ought to tread carefully when exercising their rights. Otherwise, wide swaths of the local population could turn against them, as occurred in East Germany during the reunification of the country. Returning Cubans should not be perceived as insensitive overlords taking over properties and displacing local residents. Instead of evincing greed to recover, they should exude zeal to rebuild.

The Shattered Infrastructure

Cuba's recovery will require the rebuilding of its shattered infrastructure, starting with housing. The island faces today an acute housing crisis. Too many Cubans live in dangerous, overcrowded conditions with entire families crammed in one-room apartments or lofts. Deferred maintenance and scant materials and financing has created perilous electrical, gas, and structural issues. Dilapidated buildings frequently collapse, particularly in Old Havana. Experts estimate that Cuba is lacking adequate housing by almost 1 million units.

Another major infrastructure emergency is insufficient potable water. The Pan American Health Organization estimates that only 62 percent of Cubans have reasonable access to disinfected water. To complicate matters, sewage treatment is alarmingly inadequate. Reliable sources indicate that "in the entire country, there are only five municipal wastewater plants, and an extremely low level of the sewage effluent has treatment."[19]

An efficient transportation system—by air, sea, and land—is a critical element of infrastructure that would spur the development of tourism, employment, and overall economic growth in a post-Castro Cuba. This will require upgrading Cuba's seven principal international airports and providing its ten major ports with modern container and cruise terminals, as well as links to rail, trucking, barge, and pipeline operations. High on the priority list is also the rebuilding of deteriorated roads and the modernization of Cuba's railway system.

Digitalizing the island's antiquated telecom system is an urgent must. Despite recent progress, Cuba still has one of the region's lowest density of mobile phones, computers, and internet usage. This is due, in part, to Castro's fear that their totalitarian regime could be undermined through the connectivity of the Web and social media.

Untapped Potential

As a free Cuba rebuilds its infrastructure, upgrades professional services, and opens its economy with adequate legal safeguards, investors will flock to develop the island's potential in a number of areas, including: tourism; agro-industries; mining, minerals and petroleum; biotechnology; and pharmaceuticals.

Tourism

Not surprisingly, at the top of the list is tourism. The Castro regime, mainly in partnership with European hospitality companies, stepped up construction of new hotels, mostly in Havana and beach areas and keys, like Varadero, Cayo Coco, and Cayo Largo. But owing to inadequate services and facilities (with a few exceptions), Cuba has not been able to attract the high-end, heavy-spending, repeat tourist market. Still lacking are five-star resort hotels with golf courses and villas for rent or sale.

The opportunity is there for investors in a free Cuba to take tourism to a much higher level. After all, Cuba is an archipelago of more than thirty-five hundred islands, islets, and keys, and only a fraction of its hundreds of pristine blue water beaches have been developed. Its coral reefs and diverse fisheries, particularly in the spectacular diving spot of Jardines de la Reina—often called the Galápagos of the Caribbean—have attracted both naturalists and fishing enthusiasts from all over the world.[20]

But Cuba offers visitors more than maritime splendor. It is rich in history with the grandeur of its colonial past carved in stone as evidenced in Old Havana and in the central city of Trinidad—both World Heritage Centers. It has lush fertile valleys, like Viñales, dotted with impressive dome-like limestone outcrops (*mogotes*) that rise like fortresses. It is renowned for its vast labyrinth of magnificent caves, including the Great Cavern of Santo Tomás, one of the largest in Latin America with galleries and subterranean rivers spanning more than nine miles. Cuba is also endowed with outstanding thermal springs in picturesque settings, like San Diego de los Baños and San Miguel de los Baños, which, with private sector funding and well-trained medical and administrative staff, could become first-rate wellness centers and spas.

One of the pending projects, mapped out by distinguished Cuban Americans and led by Alberto S. Bustamante, takes a page out of Spain's book of Paradores—a network of luxury hotel accommodations in or near castles, palaces, convents, and other historic buildings designed to promote tourism while preserving the country's heritage. Cuba could have its own version of Paradores in fortresses, majestic villas, vintage sugar mills, and other sites of historic significance and unusual beauty.[21]

Agro-Industries

Given its benign climate, fertile soil, and optimal topographic conditions, Cuba is ideally suited to agriculture. Yet under Castro-Communist rule it has sagged, if not collapsed. For example, in the 1950s, pre-Castro, the island was the global sugar cane leader, accounting for about 20 percent of world production. Today, with production falling to levels not seen since the early 1900s, Cuba has been surpassed by Brazil and at least five other countries.[22] With the dawn of freedom and the inflow of private capital and technology, economists predict a significant recovery of the Cuban sugar industry. Cargill, Archer Daniels Midland, Caterpillar, Deere, and other companies would seriously consider investment opportunities, but the list will most likely be headed by the

Florida-based Cuban American Fanjul family, reputed to be the largest private refiner of sugar cane in the world.

The reinvigoration of the sugar industry would also include the development of its by-products. Among these is bagasse, for the generation of bioelectricity, and molasses, for the production of clean, low-carbon ethanol—a leading renewable biofuel that is blended with gasoline. But for Cuba, the by-product that will continue to have the highest priority is the alcoholic distillate from the fermentation of cane juice, syrup, or molasses: rum. The Bacardi shareholders look forward to the day when, in a free Cuba, they can reestablish their company— the largest privately held spirits enterprise in the world—and relaunch their popular products where their amazing story began.

The word *Havana* still denotes the ultimate in quality and smoking pleasure, thanks largely to the light sandy clay soil, rich in humus, of Vuelta Abajo, where most Cuban tobacco is cultivated. Yet growth is held back by the resourceless government, which buys most of the production and pays very little to the farmers. Without the fetters of state control, reputable private investors could revitalize the industry with fresh capital and technology, and enhance its competitiveness.

The Castro regime tried to boost citrus production (focusing on oranges, grapefruits, limes, and tangerines) and installed processing, cold storage, and packing facilities in partnership with a few weak, undercapitalized foreign investors. But shortages of fuel, fertilizers, herbicides, and spare parts severely crippled those efforts. In a free and open Cuba with strong international partners, those obstacles could be overcome.

Before the Castro revolution, the growth of cattle in Cuba was keeping pace with the population. In the 1950s, the island had over six million head of cattle, or one per inhabitant, and ranked fourth in meat consumption per capita in Latin America. It even started to export meat. Today meat is severely rationed, along with various other foods. An unshackled and resurgent Cuba, however, could restore the island's rich cattle tradition, which once included fabulous ranches similar to those in western United States.

Mining, Minerals, and Petroleum

In its 1956 report on investment opportunities, the US Department of Commerce stated that, potentially, Cuba was one of the world's largest sources of nickel and iron. It was also an important supplier of chrome and manganese.[23] The Castro regime confiscated the US nickel-processing plant (Nicaro) in far-eastern Cuba, as well as the nearby Moa Bay mines owned by a subsidiary of Freeport Sulphur Co. It then authorized the Canadian company Sherritt International to extract, process, and export nickel and cobalt ores. Results were initially profitable, but later the enterprise hit roadblocks. To further develop Cuba's mining potential in a post-Castro era, investors would need to add refining capability to the nickel-processing plants, among other investments.

It is well-known that Cuba largely depends on foreign oil sources (mainly from Venezuela at present) to supply its needs. In 2012, three deep-water exploration wells were drilled by Spanish, Russian, and Venezuelan companies, but no commercial quantity of oil or gas was found. However, the area that was prospected represents only a small portion of Cuba's yet-to-be-explored 112,000-square-kilometer Gulf of Mexico Economic Exclusive Zone. Major US oil companies await a more propitious and friendly environment to tap the island's high-potential oil reserves, estimated by the 2004 US Geological Survey at 4.6 billion barrels of crude oil and 9.8 trillion cubic feet of natural gas.

Biotechnology and Pharmaceuticals

The Castro regime has reportedly invested $1 billion in biotechnology and pharmaceuticals, but hanging over this alleged investment is the suspicion that it may have included research and development of dual-use biotechnologies (for medicinal purposes and for biological weapons) shared with Iran and other rogue states. Since the regime has not authorized an independent inspection of the secluded sites, the concern persists.

Another critical question is: How reliable are Cuba's claims about its vaccines and drugs? Lacking in most cases proper validation of the touted results, we really don't know the degree of progress made with its vaccines for meningitis B, influenza type B, and hepatitis B, or for a treatment for heart attacks called streptokinase. To really make headway in this field and gain the confidence of consumers, physicians, and the World Health Organization, the solution post-Castro possibly lies in privatizing the industry and inducing reputable multinational pharmaceutical companies to partner in the development of the island's potential with capital to invest, science to innovate, credibility to advertise, and channels to distribute and sell worldwide.

The Ultimate Goal

Could a post-Communist Cuba become over the long haul a vibrant haven of freedom and prosperity? On the positive side, Cuba will benefit from its privileged geography. Sitting astride the sea-lanes that connect the Americas and adjoining the largest market in the world, the island is an ideal location for commerce and cultural intercourse. Another big advantage is its bright and resilient population 11.3 million strong—larger than Hungary, the Czech Republic, Austria, Sweden, and Portugal, and almost comparable to Greece. But the broader demographic trends are troubling and need to be addressed.

▌Demographics

As reported by Azam Ahmed of the *New York Times*, "Since the 1970s, Cuba's birthrate has been in free fall, tilting population figures into decline." The island already has the oldest population in all of Latin America. Based on current trends, some experts forecast that fifty years from now, Cuba's population will have fallen by a third. More than 40 percent of the country will be older than sixty. If this were to happen, the retirees would require a vast health-care system, which the country could not afford.[24]

What accounts for this demographic predicament? Not having much hope for a better future in Cuba, youngsters have fled the island in large numbers, searching for opportunities to uplift their lives and raise a family. Many who have remained in Cuba are reluctant to have children given the meager average salary of about $40 a month, the shortage of consumer goods, and the dearth of housing, all of which make life a daily struggle.

Yet another factor that bears on Cuba's low birth rate is the ease of obtaining abortions. In Cuba they are legal, free, and without stigma and are essentially viewed as an alternative to birth control. As a result, Cuba's abortion rate is among the highest in the world. According to a 2010 United Nations report, the island's rate of nearly thirty abortions for every one thousand women of childbearing age is only surpassed by Russia. In the United States, 2011 statistics show a rate of about seventeen per one thousand.[25]

Cuba's demographic problem is serious but not irreparable. Trends are bound to change when the government of a free Cuba unleashes the population's entrepreneurial zeal, kick-starts the economy, and palliates the housing shortage. In practical terms, young people on the island will start having babies again when they can afford it.

Luring Cuban Americans and other expatriates to relocate in the island nation where they or their forebears were born would be an important way (but not the only one) to help offset the population decline. Even attracting a fraction of the the vast diaspora of close to two million Cuban-born expatriates and descendants—many of whom have succeeded as business builders, corporate executives, professionals, educators, doctors, scientists, and artists—could be a boon for the reconstruction of the liberated island

The Quantum Leap

For a free Cuba to become a regional powerhouse, it will have to reach some audacious milestones: evolve from an import-dependent to an export-driven country; operate as a reliable trading partner with first-class harbors and airports; recapture its role as an assembler of industrial goods bound for the United States; and gear up to grab a meaningful share of the information technology outsourcing market.

Havana also will have to compete with Miami as a financial center and regional hub for multinational corporations (a scenario that started to unfold in the 1950s before the fall of the republic). Here again, Cuban Americans could be very helpful. Many were instrumental in turning Miami from a sleepy retirement spot into a throbbing metropolis.

Reeducation

To hasten the island's economic resurgence, raise productivity, and improve the island's competitiveness, large numbers of Cubans will need technical and vocational education and training. This applies both to large-scale corporate businesses and small start-ups.

An even greater challenge for the leaders of a free Cuba will be reviving the island's heritage, including its cultural legacy, ethnic roots, and national traditions—all of which were razed by the Castro regime. That's what totalitarian tyrants do to befuddle and enslave a nation: destroy the past to control the present and shape the future.

At the same time, Cubans will have to expurgate the corruption and overdependence on the state that discourages honest work and move past the cynicism that has resulted from six decades of communist dictatorship.

Both the public and the reinstated private and church-affiliated schools can help by offering civic courses to instill democratic values and shed light on crucial principles like the rule of law, human rights, separation of powers, representative government, and multiparty elections.

The objective is to build a strong civil society capable of influencing public policy decisions and holding government officials accountable. To achieve that, a democratic Cuba will need an active and involved population imbued with the virtues of self-discipline, tolerance, and respect for all regardless of background, race, gender, and political opinions.

Of critical importance will be the island's churches. Free to practice their creeds with no concern of government interference or reprisals, Cuban churches will be in a position to uplift their parishioners, give them a strong moral foundation, and preach the gospel of goodness and love.

Cultural Renaissance

As Cuba makes headway in its recovery and affluence again reaches its shores, the island must avoid becoming hedonism's new tropical headquarters, flaunting the three nocturnal R's: rum, rumba, and roulette. What the island should aspire to is a cultural renaissance such as the one Cuba enjoyed in the golden years of the republic when its splendid academies, lyceums, and theaters were flourishing.

Thanks to Pro Arte Musical de La Habana, led over more than forty-five years by six distinguished Cuban women, the world's greatest artists beat a path to Havana's doors: Sergei Rachmaninoff, Ignacy Paderewski, Arthur Rubinstein, Enrico Caruso, Renata Tebaldi, Pablo Casals, and Vaslav Nijinsky, among many others.[26]

When the island regains its cultural vitality, the luminaries of arts, letters, and science will likely flock again to the fascinating island, especially the many highly successful expatriates and their descendants. Cuba's own writers, journalists, musicians, and artists will be able to open their creative wings without fear of prison or exile. And the island's outstanding athletes will not have to defect to travel, train, and compete wherever they choose.

To enrich the culture of the new generations and broaden their perspective, it will be important to republish the great books highlighting Cuba's past precommunism achievements that were blocked by the Castro regime. Many of those books were published by Ediciones Universal under Juan Salvat and have been collected by the University of Miami's Cuban Heritage Collection, Florida International University, Miami Dade College's Freedom Tower, and the Colonial Florida Heritage Cultural Center.

Also illuminating the past, pondering the present, and projecting the future are the articles, essays and poems disseminated by Círculo de Cultura Panamericano, headed for many years by Elio Alba Buffill; Herencia Cultural Cubana, created and developed by Alberto S. Bustamante; Association for the Study of the Cuban Economy (ASCE), founded in 1990 and initially presided ex officio by Felipe Pazos; Institute for Cuban and Cuban-American Studies of the University of Miami, led by Jaime Suchlicki; Florida International University's Cuban Research Institute, directed by Jorge Duany; National Association of Cuban-American Educators (NACAE), spearheaded by Orlando Rossardi, and Academia de la Historia de Cuba en el Exilio, chaired by Eduardo Lolo.

Foreign Affairs

In the field of diplomacy and foreign relations, what role will a free Cuba play in the Organization of American States, the United Nations, and other international organizations? Hopefully an active and constructive role, upholding democratic principles, human rights, and peaceful resolution of disputes. Complaints or disappointments for not having received much support from some of those institutions during the struggle for the island's freedom should be set aside as Cuba endeavors to consolidate its democracy and regain its international standing.

Promising leaders of the future can draw inspiration and guidance from the example set by Cuba's prestigious statesmen and diplomats during the republic and by the Cuban Americans who honorably served as US ambassadors.[27]

The Long-Term Outlook

Those who know Cuba's history and its people and believe in the uplifting power of freedom—including this author—are confident that the island nation will eventually rise from the rubble left behind by Castro-Communism. They are also confident that Cuba will be able to tackle the four great challenges ahead: political democratization, economic liberalization, cultural revitalization, and moral regeneration.

Still, crucial questions hang in the balance: Could Cuba, posttransition and recovery, shun mediocrity and move from good to great? Could it, long term, become a thriving and exemplary regional powerhouse? Or is this grand and inspiring vision a feverish illusion?

Not if Cubans on the island and abroad join forces to unlock its potential, in partnership with responsible foreign investors bringing capital and technology. Not if they channel their creative energies constructively and avoid new demagogic frauds or dictatorial temptations.

If they doggedly preserve the blessings of liberty, a generation or two will pass healing, rebuilding, and developing, but their children and grandchildren will see the results of their lofty endeavor: a solid foundation for democracy under the rule of law, economic and social prosperity, and a path to moral greatness.

ACKNOWLEDGMENTS

This ten-year book project was not a light-hearted labor of love. It was an intense labor of devotion to the cause of freedom, involving my birth country (Cuba) and my adopted country (the United States of America). Along the way I encountered numerous obstacles that tested both my resolve and my endurance.

There is so much that I owe to so many who lent me a hand or gave me a word of encouragement throughout the long process that I will almost surely miss some names deserving recognition. To those individuals, I offer my sincerest apology.

I first would like to thank Pat Hass, former editor of Alfred Knopf, who introduced me to the publishing world in 1989. She provided valuable insights and guidance for my first book in English, *And the Russians Stayed: The Sovietization of Cuba*, and for this one, too.

I owe a huge debt of gratitude to Dick Detwiler, an outstanding professional, former PepsiCo colleague and unfailing friend. Throughout the critical stages of this book, I relied on Dick's expertise and good judgment as a superb editor and stylist, idea generator and trustworthy adviser. He stood by me through thick and thin and helped me cross the finish line.

For more than two years, I was represented by a very talented and highly regarded literary agent and naval historian, Jim Hornfischer. He sharpened my proposal and approached in my behalf leading book editors. Although most of the editors offered stimulating comments and generous praise, they opted to pass, mainly because Cuba was not in the limelight at the time, and the market for this book seemed narrow and difficult to reach.

Circumstances changed, however. Communist Cuba, still under Castro control, raised again its nefarious profile as a disrupter of peace and subverter of democracy in collusion with Russia, China and Venezuela. Encouraged by several experienced editors and authors, including Mary E. Curtis, former president of Transaction Publishing, and Marysue Rucci, senior editor of Simon & Schuster, I recast the manuscript and changed the title to reinforce that Cuba does indeed matter, not only to the captive Cuban people, but to the United States and the world.

That led me to Archway Publishing of Simon & Schuster, which provided all the necessary support to steer the revised book project to completion. I greatly appreciated Sarah Smith's overall coordination, as well as the assistance of line editors, design experts and publishing and marketing consultants, including Brad Wilhelm and Kelly Martin.

I also am deeply grateful to five foreign affairs luminaries who took the time to read excerpts of my manuscript and honored me with their early endorsements: former U.S. Secretary of State, Dr. Henry Kissinger; former President of the Council of the Americas, Ambassador Everett Briggs; former U.S. Director of the Central Intelligence Agency, Porter Goss; former U.S. Speaker of the House of Representatives, Newt Gingrich; and U.S. Chairman of the Senate Foreign Relations Subcommittee on the Western Hemisphere, Senator Marco Rubio.

I wish to thank those who shared with me important unpublished documents and information. Among them, Agustin de Goytisolo, who trusted me with the startling revelations of the Jesuit priest Amando LLorente, Fidel Castro's school mentor, who interviewed him in his mountain hideout a few weeks before he seized power. And Mark Falcoff, a resident scholar at the American Enterprise Institute, who chronicled the February 2001 meeting held with Fidel Castro in Havana by a delegation of the Council on Foreign Relations headed by David Rockefeller.

Three distinguished literary agents who represented me in the early stages of this book project also merit my gratitude: Joe Tessitore, and Jerrold and Leona Schecter. (Leona was my agent in 1989 when my first book in English was published.) A special mention goes to my former colleague Dave Gilman, who assisted me for several months as a literary consultant. The publisher of all my books in Spanish, which preceded and laid the groundwork for *Why Cuba Matters*, was Ediciones Universal, led by my patriotic friend Manuel Salvat.

Five former U.S. ambassadors stationed in Latin America, with whom I have a close relationship, provided first-hand information and support: Mauricio Solaún, Alberto Martínez Piedra, Otto Reich, Everett Briggs and Jim Cason. And so did the former President and the Executive Director of the Center for a Free Cuba, Manuel Jorge Cutillas and Frank Calzón. I also drew on the insightful reports and assessments of two prominent Latin America editors: Mary O'Grady of The Wall Street Journal and John Paul Rathbone of the Financial Times.

Prior to the publication of this book, John Fulkerson, John Hess and Peter Thompson invited me to lecture at their respective literary clubs—an opportunity I gladly accepted and greatly appreciated. I also was privileged to write for or speak at *Forbes* (Steve Forbes), *Foreign Policy* (Moisés Naim), *Institute for Cuban and Cuban-American Studies* (Jaime Suchlicky), *Círculo de Cultura Panamericano* (Elio Alba Buffill), *Herencia Cultural Cubana* (Alberto S. Bustamante), *M.A.R. por Cuba* (Sylvia Iriondo), *Asociación Pro-Cuba* (Camilo Fernandez) and *Centro Cultural Cubano de New York (Iraida Iturralde)*.

Univision, El Nuevo Herald, Diario Las Américas, El Nuevo Día in Puerto Rico, and the digital publication La Nueva Nación, led by Alfredo Cepero, enabled me to express and disseminate my views years before this book was brought to light.

Friends working at or for PepsiCo were very helpful; particularly, Dave Yawman, Joe Ferreti, Denise D'Arbonne, Andrea Grasso, Peter Wilcox and Michael Drucker.

Among the scholars who provided insights and guidance, I wish to thank Harvard Professor Graham T. Allison and his research associate Daniel K. Khalessi. Encouragement and support for my book came from Florida International University and from its Casa Cuba, led by Agustin Arellano, with the enthusiastic assistance of Maria Carla Chicuen, George Corton and Lily Betancourt Space.

I am particularly grateful for the stimulus and assistance I received from these very kind and cooperative friends and relatives: Allie Hanley, Micho Spring, Kathy Lubber Gingrich, Ilvi Cannon, Manuel and Joe Delgado, Claudia Puig, Gastón Arellano-Pichardo, and my dynamic sister, Maitá.

And finally, of course, my heartfelt thanks go to my entire family, without whose inspiration and unflagging support this book could not have been written. My parents and grandparents set the example of service to country and provided troves of historical information and personal experiences. My cousins, Ofelia and Ileana Arango-Puig, Eduardo Arango, Manuel and Ramón Puig, and Humberto Cortina personified the highest level of patriotism and courage in the struggle for freedom and recounted their daunting sacrifices in this book.

My daughter Rosa María, and my sons Néstor Gastón and José Manuel were very involved in the drafting of this book. They were my reliable sounding board to bounce off ideas and gauge reactions. And my wife, Rosa, who shares my dreams and convictions, gave me the zeal to overcome the obstacles and the love to keep the faith alive.

NOTES

Chapter 1—Castro's Collusion with Russia, China, and Venezuela

1 *Washington Post*, July 26, 2019.

2 José de Córdoba, "The Future of Cubazuela," *Wall Street Journal*, March 1, 2013.

3 Will Grant, "Concern over Cuba's Role in Venezuela," BBC News Latin America, June 23, 2010.

4 Antonio María Delgado, "General Rivero: Cuba Tiene a 20,000 Hombres Listos para el Combate en Venezuela," *El Nuevo Herald*, January 29, 2015.

5 Moisés Naím, "Cuba Fed a President's Fears and Took over Venezuela," *Financial Times*, April 15, 2014.

6 Ibid.

7 Pedro Roig, "Venezuela-Cuba Military Cooperation and the Narco-Terrorist Connection," Institute for Cuban and Cuban American Studies, University of Miami, Issue 212, March 18, 2014.

8 "Venezuela No Ayuda en Lucha Antidroga, Dice el Comando Sur de EEUU," Associated Press, June 3, 2015.

9 Nicholas Casey and Ana Vanessa Herrero, "How a Politician Accused of Drug Trafficking Became Venezuela's Vice President," *New York Times*, February 16, 2017.

10 Ibid.

11 Luis Fleischman, "Iran in Latin America: Identifying the Problem and How We Need to Confront It," Center for Security Policy, February 1, 2018.

12 Wanda Carruthers, "OAS Secretary General: Cuba Has Occupation Army in Venezuela," Newsmax, July 22, 2017.

13 José R. Cárdenas, "The Cubanization of Venezuela," *Washington Times*, June 14, 2013.

14 Angus Berwick, "How Cuba Taught Venezuela to Quash Military Dissent," Reuters, August 22, 2019.

15 Nora Gámez Torres, "Tropas Cubanas Participaron en Maniobra Militar en la Frontera de Venezuela con Colombia," *El Nuevo Herald*, October 3, 2018.

16 *The New York Times*, July 5, 2019.

17 Mary O'Grady, "Chilean Capitalism on Trial," *The Wall Street Journal*, October, 28, 2019.

18 Associated Press, August 19, 2019.

19 Jaime Suchlicki, "The Cuba-Iran Venezuela Relationship: Implications for the United States," Institute for Cuban and Cuban American Studies, University of Miami, February 24, 2015.

20 María C. Werlau, "Does Cuba Have Biochemical Weapons?" This article was entered into the congressional record at the hearing "Cuba's Pursuit of Biological Weapons: Fact or Fiction?" before the Subcommittee on Western Hemisphere on June 5, 2002.

21 Ibid.

22 AP Teheran, May 13, 2001.

23 *Granma International Digital* (English translation), October 18, 2001.

24 Juan O. Tamayo, "US Skeptical of Report on Cuban Biological Weapons," *Miami Herald*, June 23, 1999.

25 Senator Bob Menendez's letter to Secretary of State John Kerry, February 26, 2015.

26 "Another Gift to Castro," editorial, *Wall Street Journal*, April 15, 2015.

27 Senator Robert Menendez's letter to Secretary of State John Kerry; Mary Anastasia O'Grady, "The Castro Brothers Get Caught in the Act," *Wall Street Journal*, July 29, 2013.

28 Mary Anastasia O'Grady, "Devilish Dealmaking in Colombia," *Wall Street Journal*, April 26, 2015; Mauricio Claver-Carone, "Is Cuba Smuggling Weapons for FARC Terrorists?" Capitol Hill Cubans, April 5, 2015, http://www.capitolhillcubans.com/2015/04/is-cuba-smuggling-weapons-for-farc.html.

29 Todd Beamon, "Report: Panama Intercepts Ship from Cuba Carrying 401 Kilos of Cocaine," Newsmax, April 14, 2016; "Autoridades Panameñas Interceptan 400 Kilos de Cocaína Procedentes de Cuba," *Diario de Cuba*, April 15, 2016.

30 Carol Rosenberg, "Cuban Security Officials Toured Key West Drug-War Center," *Miami Herald*, May 4, 2016.

31 Randal C. Archibold, "Latest Talks on US-Cuba Diplomatic Ties End," *New York Times*, March 18, 2015.

32 Ernesto Londoño, "China's Long, Quiet Push into Latin America," *New York Times*, July 29, 2018.

33 *The New York Times*, December 24, 2018.

34 *The New York Times*, September 22, 2019.

35 Nick Cunningham, "China Could Be the New Owner of Venezuela's Oil Industry," *Business Insider*, April 5, 2018.

36 Foreign Policy, April 8, 2019.

37 Londoño, "China's Long, Quiet Push."

38 Admiral Kurt W. Tidd, "Posture Statement before the Senate Armed Services Committee," February 15, 2018; Ernesto Londoño, "China's Long, Quiet Push."

39 Victor Robert Lee, "Satellite Images: A (Worrying) Cuban Mystery," *The Diplomat*, June 8, 2018.

40 Kenneth Rapoza, Forbes, May 29, 2019.

41 Andrew F. Kramer, "Russia Plans to Reopen Post in Cuba for Spying," *New York Times*, July 17, 2014; Mary Anastasia O'Grady, "Putin Restores a Cuban Beachhead," *Wall Street Journal*, July 27, 2014.

42 Ibid.

43 "Russia-Cuba Announce Increase in Intelligence Cooperation," *Cuba Confidential*, posted ITAR-TASS, May 2014.

44 Diane Barnes, "Could the US Face a Cruise Missile Threat from the Gulf of Mexico?" *Global Security Newswire, National Journal*, March 21, 2014.

45 "Cuba Agrees to Host Russian Glonass Navigation Stations," *Moscow Times*, June 18, 2014.

46 O'Grady, "Putin Restores Cuban Beachhead."

47 Kramer, "Russia Plans to Reopen Post."

48 Naftali Bendavid and Gregory L. White, "Russian Dial Up Military Threats," *Wall Street Journal*, November 13, 2014.

49 David E. Sanger and Eric Schmitt, "Russian Ships near Data Cables Are Too Close for US Comfort," *New York Times*, October 26, 2015.

50 Michael Birnbaum, "Russian Submarines Are Prowling around Vital Undersea Cables. It's Making NATO Nervous," *Washington Post*, December 22, 2017.

51 Devlin Barrett and Gordon Lubold, "Missing US Missile Shows up in Cuba," *Wall Street Journal*, January 8, 2016; Mary Anastasia O'Grady, "North Korea's Cuban Friends," *Wall Street Journal*, January 11, 2016.

52 Nora Gámez Torres, "Cuba y Rusia Reestablecen Cooperación Nuclear," *El Nuevo Herald*, July 5, 2016.

53 Nora Gámez Torres and Antonio María Delgado, "Goodbye Venezuela, Hello Russia. Can Vladimir Putin Save Cuba?" *Miami Herald*, December 27, 2017.

Chapter 2—How Democracy Died in Cuba: From Batista to Castro (1952–58)

1   See Gabriel E. Taborda, *Palabras Esperadas: Memorias de Francisco H. Tabernilla Palmero* (Miami: Ediciones Universal, 2009); and Roberto Fernandez Miranda, *Mis Relaciones con el General Batista* (Miami: Ediciones Universal, 1999).

2   Taborda, *Palabras Esperadas*, pp. 99–100.

3   Ibid., p. 165.

4   Hugh Thomas, "Cuba or the Pursuit of Freedom" (London: Eyre & Spottiswoode, 1971), p. 904.

5   Theodore Draper, *Castro's Revolution: Myths and Realities* (New York: Frederick A. Praeger, 1962), p. 22. See "Socio-Economic Conditions in Pre-Castro Cuba," *Cuba Facts* 43 (December 2008); Jorge Salazar Calazar and Andro Nodarse-León, *Cuba: From Economic Take-Off to Collapse under Castro* (New Brunswick: Transaction, 2015).

6   Thomas, "Cuba or the Pursuit of Freedom," p. 1007.

7   John Paul Rathbone, *The Sugar King of Havana: The Rise and Fall of Julio Lobo, Cuba's Last Tycoon* (New York: Penguin, 2010), pp. 13, 210–11.

8   Tom Gjelten, *Bacardi and the Long Fight for Cuba* (New York: Viking, 2008), pp. 195–96.

9   Carlos Franqui, *Family Portrait with Fidel* (New York: Random House, 1984), p. 242.

10 Néstor T. Carbonell, *And the Russians Stayed: The Sovietization of Cuba* (New York: William Morrow, 1989), p. 52.

11 Taborda, *Palabras Esperadas*, p. 157.

12 Earl E. T. Smith, *The Fourth Floor: An Account of the Castro Communist Revolution* (New York: Random House, 1962), p. 156.

13 Manuel Márquez-Sterling, *Cuba 1952–1959: The True Story of Castro's Rise to Power* (Wintergreen, VA: Kleiopatria Digital Press, 2009), p. xxix.

14 Luis Conte Aguero, *Los Dos Rostros de Fidel Castro* (Mexico: Editorial Jus, 1960), p. 22.

15 Serge Raffy, *Castro el Desleal* (Spain: Santillana Ediciones Generales, 2004), pp. 618–19.

16 Ann Louise Bardach, "Fidel! Fidel!" *Talk* (August 2001): p. 87.

17 Georgie Anne Geyer, *Guerrilla Prince: The Untold Story of Fidel Castro* (Boston: Little Brown, 1991), pp. 39–40.

18 Ibid., pp. 49–50.

19 Néstor Carbonell Cortina, *Por La Libertad de Cuba: Una Historia Inconclusa* (Miami: Ediciones Universal, 1996), pp. 140–47.

20 Bardach, "Fidel! Fidel!" p. 120.

21 Juanita Castro, *Fidel y Raúl Mis Hermanos: La Historia Secreta* (Doral, FL: Santillana, 2009), p 149.

22 Thomas, "Cuba or the Pursuit of Freedom," p. 1078.

23 Paul D. Bethel, *The Losers* (New York: Arlington House, 1969), p. 95.

24 Salvador Díaz-Versón, "When Castro Became a Communist," Institute for US-Cuba Policy, November 8, 1997.

25 US Senate Internal Security Subcommittee Hearings, "Communist Threat to the United States through the Caribbean," pt. 5 (July 17, 1960), p. 284.

26 US Senate Internal Security Subcommittee Hearings, pt. 10 (September 2, 1960), p. 725.

27 Marta Harnecker, *Fidel Castro: Del Moncada a la Victoria* (Venezuela: Ediciones Centauro, 1986), p. 9.

28 Brian Latell, *After Fidel: The Inside Story of Castro's Regime and Cuba's Next Leader* (New York: Palgrave Macmillan, 2005), pp. 126–30.

29 Franqui, *Family Portrait*, p. 239.

30 Ibid., p. 241.

31 US Senate Internal Security Subcommittee Hearings (May 3, 1960), pp. 353, 355; full text of Díaz-Balart's speech held by the author.

32 Text of Díaz-Balart's speech held by author.

33 Franqui, *Family Portrait*, p. 243.

34 Christopher Andrew and Vasili Mitrokhin, *The World Was Going Our Way: The KGB and the Battle for the Third World* (New York: Basic Books, 2005), p. 34.

35 Draper, *Castro's Revolution*, p. 191.

36 Anthony De Palma, *The Man Who Invented Fidel* (New York: Public Affairs, 2006), p. 19.

37 Manuel Márquez-Sterling, *Cuba 1952–1959*, pp. 145–46.

38 Letter from Ambassador Everett Ellis Briggs to the author, April 24, 1998.

39 Wayne S. Smith, *The Closest of Enemies* (New York: W. W. Norton, 1987), pp. 36–37.

40 Alphone Chady, "After 50 Years Questions about Cuba Still Pound Wieland," *Miami Herald*, January 6, 2009.

41 US Senate Internal Security Subcommittee Hearings, pt. 12 (June 12, 1961), p. 798.

42 Ibid., pt. 9 (August 30, 1960), p. 694.

43 Lucas Morán Arce, *La Revolución Cubana* (Ponce, PR: Imprenta Universitaria, 1980), pp. 238–39.

44 Bethel, *The Losers*, p. 60.

45 Geyer, *Guerilla Prince*, pp. 189–90.

46 Alexsandr Fursenko and Timothy Naftali, *One Hell of a Gamble: Khrushchev, Castro, and Kennedy, 1958–1964* (New York: W. W. Norton, 1997), p. 12.

47 Earl E. T. Smith, *The Fourth Floor*, p. 159.

48 US Senate Internal Security Subcommittee Hearings, pt. 10 (September 2, 1960), p. 739.

49 Earl E. T. Smith, *The Fourth Floor*, p. 170.

Chapter 3—The Vatican Mystified, and the White House in the Dark (End of 1958)

1 George Anne Geyer, *Guerrilla Prince: The Untold Story of Fidel Castro* (Boston: Little, Brown, 1991), p. 38.

2 Copy of the notarized document is held by the author.

3 Dwight D. Eisenhower, *Waging Peace* (New York: Doubleday, 1965), p. 521.

4 *Foreign Relations of the United States, 1958–1960*, vol. 6, Cuba, Department of State Publication 9855, pp. 302–3.

5 Earl E. T. Smith, *The Fourth Floor: An Account of the Castro-Communist Revolution* (New York: Random House, 1962), pp. 229–30.

6 The other five US ambassadors who basically concurred with Smith when they testified at congressional hearings in 1960–61 were Spruille Braden, Arthur Gardner, William D. Pawley, Robert C. Hill, and Whiting Willauer.

Chapter 4—In the Eye of the Storm: Denouncing the Takeover (1959–Mid-1960)

1   Foreign Relations of the United States (FRUS), Department of State, 1958–60, vol. 6, pp. 580–82.

2   Philip W. Bonsal, *Cuba, Castro, and the United States* (London: University of Pittsburgh Press, 1972), pp. 59–61.

3   Senate Subcommittee of the Judiciary, Hearings on Communist Threat to the United States through the Caribbean, pt. 12 (June 12, 1961), p. 817.

4   Senate Subcommittee Hearings (July 27, 1961), pp. 867–70.

5   Néstor T. Carbonell, *And the Russians Stayed: The Sovietization of Cuba* (New York: William Morrow, 1989), pp. 61–62.

6   Bonsal, *Cuba, Castro, and the United States*, pp. 53–54.

7   Rufo López-Fresquet, *Times of Havana* (Miami), September 15–17, 1961.

8   Tad Szulc, *Fidel: A Critical Portrait* (New York: William Morrow, 1986), p. 490.

9   Juan Vivés, *Los Amos de Cuba* (Buenos Aires: Emecé, 1982), p. 34.

10 Szulc, *Fidel*, pp. 471–75.

11 Manuel Prieres, "Conspirando en Tarará y Cojímar," *Guaracabuya*, June 2, 2006.

12 Alvaro Vargas Llosa, "The Killing Machine: Che Guevara—from Communist Firebrand to Capitalist Brand," *New Republic*, July 11, 2005.

13 Rufo López-Fresquet, *My 14 Months with Castro* (New York: World Publishing, 1966), pp. 80–83.

14 Néstor T. Carbonell, *And the Russians Stayed*, p. 259.

15 FRUS, pp. 579–80.

16 Bonsal, *Cuba, Castro, and the United States*, p. 84.

17 Paul D. Bethel, *The Losers* (New York: Arlington House, 1969), pp. 186–92.

18 FRUS, pp. 595–98.

19 Bonsal, *Cuba, Castro, and the United States*, p. 19.

20 FRUS, p. 611.

21 Bonsal, *Cuba, Castro, and the United States*, p. 98.

22 Ibid., p. 104.

23 Ion Mihai Pacepa, "Who Is Raúl Castro?" *National Review Online*, August 10, 2006.

24 FRUS, p. 656.

25 Senate Subcommittee Hearings (November 5, 1959), p. 163.

26 Szulc, *Fidel*, pp. 507–9.

27 FRUS, p. 685.

28 Bonsal, *Cuba, Castro, and the United States*, p. 115.

29 Ibid., pp. 126–27.

30 Julio A. Amoedo, "Negotiating with Fidel Castro," *New Republic*, April 27, 1964.

31 Juan Vivés, *Los Amos de Cuba*, p. 81.

32 FRUS, p. 792.

33 Amoedo, "Negotiating with Fidel Castro."

34 Arthur Krock, "The Lively Issue of Castro's Justification," *New York Times*, May 18, 1961.

35 FRUS, p. 792.

Chapter 5—The Cloak and the Dagger: Joining the Exile Front (Mid-1960)

1 Foreign Relations of the United States (FRUS), 1958–60, vol. 6, Cuba, Department of State, pp. 996–97.

2 FRUS, vol. 6, pp. 850–51, 861–63.

3 Jim Rasenberger, *The Brilliant Disaster: JFK, Castro, and America's Doomed Invasion of Cuba's Bay of Pigs* (New York: Scribner, 2011), p. 58.

4 Piero Gleijeses, *Ships in the Night: The CIA, the White House, and the Bay of Pigs* (Cambridge, MA: Cambridge University Press, 1995), p. 8.

5 Peter Wyden, *Bay of Pigs: The Untold Story* (New York: Simon and Schuster, 1979), p. 33.

6 Executive Session of the Senate Foreign Relations Committee (Historical Series), vol. 13, pt. 1 (1961), p. 426.

7 David M. Barrett, "Documento Muestra Dudas sobre Invasión a Cuba," *El Nuevo Herald*, August 11, 2005.

8 Wyden, *Bay of Pigs*, p. 21.

9 Néstor T. Carbonell, *And the Russians Stayed: The Sovietization of Cuba* (New York: William Morrow, 1989), p. 90.

10 *Miami Herald*, August 17, 1960.

11 Theodore Draper, *Castro's Revolution: Myths and Realities* (New York: Praeger, 1962), p. 106.

12 FRUS, vol. 6, pp. 1057–60.

13 Ibid., p. 1149.

14 According to Juan Vivés (a pseudonym used by a former secret service officer of the Castro regime who defected), the offensive against the insurgents was

directed by Soviet antiguerrilla specialists under the command of Lieutenant Colonel of the Red Army Anastas Grigorich, Lieutenant Colonel of the KGB Valentin Trujanov, and Colonel-Political Commissar of the KGB Mijail Furmanov. Juan Vivés, *Los Amos de Cuba* (Buenos Aires: Emecé, 1982), pp. 98–100.

15 Eduard B. Ferrer, *Operation Puma: The Air Battle of the Bay of Pigs* (Miami: International Aviation Consultants, 1982), p. 70.

16 Ibid., pp. 82–83.

17 "JFK Muzzled Me," *Miami Herald*, December 1, 1961.

18 Rasenberger, *The Brilliant Disaster*, pp. 90–94.

19 FRUS, vol. 6, p. 1126.

20 FRUS, vol. 6, pp. 1126–31.

21 FRUS, vol. 6, pp. 1132–40.

22 Memorandum of meeting with the president, January 3, 1961 (January 9, 1961). National Security Archive, "Bay of Pigs: 40 Years After—Chronology," p. 22.

23 FRUS, vol. 10, Cuba (1961–62), pp. 10–43.

24 Senate Hearings, "Communist Threat to the United States through the Caribbean" (July 27, 1961), p. 875.

25 FRUS, vol. 10, p. 44.

Chapter 6—Inside a Doomed Expedition: The Bay of Pigs (January–April 1961)

1 Senate Hearings, "Communist Threat to the United States through the Caribbean" (July 27, 1961), pp. 877–78.

2 Foreign Relations of the United States (FRUS), 1958–60, vol. 10, p. 18.

3 Ibid., vol. 10, p. 200.

4 Ibid., pp. 90–91.

5 Ibid., pp. 136–43.

6 Luis Aguilar, *Operation Zapata: The Ultrasensitive Report and Testimony of the Board of Inquiry on the Bay of Pigs* (Frederick, MD: Aletheia Books, 1981), p. 13.

7 FRUS, vol. 10, pp. 145–56, 158–60.

8 Aguilar, *Operation Zapata*, p. xiii.

9 FRUS, vol. 10, p. 179.

10 Ibid., p. 185.

11 Rasenberger, *The Brilliant Disaster*, pp. 156–63.

12 Aguilar, *Operation Zapata*, p. 16.

13 FRUS, vol. 10, p. 227.

14 Ibid., pp. 235–37.

15 Wyden, *Bay of Pigs*, p. 202.

16 Gleijeses, *Ships in the Night*, p. 26.

17 Arthur M. Schlesinger, *A Thousand Days: John F. Kennedy in the White House* (New York: Fawcett Premier, 1965), p. 241.

18 Rasenberger, *The Brilliant Disaster*, pp. 81–83, 141–44.

19 FRUS, vol. 6, p. 789.

20 Rasenberger, *The Brilliant Disaster*, pp. 143–44.

21 Ferrer, *Operation Puma*, p. 144.

22 Rasenberger, *The Brilliant Disaster*, p. 283; Michael Beschloss, *The Crisis Years: Kennedy and Khrushchev, 1960–1963* (New York: Edward Burlingame, 1991), p. 122.

23 Néstor T. Carbonell, *And the Russians Stayed: The Sovietization of Cuba* (New York: William Morrow, 1989), p. 139; *US News and World Report*, February 4, 1963, p. 33; Wyden, *Bay of Pigs*, pp. 56–57.

24 Howard Hunt, *Give Us This Day: The Inside Story of the CIA and the Bay of Pigs Invasion … by One of Its key Organizers* (New York: Arlington House, 1973), pp. 157–58.

25 FRUS, vol. 10, p. 191.

26 The resistance leaders who attended the meeting, apart from Sorí Marín and Ñongo, were Rafael Díaz ("Rafael"), Rogelio González-Corzo ("Francisco"), and Domingo Trueba ("Mingo").

27 Néstor T. Carbonell, *And the Russians Stayed*, pp. 132–33.

28 FRUS, vol. 10, p. 221.

29 Néstor T. Carbonell, *And the Russians Stayed*, p. 144.

30 Ibid., pp. 150–51.

31 Ibid., pp. 151–53.

32 Aguilar, *Operation Zapata*, pp. 355–58.

33 Schlesinger, *A Thousand Days*, pp. 245–48.

34 Néstor T. Carbonell, *And the Russians Stayed*, pp. 153–54.

35 Wyden, *Bay of Pigs*, p. 246.

36 Grayston L. Lynch, *Decision for Disaster: Betrayal at the Bay of Pigs* (Washington, DC: Brassey's, 1998), p. 71.

37 Ibid., p. 218.

38 Ibid., pp. 159, 160, 259.

39 Ibid., pp. 131–32.

40 Schlesinger, *A Thousand Days*, p. 264.

41 Ibid., pp. 133–36.

42 Rasenberger, *The Brilliant Disaster*, p. 272.

43 Ibid., p. 314.

44 Michael R. Beschloss, *The Crisis Years: Kennedy and Khrushchev, 1960–1963* (New York: Edward Burlingame, 1991), pp. 144–45.

Chapter 7—The Battle of the OAS and the Mongoose Plots (Mid-1961–Early 1962)

1   Foreign Relations of the United States (FRUS), vol. 10, Cuba (1961–62), pp. 309–10.

2   FRUS, vol. 10, pp. 302–4.

3   Ibid., p. 304.

4   Ibid., pp. 305–6.

5   Ibid., pp. 306–7.

6   Ibid., p. 405.

7   Ibid., pp. 481–83.

8   Néstor T. Carbonell, *And the Russians Stayed: The Sovietization of Cuba* (New York: William Morrow, 1989), pp. 181–83.

9   Jim Rasenberger, *The Brilliant Disaster: JFK, Castro, and America's Doomed Invasion of Cuba's Bay of Pigs* (New York: Scribner, 2011), p. 347.

10 Ibid.

11 Frederick Kempe, *Berlin 1961: Kennedy, Khrushchev, and the Most Dangerous Place on Earth* (New York: G. P. Putnam's Sons, 2011), pp. 257–58.

12 Ibid., p. 262.

13 FRUS, vol. 10, pp. 621–24.

14 Ibid., p. 635.

15 Néstor T. Carbonell, *And the Russians Stayed*, pp. 192–93.

16 Carlos Franqui, *Family Portrait with Fidel* (New York: Random House, 1984), p. 242.

17 Richard N. Goodwin, *Remembering America: A Voice from the Sixties* (Boston: Little, Brown and Company, 1988), pp. 196–202.

18 FRUS, vol. 10, p. 641.

19 Juan Archibaldo Lanus, *De Chapultepec al Beagle: Política Exterior Argentina, 1945–19* (Buenos Aires: Emecé, 1984), pp. 250–51.

20 Néstor T. Carbonell, *And the Russians Stayed*, pp. 198–99.

21 FRUS, vol. 10, pp. 650–52.

22 Ibid., p. 654.

23 Ibid., pp. 657–58.

24 Néstor T. Carbonell, *And the Russians Stayed*, pp. 200–1.

25 Among the other exiles involved in the OAS battle were Luis V. Manrara, representing the Truth about Cuba Committee, Fernando García Chacón on behalf of the Student Revolutionary Directorate, and Tulio Díaz Rivera for the economic sector in exile.

26 FRUS, vol. 10, p. 720.

27 Ibid., pp. 270–71.

28 Operation Mongoose: The Cuba Project, program review by Brigadier General Lansdale, February 20, 1962, Cuban History Archive (Marxists. org), 2000.

29 FRUS, vol. 10, p. 718.

30 *Alleged Assassination Plots Involving Foreign Leaders: An Interim Report of the Select Committee to Study Governmental Operations with Respect to Intelligence Activities, US Senate* (Washington, DC: US Government Printing Office, 1975), p. 141.

31 Jim Rasenberger, *The Brilliant Disaster: JFK, Castro, and America's Doomed Invasion of Cuba's Bay of Pigs* (New York: Scribner, 2011), p. 352.

32 FRUS, vol. 10, p. 771.

33 Aleksandr Fursenko and Timothy Naftali, *One Hell of a Gamble: Khrushchev, Castro, and Kennedy, 1958–1964* (New York: W. W. Norton & Company, 1997), p. 166.

34 FRUS, vol. 10, pp. 706–9.

35 Ibid., pp. 772–76.

36 Ibid., p. 778.

37 Néstor T. Carbonell, *And the Russians Stayed*, pp. 210, 211.

Chapter 8—Unheeded Warnings: The Looming Missile Crisis (August–October 1962)

1 Aleksandr Fursenko and Timothy Naftali, *One Hell of a Gamble: Khrushchev, Castro, and Kennedy, 1958–1964* (New York: W. W. Norton, 1997), p. 170.

2 Raymond L. Garthoff, *Reflections on the Cuban Missile Crisis* (Washington, DC: Brookings Institution, 1989), p. 12.

3 Fursenko and Naftali, *One Hell of a Gamble*, p. 160.

4 Ibid., pp. 181–82.

5 Ibid., p. 187.

6 Ibid., pp 188–89.

7 "CIA Briefings for JFK Shed New Light on Cuban Missile Crisis," *Miami Herald*, October 18, 2015.

8 Sergo Mikoyan, *The Soviet Cuban Missile Crisis: Castro, Mikoyan, Kennedy, Khrushchev, and the Missiles of November* (Washington, DC: Woodrow Wilson Center Press, 2012), p. 105.

9 Fursenko and Naftali, *One Hell of a Gamble*, pp. 193–94.

10 Interim Report of the Cuban Military Buildup issued by the Senate Preparedness Investigative Subcommittee on May 9, 1963.

11 "CIA Briefings for JFK Shed New Light on Cuban Missile Crisis."

12 FRUS, vol. 10, p. 923; Lawrence Chang and Peter Kornbluh, eds., *The Cuban Missile Crisis: A Chronology of Events* (New York: New Press, 1992, 1998).

13 FRUS, vol. 10, pp. 955–56.

14 Ibid., pp. 957–58.

15 Ibid., p. 968; Fursenko and Naftali, *One Hell of a Gamble*, p. 204.

16 *Newsweek*, September 14, 1962; Fursenko and Naftali, *One Hell of a Gamble*, pp. 205–6.

17 David M. Barrett and Max Holland, *Blind over Cuba* (College Station: Texas A&M University Press, 2012), pp. 8–10.

18 FRUS, vol. 10, p. 973.

19 Hearing on the Situation in Cuba before the Senate Committees of Foreign Relations and Armed Services (September 17, 1962).

20 Ibid., pp. 58–59.

21 Ibid., p. 4.

22 Ibid., p. 18.

23 Ibid., p. 27.

24 Ibid., pp. 40–41, 71.

25 Fursenko and Naftali, *One Hell of a Gamble*, p. 209.

26 Ernest R. May and Philip D. Zelikow, eds., *The Kennedy Tapes: Inside the White House during the Cuban Missile Crisis* (New York: W. W. Norton, 2002), pp. 19–22.

27 Ibid., pp 22–29.

28 Fursenko and Naftali, *One Hell of a Gamble*, p. 216.

29 Chang and Kornbluh, *The Cuban Missile Crisis*, p. 357.

30 Fursenko and Naftali, *One Hell of a Gamble*, p. 217.

31 Mary S. McAuliffe, ed., CIA documents on the Cuban Missile Crisis (October 1992), pp. 111–12.

32 Ibid., pp. 115–16.

33 Fursenko and Naftali, *One Hell of a Gamble*, p. 219.

34 FRUS, vol. 11, p. 17.

35 Ibid., p. 18.

36 Ibid., pp. 26–29.

37 CIA documents on the Cuban Missile Crisis (1992), pp. 101–4.

38 Fursenko and Naftali, *One Hell of a Gamble*, pp. 221–22.

Chapter 9—Eyeball-to-Eyeball: Who Blinked? (October–December 1962)

1 Earnest R. May and Philip D. Zelikow, eds., *The Kennedy Tapes: Inside the White House during the Cuban Missile Crisis* (New York: W. W. Norton, 2002), pp. 60–61.

2 Ibid., pp. 45–46.

3 Ibid., pp. 36–38.

4 Ibid., pp. 70–71.

5 Ibid., p. 62.

6 Ibid.

7 Ibid., p. 61.

8 Presidential Recordings: Transcripts—Cuban Missile Crisis Meetings (October 16, 1962), the John F. Kennedy Library, pp. 14–15.

9 May and Zelikow, *The Kennedy Tapes*, p. 42.

10 Ibid., pp. 66, 67, 68.

11 FRUS, vol. 11, pp. 110–14.

12 Aleksandr Fursenko and Timothy Naftali, *One Hell of a Gamble: Khrushchev, Castro, and Kennedy, 1958–1964* (New York: W. W. Norton, 1997), p. 232.

13 FRUS, vol. 11, p. 115.

14 Ibid., p. 131.

15 Ibid., p. 134.

16 Ibid., pp. 129, 131.

17 Ibid., p. 98.

18 Ibid., p. 121.

19 Ibid.

20 Ibid., p. 140.

21 Ibid., pp. 129, 133.

22 Ibid., p. 144.

23 Fursenko and Naftali, *One Hell of a Gamble*, pp. 237, 241.

24 Néstor T. Carbonell, *And the Russians Stayed: The Sovietization of Cuba* (New York: William Morrow, 1989), p. 221.

25 FRUS, vol. 11, pp. 159–60.

26 Fursenko and Naftali, *One Hell of a Gamble*, pp. 247, 248, 259, 260.

27 Anatoly Dobrynin, *In Confidence* (New York: Times Books, Random House, 1995), pp. 81–82.

28 Fursenko and Naftali, *One Hell of a Gamble*, pp. 249, 250, 274, 275.

29 CIA documents on the Cuban Missile Crisis (1992), pp. 338–40.

30 FRUS, vol. 11, p. 253.

31 Fursenko and Naftali, *One Hell of a Gamble*, pp. 272, 277, 278.

32 Dobrynin, *In Confidence*, pp. 86–88.

33 Néstor T. Carbonell, *And the Russians Stayed*, pp. 222–24.

34 Dobrynin, *In Confidence*, pp. 84–90.

35 Michael R. Beschloss, *The Crisis Years: Kennedy and Khrushchev, 1960–1963* (New York: Edward Burlingame, 1991), pp. 541–44.

36 Ibid., p. 543.

37 Sergo Mikoyan, *The Soviet Cuban Missile Crisis: Castro, Mikoyan, Kennedy, Khrushchev, and the Missiles of November* (Stanford: Stanford University Press, 2012), p. 262.

38 Fursenko and Naftali, *One Hell of a Gamble*, pp. 298–310.

39 FRUS, vol. 1, p. 544.

40 Ibid., p. 475.

41 Ibis., p. 489.

42 C. L. Sulzberger, in *International Herald Tribune*, March 3, 1986.

43 *Miami News*, March 19, 1963.

44 Beschloss, *The Crisis Years*, p. 567.

45 Ibid., p. 562.

46 Mikoyan, *The Soviet Cuban Missile Crisis*, p. 253.

47 Beschloss, *The Crisis Years*, p. 562

48 FRUS, vol. 11, p. 541.

49 General Anatoli I. Gribkov and General William Y. Smith, *Operation Anadyr: US and Soviet Generals Recount the Cuban Missile Crisis* (Chicago: Edition Q Inc., 1994), p. 28.

50 Edwin O. Guthman and Jeffrey Shulman, eds., *Robert Kennedy in His Own Words* (New York: Bantam, 1988), p. 379.

51 James G. Blight, Joseph S. Nye Jr., and David A. Welch, "The Cuban Missile Crisis Revisited," *Foreign Affairs* (Fall 1987).

Chapter 10—Did Castro Get to Kennedy before Kennedy Got to Him? (1963)

1   Foreign Relations of the United States (FRUS), vol. 11 (1961–63), pp. 635–36.

2   Néstor T. Carbonell, *And the Russians Stayed: The Sovietization of Cuba* (New York: William Morrow, 1989), p. 185.

3   Dissatisfied with the fate of the flag and disappointed that even the post-Kennedy Republican administrations had decided to coexist with a subversive Communist Cuba, the men of the Bay of Pigs brigade tried to retrieve their emblem. Faced with bureaucratic delays, they hired a lawyer to expedite the process. They finally got their flag back in April 1976. The deeply depressed military chief of the brigade, José "Pepe" San Román, committed suicide in Miami in 1989. Néstor T. Carbonell, *And the Russians Stayed*, pp. 189–91.

4   FRUS, vol. 11, p. 669.

5   Ibid., pp. 763–64.

6   Ibid., p. 621.

7   Ibid., pp. 687–88.

8   Ibid., p. 688.

9   Peter Kornbluh, "JFK and Castro," *Cigar Aficionado*, September–October 1999.

10 Andrew St. George, "The Tension Is Already Gnawing at All of Us," *Life*, April 12, 1963.

11 Henry J. Taylor, "Our Cuban Policy's a Leaky Bean Bag," *Miami Herald*, April 5, 1963.

12 Néstor T. Carbonell, *And the Russians Stayed*, pp. 243–45.

13 Ibid., pp. 245–49.

14 *Miami Herald*, April 29, 1963.

15 Néstor T. Carbonell, *And the Russians Stayed*, p. 249.

16 Kornbluh, "JFK and Castro."

17 Ibid.

18 Interim Report of the Senate (Church Committee) issued in 1975 on Alleged Assassination Plots Involving Foreign Leaders (online version).

19　According to Edward Jay Epstein, author of *The JFK Assassination Diary*, Richard Helms, though not yet CIA director, was "receiving almost daily phone calls from [Attorney General] Robert Kennedy, demanding to know what actions he was [taking] to remove Castro from power." Mary Anastasia O'Grady, "What Castro Knew about Lee Harvey Oswald," *Wall Street Journal*, November 18, 2013.

20　Glenn Garvin, "New Book Claims Castro Knew Kennedy Would Be Assassinated," *Miami Herald*, March 19, 2012.

21　Ibid.

22　The AM/LASH plan was ultimately canceled for "security reasons." The CIA terminated all contact with Cubela in 1965. He was convicted in Cuba in 1966 for conspiring to kill Castro, but unlike with many others who were executed for similar crimes, the Cuban ruler spared his life and shortened his sentence from thirty to twelve years. While in "jail," Cubela reportedly served as the prison's doctor, lived in comfortable quarters, and was frequently seen outside driving his car. In 1977, he was allowed to resettle in Spain. Garvin, "New Book Claims Castro Knew Kennedy Would Be Assassinated."

23　O'Grady, "What Castro Knew about Lee Harvey Oswald."

24　Ibid.

25　Ibid.

26　Garvin, "New Book Claims Castro Knew Kennedy Would Be Assassinated."

27　Max Holland, "The Assassination Tapes," *Atlantic Monthly*, June 2004.

28　Ibid.

29　Ibid.

30　Joseph Califano, "Inside: A Public and Private Life," *Public Affairs* (2004): p. 126.

Chapter 11—Castro's Détente Game: From Lyndon Johnson to George H. W. Bush

1　Peter Kornbluh, "JFK and Castro," *Cigar Aficionado*, September–October 1992.

2　*US News and World Report*, March 11, 1963, p. 69.

3　Congressional Record, Senate (August 23, 1965), p. 20505.

4　Peter Felten, *Yankee, Go Home and Take Me with You—Lyndon Johnson and the Dominican Republic*, edited by H. W. Brands (College Station: Texas A&M University Press), 1999, p. 103.

5   Message to the Tricontinental Conference in Havana, January 1966.

6   Andrea Billups and Kathleen Walter, "On Anniversary of Che Killing, CIA's Felix Rodríguez Remembers," Newsmax, October 10, 2013.

7   "Che Guevara," Wikipedia, last updated September 30, 2019, https://en.wikipedia.org/wiki/Che_Guevara.

8   Christopher Whalen, "The Soviet Military Buildup in Cuba," Heritage Foundation, June 11, 1982.

9   "Russia in the Caribbean," pt. 2, Special Report issued by the Center for Strategic and International Studies of Georgetown University (Washington, DC: 1973), p. 108.

10 Documents 82–84, "A Turning Point in their Relationship": Kissinger and Dobrynin records of meetings (September 25, 1970), pp. 191–97. National Security Archive—Electronic Briefing Book No. 233, edited by William Burr, posted November 2, 2007.

11 Christopher Andrew and Vasili Mitrokhin, *The KGB and the Battle for the Third World* (New York: Basic Books, 2005), pp. 70–71.

12 Ibid., pp. 71–72.

13 Ibid., p. 69.

14 Henry Kissinger, *White House Years* (Boston: Little, Brown & Co., 1979), p. 671.

15 Christopher Andrew, *For the President's Eyes Only—Secret Intelligence and the American Presidency from Washington to Bush* (New York: HarperCollins, 1995), p. 371.

16 Kissinger, *White House Years*, p. 671.

17 Jack Devine, "What Really Happened in Chile: The CIA, the Coup against Allende, and the Rise of Pinochet," *Foreign Affairs* (July–August 2014): pp. 26–35.

18 Richard M. Nixon, *RN: The Memoirs of Richard Nixon* (New York: Touchstone, 1990), p. 490.

19 Kissinger, *White House Years*, p. 674.

20 Andrew and Mitrokhin, *The KGB and the Battle for the Third World*, p. 74.

21 Ibid., pp. 73, 74, 84.

22 Ibid., p. 74.

23 Devine, "What Really Happened in Chile."

24 Andrew and Mitrokhin, *The KGB and the Battle for the Third World*, p. 85.

25 Christopher A. Swiggum, "American-Cuban Détente in the 1970s and Its Collapse: Conflicts and Confrontations in American and Cuban Foreign

Policy Blocking the Road to Normalization," *Archive: A Journal of Undergraduate History*.

26 Henry Kissinger, *Years of Renewal* (New York: Simon and Schuster, 1999), p. 773.

27 Ibid.

28 Raymond L. Garthoff, *Détente and Confrontation: American-Soviet Relations from Nixon to Reagan* (Washington, DC: Brookings Institute, 1994), p. 47.

29 "Cuba and the US Road Map on Efforts to Improve Relations Revealed in Declassified Documents," National Security Archive Electronic Briefing Book No. 269, posted by Peter Kornbluh, January 22, 2009.

30 Ibid.

31 *Granma Weekly Review*, December 12, 1976, p. 1.

32 Jorge I. Domínguez, *To Make a World Safe for Revolution: Cuba's Foreign Policy* (Cambridge, MA: Harvard University Press, 1989), p. 152.

33 State Bulletin, vol. 74 (January 19, 1976), p. 78.

34 William M. LeoGrande and Peter Kornbluh, *Back Channel to Cuba: The Hidden History of Negotiations between Washington and Havana* (Chapel Hill: University of North Carolina Press, 2014), p. 149.

35 Ibid., pp. 149–50.

36 Ibid. (The "Cuban Contingencies" paper—a summary, a detailed thirty-eight-page outline, and a twenty-seven-page options paper—was obtained by Peter Kornbluh through a Mandatory Declaration request to the Presidential Library. See pages 2 and 18.)

37 National Security Archive, "Jimmy Carter Directive on Normalizing Cuba Relations," posted by Peter Kornbluh on May 15, 2002.

38 Personal correspondence with Jimmy Carter, May 12, 1977, White House Central Files. Subject File—Countries: Executive Country 38. Cuba: June 1, 1977–June 30, 1977, Jimmy Carter Library, Atlanta, Georgia. Quoted by Catherine Loiacano, "A Community Divided: Cuban American Attempts to Influence Jimmy Carter's Cuba Policy," January 1977–May 1978, posted online.

39 Brzezinski response to Juanita Castro, June 7, 1977. White House Central File, Countries, Executive 38, June 1, 1977, Jimmy Carter Library, Atlanta, Georgia. Quoted by Catherine Loiacano.

40 Zbigniew Brzezinski, *Power and Principle: Memoirs of the National Security Adviser, 1977–1981* (New York: Farrar, Straus, and Giroux, 1983), pp. 181–82.

41 Wayne S. Smith, *The Closest of Enemies: A Personal and Diplomatic History of the Castro Years* (New York: W. W. Norton, 1987), p. 135.

42 Zbigniew Brzezinski, *Power and Principle*, p. 182.

43 Ibid., p. 184.

44 Catherine Loiacano, "A Community Divided—Cuban American Attempts to Influence Jimmy Carter's Cuba Policy, January 1977–May 1978," posted online.

45 John Woolley and Gerhard Peters, "The American Presidency Project: Jimmy Carter—Peace and National Security Address to the Nation on Soviet Combat Troops in Cuba and the Strategic Arms Limitation Treaty," October 1. Text posted online.

46 Néstor T. Carbonell, *And the Russians Stayed: The Sovietization of Cuba* (New York: William Morrow, 1989), p. 270.

47 Anne Marie García, "Carter Sought to Normalize Relations with Cuba" (translation), Associated Press, October 13, 2014.

48 Robert A. Pastor, *Condemned to Repetition: The United States and Nicaragua* {Princeton, NJ: Princeton University Press, 1987), p. 53.

49 Néstor T. Carbonell, *And the Russians Stayed*, pp. 272–73.

50 Pastor, *Condemned to Repetition*, p. 69.

51 Ibid., p. 318.

52 Ibid., p. 194.

53 Ibid., p. 206.

54 Christopher Andrew, *For the President's Eyes Only: Secret Intelligence and the American Presidency from Washington to Bush* (New York: HarperCollins, 1995), p. 461.

55 Pastor, *Condemned to Repetition*, p. 231.

56 Andrew, *For the President's Eyes Only*, p. 462.

57 Alexander M. Haig Jr., *Caveat: Realism, Reagan, and Foreign Policy* (New York: Macmillan, 1984), pp. 123, 129.

58 Pastor, *Condemned to Repetition*, pp. 236–37.

59 Ibid., pp. 234–35.

60 Haig, *Caveat*, pp. 133–34.

61 Document obtained by Carter-Brezhnev Project and on file at the National Security Archive. Translation by Bruce McDonald.

62 Vernon A. Walters, *The Mighty and the Meek* (London: St. Ermin's Press, 2001), pp. 149–57.

63 Ibid.

64 Pastor, *Condemned to Repetition*, pp. 245–46.

65 Geyer, *Guerilla Prince*, pp. 374–75.

66 Ibid., p. 376.

67 Andrew, *For the President's Eyes Only*, pp. 478–79.

68 Pastor, *Condemned to Repetition*, p. 254.

69 Andrew, *For the President's Eyes Only*, pp. 479–82.

70 President Reagan's Address to the Nation on June 24, 1986, reprinted by Department of State, Policy No. 850.

71 Pastor, *Condemned to Repetition*, p. 258.

72 Andrew, *For the President's Eyes Only*, pp. 490–91.

73 Ibid., pp. 493–94.

74 Peter Schweizer, *Victory: The Reagan Administration's Secret Strategy that Hastened the Collapse of the Soviet Union* (New York: Atlantic Monthly Press, 1994).

75 Christopher Andrew and Vasili Mitrokhan, *The Sword and the Shield: The Mitrokhan Archive and the Secret History of the KGB* (New York: Basic Books, 1999), pp. 523–43.

76 Antonio R. de la Cova, "US-Cuba Relations during the Reagan Administration." Paper published by Greenwood Press, Westport, CT, and circulated online as part of the study "President Reagan and the World," edited by Eric J. Schmertz, Natalie Datkof, and Ursula Ugrinsky.

77 "Inaugural Addresses of the Presidents of the United States," Bartleby.com.

78 Andrew, *For the President's Eyes Only*, p. 511.

79 Philip Shenon, *New York Times*, February 6, 1988.

80 After serving for two decades in the United States, Noriega was extradited to France, where he was convicted for money laundering through French banks. In December 2011, he was extradited back to Panama, where he served for crimes committed under his rule until his passing.

81 Jeff Lean, Knight-Ridder Newspapers, April 8, 1993.

82 Ibid.

83 Julia Preston, "The Trial that Shook Cuba," *New York Review of Books*, December 7, 1989.

84 Lean, Knight-Ridder Newspapers.

85 Brian Ross and Vic Walter, ABC News, August 14, 2006.

86 John Hughes, "What Gorbachev Planted in Cuba," *Christian Science Monitor*, April 7, 1989.

87 Carlos Alberto Montaner, "Adolfo Suárez y Cuba," *El Nuevo Herald*, March 29, 2014.

88 Evelyn Larrubia, "Bush Rechaza Petición de Exiliados," *El Nuevo Herald*, May 8, 1992.

Chapter 12—Clinton, Castro, and the Pope (1993–2001)

1   Inter-American Commission on Human Rights, OAS, Report No. 47/96, Case 11.436, Victims of the Tugboat *13 de Marzo* vs. Cuba, October 16, 1996.

2   Operation Sea Signal, GlobalSecurity.org website; retrieved October 19, 2008; Cuba: US Response to the 1994 Cuban Migration Crisis, USAID—95–211, publicly released October 3, 1995.

3   Harvey Weinstein, "A Man of Magic in the Real World," *New York Times,* April 23, 2014.

4   Peter Grier, "Raft Crisis Points Out Need for Long-Term Cuba Policy," *Christian Science Monitor,* September 12, 1994.

5   Madeline Baro Díaz, "1994 Cuban Exodus Remembered," *Orlando Sentinel,* May 14, 2014.

6   Lili Prellezo with José Basulto, *Seagull One: The Amazing True Story of the Brothers to the Rescue* (Gainesville: University Press of Florida, 2010), pp. 48–49.

7   Ibid., pp. 243–44.

8   The four Brothers to the Rescue who were shot down were Armando Alejandre Jr., forty-five, Vietnam veteran, married with one daughter, who had recently started law school; Carlos Costa, twenty-nine, a devoted pro-democracy militant who had a job at Miami International Airport; Pablo Morales, twenty-nine, a Cuban rafter who had been saved by Brothers to the Rescue and was about to get married; and Mario de la Peña, twenty-four, who had just started his internship with American Airlines in Miami. Ibid., pp. 226–27.

9   Ibid., pp. 226, 228, 243.

10 Inter-American Commission on Human Rights, OAS, issued September 29, 1999.

11 Prellezo Basulto, *Seagull One,* p. 223.

12 Ibid., p. 281.

13 See Govtrack, HR (104th) Cuban Liberty and Democratic Solidarity (LIBERTAD) Act, enacted March 12, 1996.

14 Néstor Carbonell Cortina, *Luces y Sombras de Cuba* (Miami: Ediciones Universal, 2008), pp. 411–17.

15 Néstor Carbonell Cortina, *El Cardenal, la Iglesia, y Cuba: La Cuba Eterna* (Miami: Ediciones Universal, 2004), pp. 165–72.

16 Alberto M. Piedra, "A View of Pope John Paul II's Trip to Cuba," Institute for US-Cuba Relations Occasional Series, April 30, 1998, pp. 6–7.

17   Ibid., p. 12.

18   Alberto M. Piedra, "Pope Urges Freedom of Expression in Cuba," CNN Interactive, January 24, 1998; official text of Archbishop Pedro Meurice welcoming remarks at the pope's Mass in Santiago, January 24, 1998.

19   Ibid., pp. 27–30; "Le Pape a Cuba," *Paris Match*, January 1998; Néstor Carbonell Cortina, *Luces y Sombras de Cuba*, p. 422.

20   The Immigration and Naturalization Service justified the show of force to seize Elián because his great-uncle and other relatives in Miami had refused to release him voluntarily and had enlisted sympathizers to resist any attempt by the authorities to remove him from their house.

21   Frances Robles, "Cuban Diplomats Visit Elian at the Plantation," *Miami Herald*, May 5, 2000.

22   "*60 Minutes*: Elian González Calls Castro Friend," *Palm Beach Post*, September 29, 2005.

Chapter 13—Divergent Paths: George W. Bush and David Rockefeller (2001–2009)

1   David Rockefeller, *Memoirs* (New York: Random House, 2012), p. 405.

2   Ibid.

3   Ibid., p. 328.

4   Copies of the letters I exchanged with David Rockefeller are in my files.

5   Lizette Alvarez, "The UN at 50: Castro Back in Fatigues and Harlem," *New York Times*, October 23, 1995.

6   Rockefeller, *Memoirs*, p. 410.

7   Jim Popkin, *Washington Post Magazine*, April 18, 2013.

8   William M. LeoGrande and Peter Kornbluh, *Back Channel to Cuba: The Hidden History of Negotiations between Washington and Havana* (Chapel Hill: University of North Carolina Press, 2014), pp. 348–55; Pastor interview, "President Carter's Cuba Trip Report," July 1, 2004.

9   Carlos Lauría, Mónica Campbell, and María Salazar, "Cuba's Long Black Spring," Committee to Protect Journalists, posted March 18, 2008.

10   Carlos M. Gutierrez, "The Commission for Assistance to a Free Cuba and the Promise of a Free Cuba," Council of American Ambassadors (Spring 2007).

11   President's Remarks to the Commission for Assistance to a Free Cuba on May 6, 2004; US Department of State Archive released online from January 20, 2001, to January 20, 2009.

12 "Dissidents, Spies, and Attack Cartoons—Life at the Interests Section in Havana," Association for Diplomatic Studies and Training, posted online October 2013.

13 LeoGrande and Kornbluh, *Back Channel to Cuba*, p. 363.

14 James C. McKinley Jr., "Fidel Castro Resigns as Cuba's President," *New York Times*, February 20, 2008.

15 LeoGrande and Kornbluh, *Back Channel to Cuba*, p. 364.

Chapter 14—Raúl Castro's Rule and Bogus Opening

1 Michael Voss, "Raúl Castro Says Cubans Must Back Economic Reforms," BBC News, Havana, December 18, 2010.

2 Rigoberto Díaz, "Power Cuts and Fewer Beans for Crisis-Hit Cubans," Havana, AFP, June 12, 2009.

3 Juan O. Tamayo, "Cubans 'Make Do' with Odd Inventions," *Miami Herald*, April 26, 2014.

4 Marc Frank, "Cuban Payment Crisis Goes on, Business in Limbo," Reuters, June 23, 2010.

5 Mario J. Penton, "Cuba Set to Kick Off the New School Year with a Shortage of 10,000 Teachers," *El Nuevo Herald*, August 22, 2018.

6 José Manuel Prieto, "Havana: The State Retreats," *New York Review of Books*, May 26, 2011, pp. 15–17.

7 Ibid.

8 "Health Care Realities in Cuba: Pawning the Jewel of the Revolution," Institute for Cuban and Cuban American Studies, University of Miami, November 2003; "Cuba Facts—Socio-Economic Conditions in Pre-Castro Cuba," Institute for Cuban and Cuban American Studies, University of Miami, December 2008.

9 María C. Werlau, "Cuba's Health-Care Diplomacy: The Business of Humanitarianism," *World Affairs Journal* (March–April 2013); Janis Hernández, "On Cuba's Missions Abroad," *Havana Times*, February 27, 2015.

10 Andrew Cawthorne, "Maradona in Cuba to Kick Drugs, Thanks Castro," Reuters, January 18, 2000.

11 Laurie Garrett, "Castrocare in Crisis: Will Lifting the Embargo Make Things Worse?" *Foreign Affairs*, July–August 2010.

12 Christopher P. Baker, "Cuba's Healthcare System Has Its Downside," Moon Travel Guides, January 20, 2012.

13 Charles Tweed, "Oak Lake Family Reeling from Cuba Tragedy, Death of Mother," *Brandon Sub*, posted on January 12, 2016.

14 For background on Cuba's agricultural resources pre-Castro, see *Atlas of Cuba*, published by Harvard University Press in 1949, and US Department of Commerce Report on Cuba of 1956.

15 Tripp Mickle, "Can Cuba Make Enough Cigars?" *Wall Street Journal*, May 21, 2016.

16 Nora Gámez Torres, "Cuba's Food Odyssey," *Miami Herald*, October 24, 2016.

17 Nora Gámez Torres, "Cuba Impone Más Controles e Impuestos al Sector Privado y Censura a los Artistas," *El Nuevo Herald*, July 10, 2018.

18 Andrea Rodríguez, "Pese a Buen Resultados de Emprendedores, Cuba Guarda Cautela," Associated Press, July 31, 2018.

19 Nora Gámez Torres, "Cuba Impone Más Controles e Impuestos al Sector Privado y Censura a los Artistas,"op. cit.

20 Mario J. Pentón, "If You Send Packages to Relatives or Friends in Cuba, Goods Could Get Confiscated," *El Nuevo Herald*, June 7, 2018.

21 Marc Frank, "Cubans' Hopes Dashed as New and Used Cars Go on Sale," Reuters, January 3, 2014.

22 Victoria Burnett, "Cuba Unleashes the Pent-Up Energy of Real Estate Dreams," *New York Times*, February 16, 2012.

23 Joaquin P. Pujol, "Raúl Castro's Economic Policies: What Are the Results So Far?" Center for a Free Cuba, 2012.

24 Marc Frank, "Foreign Executives Arrested in Cuba in 2011 Await Charges," Reuters, October 9, 2012.

25 Colin Freeman, "The Briton Who Languished in a Cuban Jail after Being Accused of Spying," *The Telegraph*, July 6, 2013.

26 Ibid.

27 "Cuba Opens 'Megaport' with High Hopes for More Trade," Tengri News, March 11, 2015.

28 Mario J. Pentón, "The Mariel Special Development Zone," *14yMedio*, June 14, 2018.

29 Ibid.

30 Mario J. Pentón, "Cuban Economy's 1.1% Growth Is Not Felt on Cubans' Dinner Tables," *14ymedio*, July 27, 2018.

Chapter 15—The Delusive Obama-Castro Thaw and the Trump Aftermath

1   Barack Obama's remarks to the Cuban American Foundation in Miami, Florida, May 23, 2008. The American Presidency Project.

2   "Reaching Out to the Cuban People," White House Office of the Press Secretary, Fact Sheet, April 13, 2009.

3   Emilio Morales, "Remittances Have Become the Driving Force of the Cuban Economy," *Havana Times*, June 11, 2013.

4   "Reaching Out to the Cuban People," White House Office of the Press Secretary, January 14, 2011.

5   Ben Rhodes, *The World as It Is* (New York: Random House, 2018), p. 212.

6   Warren Strobel, Matt Spetalnick, and David Adams, "How Obama Outmaneuvered Hardliners and Cut a Cuba Deal," Reuters, March 23, 2015.

7   Ibid.

8   Ibid.

9   "US Brokered Deal to Help Wife of Cuban Spy Become Pregnant through Artificial Insemination," Fox News Latino, December 23, 2014.

10 "Republicans: Shameful that Feds Shipped Sperm for Imprisoned Spy," *The Hill*, February 12, 2015.

11 Rhodes, *The World as It Is*, pp. 285–86.

12 Nora Gámez Torres, "Catholic Archbishop in Cuba Criticizes Government," *Miami Herald*, August 29, 2014.

13 Frances Robles, "In Talks Over Seized US Property, Havana Counters with Own Claims," *New York Times*, December 13, 2015; Raúl Castro, "Remarks by Army General at the Third CELAC Summit," Belén, Costa Rica, January 28, 2015; "Castro at the UN Calls for End to the Embargo and Return of Guantánamo," *Latin America Daily Briefing Blog*, September 29, 2015.

14 David Samuels, "The Aspiring Novelist Who Became Obama's Foreign Policy Guru," *New York Times Magazine*, May 5, 2016.

15 "Who Is Ricardo Zuñiga, the Man Who Helped Broker the White House Deal with Cuba?" *Washington Post*, December 22, 2014.

16 Chris Simmons, "Senior Cuban Spies Leading Normalization Talks in the US," *Cuba Confidential*, January 20, 2015, https://cubaconfidential.wordpress.com/2015/01/20/exclusive-senior-cuban-spies-leading-normalization-talks-with-us/; "Cuban Diplomat Heading Talks with US Doesn't Hesitate to Speak her Mind," *Miami Herald*, January 21, 2015.

17 Charles Krauthammer, "Nylons for Nothing in Cuba," *Washington Post*, January 1, 2015.

18 "Open Letter to President Obama: Support Civil Society in Cuba," Council of the Americas and signatories, May 19, 2014; "Open Letter to President Obama: Support for a New Course in Cuba," Council of the Americas and signatories, January 19, 2015.

19 "The New Cuba Policy: Breakthrough or Bailout?" open letter to Congress, *Washington Post*, February 11, 2015.

20 "President Obama Must Make Trip to Cuba Count," Editorial Board, *Washington Post*, February 19, 2016.

21 Remarks by President Obama to the people of Cuba, the White House, March 22, 2016.

22 Ibid.

23 Adriana Cohen, *Boston Herald*, May 15, 2016.

24 Rhodes, *The World as It Is*, p. 353.

25 Bello, "Fidel's Last Stand—the Communist Party Blocks Change," *The Economist*, April 30, 2016.

26 Victoria Burnett, "Raúl Castro Urges Cubans to Remain Alert to US Efforts to Alter Communist System," *New York Times*, April 16, 2016.

27 Nora Gámez Torres, "Raúl Castro Proposes Age Limits on Key Jobs in CCP," *Miami Herald*, April 16, 2016.

28 Karen DeYoung, "Fidel Castro Says Obama's Syrupy Words Were Enough to Cause a Heart Attack," *Washington Post*, March 28, 2016.

29 "Cuban Military Expands Its Economic Empire Under Détente," Associated Press, September 9, 2016.

30 Nora Gámez Torres, "Controversy Erupts Over Workers from India Building Cuban Hotel," *Miami Herald*, October 24, 2016.

31 Sarah Marsh, "Communist-Run Cuba Puts Brakes on Private Sector Expansion," Reuters, August 1, 2017.

32 Andrés Oppenheimer, "Cuba's Human Rights Abuses Worse despite US Ties," InCubaToday.com, July 16, 2017.

33 José María Aznar's remarks during the Concordia Summit on the Americas held at Miami-Dade College on May 13, 2016.

34 Fabiola Santiago, "Cuban Troop's Bizarre Chant: We'll Make Obama a Hat out of Bullets to the Head," *Miami Herald*, January 6, 2017.

35 Karen DeYoung, "White House Implements New Cuba Policy Restricting Travel and Trade," *Washington Post*, November 8, 2017.

36 Carol Morello, "US Slashing Embassy Staff in Cuba, Issuing Travel Warning because of Apparent Sonic Attacks," *Washington Post*, September 28, 2017; Karen DeYoung, "Doctors Find Neurological Damage to Americans who Served in Cuba," *Washington Post*, February 14, 2018.

37 Steven Lee Myers, "More Sonic Attacks on Americans in China," *New York Times*, July 1, 2018.

38 William J. Boad, "Invisible Strike May Be Cause of Envoys' Ills," *New York Times*, September 2, 2018.

39 "Cuba's New Constitution Preserves Communist Power," *The Economist*, July 26, 2018.

Chapter 16—Two Sides of the Cuban Saga: Repression and Resistance

1 "Mario Chanes de Armas," *The Economist,* March 1, 2007.

2 Lee Habeeb, "The Dictator and the Dissident," *National Review*, November 28, 2016; Ronald Radosh, "When Did the Left Know the Truth about Cuba?" (Hudson Institute, November 28, 2016).

3 Paul Kidd, "Cuba Expels Reporter," *Edmonton Journal*, September 10, 1966.

4 Enrique Ros, *La UMAP: El Gulag Castrista* (Miami: Ediciones Universal), 2004; Néstor Almendros and Orlando Jimenez Leal, *Improper Conduct*, VHS tape (CineVista, 1984).

5 Joseph Tahbaz, "Demystifying las UMAP: The Politics of Sugar, Gender, and Religion in 1960s Cuba," *Delaware Review of Latin American Studies* (December 31, 2013); Norberto Fuentes, *Dulces Guerreros Cubanos* (Barcelona: Seix Barral, 2000).

6 Gustavo López, "Hispanics of Cuban Origin in the United States, 2013," Pew Research Center, September 15, 2015.

7 Ivonne M. Conde, *Operation Pedro Pan: The Untold Exodus of 14,048 Cuban Children* (New York and London: Routledge, 1999).

8 Carlos Eire, *Learning to Die in Miami: Confessions of a Refugee Boy* (New York: Free Press, 2010).

9 John Pearly Huffman, "Sail to the USA in a Chevrolet—How Luis Grass Turned Some Very Old Detroit Iron into a Seagoing Escape Vehicle," *Car and Driver*, August 2006.

10 "More than 43,000 Cubans Came to the US over Past Year," EFE Agency, November 4, 2015.

11 David Adams, "Cuba Aims to Ramp Up Internet Access: US Department Official," *Reuters*, March 20, 2015.

12 Ibid.

13 Lizette Alvarez, "Out of Cold War Past, Broadcasts to Cuba Face an Uneasy Future," *New York Times*, March 25, 2015.

14 Posted by Capitol Hill Cubans on July 7, 2015.

15 AFP, "Cuba Busca Aumentar Acceso a Internet Sin Ceder Control Estatal," *El Nuevo Herald*, March 30, 2015.

16 "Cuba and the Internet—Wired at Last," *The Economist*, March 5, 2011.

17 Juan O. Tamayo, "Cuba Clamps Down on Wi-Fi Networks," *Miami Herald*, June 16, 2014.

18 José de Córdova, "Cuban Dissident Starts Website," *Wall Street Journal*, May 22, 2014.

19 "Cuban Dissident Wilmar Villar Dies on Hunger Strike," *The Telegraph*, January 20, 2012.

Chapter 17—The Dawn of Freedom

1 Nora Gámez Torres, "Cuban Leader Takes a Jab at Trump at the UN, Blaming Capitalism for World's Woes," *Miami Herald,* September 26, 2018.

2 Among the soon-to-exit octogenarians of the Old Guard are José Machado-Ventura, eighty-eight, Raúl Castro's hard-line crony, and Ramiro Valdés, eighty-six, the dreaded former interior minister who became the chief architect of Venezuela's current intelligence and repression apparatus.

3 The military officers expected to succeed Castro's "historic" Old Guard include General Leopoldo Cintra, seventy-seven, General Alvaro López-Miera, seventy-five, Admiral Julio C. Gandarilla, seventy-eight, and General Onelio Aguilera, sixty-five.

4 Juan Reinaldo Sánchez, *The Double Life of Castro: My 17 Years as Personal Bodyguard to El Líder Máximo* (New York: St. Martin's Press, 2014).

5 Daniel Trotta, "A Castro Son Rises in Cuba," *Reuters*, June 17, 2015.

6 "Raúl Castro's Daughter, Mariela Castro, in US Blasts 'Cuban Mafia' Supporting Cuban Restrictions," Associated Press, October 10, 2012.

7 "Reform in Cuba: Trying to Make the Sums Add Up," *The Economist*, November 13, 2010.

8 Michael Smith, "Want to Do Business in Cuba? Prepare to Partner with the General," *Bloomberg*, September 30, 2015.

9   "Caribbean Contagion: Venezuela's Pneumonia Infects the Communist Island," *The Economist*, July 23, 2016; Victoria Burnett, "Amid Weakening Economy, Cubans Fear Return to Darker Times," *New York Times*, July 13, 2016.

10   "Caribbean Contagion," *The Economist*.

11   Nora Gámez Torres, "Cuba Is a Lot Poorer than the Government Reports, a New Study Shows," *Miami Herald*, January 22, 2018. (The study shows that Cuba's GDP dropped by more than 50 percent following the loss of Soviet subsidies in the 1990s, not 35 percent as originally reported.)

12   María C. Werlau, "Get It Right This Time: A Victims-Centered Trafficking in Persons Report," Hearing of the Subcommittee on Africa, Global Health, and Global Human Rights, and International Organizations Committee on Foreign Affairs, US House of Representatives, March 22, 2016.

13   Ibid.; Martin Camoy, "Cuba's Biggest Export Is Teachers, Doctors—Not Revolution," Reuters.com great-debate, December 23, 2014.

14   These are some of the most active Cuban American organizations denouncing repression in Cuba and calling for a democratic change on the island. Under the umbrella of the Asamblea de la Resistencia Cubana are the following (with the founders' names in parentheses: Directorio Democrático Cubano (Orlando Gutierrez); MAR por Cuba (Sylvia Iriondo); Asociación de Veteranos de Bahía de Cochinos—Brigada 2506 (Ret. Colonel Johnny López); Plantados por la Libertad y la Democracia Cubana (Angel de Fana); and Fundación Inspire América (Marcel Felipe). Other prominent organizations include the Center for a Free Cuba (Everett Ellis Briggs and Otto Reich), Fundación Cubano-Americana (José "Pepe" Hernández), Cuba Decide (Rosa María Payá), Junta Patriótica Cubana (Antonio Esquivel), Encuentro Nacional Cubano (Severiano López), La Nueva Nación (Alfredo Cepero), Cuban Studies Institute (Jaime Suchlicki), Cuban Archive (María Werlau), Movimiento Democracia (Ramón Raúl Sánchez), Alpha 66 (Ernesto Díaz Rodríguez), and Instituto de Memoria Histótica Cubana Contra el Totalitarismo (Pedro Corzo), among others.

15   Néstor Carbonell-Cortina, "A Constitutional Framework for a Democratic Transition in Cuba," Center for a Free Cuba, Washington, DC, 2004. Other Cuban American attorneys who have diligently worked on constitutional adjustments to Cuba's 1940 charter for a democratic transition are Alberto Luzárraga, Luis Figueroa, and Roberto Godoy. A strong supporter of the initiative was Hector Lans, who organized a forum with the participation of dissident leaders on the island.

16 "A Road Map for Restructuring Future US Relations with Cuba," the Atlantic Council of the United States, June 1995.

17 Juan J. Linz and Alfred Stepan, *Problems of Democratic Transition and Consolidation* (Baltimore: Johns Hopkins University Press, 1966).

18 "Property Restitution in Central and Eastern Europe," US Department of State—Archive (January 20, 2001–January 20, 2009).

19 Commission for Assistance to a Free Cuba, report to the president; Condoleezza Rice, secretary of state, chair; and Carlos Gutierrez, secretary of commerce, cochair (July 2006), p. 46.

20 Erica Goode, "Cuba's Crown Jewel," *New York Times*, July 14, 2015.

21 Alberto S. Bustamante Jr., "The Free Enterprise in Function of Historic and Patrimonial Preservation: The Project Paradores de Cuba," (Miami: Cuban Cultural Heritage, 2008).

22 Marc Frank, "Cuban Raw Sugar Output Tops 1.8 Million Tons," Reuters, May 26, 2015.

23 "Investment in Cuba," US Department of Commerce (July 1956), p. 59.

24 Azam Ahmed, "In Cuba, an Abundance of Love but a Lack of Babies," *New York Times*, October 27, 2015.

25 Ibid.

26 The presidents of Pro Arte Musical were María Teresa García Montes de Giberga, Oria Varela de Albarrán, Laura Rayneri de Alonso, María Teresa Velasco de González Gordón, Dulce María Blanco de Cárdenas, and Conchita Giberga de Oña. (Mrs. Cárdenas was reelected president after Mrs. Oña.)

27 These are some of the Cuban Americans who have served the United States as ambassadors: Otto Reich, ambassador to Venezuela and assistant secretary of state for Western Hemisphere affairs; Lino Gutierrez, ambassador to Nicaragua and Argentina; Alberto Martínez Piedra, ambassador to Guatemala; Mauricio Solaún, ambassador to Nicaragua; José Sorzano, ambassador and US deputy to the United Nations; Armando Valladares, ambassador to the United Nations Human Rights Council; Paul Cejas, ambassador to Belgium; and Simón Ferro, ambassador to Panama.

SELECTED SOURCES

Aguilar, Luis. *Operation Zapata: The Ultrasensitive Report and Testimony of the Board of Inquiry on the Bay of Pigs.* Frederick, MD: Aletheia Books, 1981.

Allison, Graham T. *Essence of Decision: Explaining the Cuban Missile Crisis.* Boston: Little, Brown and Company, 1971.

Andrew, Christopher. *For the President's Eyes Only: Secret Intelligence and the American Presidency from Washington to Bush.* New York: Harper Collins, 1995.

Andrew, Christopher, and Vasili Mitrokhin. *The Sword and the Shield: The Mitrokhin Archive and the Secret History of the KGB.* New York: Basic Books, 1999.

———. *The World Was Going Our Way: The KGB and the Battle for the Third World.* New York: Basic Books, 2005.

Antón, Alex, and Roger E. Hernández. *Cubans in America: A Vibrant History of a People in Exile.* New York: Kensington, 2002.

Applebaum, Anne. *Iron Curtain: The Crushing of Eastern Europe, 1944–1956.* New York: Doubleday, 2012.

Aragón, Ernesto. Executive assistant to the president of the Cuban Revolutionary Council (in exile), José Miró-Cardona. Records and notes taken as interpreter during private meetings between Miró-Cardona and President Kennedy, Attorney General Robert Kennedy, and other US government officials (1961–63).

Bardach, Ann Louise. *Without Fidel: A Death Foretold in Miami, Havana, and Washington.* New York: Scribner, 2009.

Barquin, Ramón M. *El Día Que Fidel Castro Se Apoderó De Cuba.* San Juan: Editorial Rambar, 1978.

Barrett, David M., and Max Holland. *Blind Over Cuba: The Photo Gap and the Missile Crisis.* College Station: Texas A&M University Press, 2012.

Batista, Fulgencio. *Respuesta.* Mexico: Manuel León, Sánchez, 1960.

————. *The Growth and Decline of the Cuban Republic*. New York: Devin-Adair, 1964.

Berman, Ilan, and J. Michael Waller. *Dismantling Tyranny: Transitioning beyond Totalitarian Regimes*. New York: Rowman and Littlefield, 2006.

Beschloss, Michael R. *The Crisis Years: Kennedy and Khrushchev, 1960–1963*. New York: Edward Burlingame, 1991.

Bethel, Paul D. *The Losers: The Definitive Report, by an Eyewitness of the Communist Conquest of Cuba and the Soviet Penetration in Latin America*. New Rochelle, NY: Arlington House, 1969.

Bissell, Richard M. *Reflections of a Cold Warrior: From Yalta to the Bay of Pigs*. New Haven, CT: Yale University Press, 1996.

Blight, James G., and Peter Kornbluh. *Politics of Illusion: The Bay of Pigs Invasion Reexamined*. Boulder, CO: Lynne Rienner, 1998.

Blight, James G., and David A. Welch. *On the Brink: Americans and Soviets Reexamine the Cuban Missile Crisis*. New York: Hill and Wang, 1989.

Bonsal, Philip W. *Cuba, Castro, and the United States*. London: University of Pittsburgh Press, 1971.

Botín, Vicente. *Los Funerales de Castro*. Barcelona: Editorial Ariel, 2009.

Brugioni, Dino A. *Eyeball to Eyeball: The Cuban Missile Crisis*. New York: Random House, 1990.

Brzezinski, Zbigniew. *Power and Principle: Memoirs of the National Security Adviser, 1977–1981*. New York: Farrar, Straus, and Giroux, 1983.

Carbonell, José Manuel. *Evolución de la Cultura Cubana*. La Habana: Imprenta Montalvo y Cárdenas, 1928.

Carbonell, Néstor T. *And the Russians Stayed: The Sovietization of Cuba*. New York: William Morrow, 1989.

Carbonell-Cortina, Néstor. *Por la Libertad de Cuba: Una Historia Inconclusa*. Miami: Ediciones Universal, 1996.

————. *Grandes Debates de la Constituyente Cubana de 1940*. Miami: Ediciones Universal, 2001.

————. *La Cuba Eterna: Ayer, Hoy, y Mañana*. Miami: Ediciones Universal, 2004.

————. *Luces y Sombras de Cuba: Reflexiones sobre la República, la Revolución Comunista, el Exilio, y la Añorada Libertad*. Miami: Ediciones Universal, 2008.

Castro, Fidel. *La Historia Me Absolverá*. La Habana: Editorial de Ciencias Sociales, 1985.

Castro, Juanita. *Fidel y Raúl Mis Hermanos: La Historia Secreta—Memorias de Juanita Castro Contadas a María Antonieta Collins*. Doral, FL: Santillana, 2009.

Christian, Shirley. *Nicaragua: Revolution in the Family*. New York: Random House, 1985.

Clark, Juan. *Cuba Mito y Realidad: Testimonios de un Pueblo*. Miami: Saeta Ediciones, 1990.

Committee on Armed Services, US Senate. *Interim Report by Preparedness Investigating Subcommittee on the Cuban Military Buildup*. Washington, DC: US Government Printing Office, 1963.

Committee on Foreign Relations. Executive Sessions of the Senate Foreign Relations Committee: Historical Series. *Briefing on the Bay of Pigs Invasion and on the Cuban Situation, April 28, 1961, and May 1, 1961*. Washington, DC: US Government Printing Office, 1984.

Conde, Yvonne M. *Operation Pedro Pan: The Untold Exodus of 14,048 Cuban Children*. New York: Routledge, 1999.

Cortina, José Manuel. *Caracteres de Cuba*. La Habana: Editorial Lex, 1945.

Corzo, Pedro. *Confrontación: Lucha Cívica, Clandestina, Guerrillas*. South Carolina: CreateSpace Independent Publishing, 2017.

Courtois, Stéphane, et al. *The Black Book of Communism: Crimes, Terror, Repression*. Cambridge, MA: Harvard University Press, 1999.

Daniel, James, and John G. Hubbell. *Strike in the West: The Complete Story of the Cuban Crisis*. New York: Holt, Rinehart, and Winston, 1963.

DePalma, Anthony. *The Man Who Invented Fidel: Castro, Cuba, and Herbert L. Matthews of the New York Times*. New York: Public Affairs, 2006.

Djilas, Milovan. *Conversations with Stalin*. New York: Harvest/HBJ, 1962.

Dobbs, Michael. *One Minute to Midnight: Kennedy, Khrushchev, and Castro on the Brink of Nuclear War*. New York: Alfred A. Knopf, 2008.

Dobrynin, Anatoly. *In Confidence: Moscow's Ambassador to America's Six Cold War Presidents (1962–1986)*. New York: Times Books, 1995.

Domínguez, Jorge I. *Cuba: Order and Revolution*. Cambridge, MA: Harvard University Press, 1978.

———. *To Make a World Safe for Revolution: Cuba's Foreign Policy*. Cambridge, MA: Harvard University Press, 1989.

Dorschner, John, and Roberto Fabricio. *The Winds of December: Cuba 1958—the Dramatic, Behind-the-Scenes Story of Castro's Revolution*. New York: Coward, McCann, and Geoghegan, 1980.

Draper, Theodore. *Castro's Revolution: Myths and Realities*. New York: Frederick A. Praeger, 1962.

Duarte Oropesa, José. *Historiología Cubana: Desde 1959 hasta 1980*. Miami: Ediciones Universal, 1993.

———Historiología Cubana: Desde 1980 hasta 2000 (La Revolución Traidora). Miami: Ediciones Universal, 2003.

Eire, Carlos. Waiting for Snow in Havana: Confessions of a Cuban Boy. New York: Free Press, 2003.

———. Learning to Die in Miami: Confessions of a Refugee Boy. New York: Free Press, 2010.

Eisenhower, Dwight D. Waging Peace: The White House Years—a Personal Account, 1956–1961. New York: Doubleday, 1965.

Encinosa, Enrique. Escambray: La Guerra Olvidada. Miami: Editorial Sibi, 1988.

Epstein, Edward Jay. Deception: The Invisible War between the KGB and the CIA. New York: Simon & Schuster, 1989.

Falcoff, Mark. The Cuban Revolution and the United States. A History in Documents, 1958–1960. Washington, DC: US-Cuba Press, 2001.

Ferrer, Edward B. Operation Puma: The Air Battle of the Bay of Pigs. Miami: Trade Litho, 1982.

Fontova, Humberto. Fidel: Hollywood's Favorite Tyrant. Washington, DC: Regnery, 2005.

Foreign Relations of the United States (FRUS). Cuba 1958–1960: Volume VI. Washington, DC: Department of State Publication, 1991.

———. Cuba 1961–1962: Volume X. Washington, DC: Department of State Publication, 1997.

———. Cuba 1961–1963: Volume XI—Cuban Missile Crisis and Aftermath. Washington, DC: Department of State Publication, 1996.

Frank, Marc. Cuban Revelations: Behind the Scenes in Havana. Gainesville: University Press of Florida, 2013.

Frankel, Max. High Noon in the Cold War: Kennedy, Khrushchev, and the Cuban Missile Crisis. New York: Ballantine, 2004.

Franqui, Carlos. Retrato de Familia con Fidel. Barcelona: Editorial Seix Barral, 1981.

———. Vida, Aventuras, y Desastres de un Hombre LLamado Castro. Barcelona: Planeta, 1988.

———. Cuba, La Revolución: ¿Mito o Realidad? Barcelona: Ediciones Peninsula, 2006.

Fromm, Erich. Escape from Freedom. New York: Avon, 1969.

Furet, François. The Passing of an Illusion: The Idea of Communism in the Twentieth Century. Chicago: University of Chicago Press, 1999.

Fursenko, Aleksandr, and Timothy Naftali. One Hell of a Gamble: Khrushchev, Castro, and Kennedy, 1958–1964. New York: W. W. Norton, 1997.

Garthoff, Raymond L. *Reflections on the Cuban Missile Crisis.* Washington, DC: Brookings Institution, 1989.

Geyer, Georgie Anne. *Guerrilla Prince: The Untold Story of Fidel Castro.* Boston: Little, Brown and Company, 1991.

Gjelten, Tom. *Bacardi and the Long Fight for Cuba: The Biography of a Cause.* New York: Viking, 2008.

Golitsyn, Anatoliy. *New Lies for Old: The Communist Strategy of Deception and Disinformation.* New York: Dodd, Mead & Co., 1984.

Goodwin, Doris Kearns. *Leadership in Turbulent Times.* New York: Simon & Schuster, 2018.

Goodwin, Richard N. *Remembering America: A Voice from the Sixties.* Boston: Little, Brown and Company, 1988.

Gribkov, Anatoli I., and William Y. Smith. *Operation Anadyr: US and Soviet Generals Recount the Cuban Missile Crisis.* Chicago: Edition Q Inc., 1994.

Haass, Richard. *A World in Disarray: American Foreign Policy and the Crisis of the Old Order.* New York: Penguin, 2017.

Haig, Alexander M. *Caveat: Realism, Reagan, and Foreign Policy.* New York: Macmillan, 1984.

Hansen, Jonathan M. *Young Castro: The Making of a Revolutionary.* New York: Simon & Schuster, 2019.

Havel, Václav. *Living in Truth.* New York: Faber & Faber, 1986.

Hayek, Friedrik A. *Sobre la Libertad.* Costa Rica: Libro Libre, 1992.

Helms, Richard. *A Look over My Shoulder: A Life in the Central Intelligence Agency.* New York: Random House, 2003.

Hersh, Seymour M. *The Dark Side of Camelot.* Boston: Little, Brown and Company, 1997.

Hidalgo, Ariel. *Disidencia: ¿Segunda Revolucion Cubana?* Miami: Ediciones Universal, 1994.

Higgins, Trumbull. *The Perfect Failure: Kennedy, Eisenhower, and the CIA at the Bay of Pigs.* New York: W. W. Norton & Company, 1987.

Horowitz, Irving Louis. *Cuban Communism.* New Brunswick: Transaction Books, 1987.

International Commission of Jurists. *Cuba and the Rule of Law.* Geneva: H. Studer, 1962.

Isaacson, Walter. *Kissinger: A Biography.* New York: Simon & Schuster, 1992.

Johnson, Haynes. *The Bay of Pigs: The Leaders' Story of Brigade 2506.* New York: Dell, 1964.

Kempe, Frederick. *Berlin 1961: Kennedy, Khrushchev, and the Most Dangerous Place on Earth*. New York: G. P. Putnam's Sons, 2011.

Kennedy, Robert. *In His Own Words: The Unpublished Recollections of the Kennedy Years*. Edited by Edwin O. Guthman and Jeffrey Shulman. New York: Bantam, 1988.

———. *Thirteen Days: A Memoir of the Cuban Missile Crisis*. New York: W. W. Norton, 1969.

Khrushchev, Nikita. *Khrushchev Remembers*. Edited by Edward Crankshaw. Boston: Little, Brown & Company, 1970.

Kintner, William R. *Soviet Global Strategy*. Fairfax, VA: Hero Books, 1987.

Kirkpatrick, Jeane J. *The Withering Away of the Totalitarian State ... and Other Surprises*. Washington, DC: AEI, 1990.

Kissinger, Henry. *White House Years*. Boston: Little, Brown & Company, 1979.

———. *Years of Renewal*. New York: Simon & Schuster, 1999.

———. *World Order*. New York: Penguin, 2014.

Kornbluh, Peter. *Bay of Pigs Declassified: The Secret CIA Report on the Invasion of Cuba*. New York: The New Press, 1998.

Latel, Brian. *After Fidel: The Inside Story of Castro's Regime and Cuba's Next Leader*. New York: Palgrave Macmillan, 2005.

———. *Castro's Secrets: The CIA and Cuba's Intelligence Machine*. New York: Palgrave Macmillan, 2012.

Lazo, Mario. *Daga en el Corazón: Cuba Traicionada*. New York: Minerva, 1972.

LeoGrande, William M., and Peter Kornbluh. *Back Channel to Cuba: The Hidden History of Negotiations between Washington and Havana*. Chapel Hill: University of North Carolina Press, 2014.

Linz, Juan J., and Alfred Stepan. *Problems of Democratic Transition and Consolidation (Southern Europe, South America, Post-Communist Europe)*. Baltimore: Johns Hopkins University Press, 1996.

Llerena, Mario. *Mito y Espejismo de la Revolución*. Washington, DC: Fundación Nacional Cubano Americana, 1995.

López-Fresquet, Rufo. *My 14 Months with Castro*. New York: World Publishing, 1966.

Lynch, Grayston L. *Decision for Disaster: Betrayal at the Bay of Pigs*. Washington, DC: Brassey's, 1998.

Márquez-Sterling, Carlos, and Manuel Márquez-Sterling. *Historia de la Isla de Cuba*. New York: Regents, 1975.

Márquez-Sterling, Manuel. *Cuba 1952–1959: The True Story of Castro's Rise to Power*. Wintergreen, VA: Kleiopatria Digital Press, 2009.

Martí, José. *Obras Completas*. La Habana: Editorial Lex, 1946.

Martin, Lionel. *El Joven Fidel: Los Orígenes de su Ideología Comunista*. Barcelona: Ediciones Grijalbo, 1982.

Matos, Huber. *Cómo Llegó la Noche: Revolución y Condena de un Idealista Cubano*. Barcelona: Tusquets Editores, 2002.

Matthews, Herbert L. *The Cuban Story*. New York: George Braziller, 1961.

May, Ernest R., and Philip D. Zelikow. *The Kennedy Tapes: Inside the White House during the Cuban Missile Crisis*. New York: W. W. Norton, 2002.

McAuliffe, Mary S. *Cuban Missile Crisis: CIA Documents, 1962*. Washington, DC: Central Intelligence Agency, 1962.

Mesa-Lago, Carmelo. *The Economy of Socialist Cuba: A Two-Decade Appraisal*. Albuquerque: University of New Mexico Press, 1981.

———. *Market, Socialist, and Mixed Economies: Chile, Cuba, and Costa Rica*. Baltimore: Johns Hopkins University Press, 2000.

———. *Cuba en la Era de Raúl Castro: Reformas Económicas-Sociales y sus Efectos*. Madrid: Colibrí, 2013.

Mikoyan, Sergo. *The Soviet Cuban Missile Crisis: Castro, Mikoyan, Kennedy, Khrushchev, and the Missiles of November*. Stanford: Stanford University Press, 2012.

Miró-Cardona, José. *Resignation as President of the Cuba Revolutionary Council (in Exile) on April 9, 1963*. Including copies of records and private correspondence with President Kennedy and other US government officials (1961–63).

Montaner, Carlos Alberto. *Fidel Castro y la Revolución Cubana*. Madrid: Editorial Playor, 1983.

———. *La Libertad y sus Enemigos*. Buenos Aires: Editorial Sudamericana, 2005.

Moran Arce, Lucas. *La Revolución Cubana: Una Versión Rebelde*. Ponce, PR: Imprenta Universitaria, 1980.

Nabokov, Vladimir. *Speak, Memory*. New York: Putnam, 1966.

Newsom, David D. *The Soviet Brigade in Cuba: A Study in Political Diplomacy*. Bloomington: Indiana University Press, 1987.

Nixon, Richard. *The Real War*. New York: Warner Books, 1980.

Oppenheimer, Andrés. *Castro's Final Hour*. New York: Simon & Schuster, 1992.

Orwell, George. *1984*. New York: Houghton, Mifflin, Harcourt, 2003.

Pastor, Robert A. *Condemned to Repetition: The United States and Nicaragua*. Princeton, NJ: Princeton University Press, 1987.

Pérez-Stable, Marifeli. *Looking Forward: Comparative Perspectives on Cuba's Transition*. Notre Dame, IN: University of Notre Dame Press, 2007.

Pfeiffer, Jack B. *Official History of the Bay of Pigs Operation, Volume III, 1959–January 1961.* Washington, DC: Books Express, 2011.

Pipes, Richard. *The Russian Revolution.* New York: Alfred A. Knopf, 1990.

Portell-Vilá, Herminio. *Historia de Cuba en sus Relaciones con los Estados Unidos.* Montero: La Habana, 1938.

Prellezo, Lily, and José Basulto. *Seagull One: The Amazing Story of Brothers to the Rescue.* Gainesville: University Press of Florida, 2010.

Quirk, Robert E. *Fidel Castro: The Full Story of His Rise to Power, His Regime, His Allies, and His Adversaries.* New York: W. W. Norton, 1993.

Raffy, Serge. *Castro el Desleal.* Miami: Santillana Ediciones Generales, 2004.

Rangel, Carlos. *Del Buen Salvaje al Buen Revolucionario.* Caracas: Monte Avila Editores, 1976.

Rasenberger, Jim. *The Brilliant Disaster: JFK, Castro, and America's Doomed Invasion of Cuba's Bay of Pigs.* New York: Scribner, 2011.

Rathbone, John Paul. *The Sugar King of Havana: The Rise and Fall of Julio Lobo, Cuba's Last Tycoon.* New York: Penguin, 2010.

Ratliff, William E. *The Selling of Fidel Castro: The Media and the Cuban Revolution.* New Brunswick: Transaction Books, 1987.

Ravines, Eudocio. *La Gran Estafa.* La Habana: Editorial Librerías Unidas, 1960.

Revel, Jean-François. *Totalitarian Temptation.* London: Secker & Warburg, 1976.

———. *Democracy against Itself.* New York: The Free Press, 1993.

———. *Cómo Terminan las Democracias.* Barcelona: Planeta, 1983.

Rhodes, Ben. *The World as It Is: A Memoir of the Obama White House.* New York: Random House, 2018.

Ritter, Archibald R. M. *The Cuban Economy.* Pittsburgh: University of Pittsburgh Press, 2004.

Ritter, Archibald R. M., and Ted A. Henken. *Entrepreneurial Cuba: The Changing Policy Landscape.* Boulder, CO: First Forum, 2015.

Robbins, Carla Anne. *The Cuban Threat.* New York: McGraw-Hill, 1983.

Rockefeller, David. *Memoirs.* New York: Random House, 2002.

Rodriguez, Felix I., and John Weisman. *Shadow Warrior: The CIA Hero of a Hundred Unknown Battles.* New York: Simon & Schuster, 1989.

Ros, Enrique. *Girón: La Verdadera Historia.* Miami: Ediciones Universal, 1994.

———. *De Girón a la Crisis de los Cohetes: La Segunda Derrota.* Miami: Ediciones Universal, 1995.

———. *El Clandestinaje y la Lucha Armada Contra Castro.* Miami: Ediciones Universal, 2006.

Salazar-Carrillo, Jorge, and Andro Nodarse-León. *Cuba: From Economic Take-Off to Collapse under Castro*. New Brunswick: Transaction Publishers, 2015.

Sánchez, Juan Reinaldo. *The Double Life of Fidel Castro: My 17 Years as Personal Bodyguard to El Líder Máximo*. New York: St. Martin's Press, 2015.

Sánchez Rebolledo, Adolfo. *Fidel Castro: La Revolución Cubana, 1953–1962*. Mexico: Ediciones Era, 1972.

Schapiro, Leonard. *The Russian Revolutions of 1917: The Origins of Modern Communism*. New York: Basic Books, 1984.

Schlesinger, Arthur M. *A Thousand Days: John F. Kennedy in the White House*. New York: Fawcett Premier, 1965.

Schmidt, Dana Adams. *Anatomía de un Estado Satélite*. Buenos Aires: Editorial Bell, 1952.

Schweizer, Peter. *Victory: The Reagan Administration's Secret Strategy that Hastened the Collapse of the Soviet Union*. New York: Atlantic Monthly Press, 1994.

Service, Robert. *Lenin: A Biography*. Cambridge, MA: Harvard University Press, 2000.

Smith, Earl E. T. *The Fourth Floor: An Account of the Castro Communist Revolution*. New York: Random House, 1962.

Smith, Wayne S. *The Closest of Enemies: A Personal and Diplomatic History of the Castro Years*. New York: W. W. Norton & Company, 1987.

Solaún, Mauricio. *US Intervention and Regime Change in Nicaragua*. Lincoln: University of Nebraska Press, 2005.

Sorensen, Theodore C. *Kennedy*. New York: Harper & Row, 1965.

———. *Counselor: A Life at the End of History*. New York: HarperCollins, 2008.

Stent, Angela. *Putin's World: Russia against the West and with the Rest*. New York: Twelve, 2019.

Stern, Sheldon M. *The Cuban Missile Crisis in American Memory: Myths versus Reality*. Stanford: Stanford University Press, 2012.

Strausz-Hupé, Robert, et al. *Protracted Conflict*. University of Pennsylvania; New York: Harper & Brothers, 1959.

Suárez Rivas, Eduardo. *Un Pueblo Crucificado*. Coral Gables, FL: Service Offset Printers, 1964.

Suchlicki, Jaime. *Cuba: From Columbus to Castro*. New York: Charles Scribner and Sons, 1992.

Sweig, Julia E. Cuba: *What Everyone Needs to Know*. New York: Oxford University Press, 2009.

Szulc, Tad. *Fidel: A Critical Portrait*. New York: William Morrow, 1986.

Szulc, Tad, and Karl E. Meyer. *The Cuban Invasion: The Chronicle of a Disaster*. New York: Ballantine, 1962.

Taubman, William. *Khrushchev: The Man and His Era*. New York: W. W. Norton & Company, 2003.

Thomas, Hugh. *Cuba or the Pursuit of Freedom*. London: Eyre & Spottiswoode, 1971.

Tidd, Kurt W. *Posture Statement to the Senate Armed Services Committee on February 15, 2018, as Commander of the US Southern Command*.

Treverton, Gregory F. *Covert Action: The Limits of Intervention in the Postwar World*. New York: Basic Books, 1987.

Triay, Victor Andres. *Bay of Pigs: An Oral History of Brigade 2506*. Gainesville: University Press of Florida, 2001.

Urrutia, Manuel. *Fidel Castro y Compañia, S.A.* Barcelona: Editorial Herder, 1963.

Valladares, Armando. *Against All Hope*. New York: Alfred Knopf, 1986.

Vivés, Juan. *Los Amos de Cuba*. Buenos Aires: Emecé Editores, 1982.

Walter, Vernon A. *The Mighty and the Meek: Dispatches from the Front Line of Diplomacy*. London: St. Ermin's Press, 2001.

Weigel, George. *The Final Revolution: The Resistance Church and the Collapse of Communism*. Oxford: Oxford University Press, 1992.

Werlau, María C. *Cuba's Intervention in Venezuela: A Strategic Occupation with Global Implications*. Washington, DC: Free Society Project, 2019.

White, Mark J. *The Kennedys and Cuba: The Declassified Documentary History*. Chicago: Ivan R. Dee, 1999.

Wyden, Peter. *Bay of Pigs: The Untold Story*. New York: Simon & Schuster, 1979.

PHOTO CREDITS

INDEX

M